Journey on Parallel Roads

AUTOBIOGRAPHY & MEMOIR

NEW EDITION,

EDUCATION 23YRS

COMMUNITY 34YRS

PROFESSION 41YRS

FAMILY 51YRS

CHALLENGES

Naiyer Habib & Mahlaqa Naushaba Habib

Autobiography and Memoir

NAIYER HABIB & MAHLAQA NAUSHABA

JOURNEY ON PARALLEL ROADS

Autobiography and Memoir

Naiyer Habib & Mahlaqa Naushaba Habib

Bismillah ir Rahman ir Rahim —
In the name of God, most Gracious, most Compassionate

AMAZON PUBLISHERS ONLINE

539 W. Commerce St #1852
Dallas, Texas 75208

www.amzpublishersonline.com

ISBN

978-1-964712-89-5 (Hardcover)
978-1-964712-90-1 (Paperback)

1. BIOGRAPHY & AUTOBIOGRAPHY, CULTURAL HERITAGE

JOURNEY ON PARALLEL ROADS

Autobiography and Memoir

Naiyer Habib & Mahlaqa Naushaba Habib

TABLE OF CONTENTS

vi

INTRODUCTION

We dedicate this book to those who loved and respected us during our lives. There are too many to mention but we include our parents, whose memories revolve in our minds with love and respect.

We walked holding the fingers of our children as baby birds until they flew away when they matured.

We named our autobiography and memoir *Journey on Parallel Roads* because it is a recounting of the journey of our lives, which took place along parallel roads, and we have always been devoted to serving the profession and the community with leadership and a sense of caring for the family, giving priority to each of its members without any neglect or compromise. We feel content with the outcome of our walk along these parallel roads and hope it serves as a tribute to our descendants and a source of inspiration to our readers. It is our autobiography *and* our memoir; we could not separate them.

We are a son and a daughter of India before Partition, and the book covers the ebbs and tides of our lives. Our journey begins in undivided India and winds through Pakistan, the US, and the UK before returning to Pakistan. We land, at last, in Canada, having chosen that country as our adopted home not for dollars but in response to the circumstances we faced elsewhere. We were affected by the regrettable Partition of India, but Canada took us in with open arms. We have returned the gesture by serving Canada as its loyal citizens in a great number of walks of life.

We have tracked our journey back to some of our very ancestors, a stop we make only briefly because of the paucity of historical information, including a lack of knowledge about our family names. For the most part, our ancestors' history has not been documented. There is no mention, for example, of the Zamindars of Mahammadia, a very important family in Purnea, The information we did obtain about our ancestors came from Dr. Abdus Salaam, who was part of our family.

Our journey on parallel roads has been memorable and filled with lesson-learning. We are not suggesting that this is unique; all families have their own complex, ebb-and-tide-filled stories. It is up to family members to attempt to unfold the facts of his or her life. Lives of many never unfold. As Caius Titus of the Roman Senate said, "Spoken words fly away, written words remain."[1]

We have provided the details of our lives in the briefest way we could. Our intent is simply to have them available for our interested descendants, to whom we leave the book as an answer to the questions that underscore all of

---

[1] Jean-Pierre Bois, Centre de recherches sur l'histoire du monde atlantique, Université de Nantes (2004). Dialogue militaire entre anciens et modernes. Presses universitaires de Rennes. ISBN2-753500789. (Wikipedia)

our lives: "Who were our ancestors? Who settled in the West? Why? Where? How did they tumble, fail, correct themselves, and succeed? What were the circumstances of their lives?"

We have not included our children in this book because they, quite rightly, did not wish to have their lives made public. We intend to write their editable biographies separately and hand them to them to make use of as they consider fit.

We have touched on the geographical locations of relevant places, as well as some aspects of ancestral cultural habitation, given that they are very different from the West. We included dates of events wherever possible. Precise points in time could not be recollected for every event.

Each page, chapter, and subchapter have facts for the observer to ponder and draw conclusions from. We have lived in the most remote villages of India and the most modern cities in the world. We are the first couple from our family to settle in Canada. For the general reader, here is a story of a young man from a faraway Indian village who was determined to become a doctor due to the influence of his maternal grandfather, a physician named Dr. Amir ul Hussain Khan. It shows the sacrifice of a parent to let their son be away from them almost all of his life in order to achieve his dreams, even if it meant bearing the pain of not living together as one family, as fate dictated.

It is also a story of a girl from a village family of repute who was forced out as a refugee to Pakistan, where she became an orphan at age ten, vowing then to educate herself so she might support her three sisters and mother after the death of her father. From the ashes of her misery as an orphan, she achieved her goal. She joined her husband in all his endeavours—family, professional, community, and political—in addition to assuming her own leadership role among women in the Muslim community, along with women in general, all the while raising her family with religious guidance.

We did not forget our families back home in India or those in Pakistan. We looked after them jointly and spontaneously as the need arose, without ever asking if or when. The book reflects this point of view. Naushaba, who educated herself to support her family, left with her husband for foreign lands. She never placed any precondition on this arrangement regarding what was to be done for her family back home—there was no need. There was a natural, built-in trust between both families.

Our efforts to present a guideline to preserve our religion and culture while integrating with the society at large are detailed in our book, History of the Muslims of Regina, Saskatchewan, and Their Organizations: Islamic Association, Canadian Council of Muslim Women, Muslim for Peace and Justice: "A Cultural Integration." (HMR).[2]

Our living in the multicultural and multi-religious society of the West was an experience that illustrated mutual respect for and acceptance of one another.

---

[2]Available at Amazon.com

A human with a life goal who is exposed to mentors and challenges to negotiate a set of circumstances, picking up the desirables and warding off the undesirables, will achieve their goal, even if the goal needs to be modified along the way. The stories of our lives reflect this reality. We had to give up something to get something.

Iron ore, if left in its habitat, may degenerate, but if put through certain processes, it becomes excellent and usable equipment.

My forefathers started with nothing but became a governing family in the times of the Mughals and the British. After India's independence, the family adopted a lifestyle of respectable farming, education, and charity and advanced continually toward professional and political careers. The lessons about the determination and persistence that delivered it are featured in our book.

We hope and pray that this global village will become a better place for all to live. Ego and selfishness have transformed the world into a place of chaos where peace does not exist, geographically or in our souls. The dictum calling for the separation of politics and religion came into being as a result of religious scholars' misinterpretation of religions. Can the world take another look at its religions and adopt the elements most suited for implementation that don't give any preferential treatment to one over another? God bless and guide us all!

—*Naiyer Habib and Mahlaqa Naushaba Habib.*

ABOUT THE AUTHORS

I have known Dr. Naiyer and Mrs. Naushaba Habib for over forty years. It was a very interesting coincidence that we bumped into each other at a community picnic in Wascana Park in Regina, Saskatchewan. Over time, we became family friends and experienced several changes in the community.

Dr. Naiyer Habib was born in India and has settled in Canada. He is married to Mahlaqa Naushaba Khanam, and they have two sons. Dr. Habib describes the circumstances around his marriage in a later chapter. It was the Partition of India that led them to move and settle in Canada. The couple celebrated their fiftieth anniversary privately in December 2016. From his very happy relationship with his wife, he has formed an opinion that women are more mature, considerate, and tolerant than their husbands. I consider him lucky to have a marriage happy enough for him to form this opinion about women at large, an opinion with which not everyone might agree. His good fortune has translated into an attitude of equality and justice toward women.

Mrs. Habib was born in India, but she, with her family, moved as refugees to Pakistan after the Partition of India.

Dr. Habib received his earliest education from his mother, Madina Khanam. The family lived in a rural setting, and his mother educated him until fifth grade. This was followed by formal education in various schools and institutions and then by his acquisition of a medical degree from Patna University in Bihar, India, in 1966, the highest degree of medical science at the time.

Mrs. Habib completed her Master of Political Science at the University of Karachi, Sindh, Pakistan. She had a hard life, with her father passing away in her very early childhood.

The Habibs came to the United States for higher learning in 1967 and to live together, as Dr. Habib could not take his wife to India due to the ever-strained relations between the two countries. Dr. Habib received his training and education in internal medicine and interventional cardiology at various renowned institutions in the US. He earned recognition and received awards during these academic periods.

Mrs. Habib also upgraded her education with research and higher training to enable her to manage Dr. Habib's practice and research arm. In addition to her career, she, together with her husband, raised two fine sons who are well-educated professionals in their own right.

After completing their higher education, they decided to return to their native countries. Unfortunately, though, the communal and political problems that resulted from the Partition of India disappointed them, and so they reluctantly decided to migrate. They came to Canada on July 14, 1973—a gain for Canada, which acquired two highly educated professionals. They lived in Saskatoon from 1973 to 1976, where they were in the medical practice. From Saskatoon, they moved to Regina, where Dr. Habib was appointed by the University of Saskatchewan to the Plains Health Centre, to establish cardiology for southern Saskatchewan.

The University of Saskatchewan appointed Dr. Habib to an assistant professor position at the Plains Health Centre in Regina on August 14, 1976. There, he was tasked with initiating and establishing a cardiology program for southern Saskatchewan. He started the program—which became the Interventional Cardiology Centre at the Plains Health Centre—from scratch and headed up the cardiology department there from 1976 to 2001. As head of the cardiology section, Dr. Habib was an active member of several committees designed to improve the quality and utilization of services. He was elected and served as the vice president of the medical staff.

Over the years, the media have regularly consulted him on various issues in the health-care system, and he has never been hesitant in discussing the weaknesses of the system, including the role of the government. He supports his presentations with facts and offers meaningful advice about improving the system. He has always been an active and strong defender of patients' rights, as well as the rights of physicians.

Dr. Habib was elevated to the position of clinical professor of cardiology at the University of Saskatchewan, Regina, where he actively involved himself in teaching and ensuring evidence-based practice. He has served as a member of several local, provincial, national, and international medical associations. He is a Fellow of the Royal College of Physicians and Surgeons of Canada and a member of many prestigious societies and organizations— professional and otherwise.

Dr. Habib was a founder of the Regina Cardiac Society, where he also served as president. He has also generously shared his time and knowledge on committees with the Saskatchewan Medical Association, the Saskatchewan Heart Foundation, and the College of Physicians and Surgeons of Saskatchewan.

Dr. Habib was involved in numerous research trials, as noted in the research and publications section of this book. His studies earned him a reputation for being results-oriented and productive. He has considerable experience in research methods. In addition to his many clinical and administrative duties, Dr. Habib has remained an active contributor to scientific literature and has published extensively in peer-reviewed journals.

He has often been invited as a guest speaker on various topics regarding cardiology over the years. He organized and chaired many continuing medical educational conferences and seminars in Saskatchewan.

For her part, Mrs. Habib very capably managed her husband's medical practice for him, as well as the office's day-to-day nursing and clerical staff, who respected and adored her. She was his right-hand person in his medical research, administrative work, and academic and professional career. In addition, she and her husband managed their household, including a family of two sons. She was involved in research and was a co-investigator in the renowned HOPE trial. Dr. Habib considers her intelligent contribution a significant factor in his achievements.

Dr. Habib served as head of cardiology from 1976 to 2001, when he decided to step down. This decision was at least partly a reaction to the bureaucracy that had entered the medical system. He continued his practice as an interventional cardiologist with continued academic involvement. Since stepping down as cardiology head and subsequently leaving Regina in 2004, he practiced office cardiology in a semi-retired position, with his wife managing the office and staff in Abbotsford, Surrey, and Hope, BC, from 2005 to December 2011, when they retired from all practice.

Complete retirement has given this husband-and-wife team an opportunity to write about their careers and life experiences. One product of their efforts is now in your hands.

Dr. Habib's administrative and academic contributions to medical care have been the subject of much praise over the years by many illustrious individuals, including the head of the Department of Medicine, Regina, Dr. James D. McHattie; the administrative heads of the Regina Health District, Media, Dr. Marvin Balla, head of the University of Saskatchewan, and Dr. Gerald Sinclair, former head of the department of medicine at the Plains Health Centre. He was recognized as a pioneer of cardiology for Southern Saskatchewan by the cardiology staff of the Regina General-Plains Health Centre hospitals and by the Regina Cardiac Society. When Dr. and Mrs. Habib left Regina in October 2004, the cardiology staff, along with others from the Regina Health District of Southern Saskatchewan, gave him an emotional farewell.

Dr. Habib and Mrs. Habib have been serving the Muslim community since their arrival in Canada in 1973. They continued to do so in Regina until 2005, when they moved to Abbotsford, BC. Their service was recognized in the sendoff given to them by the Regina Muslim community and Muslims for Peace & Justice in October 2004. The event, the recognition, and the love shown at that function were overwhelming and joyful to the couple; a memorable day etched in their memory. The only regret I have is I could not be there to share it with them. The premier of Saskatchewan, Honourable Brad Wall, has praised them both for their contribution to the province and His Worship the mayor of Regina, Michael Fourgere, has honoured them by entering the name "Habib" in his master list for naming Street or Park in Regina.

The Islamic Association of Saskatchewan, led by then-president, Dr. Ahmad Aboudheir, and Dr. Ayman Aboguddah, president and founder of the Huda School of Regina, recognized Dr. Habib's contribution to the community. The Canadian Islamic Congress recognized Dr. and Mrs. Habib with an award for lifelong service to the Muslim community.

In 1975-1976, Dr. Habib was the vice president of the Islamic Association of Saskatchewan, Saskatoon.

Mrs. Habib taught and took over the charge of the Sunday Islamic School there when the first teacher moved away. Mrs. Habib and Dr. Habib started a once-a-week evening Islamic School at their residence in Regina, and Mrs. Habib taught and managed that school for eight years, from 1976 to 1984.

Dr. Habib was elected president of the Islamic Association of Saskatchewan, Regina, in 1977 and served as the president on multiple terms by being unanimously re-elected by the community. Mrs. Habib served as a director on the board of the Islamic Association of Saskatchewan, Regina, for two terms.

During these stretches of service, both put the interest of the community ahead of all other needs yet managed to balance those needs with those of their family. Managing not to neglect either is a great achievement. An emphasis that others might do the same and fulfill family and community needs at the same time was a big part of Dr. Habib's message during his leadership. He believes that the entire family unit, including children, must be involved in community work and leadership. He set a personal example and was seen escorting children from the playground to attend Islamic lectures and participate in functions and activities. During his term, the couple started and maintained various programs for Muslim communities, some of which are described in this book.

The couple stood up for Islam and Muslims in the media where necessary, as well as in the political arena. Dr. Habib was quoted in *Maclean's* and *Time*. He appeared on local TV stations and in local newspapers several times. He was instrumental in starting a local TV program on Islam, "Islam in Focus." He contributed significantly to the interfaith program. He was invited to be a guest speaker on Islamic topics by various organizations.

He regularly attended meetings of the Council of Muslim Communities of Canada as a representative of the Islamic Association of Saskatchewan, Regina. He organized the sending of two youths from the community as representatives to Toronto to attend the first National Conference on Youth. This led to the organization of the first youth camp in 1985 for boys and girls from Regina, Saskatoon, Swift Current, and Winnipeg at Camp Monahan in the Regina area, under the supervision of parents and arranged by Regina youths.

During the first Iraq war and Bosnian crisis, Dr. Habib, along with other members of the community, played a critical and active role in a public forum on behalf of the Islamic Association of Saskatchewan, Regina. Dr. Habib contacted the major Muslim organizations across the United States and Canada to form a Muslim Confederation to meet the new challenges of this overseas conflict—unfortunately, no organizations showed any interest.

He addressed the Muslim community of a Richmond, British Columbia masjid at a Friday prayer, asking them to unite together and attempt to form a Muslim confederation. To this day, he continues to remind major Muslim organizations in Canada to unite on a single platform to meet the needs of Muslim communities, as well as the interests of Canada.

On the day after the 9/11 crisis in 2001, Dr. Habib met with Drs. Ejaz Ahmad and Abdul Jalil. This meeting led to the formation of Muslims for Peace & Justice (MPJ). Dr. Habib was elected MPJ's first president in 2002 and served until 2005. This organization was the active advocacy group on behalf of Muslims in Saskatchewan and played a role as a point of contact wherever necessary.

In most of these social activities, Mrs. Habib was a strong support for Dr. Habib, a fact he gratefully recognizes at every opportunity. No doubt this gesture from him leads to a very healthy relationship in the husband-wife team, not limited to this joint venture and collaboration of authorship.

Dr. Habib was a life member of the Canadian Islamic Congress (CIC), serving as a director on the national board after a term as a regional director in Regina. He established this organization in British Columbia with various activities, including Islamic History Month, the brainchild of the then-national president Dr. Elmasry.

The late Dr. Lila Fahlman, the founder of the Canadian Council of Muslim Women, visited Mrs. Habib in the fall of 1981 in Regina. This meeting led to the foundation of the Regina chapter of the Canadian Council of Muslim Women. Mrs. Habib was the founding president, and she served for several terms. The council took a leading role with others in the support of women in Bosnia during the Bosnian massacre and represented the council at various women's organizations in Regina and nationally. During her last term in office, in 2004, she started a scholarship for Muslim girls at the University of Regina.

While in Regina in the late 1980s, Dr. Habib learned about a large Muslim community in Swift Current, Saskatchewan, that was primarily of Lebanese origin. The children and young people of this community lacked the opportunity of exposure to Islam. Dr. Habib visited Swift Current with a team consisting of Abdul Qayyum,

Mohammed Sadeque, and Zubair Akhtar. They met a few Muslims from the community there at the house of Abdullah Gader.

Subsequently, Dr. Habib arranged another meeting in Swift Current, inviting a range of national and community-based Muslim leaders from across Saskatchewan to attend. This resulted in the formation of a Muslim community group in Swift Current. As a result of his efforts, there is now an Islamic centre in Swift Current.

Dr. Habib believes all religions should be respected and that the followers of all religions should be able to preach their religion without any comment on the religions of others because no one has the right to be the judge. He believes that adverse or biased comments about other religions are the main cause of the conflicts that brew all over the world. People who discriminate against others' religion, he believes, know neither their religion nor that of others.

The Habibs' view is to support women in Islam and uphold their status as raised by Islam. They believe that Muslims should stop splitting into sects and groups and go back to Islam as the Prophet preached. They feel strongly that the Muslim community is a part of the Canadian mosaic and that maintaining an Islamic identity while integrating with society at large is critical. They, a successful Canadian family, who also are Muslims, are an example of this. They demonstrated this in their first book, *The History of Muslims of Regina, Saskatchewan, and their Organizations... "A Cultural Integration."*

The Habibs recognize that Canada is the best nation in the world because of the contributions of all Canadians. They salute the people and members of other faiths for defending Muslims and Islam across the country. It is inspiring to note how the couple rose professionally, serving the community religiously, socially, and politically, irrespective of race or religion, and then, in retirement, became authors of a well-praised book.

Finally: They establish Scholarship at the University of Regina: Dr. Naiyer Habib & Mrs. Mahlaqa Naushaba Habib: Pioneers of Community, Cardiology, and Health Scholarship for an endowed graduate scholarship in the Faculty of Graduate Studies and Research at the University of Regina.

They are donors to Hospitals:Regina General,Pasqua in Regina&Abbotsford Regional,Surrey Memorial &Royal Columbia in BC.

Of it, the US Review of Books says, ". . . arriving in Canada, they began establishing numerous civic and cultural organizations based in their faith. The book admirably highlights the intention of this immigrant group to integrate into local society while sustaining critical aspects of culture and religion. It is exhaustively researched, presenting extensive information about Muslim civic activities in the greater Saskatchewan area in an organized format. It can serve as an excellent reference for anyone needing to gather material about the history of Muslim expatriate communities in Canada, either for family or civic purposes."

Our friendship has gone on for well over forty years. Together, we saw, took part in, and often were instrumental in effecting many changes in society, our communities, the nation at large, and, indeed, the world. There is a lot more I can write about the Habibs, but I will let their own words take over from here. I will, however, say this: I have been most fortunate to have met a couple like them, and it is my privilege to be counted among their friends.

The Habibs signing their authored book, History of the Early Muslims of Regina..at Toronto.

Surprisingly, in answer to the question of why the Habibs did not receive the Order of Saskatchewan for their numerous civic and religious achievements and acts of service, where others inferior to them did, Dr. Habib smilingly answered, "We are happy to do what we could, for which people loved and respected us. God knows it, as well. No one thought of us, nor did we initiate it ourselves, which many do!"

Akram Din, former secretary,
Islamic Association of Saskatchewan, Regina.

ACKNOWLEDGEMENTS

In writing *Journey on Parallel Roads—Autobiography and Memoir*, we would like to acknowledge the various organizations and individuals who allowed us their assistance and provided material to complete this book that represents our life. We could not have completed it without their help.

The information about our ancestors was obtained from my uncle, Dr. Abdus Salaam, my father's second cousin. No one in the family thus far has accumulated this information related to our ancestors.

We offer our great appreciation and thanks to the following news media and organizations for helping us and allowing us to include important information without which the book would have remained incomplete.

- Canadian Broadcasting Corporation for the news, interviews, and pictures. The CBC's Darren Yearsley made it possible.

- *Briar Patch Magazine* for the article, "When Cultures Differ."

- *Regina Leader-Post* and managing editor Marion Marshall for allowing me to publish many letters, articles, and news items from this newspaper.

- *The Toronto Star*, TorStar syndication services, and Joanne MacDonald for the write-up, "Nod to Ramadhan."

- *Prairie Messenger*, for the article, "Muslims Reach Out to Larger Community," an interview by Frank Flegel.

- Access Communication Co. Ltd., Katherine Wilson, and Tami Mitchell, for allowing us to publish important aspects of "Muslims in Focus" with pictures. It includes all pictures and inserts for the conference from 2002, 2003, and 2004 of "Muslims for Peace and Justice."

- Global TV (formerly STV), marketing manager Lyndon Bray, and executive assistant Cynthia Waite, and thanks to former CK for news broad cast for allowing us to publish the news, interviews, and pictures.

- Google and Wikipedia. We appreciated the information from Google, which we included with the Google logo and permission within the book, and Wikipedia, whose data we employed according to the company's general guidelines.

We highly appreciate my nephew, Nazish Rahman of Mahammadia, Purnea, India, for sharing pictures and other information about our ancestors and home. We thank Ayesha Khokhar of Abbotsford, BC, for her excellent drawings, which enriched our book.

Lisa Kenney was very helpful with her suggestions about the manuscript before its final submission for editing and printing with Friesen Press.

We are very thankful to receive information and permission to include the picture of Watts Hospital from Preservation Durham and Lisa Watts, the communications director at the North Carolina School of Science and Mathematics.

We extend our thanks to Kristin Rodgers, the collection curator at Ohio State University, Columbus, and Judith A. Wiener, an associate professor and the assistant director of the university's Health Science Library, Collections, and Outreach, for letting us publish the picture of the Mount Carmel Hawke's Hospital. This has enriched our book.

We extend our thanks and appreciation to Helen Galloway of Orlando Health Foundation for sharing and helping us procure the picture of the Orange Memorial Hospital for inclusion in the book and to Aidybert Silva-Ortiz, system librarian of Graese Community Health Library and Health Science Library of Orlando Health for the permission.

We are very grateful for the permission of Compare Infobase Limited of Maps of India, in New Delhi, to include various maps in the book. Harneet Kaur and others helped us to turn this into a successful outcome.

We highly appreciate Madeeha Ahmed for designing the theme of the book cover and Mujtaba Aly of bringing life to it.

Finally, we appreciate Akram Din for going out of the way to write About the Authors. He invited me to lead the Muslim community and has helped along the way. With his participation, we felt content to serve the Muslim community by integrating into the society at large while maintaining our culture and religion.

The quality of some pictures is not high because they were extracted from video recordings, and some are as old as 60 years. They were included because of their importance in our lives. *Readers to look at each page to focus on all content.*

ANCESTRY OF NAIYER HABIB

by

Dr. Naiyer Habib

From an interview with Dr. Abdus Salaam

Origins

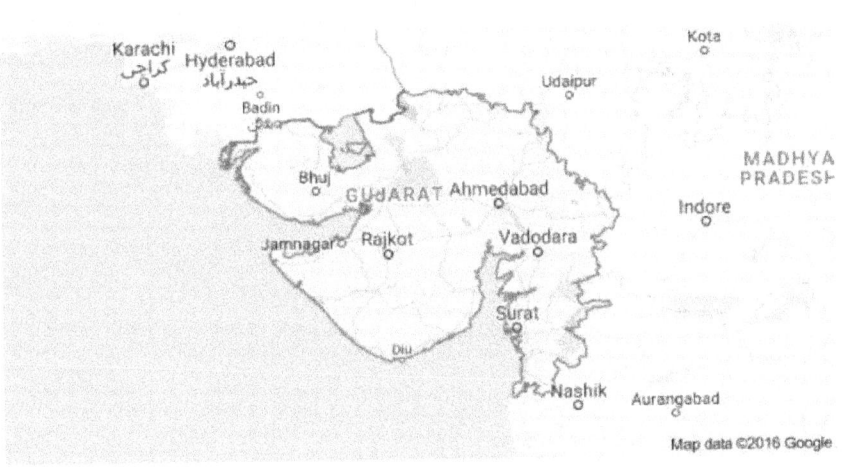

Gujarat

Dr. Abdus Salaam, a first cousin of my father, was an inquisitive person when it came to his family. According to him, my family most likely originated from the Indian state of Gujarat. The official language used in this territory is Gujarati (for example: *jai chha* [going], *khai chha* [eating]). The dialect is somewhat like Kathiyawadi, which is locally known as "Kathy," but different.

Gujarat is the western state[3] of India. It has a very rich history that dates back to 5000 years BC. Mahatma Gandhi was a Gujarati. It has seen the rules of Maurya, Rajput, Muslim, and European applied to its existence right up to its independence.

---

[3] Over the period of its history, as with other areas of India, Gujarat has been known as a kingdom, a presidency, a province, and a state. Since 1947, it has been a state, which is the term we are using throughout this book, even when referring to earlier periods of history.

Dr. Salaam suspected that Gujarat was settled during the time of Emperor Shah Alam II, 1728-1806 CE (Ali Gauhar).

Bengal had three sovereign states: Dacca, Murshidabad, and one whose name Dr. Salaam could not recall. These three states refused to pay revenue/tax to the Mughal government. In response, a subordinate of the Mughal sent two army battalions to deal with this rebellion. One battalion marched from the south, and the other from the north of the Ganges River. On arriving at the Purnea[4] district, there was an apparent change in the administration of the subordinate position of the emperor. The supply for the maintenance of the army stopped, so the army fell into disarray. The battalion from the south moved toward Bihar Sharif and sought settlement there, while the battalion from the north stayed in the Purnea area. My descendants were part of this latter group.

---

[4] Also known as Purnia; it is spelled on my passport as Purnea

ANCESTORS

Introduction To Ancestry Charts

The names of my earliest-known ancestors are listed as they were called. These names were given by parents randomly. For example, Moinuddin could be called either Moin or Moinuddin. There was no trend to follow any family name. Some attached their first name, as in my case, Naiyer *Habib*, and some added their last name, as in my brother's case, Mahboob *Ur Rahman*. Our father's full name was *Habib Ur Rahman*. Women's names were rarely common knowledge. The majority of them were called by the name of the city from where they came from: for example, Danapur Wali.[5] My mother came from Danapur. Hence, she was generally called Danapurwali (i.e. from Danapur). This created problems for tracing family ancestries. My ancestry can be traced from its beginning to the present day; others are cut short.

The gender symbol "♀" is used to indicate female, and the "♂" symbol is used to indicate male. As the chart flows, these represent daughter and son. A wife is indicated as "wife" in the box. When a box ends, that means no further information is available about the member.

Significant Ancestors
Moinuddin I

Moinuddin I was the first ancestor known to us. Moinuddin was his full name, but he was also called Moin. Another Moinuddin appears in the descendants list, but this is the *first* Moinuddin. He had a son by the name of Faqeer Mohammad. Another person mentioned that he was Fakhruddin, not Faqeer Mohammad.

We could not identify Moinuddin I's wife, the mother of Faqeer Mohammad, in our research. Progeny of Moinuddin I
Ancestry Chart #1
WITH WIFE- unknown

Faqeer Mohammad♂

Faqeer Mohammad had two sons with Wife 1 and one son with Wife 2. One of them was Rahmatullah. I am a descendant of Rahmatullah.
Progeny of Faqeer Mohammad
Ancestry Chart #1
WITH WIFE 1
Bhattu♂
Ramzani♂

---

[5] Wali- belonging to (in this example) the town of Danapur

WITH WIFE 2

Rahmatullah♂

Rahmatullah

Rahmatullah was a son of Faqeer Mohammad and grandson of Moinuddin I. I am a descendant of him.
Progeny of Rahmatullah

Ancestry Chart #4

Mohammad Agha♂

Ameer Bakhsh♂

Elahi Bakhsh♂

Moqeeban ♀

Mohammad Agha

Mohammad Agha: I am descended from him. He had three sons and a daughter with his first wife, Motiban, who was from the village of Jalkar. These three sons were: Majid Ur Rahman, Abdus Sattar, and Mohammad Siddique. He also had a daughter with his first wife. Her name was Rahim Un Nisa. We used to call her Jalkar Wali Dadi (grandmother from the village of Jalkar). I am a descendant of Mohammad Agha.

Mohammad Agha had four sons with his second wife, who was from Belgachchi Village: Abdul Jabbar, Abdul Ghaffar, Abdul Wahab, and Abdus Samad.

Mohammad Agha did not go to Mahammadia to settle. He passed away on the *6th* of Aghan 1311 (according to the Indian calendar) and was buried in Kunaily. His sons and others were buried in Mahammadia when they died. He and his brother Ameer Bakhsh lived, worked, and achieved together. Progeny of Mohammad Agha

Ancestry Chart #7

WITH WIFE 1 (*Motiban*, from Jalkar)

Majid Ur Rahman♂

Abdus Sattar♂

Mohammad Siddique♂

Rahim Un Nisa♀

WITH WIFE 2 (from Belgachchi)

Abdul Jabbar♂

Abdul Ghaffar♂

Abdul Wahab♂

Abdus Samad♂

Ameer Bakhsh

Ameer Bakhsh was a son of Rahmatullah. He had only two children, both daughters, as noted in **Ancestry Chart #4** Progeny of Ameer Bakhsh

Ancestry Chart #4

Kulsum Nisa♀
Tahir un Nisa♀

Elahi Bakhsh

Elahi Bakhsh lived separately from his two brothers, a joint decision with his wife. One of his descendants was my stepmother, Maimoona Saheba[6] , after whose passing my father married my mother. Shirf Ud Din Ahmad (son of Moinuddin II) was another descendant who stood by my mother as if she were his own sister and who was very close to us, as was his mother, who treated us as her own grandchildren.

Progeny of Elahi Bakhsh

Ancestry Chart #5

WITH WIFE 1 (from Chanderdai)

Sayeed Ur Rahman♂

Ibrahim♂

WITH WIFE 2 (from Araria)

Zaib Un Nisa♀

Moinuddin II♂

We were unable to get any details about the members of Elahi Bakhsh's family other than establishing the names of his descendants. Naushaba and I are very close to Shirfuddin (**Ancestry Chart #6**), a son of Moinuddin II and a grandson of Elahi Bakhsh. Habib Ur Rahman's first wife was Shirfuddin's sister.

Majid Ur Rahman

Majid Ur Rahman (son of Mohammad Agha)

Progeny of Majid Ur Rahman

Ancestry Charts #7, 8, 9

WITH WIFE 1 (*Asia Sabra*)

Ancestry Chart #7

Habib Ur Rahman♂ (my father)

Hasib Ur Rahman♂

Zahida Khatoon♀

Aamna Khatoon♀

WITH WIFE 2 (from Dimhia)

Ancestry Chart #8

Najib Ur Rahman♂

Wahid Ur Rahman♂

---

[6] Saheba: not a surname, but a word used as a title of respect for ladies, as "Esquire" would be used for men.

Hafiz Ur Rahman♂
WITH WIFE 3 (from Balwa)

Ancestry Chart #9
Mojib Ur Rahman♂

Mohammad Siddique

Mohammad Siddique (son of Mohammad Agha)
<u>Progeny of Mohammad Siddique</u>
<u>Ancestry Chart #10</u>
WIFE: *Naushaba*
Abul Kalam♂
Abdus Salaam♂
Arsheda♀
Rafi Ahmad♂

Habib Ur Rahman

Habib Ur Rahman (son of Majid Ur Rahman)
<u>Progeny of Habib Ur Rahman</u> **Ancestry Chart #12**
WITH WIFE 1(*Maimoona*)
Noor Jahan♀
WITH WIFE 2 (*Madina Khanam*)

Ancestry Chart #12
Najam Habib♂
Naiyer Habib♂
Nilofer Habib♀
Yasmin Habib♀
WITH WIFE 3 (*Najmun Nisa*)

Ancestry Chart #13
Sanober Habib♀
Mahboob Ur Rahman♂
Rizwan Ur Rahman♂

History Of Ancestors

Rahmatullah

Rahmatullah was one of the three grandsons of Moinuddin I. Faqeer Mohammad was the father of Rahmatullah (**Ancestry Chart #1**). He was the only child of Faqeer Mohammad and his second wife. I am a descendant of his.

Rahmatullah settled in Kunaily (maybe 1.5 kilometres south of Mahammadia) in Purnea. He owned and raised buffalos.

Rahmatullah settled in Mahammadia on the advice of a saint. One day, a stranger arrived on his doorstep, and Rahmatullah inquired of him. The stranger replied that he was a musafir (traveller). Rahmatullah offered him his own food. On the third day, the musafir asked Rahmatullah to join him for a meal and told Rahmatullah that he would not eat unless Rahmatullah joined him. They started eating, but as much as they consumed, the amount of food remained unchanged. They sent the food to the ladies of the house, and they were able to enjoy it, too. It was perceived that the musafir was a saint. The saint asked Rahmatullah to settle where Mahammadia is located today. He defined the boundary of the residence and masjid[7] and said the family would flourish there. He also gave Rahmatullah two copper coins, which were passed on to my father, as I am told, and I recall seeing them in his office box, not knowing their significance. The saint said to keep these coins and that money would never run out. What eventually happened to the coins is unknown.

Rahmatullah moved from Kunaily to Mahammadia, on plot #532, according to the survey of 1901. Then, his two brothers, Bhattu and Ramzani, also moved to Mahammadia. There was land adjacent to plot #532. In the survey of 1956, plot #532, along with the adjacent area, had become plot #1040.

His Achievements

While Rahmatullah was living on plot #532, the Hindu Zamindar[8] had a tehsildar (tax collector) who had a basta carrier.[9] He died, and Rahmatullah got his job. He got interested in studying during his off hours. Then the tehsildar died. Rahmatullah was the only literate person around, and so got this job. He continued to acquire property.

Rahmatullah put a lot of importance on education. He worked and studied during his off hours. He built the first madrasa[10] of bamboo and grass. Its foundation can still be seen west of the existing madrasa, separated by a walking road between Mahammadia and Harahi. He also built and equipped the first masjid with an adjacent family graveyard and a musafir khana (travellers' inn).

---

[7] Mosque
[8] A rich, influential family that holds large areas of land and has control over peasants, from whom the Zamindars collect taxes, often for themselves and the government.
[9] Basta is a collection of files and folders.
[10] Madrasa- School based on Islamic curriculum

A Caring Brother

Rahmatullah was planning for his Hajj.[11] He invited people to meet prior to this intended journey, which is an Islamic tradition. People told him that he had two brothers yet unmarried and that he should look after them first. So he cancelled his Hajj for that point and went three years later. This is an example of a brother caring for his brothers. He settled his two brothers, Bhattu and Ramzani, who were from his father's first marriage, in Rahka village just southwest of Mahammadia, where their descendants are still.

His Children

Rahmatullah had three sons, Mohammad Agha, Ameer Bakhsh, and Elahi Bakhsh, and a daughter, Moqeeban. Details about Moqeeban are not available. Rahmatullah had only one wife, as far as is known to us. Ameer Bakhsh and Mohammad Agha stayed together, whereas Elahi Bakhsh separated from the other two brothers at his wife's urging. Dr. Salaam told us that Ameer Bakhsh was the think-tank and Mohammad Agha was the chief executive officer. They cooked and ate together. Ameer Bakhsh would sit with the cattle grazer to get advice about how to become a Zamindar.

Ameer Bakhsh

He had two daughters.

His Achievements

He achieved the most. Elahi Bakhsh and Ameer Bakhsh worked together. Ameer Bakhsh was instrumental in building a new madrasa and a bridge over the Bhesna River. These structures were funded by his brother, Mohammad Agha, and nephews, Majid Ur Rahman and Mohammad Siddique (Mohammad Agha's sons). He also built a road across the bridge from Hichha Moti Hat (the weekly market) to Mahammadia with his own money. The proprietors of the Hat, Masjid (after Rahmatullah), and the new Mahammadia Madrasa belonged to Ameer Bakhsh and his brother Mohammed Agha.

Ameer Bakhsh created a waqf,[12] assigning a portion of the property for the maintenance of these Bridge Hat (Market), Masjid, and Madrasa. This waqf was in Ameer Bakhsh's original will. He assigned the use of certain parts of the property for the purpose of maintaining the facilities mentioned above. He was the first mutawalli (manager) to look after these properties' welfare.

Subsequent to that, his eldest daughter, Tahir Un Nisa, was to be the mutawalli. It should be noted that, even in those days, and even in a conservative family, women held managerial functions.

Ameer Bakhsh obtained the title of the estate of Ameer Bakhsh of Mahammadia from the British government. He qualified to do so according to the government's set criteria. A certain amount of revenue collection and some

---

[11] The Hajj is a five-day annual pilgrimage undertaken by Muslims to Mecca in Saudi Arabia. It is the world's biggest annual gathering of people.

[12] A waqf is an endowment under Islamic law that typically involves donating a building, plot of land, or other assets for Muslim religious or charitable purposes with no intention of reclaiming the assets (Wiki).

public services were required for a person in this role. He had such qualifications and experience, particularly in the madrasa, bridge, hat, masjid, and musafir khana. Funding was to be provided by the owner of the estate, and work was to be done by the government.

The estate belonged to Ameer Bakhsh and his two daughters, Kulsum Nisa and Tahir Un Nisa. According to the will and last wishes of Ameer Bakhsh, the estate was to be managed in perpetuity by an administrator who was a family member. They were also to be shareholders. The judge was to appoint an administrator from the shareholders on their approval. If no suitable person was found among the shareholders, he could appoint from outside in consultation with the shareholders. The first administrator was Abdul Samad. The next joint administration was looked after by Habib Ur Rahman and Hasib Ur Rahman (my father and uncle). The last was Abul Kalam. After him, and with the change of government from British rule to Congress, the landlordship was dissolved.

Abdul Rahman Haqqani, John Puri, and Ameer Bakhsh

John Puri was the title of Abdul Rahman. Abdul Rahman, John Puri was a student of the madrasa built by Ameer Bakhsh. After graduating, he moved to Saharanpur, Bihar. He established a madrasa there and was its mudassir (head of school).

Abdul Rahman Haqqani published the book *Tafseer e Haqqani* (see image below), a translation and detailed commentary (Tafseer) of the Quran in Urdu. The costs for its first publication were covered by Ameer Bakhsh. We tried to establish this connection by the time this book was published but could not!

Cover of *Tafseer e Haqqani*[13] which, as far as we know, was financed by Ameer Bakhsh

Majid Ur Rahman

Majid Ur Rahman was my grandfather. He was close to his brother Mohammad Siddique, and they were active in the affairs of the family, whereas Abdus Sattar used to avoid getting involved in that kind of thing.

Balwa Estate

Majid Ur Rahman and his brothers owned part of the Balwa Estate, which was acquired from the Thakur (landowner) by Majid Ur Rahman under the following circumstances:

Nawab[14] of Khagaria obtained the first car in the district of Purnea. He invited the VIPs of Purnea to celebrate, and Majid Ur Rahman was one of the guests. At this gathering, he met a proprietor of Balwa Estate from the Thakur family. During the conversation with Majid Ur Rahman, the Thakur asked how much debt he carried.

---

[13] Courtesy of besturdubooks.wordpress.com.

[14] Semiautonomous Muslim ruler-title by Mughal.

Majid Ur Rahman replied, "None." The Thakur told him, "Then you do not belong to this group." Majid Ur Rahman left.

After a while, the Thakur needed to pay his hundi[15] a loan on demand, with a guarantee of property. If the hundi was not paid on demand, the property was to be confiscated by the lender. The Thakur was looking for someone who could loan him money to pay the hundi, and he could not find anyone. Someone told him that he should go to Majid Ur Rahman, who gave him a loan without interest, on demand, to be paid on a fixed date. Majid Ur Rahman was not dealing with any interest.

As it happened, the Thakur could not repay the loan by the due date. So Majid Ur Rahman had to auction two and a half parts of the property of the Balwa Estate that was the security against the loan to the Thakur and took possession of this portion after a battle.

But the Thakur did not allow its possession by Majid Ur Rahman, so Majid Ur Rahman sent his brothers Mohammad Siddique and Abdul Sattar with armed forces to occupy the property. These brothers used to drink and were doing so in the camp. While drinking, they heard the news that the Thakur was coming with armed forces to attack them in their camp. Abdul Sattar was scared and wanted to run away. The Thakur's forces arrived, and Mohammad Siddique took a gun and shot six of the men. Mohammad Siddique reported this to Majid Ur Rahman and was advised by Majid Ur Rahman to stay put.

Majid Ur Rahman then met the superintendent of police and district magistrate of the Purnea district. He told him about the Thakur's army incursion and about not allowing Majid Ur Rahman to possess the property. The district magistrate and the superintendent of police went on site and justified the response.

Majid Ur Rahman and the family became owners of 6+ Aanas (one-sixteenth Aana of 16 Aanas of one Indian rupee then) of the Balwa estate. According to an act in 1888, for the mismanagement of a property (here, the two parties), a district judge would appoint a common manager to look after the property who would continue to do so on an ongoing basis on the consultation of two-party shareholders. The shareholders had no power to challenge the common manager but could petition the judge over any concern. The common manager managed the revenue and land belonging to the two parties and distributed the income among the shareholders. The Balwa Estate was dissolved upon the abolition of the Zamindari on the departure of the British, in the Congress era. The government took the property for revenue and paid compensation. The land was distributed among the shareholders.

Head of the Family, Family Conflict

Majid Ur Rahman was the eldest of the three brothers from Wife #1 and also of the other four brothers from Wife #2 of Mohammad Agha. Thus, he was managing the family. He built dwelling houses as single units for each of his brothers' families in the same compound. Things were progressing fine, but conflict occurred between the

---

15 A hundi is like a promissory note for a loan.

brothers of the two mothers. A car purchase by Siddique was the initiator of the conflict. The other group of brothers also wanted a car. Division took hold of the family, and, ultimately, separation ensued.

Majid Ur Rahman, who was my grandfather, moved to the north, where he had his own dwelling. When my grandfather separated from the others, he built his own house just north of his previous home site. A picture of it is included in this book. This was in the village of Harahi. Very few people know this by name and associate this area with Mahammadia Estate. Although the inhabitants who descended from my grandfather lived in Harahi, they belonged to the Mahammadia Estate.

The others stayed in the houses in the compound built by Majid Ur Rahman. Property was also divided.

I do not know much about Abdus Sattar. He was one of the three brothers. He respected his brother Majid Ur Rahman very much and sat in step, letting his elder be seated on higher ground. He called Uncle Salaam from time to time for socialization. Majid Ur Rahman and his other brother, Mohammad Siddique, stayed together.

Majid Ur Rahman was a man of principle and justice who was invested in caring for the needy. He married each of his wives only after the death of the previous wife.

Majid Ur Rahman's first wife, *Asia Sabra* (my grandmother), came from the village of Chanderdai in the district of Purnea. She was the sister of Zia Ur Rahman and Bhola Dada.[16] Majid Ur Rahman and Sabra had two sons and two daughters, as listed in the ancestry. He had three sons with the wife from Dimhia and one son with the third wife from Balwa.

He was interested in educating his children. He sent his two sons—my father, Habib Ur Rahman, and uncle Hasib Ur Rahman—to the Aligarh Muslim University.

Majid Ur Rahman passed away in 1937 when I was not yet born.

When my grandfather died, my father, being the eldest, had to return home to look after the affairs of the family. Thus, he could only finish Intermediate Arts. My uncle Hasib Ur Rahman studied law.

Habib Ur Rahman

Habib Ur Rahman was my father. His details can be found on page 74.

Hasib Ur Rahman

Hasib Ur Rahman was my father's full brother. He studied at Aligarh Muslim University and became a lawyer. He started practice in Purnea. He was intelligent and had a good law practice. Unfortunately, he fell victim to alcoholism because of bad company. His practice met with failure to a great extent. One time, his brother-in-law made a remark that my uncle's family would become his responsibility, as Hasib was not looking after himself. The brother-in-law was bitter about it. My uncle heard this comment. He was then discovered to have tuberculosis of the lungs. These two factors influenced my uncle very much, and he became a changed man. He

---

[16] Dada=paternal grandfather, and generally follows the first name.

quit alcohol, and fortunately, his tuberculosis was cured. He became religious. His law practice picked up. He performed Hajj. He entered politics. He served as an MLA from Baisi Thana of the Purnea district. He joined the Praja Socialist Party and subsequently entered Congress. He became a minister in Bihar, and then he stood for Member of Parliament and was elected. He was stationed in New Delhi.

We had a good relationship with Hasib Ur Rahman. He had a son, Nasim, who did not do well in school and, after marriage, passed away. His second son, Shamim, became a professor and taught at a college in Kasba in the district of Purnea. His eldest son, Akhtar, passed away, and this was a shock to the family. The next son after Shamim was Waseem, and he became a lawyer and practiced in Purnea. He had two daughters, one married in the village of Hakka, and another daughter whom we call Bunni, was married to Qamar, the son of my uncle Shamsh Uz Zaman. **Zahida Khatoon** and **Amna Khatoon** were the two daughters of Majid ur Rahman. Details are deferred.

My grandfather had three sons from Wife #2. **Najib Ur Rahman** was the eldest. He drowned when he was coming from school on foot and crossing the river. **Wahid Ur Rahman** was the second son. He finished his matric and did not undertake further study. He is living, and in 2017, was eighty-eight. **Hafiz Ur Rahman** earned a bachelor of commerce. He passed away in 2016 at the age of eighty-three. These three sons were young when their mother passed away and were very much attached to my mother. My mother did what she could to raise them and look after them. Wahid Ur Rahman had a great deal of affection for my mother.

Mojib Ur Rahman

Mojib Ur Rahman was the only son of my grandfather with Wife #3 from Balwa village. My grandfather passed away soon after Mojib's birth.

Mojib was about a year older than me. We grew up together as friends and were together till high school. We played all kinds of things. We went to pick up birds from the nest in the hot summer, violating the disciplinary boundary of our parents. We dramatized in the orchard of mango trees next to the house. One day, my father was watching us play drama. We were shooting each other with toy guns. When we realized we had an audience, we were very shy, and my father was very happy to see it. We were much more friends than uncle and nephew. We went to high school at Purnea Zila School together.

During adulthood, when we were visiting home, he entertained Naushaba, Mahboob, and the children by narrating a story of my attempts to smoke in a very dramatic manner. I have this in a video recording.

He said, "Naiyer told me, 'I need to smoke and wear glasses to be a doctor.'" He said that he gave me a cigarette and said that I told him, "Not here, maybe in the toilet." Then he described me coming out with red eyes, coughing, and with tears flowing down my cheeks. I told him, "No, no smoking! It's just the glasses." There was big laughter, and then, turning to Naushaba, Mojib asked, "Naiyer does not smoke, does he, as he had promised to me not to smoke?" More laughter. Those days!

He passed away in his fifties. He performed Hajj. Of course, we miss him more as a friend than as an uncle. His family is in Mahammadia, and they are doing fairly well.

Mojib Ur Rahman, in his youth

Mohammad Abdus Siddique

Mohammad Abdus Siddique and his brother (my grandfather) Majid Ur Rahman were close.

Mohammad Siddique acquired the second car in the district of Purnea. After Nawab's gathering to celebrate his purchase of the first car, Mohammad Siddique could not accept not having a car himself. So he secretly copied the key to his brother's safe using wax and had a real key made. He took money from the safe when Majid Ur Rahman was away, went to Calcutta, and brought a car. This secret act was then confessed to Majid Ur Rahman, who had to accept his brother's doing.

Mohammad Siddique was instrumental in defeating the armed forces of the Thakur to acquire Balwa Estate as sent by Majid Ur Rahman, described earlier.

All of a sudden, one day, Mohammad Siddique disappeared for unknown reasons. Majid Ur Rahman kept looking for his brother. After a few years, he found him in the district of Chapra, in Bihar. He had married and was living there. Majid Ur Rahman went himself and brought his brother back, and they lived together again.

Mohammad Siddique married in Chapra and had three sons, Abul Kalam, Abdus Salaam, and Rafi Ahmed, and a daughter, Arsheda. After the passing away of their father and Uncle Majid Ur Rahman, they faced much hardship from the rest of the uncles.

Abul Kalam

Abul Kalam completed his bachelor's degree despite hardship. He worked as a surveyor of land for the Congress government. Abul Kalam opened a school on the border of Ichalo and Mahammadia. It has been a high school in his name since the early 1990s. He also established a market called Abul Kalam in the vicinity during the same period. He and his wife have passed away. He had two sons.

Dr. Abdus Salaam

Dr. Abdus Salaam, the second son of Mohammad Siddique, was born in 1933. He had a hard time after the death of his father. Despite this, he was educated to be a doctor and became the first doctor in our family. He married the niece of a district judge. The government gave him the job of an officer of malaria in the district of

Purnea. This was not a good posting. He worked in that position, then subsequently moved to the UK and practiced medicine there for years. He flourished. His wife has passed away, and he is alone. He spends time in Yorkshire, England, in his house where his younger son and his two sons also live. He has two sons and two daughters. His sons and daughters were well-placed professionally and financially. He sometimes returns to Mahammadia and stays for a while. He has a very special attachment with Mahammadia. He always had a close relationship with my parents, and he continues to maintain that closeness. He even visited us and my sister Yasmin in Regina, Canada, and talked to my children. He said that he came to visit his lost tribe. We went especially to visit him in October 2015 in Yorkshire. May Allah keep him alive, maintaining his good health.

Rafi Ahmed

Rafi Ahmed stayed home and did not study. Rafi has also passed away. His granddaughter was married to my brother's son, Danish Mahboob, in 2013. We were there and negotiated the marriage.

Arsheda

Arsheda, Mohammad Siddique's daughter, was married to Mir Nayyar Ali from the Nawab family of Purnea city. She and her husband have passed away. They had two sons, Shakir and Sarwar.

Mohammad Agha

Mohammad Agha had four sons with Wife #2, from Belgachchi.

Abdul Jabbar

I do not know much about Abdul Jabbar. He had children, as listed in the ancestry rolls, whom I knew well. His wife was Asma from Chanderdai, a sister of Bhola Babu and Zia Ur Rahman and my father's aunt. He had two sons, Badi Uz Zaman and Shamsh Uz Zaman, and a daughter, Akhtari Begum, who is married to my uncle Hasib Ur Rahman.

Abdul Ghaffar

He was a man who lived with dignity and influence. He also owned a car. He would wake up in the morning with prayer and sit outside his bungalow. At 10 a.m., he would go in to have a shower and eat breakfast, and then he would come out in the evening to sit outside the bungalow and look after the family affairs. He had no children of his own. He adopted his grandson from Shamsh Uz Zaman.

Abdul Wahab

He respected his brother, Abdul Ghaffar, very much. He used to sit in the corner of the bungalow while Abdul Ghaffar sat in the main sitting area. If Abdul Ghaffar would go away from the main sitting area, Abdul Wahab would sit in the main area of the bungalow. He had two sons and two daughters from his first marriage and two daughters from his second. The sons were Sulaiman Akhtar and Naoman Akhtar, and the daughters were Jahan Ara and RukhSana Ara with Wife #1, and Roshan and a sister with Wife #2.

Abdus Samad

His illustrated incident with the police is noted to show the influence of the Mahammadia family in the area. He was a man of temper, and he would not approve of anyone being undisciplined in his presence. He used to live secluded in an area of the building, in his room. If he went somewhere, he would have guards accompany his carriage. He used to travel on a bullock cart. These bulls were very robust and astoundingly fast runners. I am told that one time, he was travelling to the city in his carriage on the paved road (the Grand Trunk Road built by Shah Suri from Bengal to Delhi), and a police car was travelling in the same direction. The police car blew the horn, and the carriage driver of Abdus Samad moved his cart but left one wheel running on the road. Apparently, this was to maintain the dignity and honour of Abdus Samad, as known to his servants. The police car kept blowing the horn and then pulled in front and stopped his carriage. Abdus Samad was sleeping, and he woke up. I am told that he took the whip out and whipped the police officer and his driver badly. He did this because their treatment of him was below his dignity and to tell them that he had already allowed them half of the road. Anyway, police action was carried out, and Abdus Samad dealt with it with dignity, being an influential individual. We had such personalities in the family. He was married to Zubaida from Elahi Bakhsh Family **Ancestry Chart #5**. He had two daughters: Ahmadi, who is married to Naeem Registrar, and Mohammadi, who passed away at an early age.

Other Relatives

Mohammad Shirfuddin

Mohammad Shirfuddin was the brother of my father's first wife, Maimoona, who passed away, as previously noted. He was as close to my mother as his own sister, as were his mother and wife. He was standing by for any problem that we faced. We still have links with his family. We miss him very much. Whenever I returned from my school during a holiday, he would invite us. He participated in and celebrated all the happy occasions that came around, with special attention to my mother and her children. His mother used to send food whenever she cooked something special. He was richest from the share that he received from his ancestors. He passed away. He had sons who were looking after the family and were in touch with us.

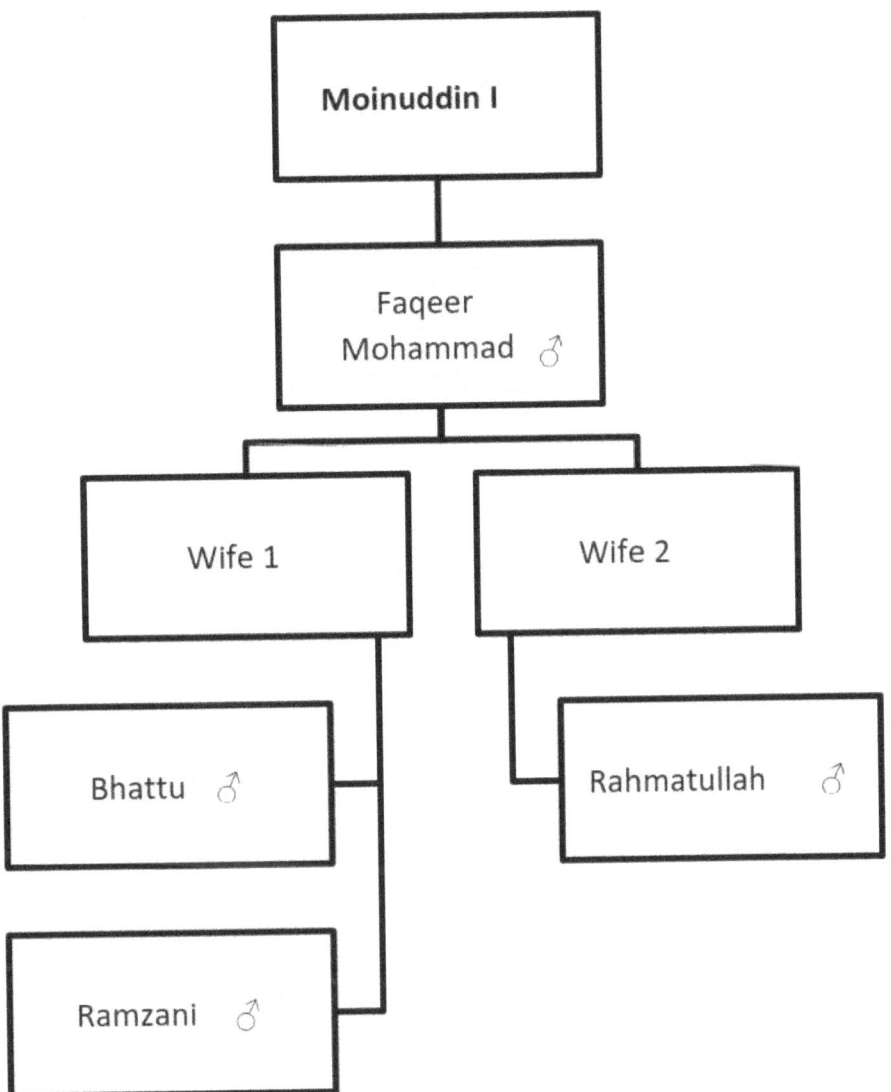

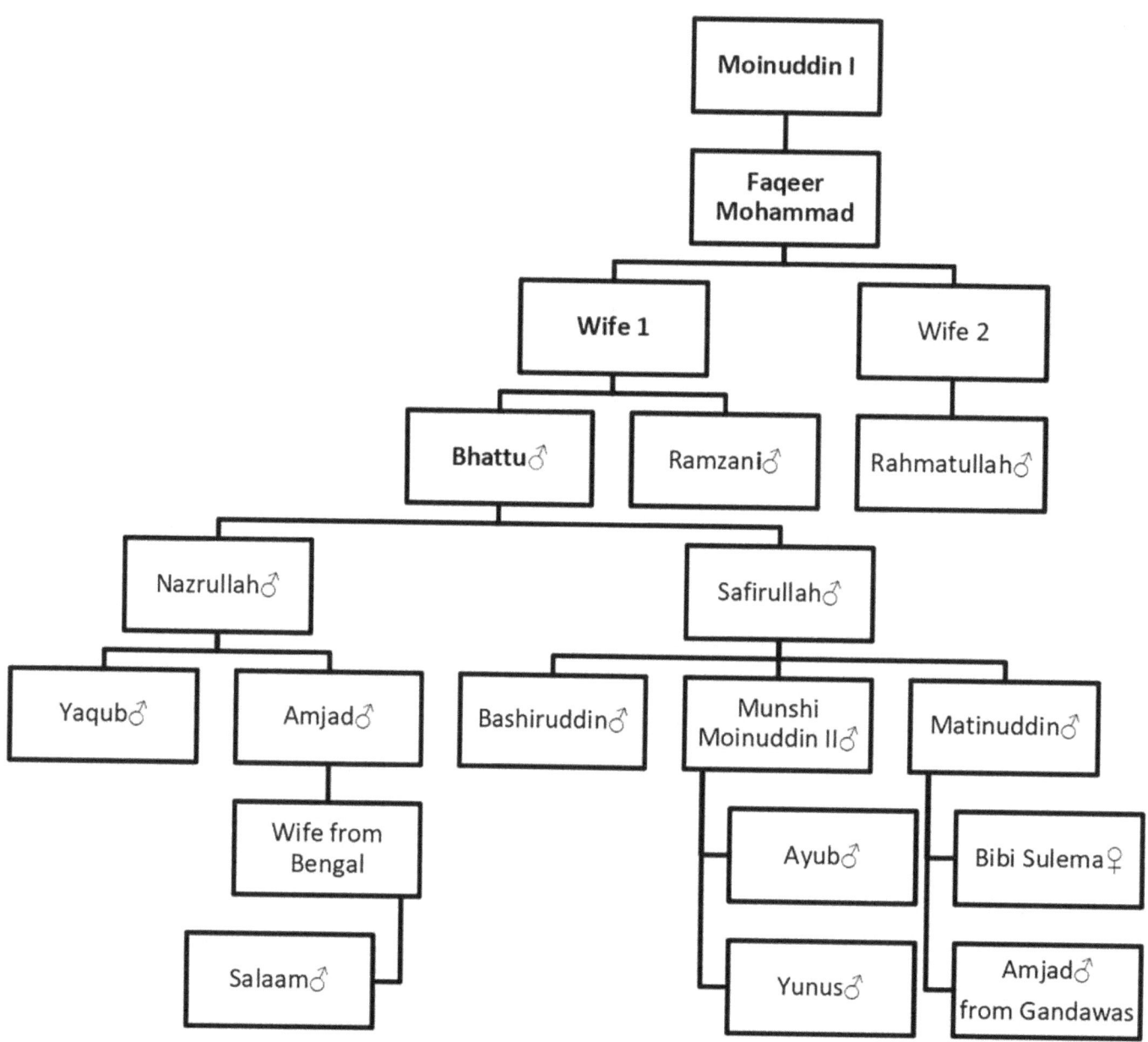

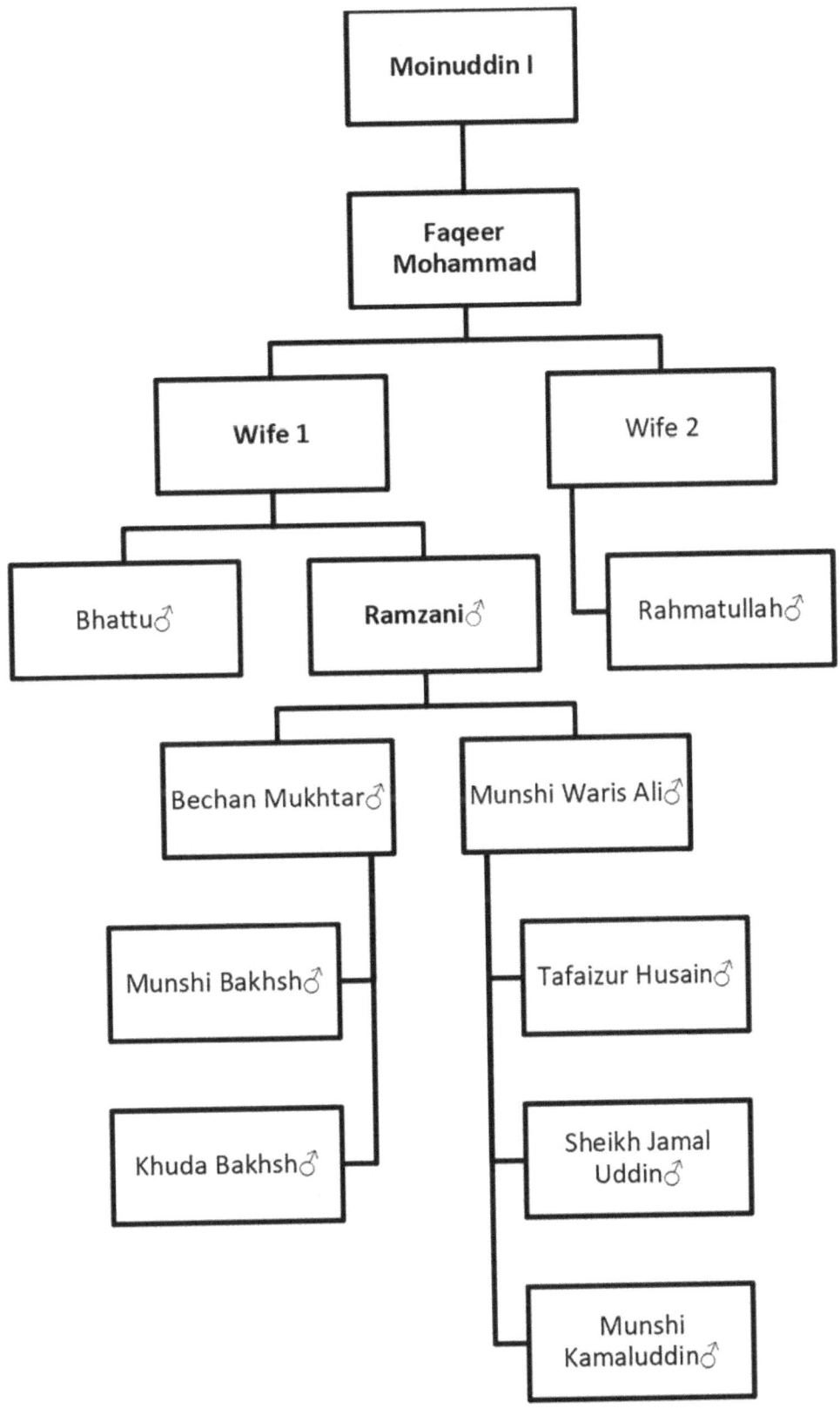

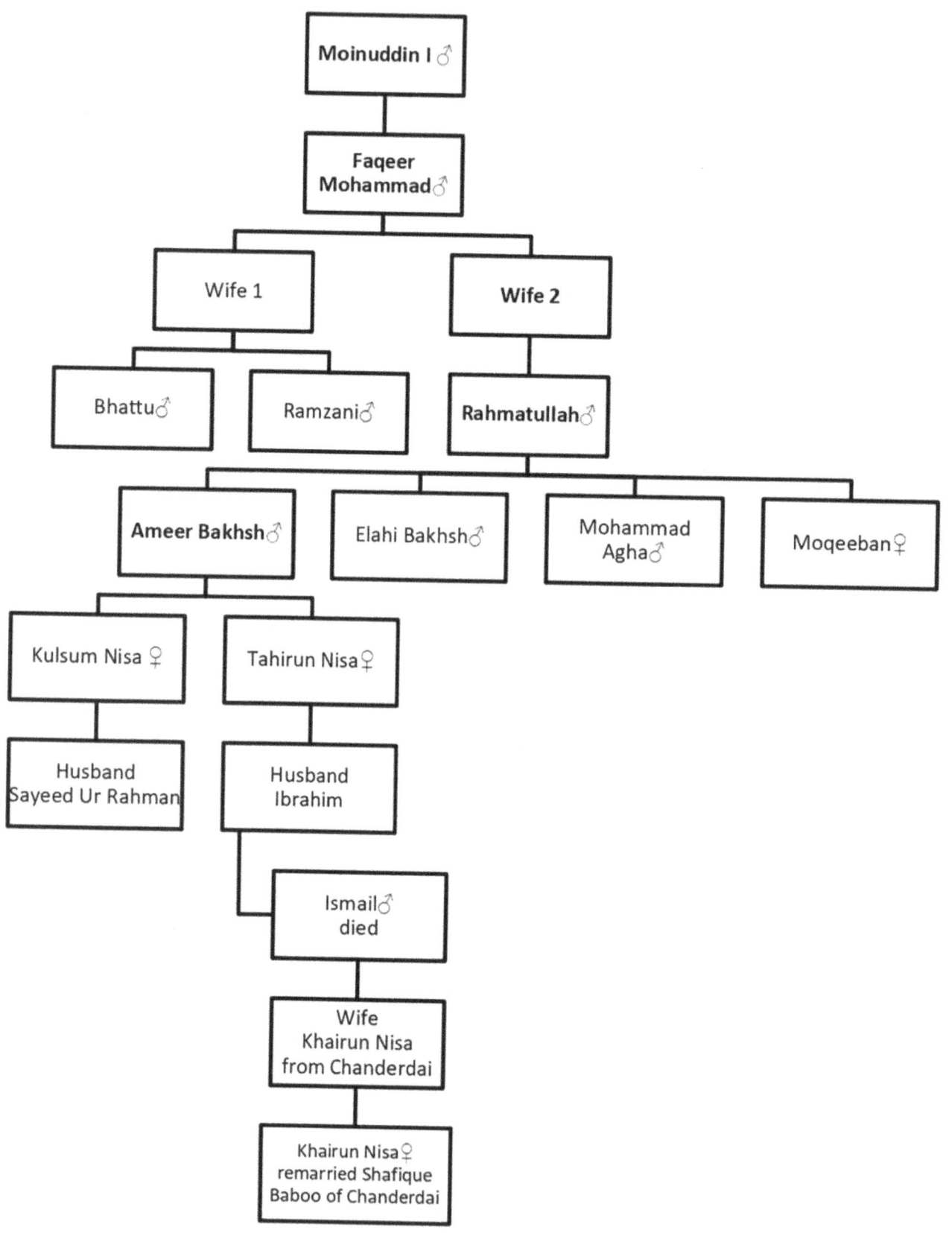

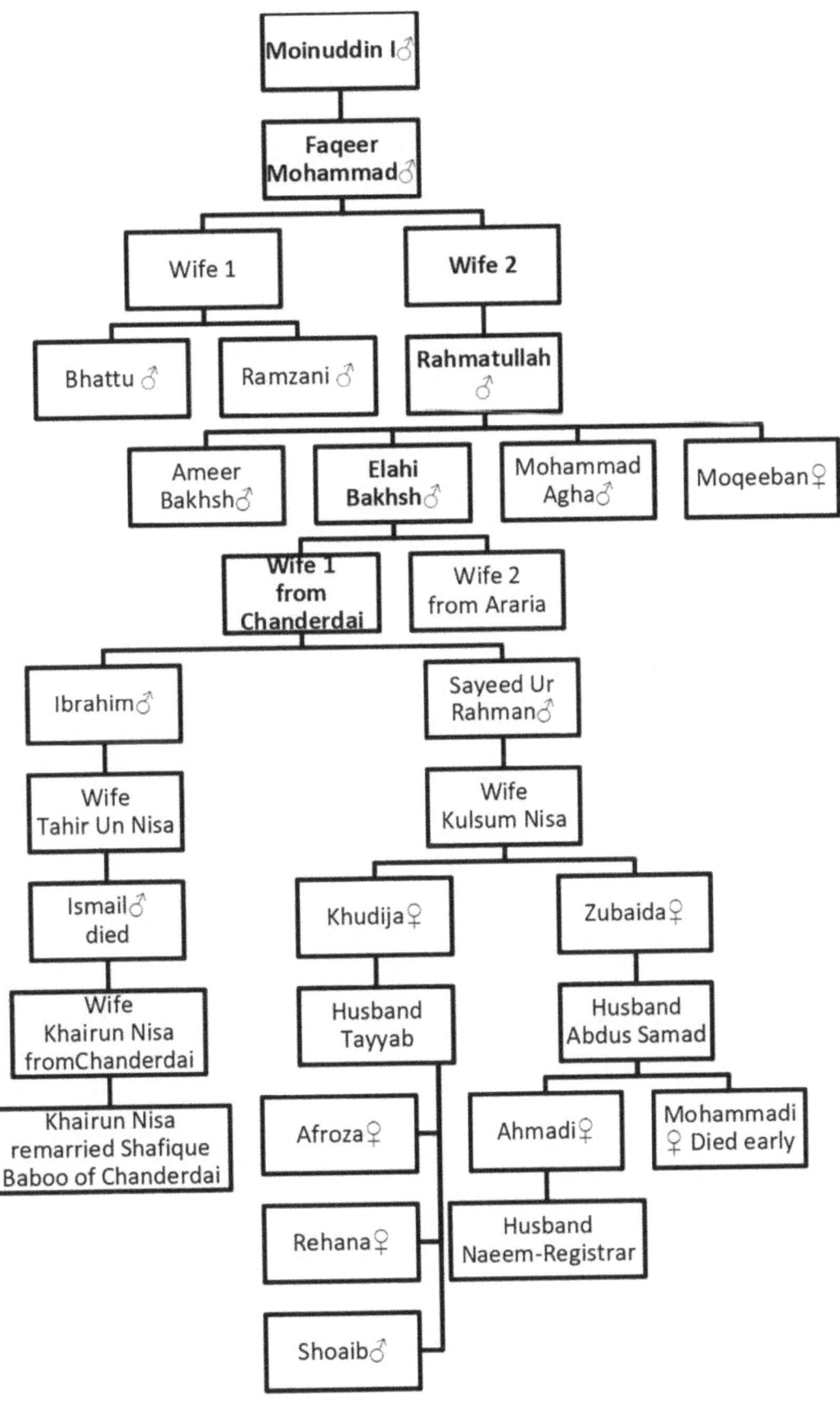

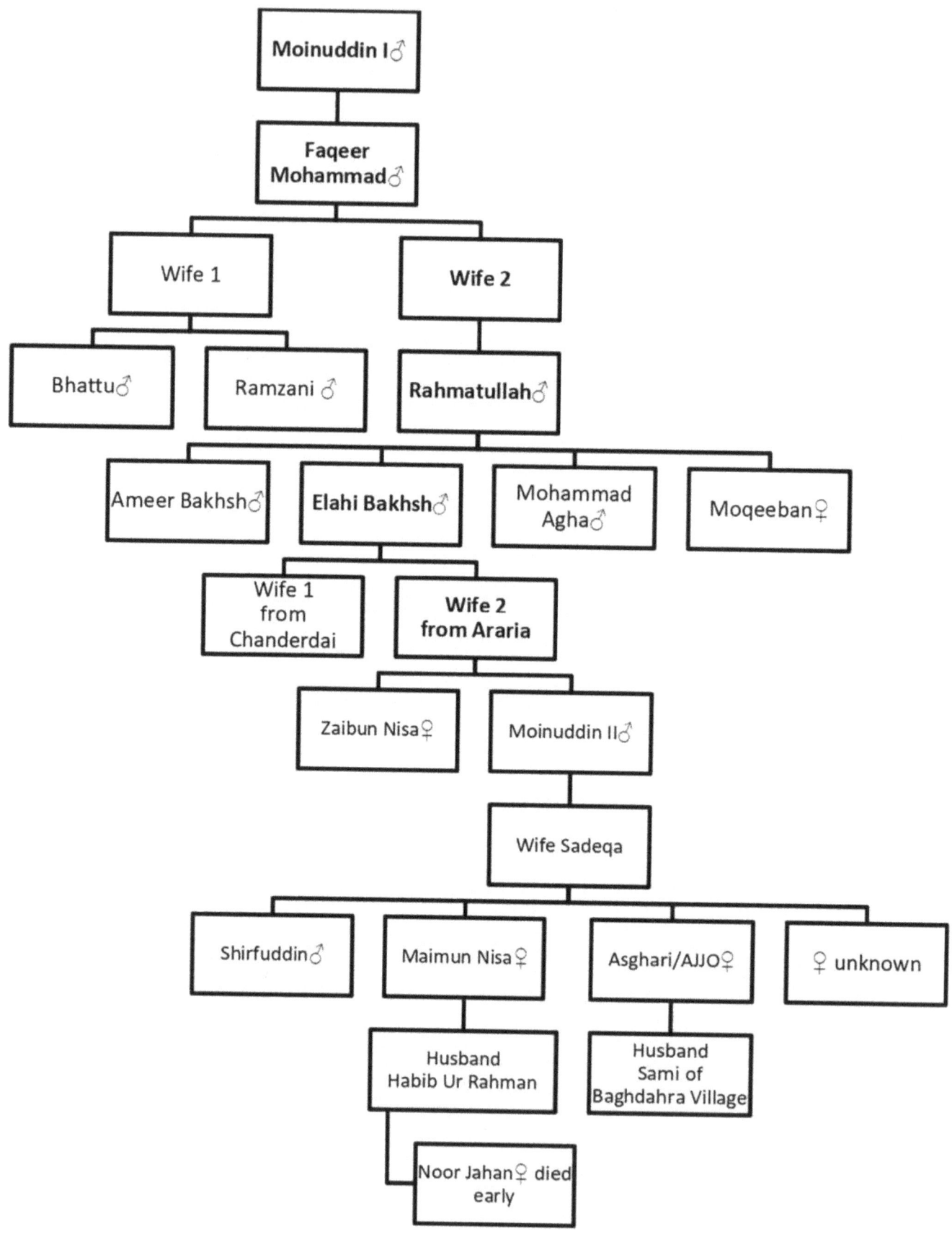

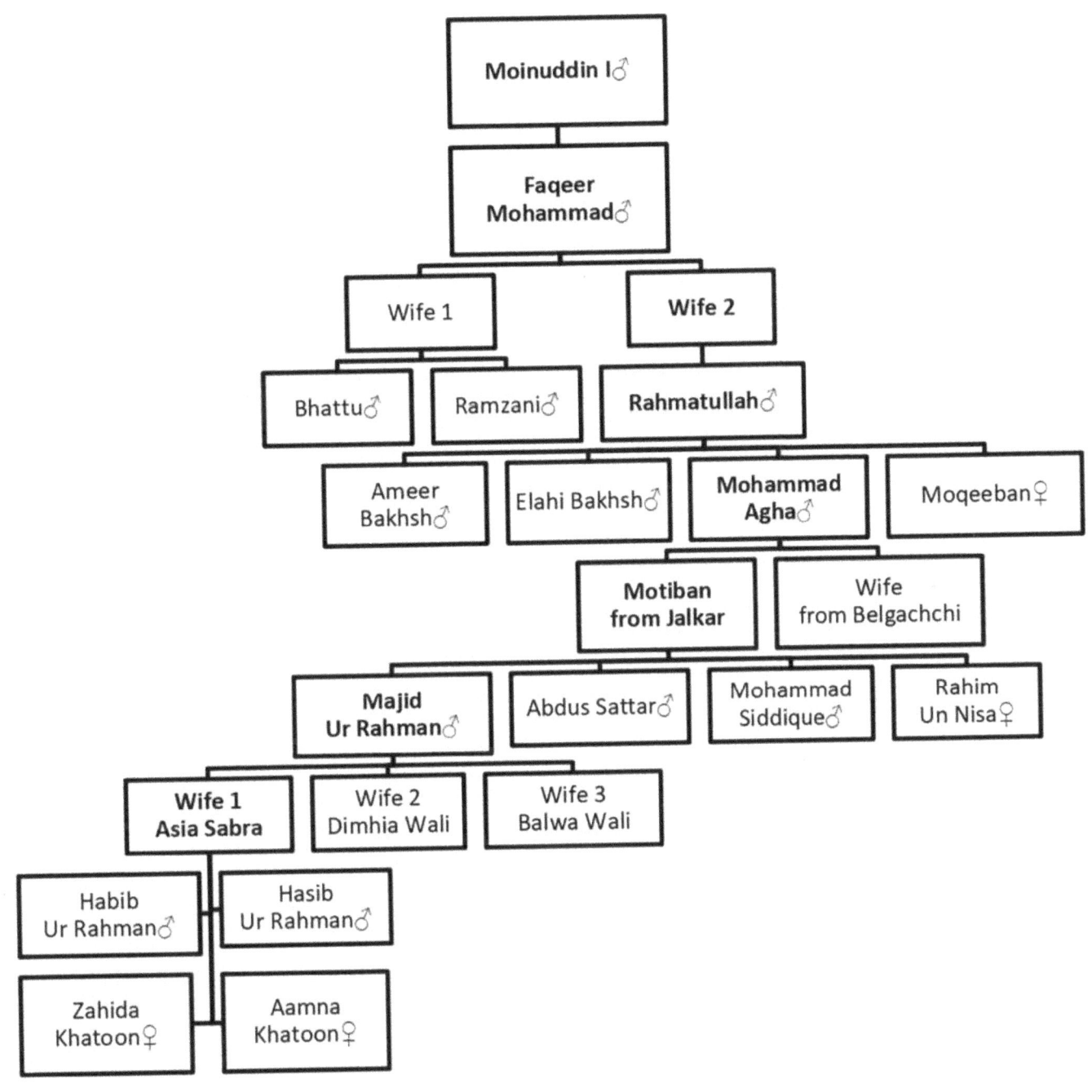

Faqeer & Wife #2/Rahmatullah/Mohammad Agha & Motiban/Majid Ur Rahman & Wife #2

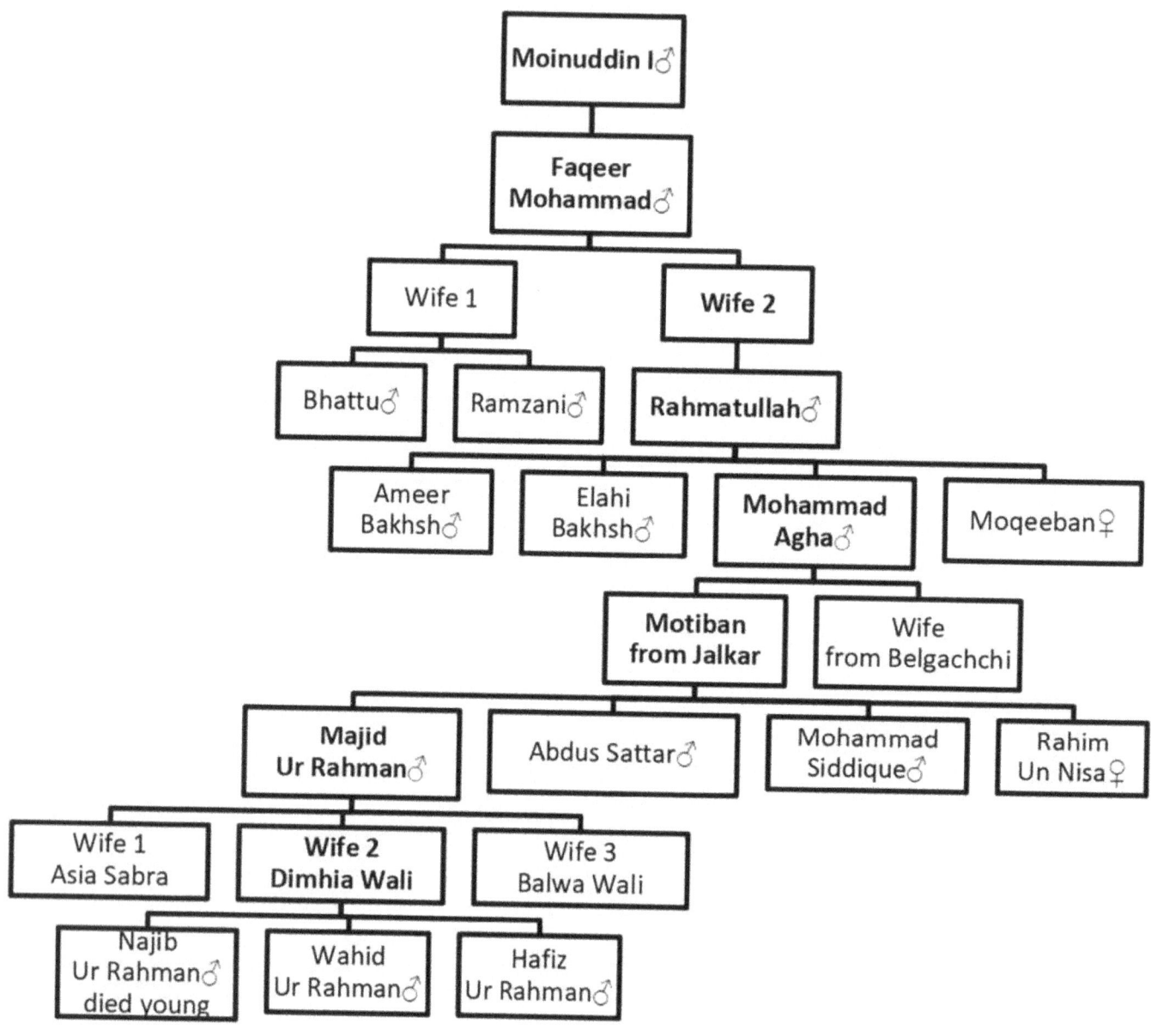

Faqeer & Wife #2/Rahmatullah/Mohammad Agha & Motiban/Majid Ur Rahman & Wife #3

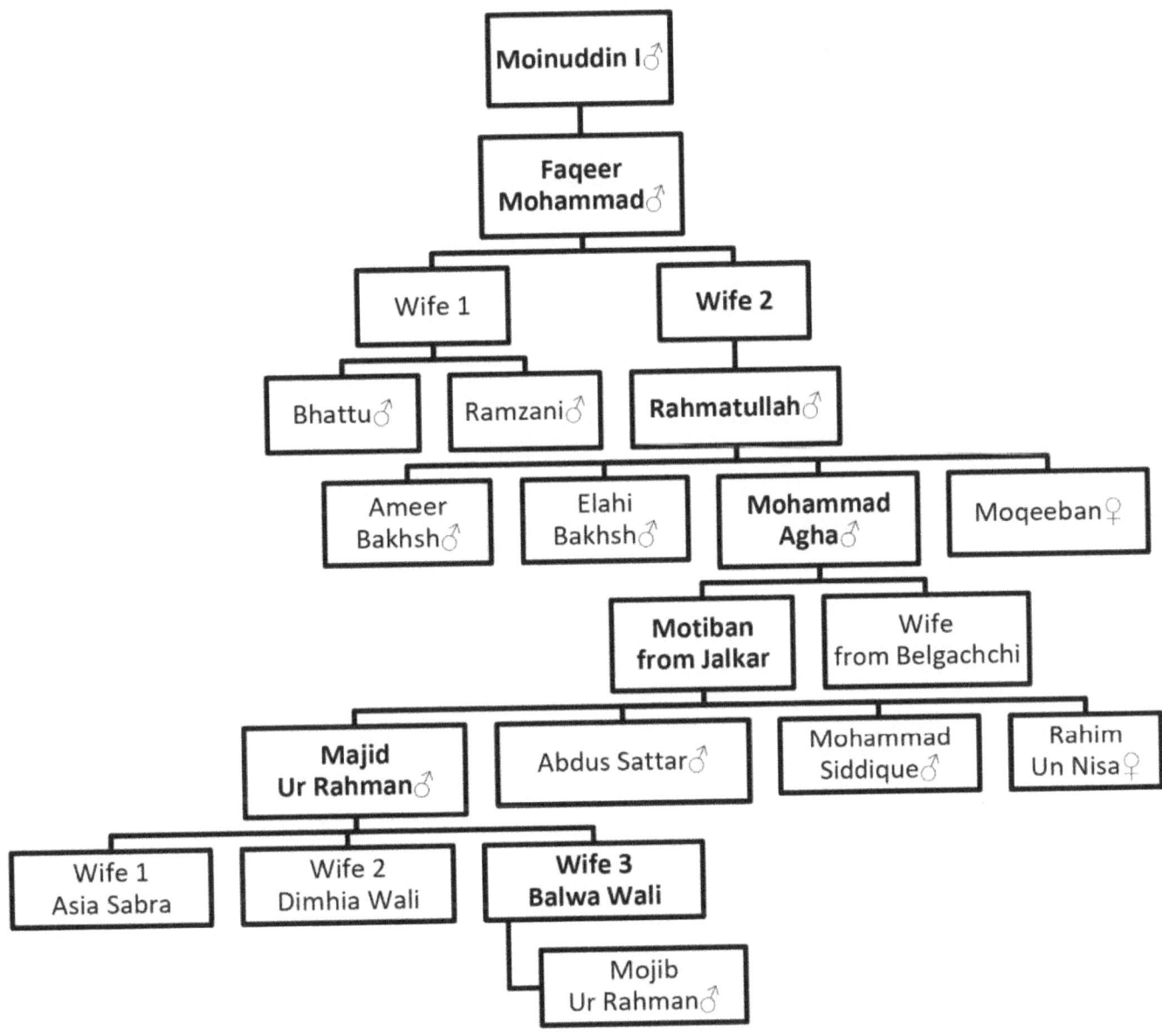

Faqeer & Wife #2/Rahmatullah/Mohammad Agha & Motiban/Mohammad Siddique & Naushaba

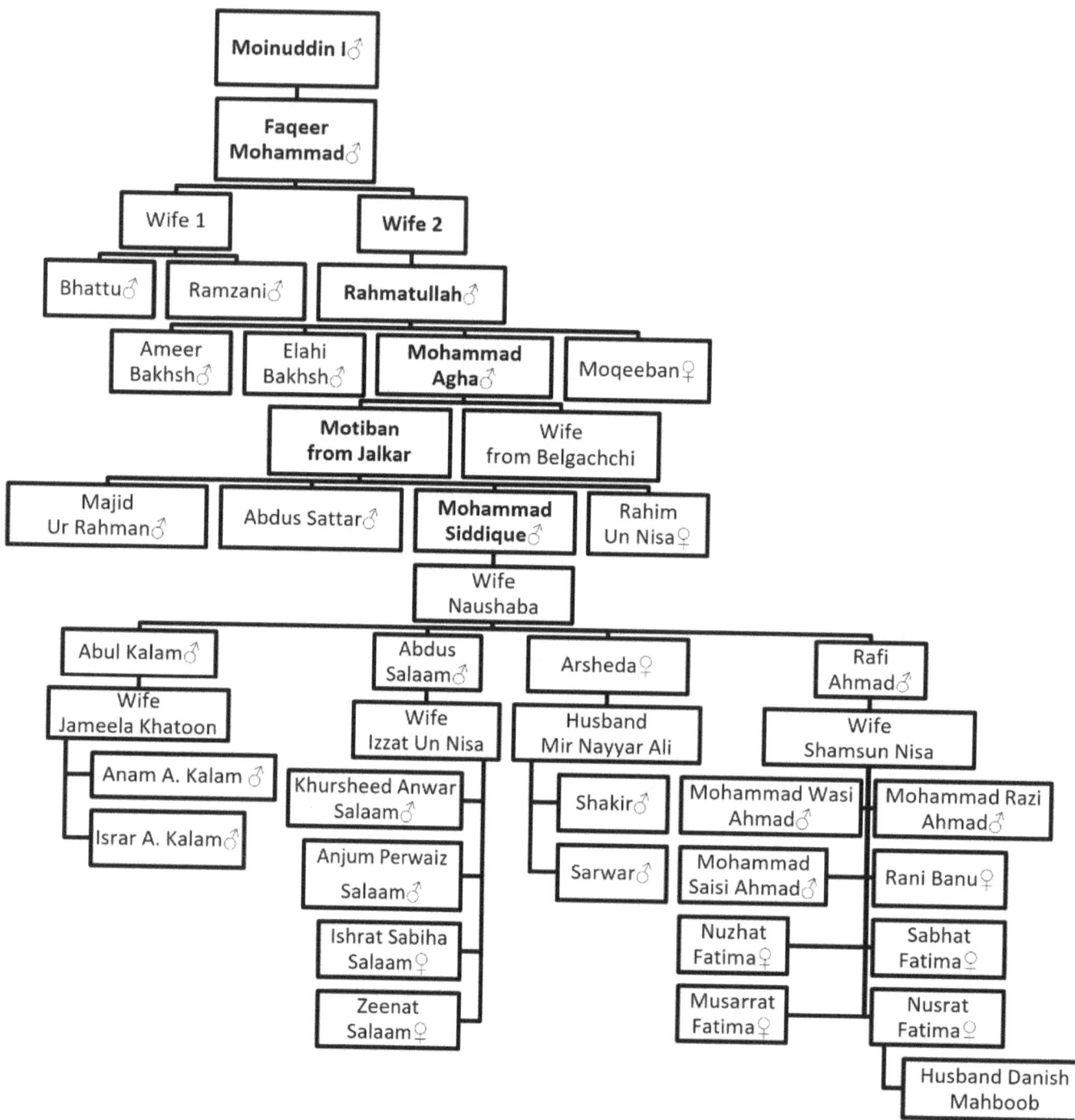

Faqeer Mohammad &Wife 2/Rahmatullah/Muhammad Agha & Wife 2

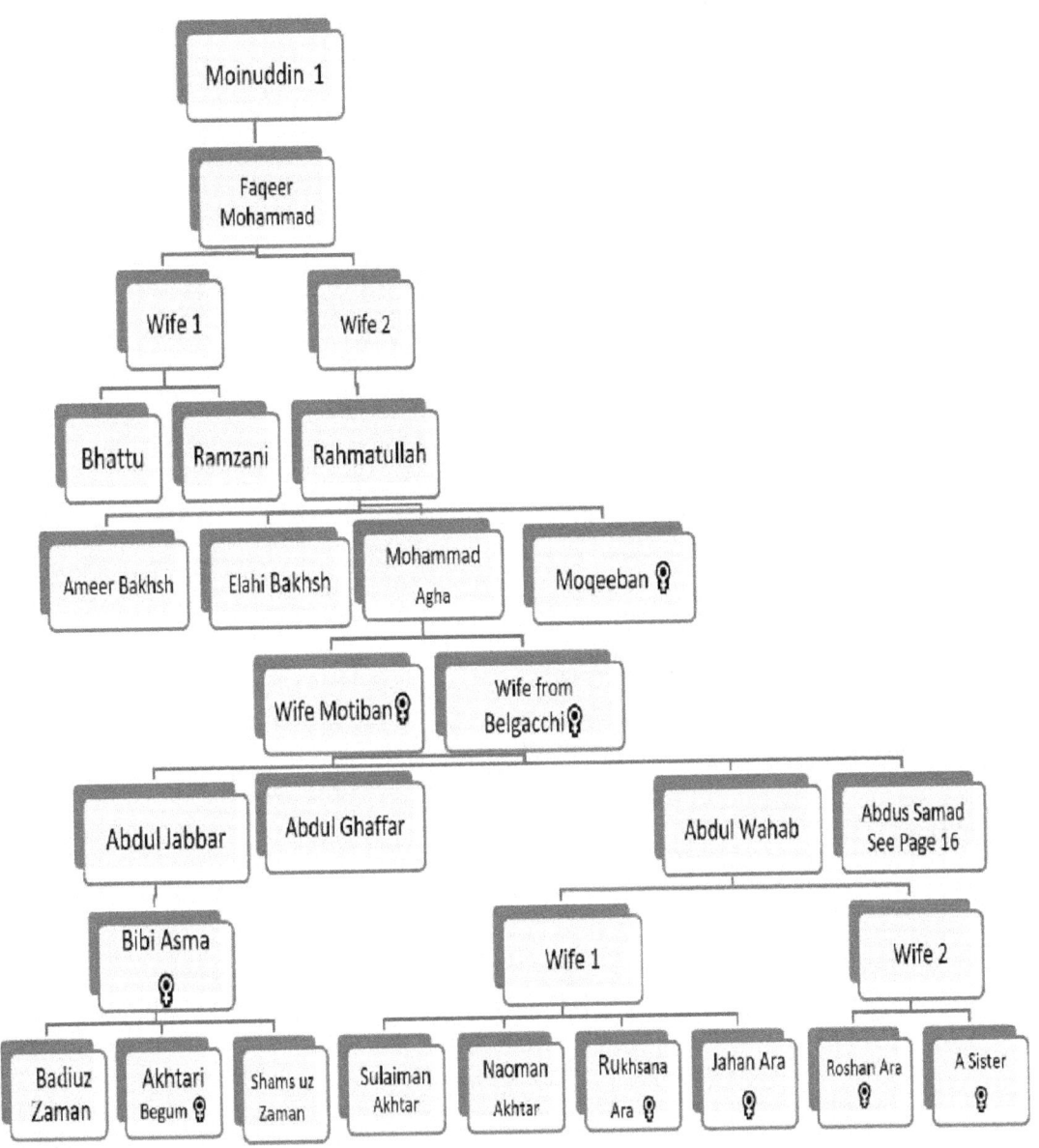

: Akhtari Begum: See Ancestry Chart # 14 on Page 30 for her progeny: Only females are Identified with ♀
Ancestry of Badiuz Zaman and Shamsuz Zaman had to be moved to pages 555 and 556, respectively, because of
their insertions in the post-print status of the book to maintain continuity of page numbers of all topics in the
content of the book.

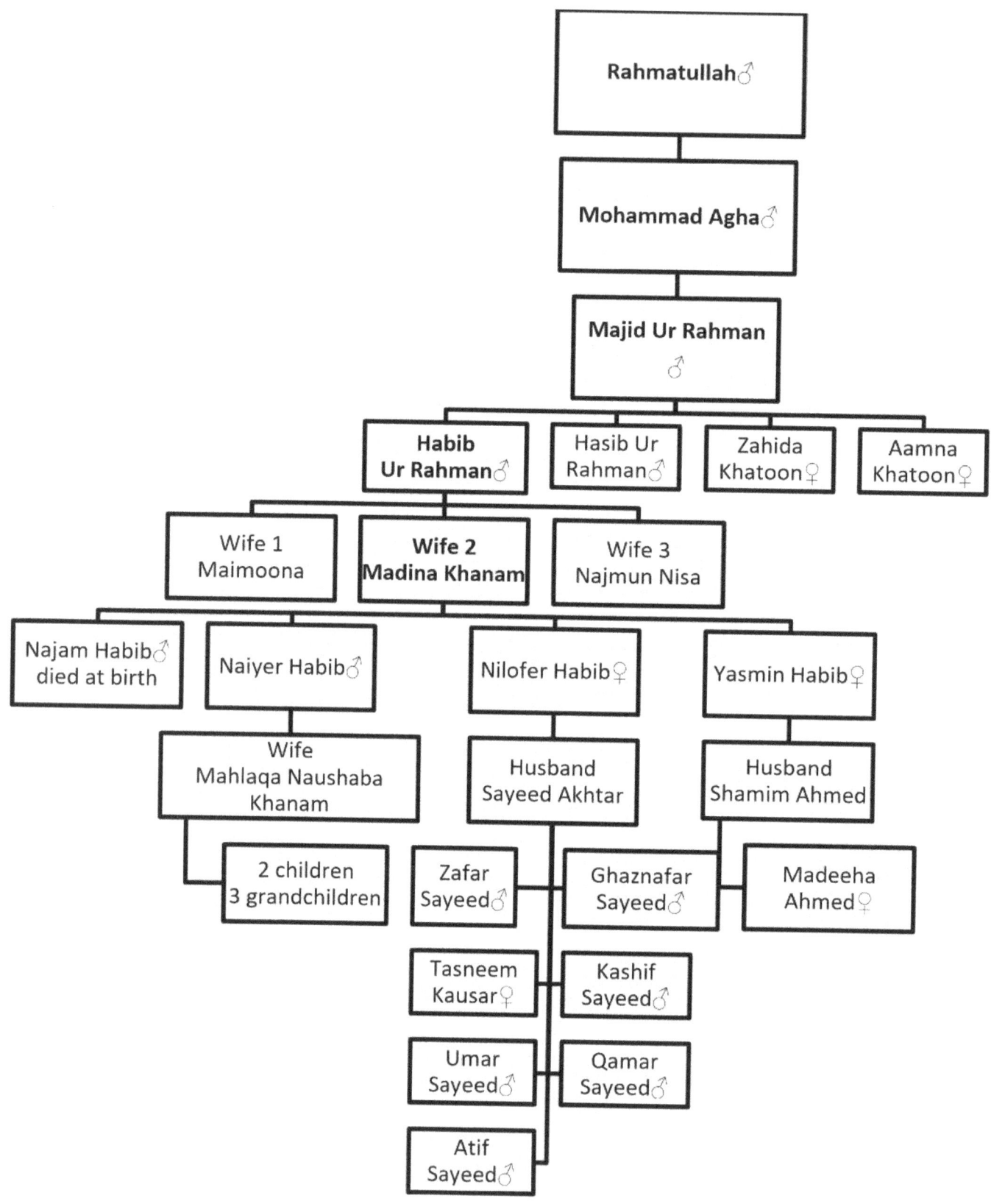

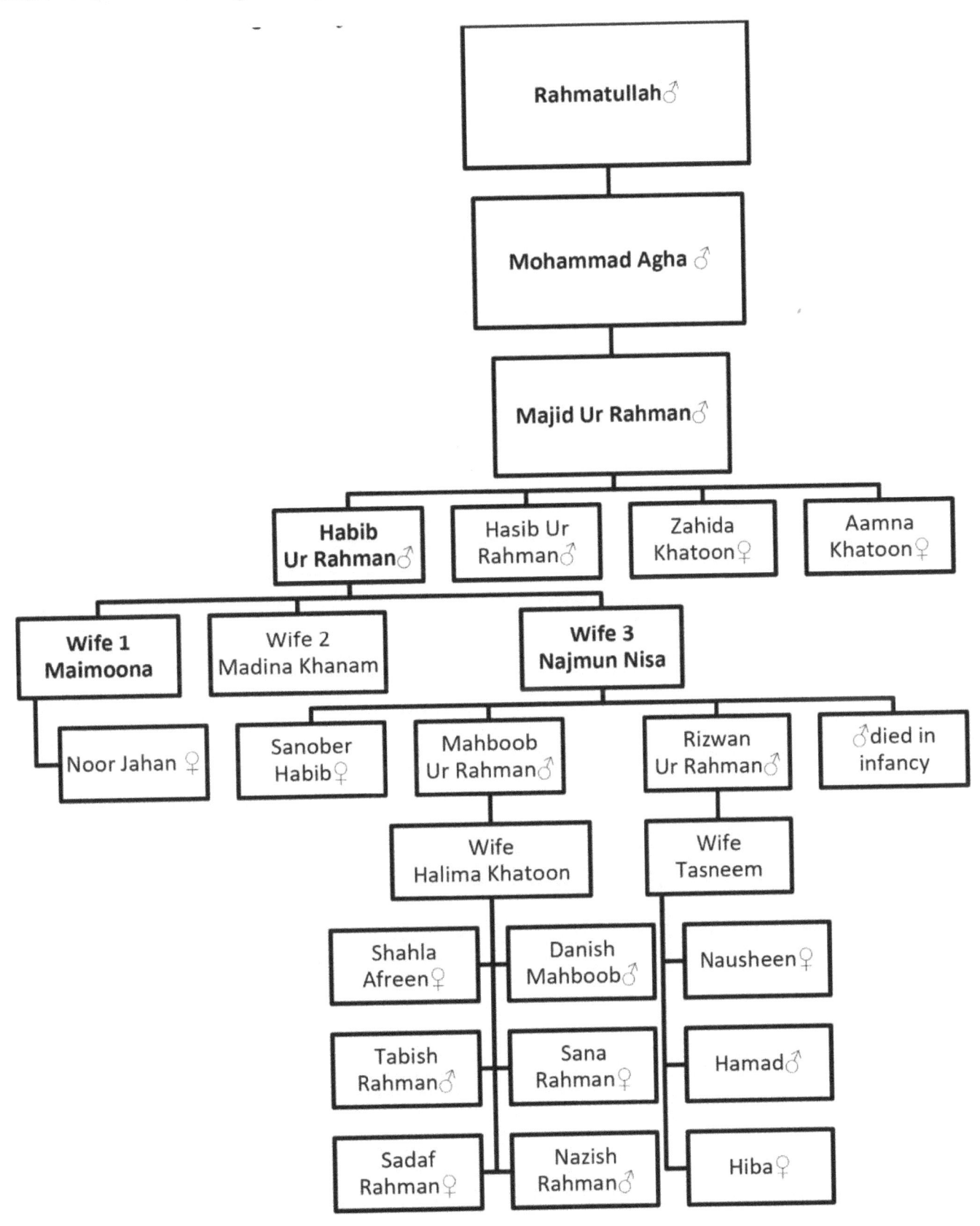

Rahmatullah/Mohammad Agha//Majid Ur Rahman//Hasib Ur Rahman & Wife Akhtari Begum

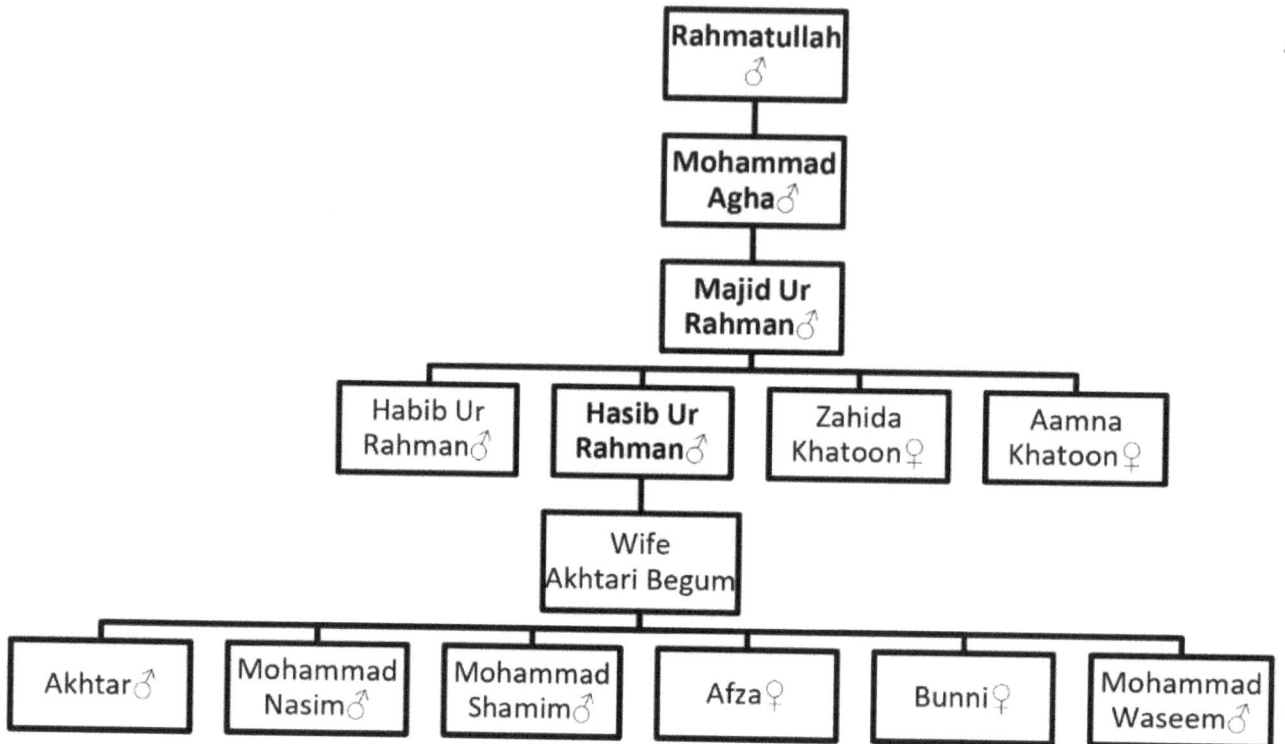

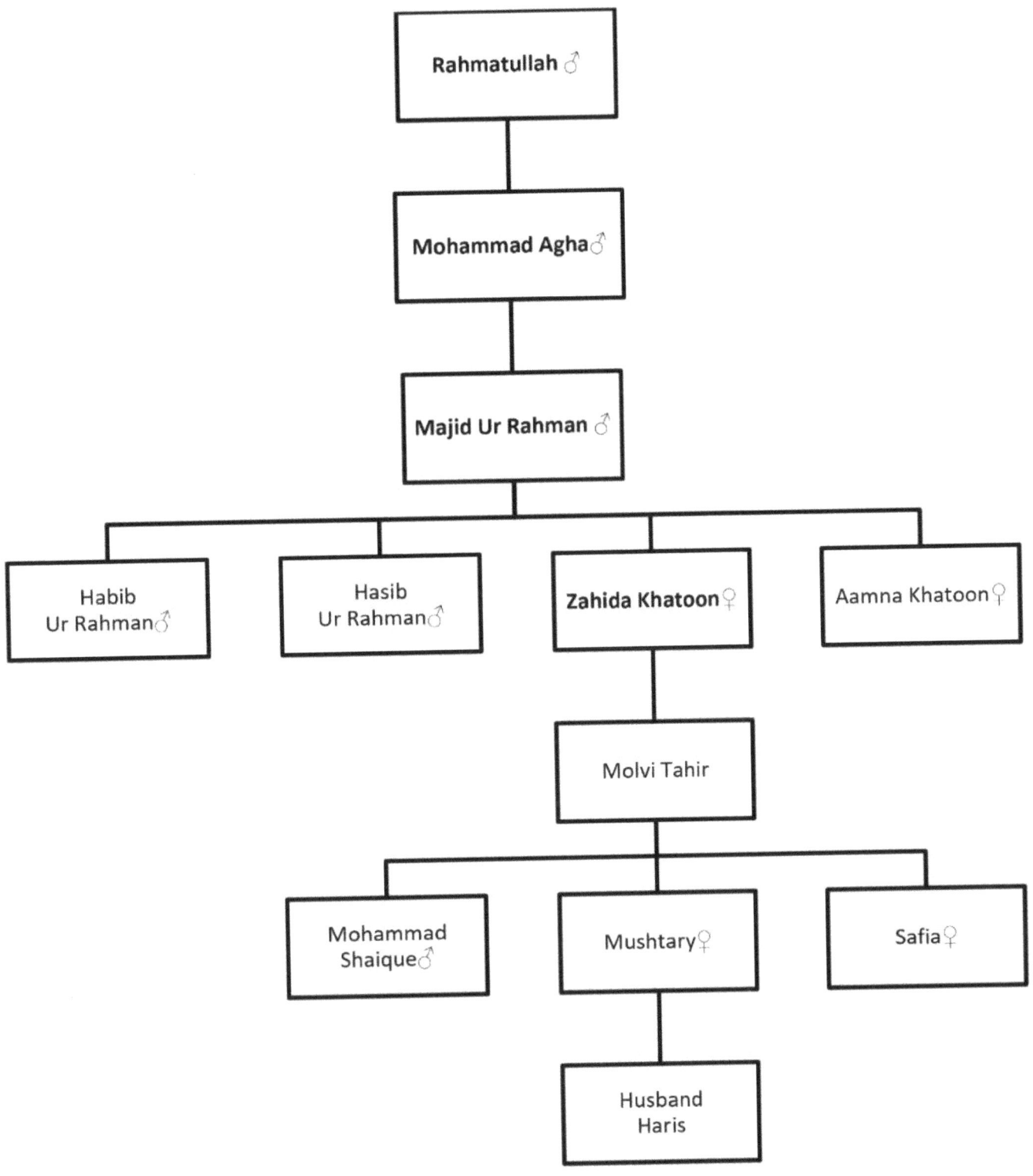

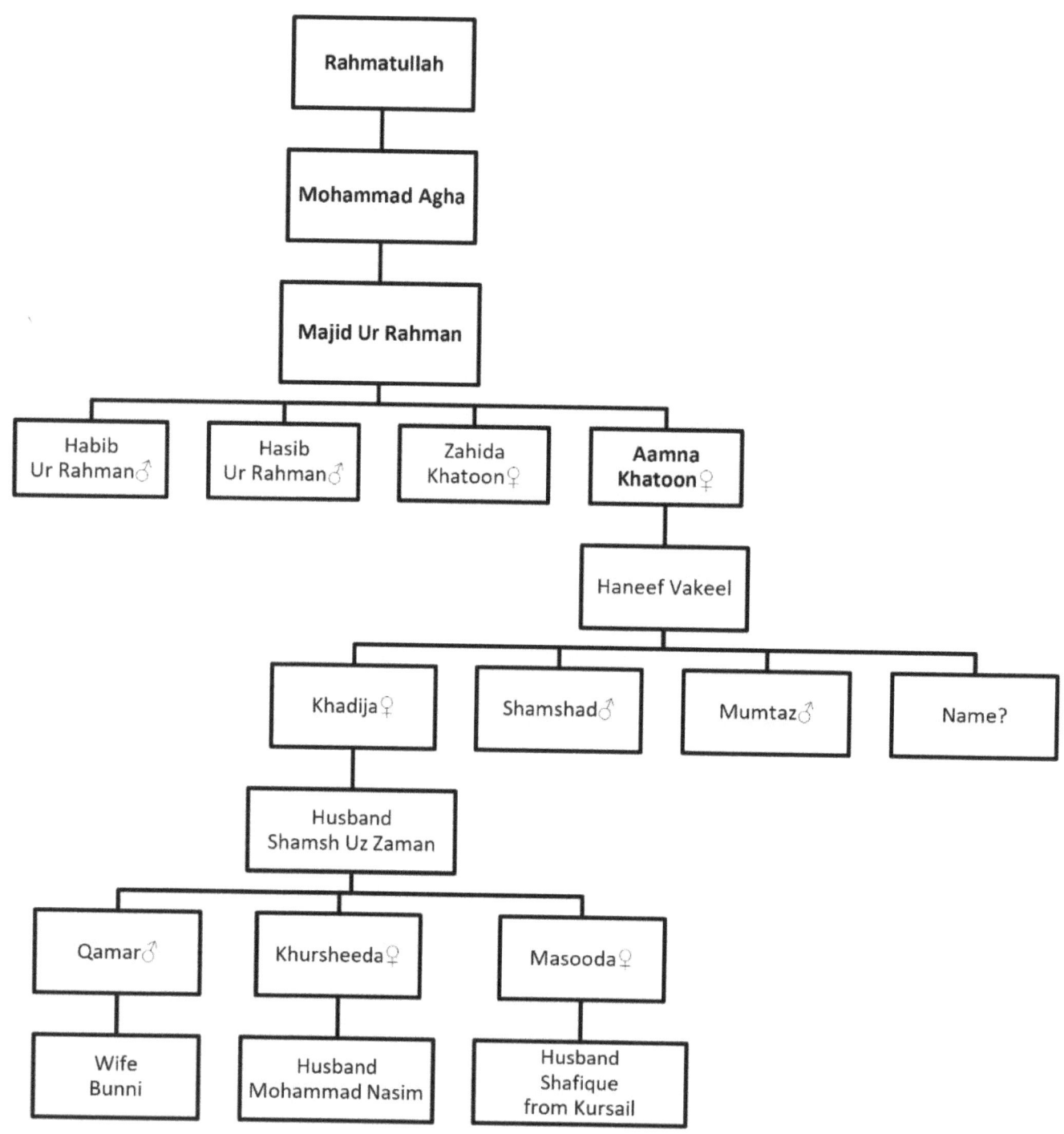

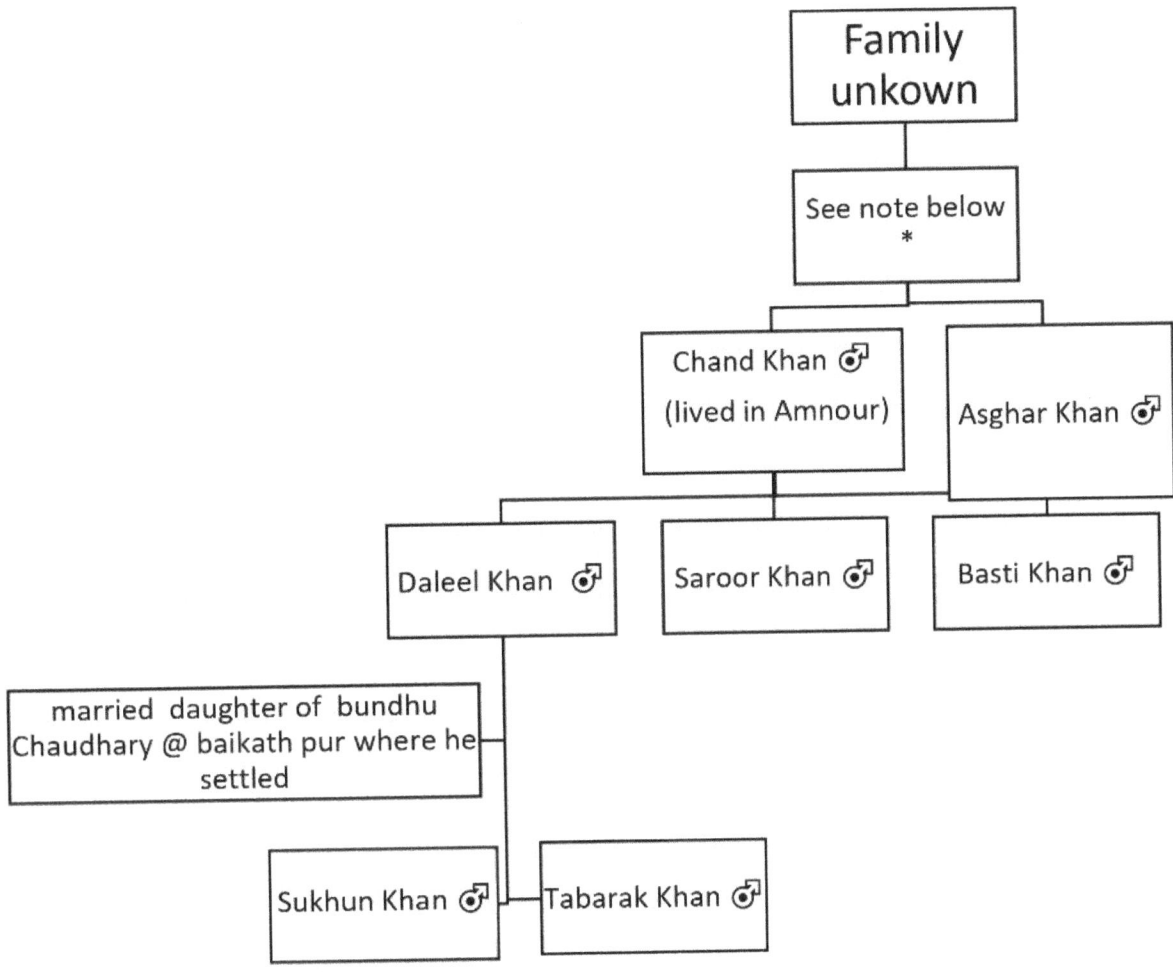

- Ancestors of our mothers (Chart No 17) came from Afghanistan to Delhi during the Akbar Emperor period, called the Yusuf Zai Pathan family. Some moved to Nagpur, Khatak Pur. After decades, what is known is that there were two brothers. Their names are not known. A brother's son married at Amnourr, Chhapra, and second brother's son married at Kona Sarai, Bihar Sharif, both in the State of Bihar. They settled at Amnour and Kona Sarai, respectively.
- Names of the wives are not available.

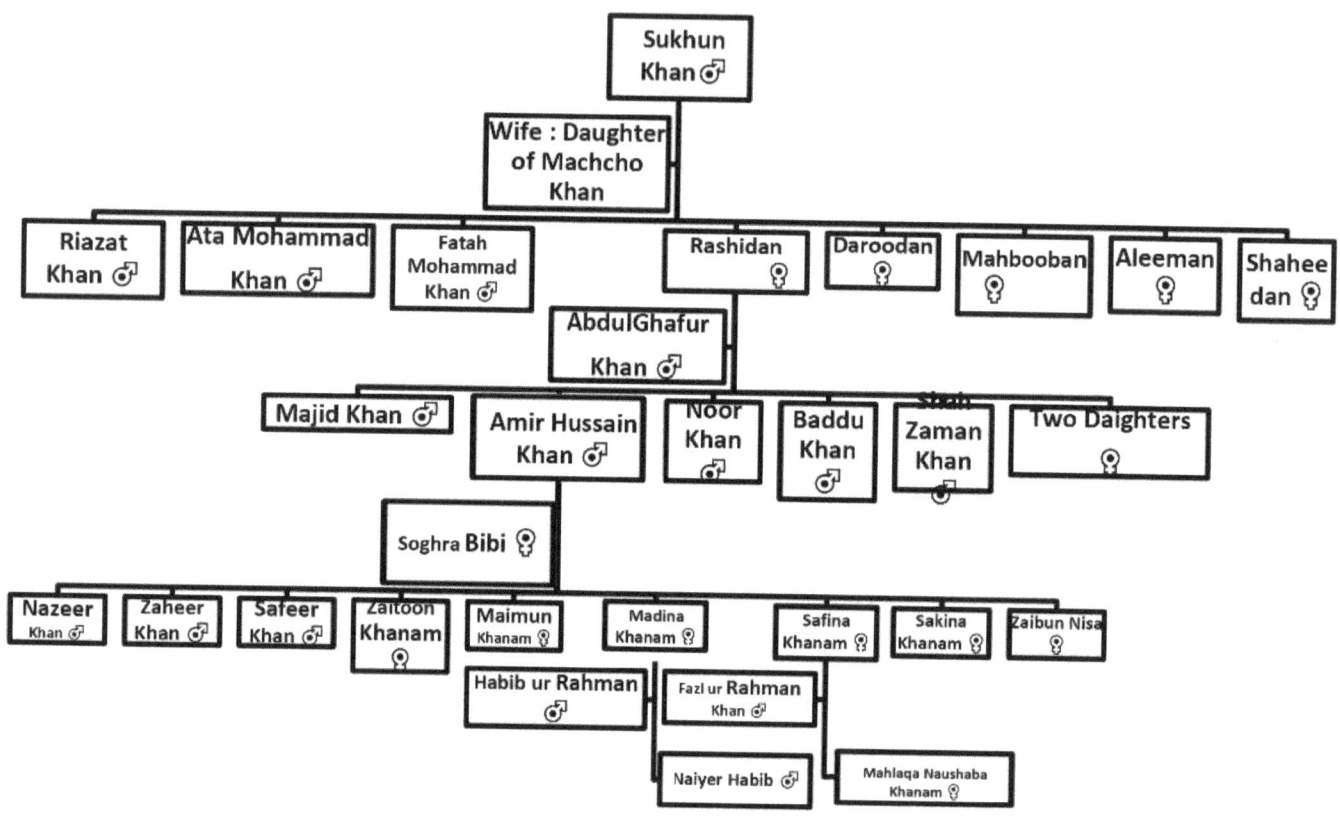

NOTE: Our mothers were sisters. Paternal grandfather of Mahlaqa Naushaba Habib and the Maternal grandfather of her and of Naiyer Habib were 1st cousins, but we could not link their parents.

*Zaheer khan

Pictures of some family members who are in the ancestry charts

Dr. Abdus Salaam, at young age and at senior age

Wahid Ur Rahman and Hafiz Ur Rahman, with wives

Hasib Ur Rahman, with wife Akhtari Begum

L to R: Rizwan, s/o Shirfuddin, Shirfuddin, Abul Kalam, Wahid Ur Rahman, Hasib Ur Rahman, Javed, Mahboob, Shamim (being seen off on our 1979 visit to Mahmmdia by my uncles, brothers, and cousins).

Our State, District, And Village

My ancestral family finally settled and lived in the village of Mahammadia, in the district of Purnea, state of Bihar, India.

Naushaba's family settled in the village of Nathupur, in the district of Patna, state of Bihar, India.

Bihar

Ancient Bihar, known as Magadha, was the centre of power, learning, and culture in India for a thousand years. India's "first empire," the Maurya Empire, as well as one of the world's religions, Buddhism, arose from the region in Gaya. The capital, Patna, earlier known as Pataliputra, was an important political, military, and economic centre of Indian civilization during the ancient and classical periods of history. Many of the ancient Indian texts that were written outside of the religious epics were written in ancient Bihar, Abhijñānaśākuntala[17] being the most prominent. The state played a vital role in the movement toward independence from the British. The first president of India, Dr. Rajendra Prasad, was from here. He was with Mahatma Gandhi.[18] See a rich history on him online.

---

[17] Sanskrit, with English translation, meaning: the Recognition of Shakuntala.
[18] See rich history in Wikipedia.

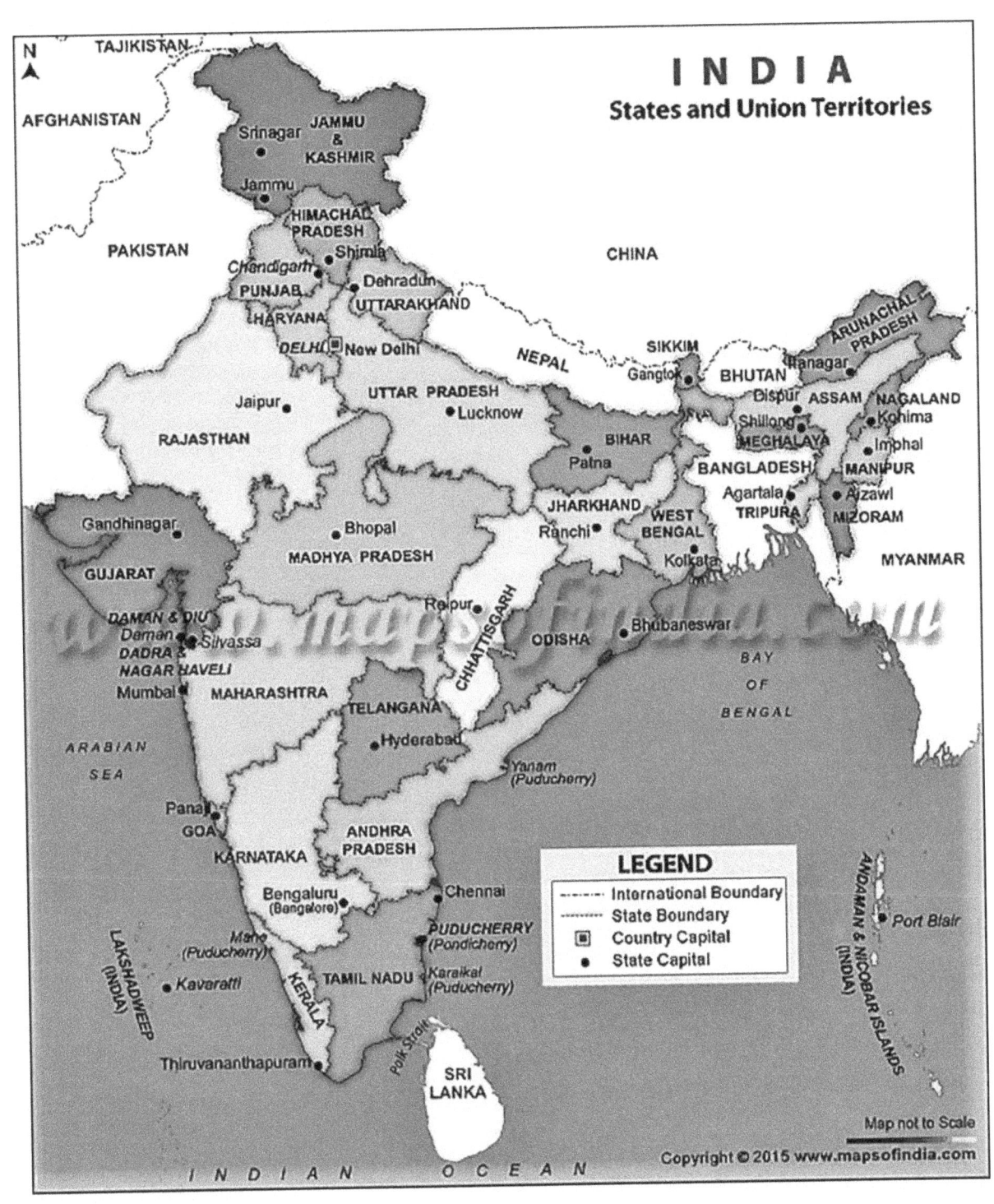

States of Bihar and Gujarat in India.[19]

[19]Map reprinted with the permission of MapsofIndia.com.

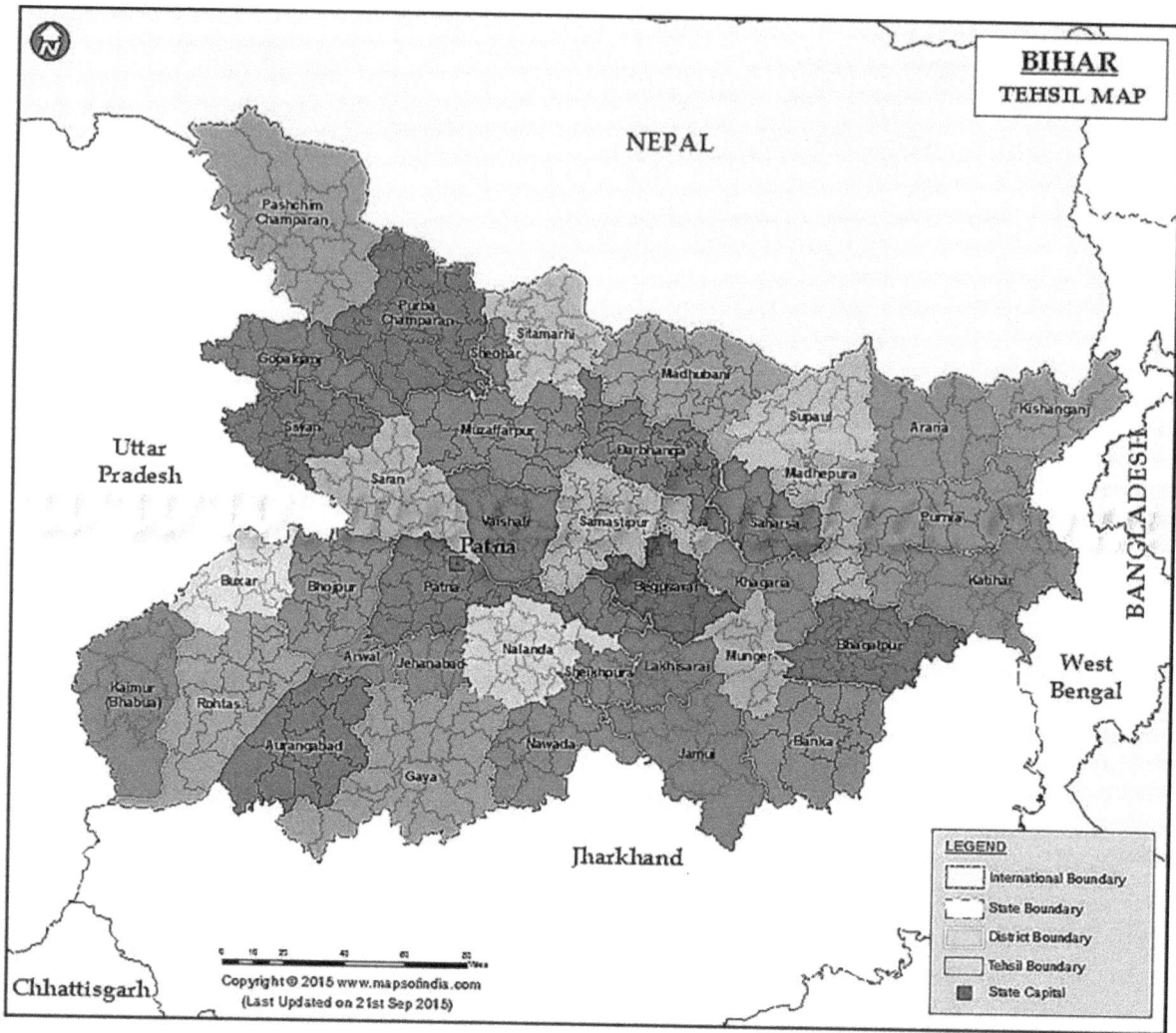

Purnea

During the Mughal rule, Purnea was an outlying military province, and its revenue was mostly spent on protecting its borders against tribes from the north and east. Its local governor raised a rebellion against Siraj Ud Din in 1757 after the capture of Calcutta. In 1765, along with the rest of Bengal, the district became a British possession. The district of Purnea, in modern history, was formed by the East India Company in February 1770. Purnea city is the fifth largest city of Bihar and is located about 300 kilometres from Patna, the capital city. The Indian army, Indian air force, border security force, and Sashastra Seema Bal (armed border force) have their bases around the district.[20]

---

[20] Edited from https://en.wikipedia.org/wiki/Purnia_district. Map reprinted with permission from Maps of India.

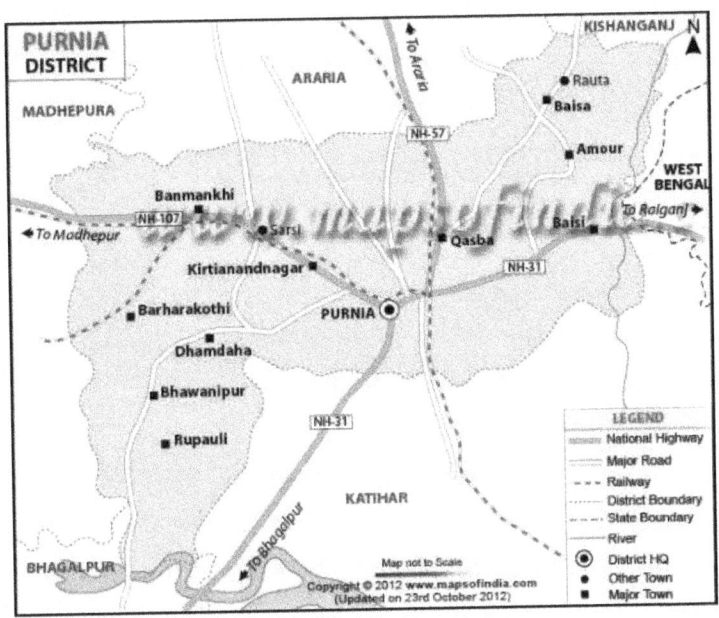

Mahammadia

Mahammadia is a small village in Dagarua Block of Purnea District of Bihar State, India. It is located twenty-two kilometres east of district headquarters in Purnea. Mahammadia is about seven kilometres east of Kasba and is surrounded by Kasba Block to the west, Baisi Block to the east, and Jalalgarh Block to the northwest. Purnea, Dalkhola, Araria, and Kishanganj are nearby cities to Mahammadia.

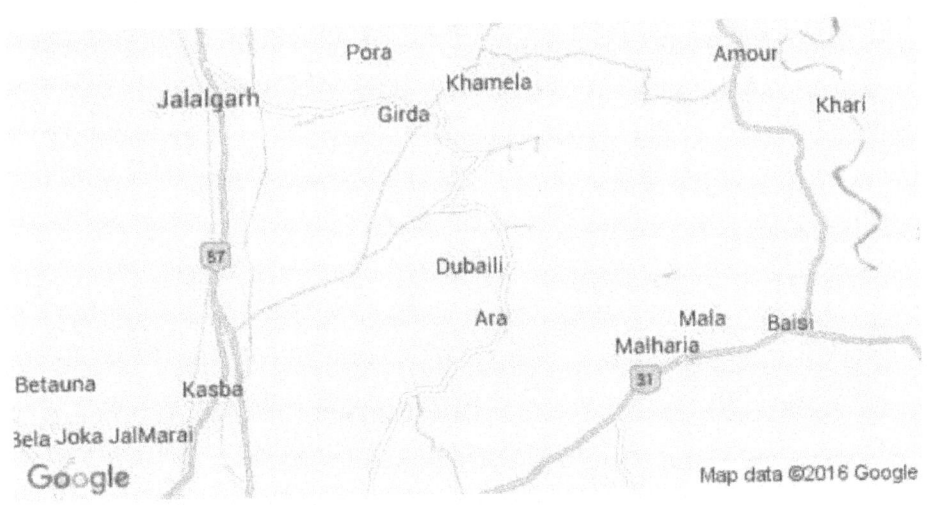

Mahammadia, seven kilometres from Kasba to the east—
credit to Google, with universal permission.

Villages

Here one will find a typical village view of India representing the lifestyle of day-to-day living. This is represented in pictures at the end of the chapter, to the best of my ability to obtain them. No doubt, many cities and villages are well-modernized. We have shown here some reflections of the old days, which we saw continue to exist in many villages when we visited in 2013.

I come from Mahammadia Village. I was educated in the village and then mostly in the city. My intent is to present village life. Indian cities are as modern as anywhere and vary in amenities.

India is divided into many villages. Mahammadia is one of them. The villages are no longer as ancient as they used to be. However, the more remote villages, especially those inhabited by the poorer population, have not caught up with modernity.

Although modern amenities have reached (and are still reaching) many other villages, their inhabitants' day-to-day living has not changed in many areas, including food, clothing, transportation, and even agriculture.

When I lived there in the 1960s and early 1970s, my village had not fully received this modern advance, but it had started to be affected. We had no phone, and if we had a need for one, we had to travel to a city to find one. From my village, when a member of my family wanted to contact us in the US, they would go to the post office in the city, about ten kilometres away, and the post office clerk would try to reach us. There may be a wait of hours, and sometimes contact could not even be established, and they would have to try another time. It was the same situation for trying to contact someone in another city. Calls required appointments. There were no pagers then, either. The fax, cell phone, and internet could not have even been imagined (though they have reached most villages now). Postal mail service was and is available. Transportation by ox-driven carts has been replaced by automobiles and buses, and for carrying loads, trucks now stand in for Saggarh carts. Motorcycles are common. Roads have now been made modern, but are not paved yet in many areas.

Our ox-driven passenger cart. I travelled to my Kanharia School on it.
Ox-driven Saggarh cart for loads

Electricity, radio, and television have now reached the villages, but there was none in the 1960s and 1970s when kerosene lamps were in use. For larger functions, we used a Petromax.

Kerosene lamp   Petromax   Wick lamp

Barbers may come to the home to cut hair, and simple barber shops in shopping areas of the village provide such services, even today.

Barber at home   Barbershop in village market

Oil used to be extracted by manual machines powered by oxen.

Mustard oil extraction[21]

---

[21] Drawing courtesy of Ayesha Khokhar.

Water was obtained from a ground well and/or a water pump.

Wellwater pulled with a bucket on rope ,
or pulley system

Tube well

Flour from the wheat to make bread was obtained by grinding wheat manually. The equipment is called *Janta* in the local language.

Equipment for grinding grains

There is an example of making rice flour for bread using soaked rice and then smashing it, as illustrated here by two ladies. They are using a village version of a wooden okhli (mortar). They had put the water-soaked rice generally overnight in it. The village version of a mosal (pestle) made of wood with a metal ring at the bottom half is fitted on the wood piece, and half is left bare to cut the rice with each stroke. This was used as recently as 2013, and actually produced the special flour made for Naushaba and me when we visited.

Preparation of rice flour with okhli and mosal by my own family on our most recent visit

Spice crushing: garlic, onion, etc.

Land was ploughed manually by oxen. People from several families joined forces to plough the land together to cover a larger area in a shorter time. After the land was ploughed and seeded by hand with a basket, it would be levelled with a wooden plank pulled by oxen, with a man standing on that plank, as shown in the picture below. Seeding by hand and basket, which was still done in some areas as late as 2013, is enjoyable to watch. Men hold the basket filled with seeds with one hand; with the other, they pick the seed out quickly and strike it against the basket as they walk fast. The seeds spread out as they fall on the ground.

Ploughing land[22]

Leveling land[23]

Land irrigation

All these are still used (or were in 2013), but so are mechanical and more modern systems.

---

[22] Purchased from Visual Photos LLC.
[23] Courtesy of Ayesha Khokhar.

Farming in my neighbourhood by men and women   Child helping family
in farming

People still live in houses that are tin or built with thatched roofs and walls. There is a great range of building types, from simple to palatial brick buildings. These reflect the strata of the family. A house with bricks and plaster is also featured below.

Villagers with their houses, the first better off economically than the second (2013 visit).

My uncle Mojib Ur Rahman's house, equivalent to a living room, isolated from ladies culturally.

Mahboob's house of brick and plaster

Bicycle vendor

Villager selling vegetables on the roadside.

Casual snack bar on the village street

Naushaba with my grand Ma in the Kitchen

Naushaba with relatives in another Kitchen

A bus station

A village farm near a residence

Milk-giving buffalos near a residence.

The village is surrounded by natural scenes and sounds, including those generated by birds, a rooster with its family, playing goat kids, and buffalos returning home from grazing. There are also cattle, the calling of Adhan from the mosques in Muslim villages, and the song of Kirtan with music by Hindus. No one can hear the sound of buses, cars, or motorcycles. There used to be some horse-driven carriages, as well, and my father had one.

Bhesna Bridge, by Ameer Bakhsh. A modern bridge has now been added above.

Masjid, built by Rahmatullah.

Masjid, upgraded recently by Abdus Salaam and Naiyer Habib.

Family graveyard adjacent to the masjid.

Remains of the first madrasa, built by Rahmatullah.

Second madrasa, built by Ameer Bakhsh.

Palatial buildings built by my ancestors.

Deserted building for stay of official work in Purnea town related to Zamindari.

House in Harahi, where we lived, built by Majid Ur Rahman.
L to R: Shafiq Ur Rahman, Naiyer Habib, Mahboob Ur Rahman.

A Unit of Indoor Residential Building

Zamindars Of Mahammadia

My family was known as Zamindars of Mahammadia Estate. It was one of the three influential families in the district of Purnea. The other two were the families of Raja P. C. Lal and Nawab of Khagaria. Raja P. C. Lal was during my time. We do not know the details of his ancestors. One of his sons was Victor from his English wife. He ran a cinema hall in Purnea town near the Purnea Zila School. We used to go there to see movies.

My family owned the Mahammadia Estate and part of the Balwa Estate in the district of Purnea. Ameer Bakhsh acquired the Mahammadia Estate, and Majid Ur Rahman acquired part of the Balwa Estate.

These Zamindars of Mahammadia Estate and part of Balwa Estate were well known for their influence, power, wealth, and dignity in the region. Their estate was a mini-government or mini-kingdom, but it was the time of the British government. This family was an extension of the British government in the region. They collected taxes from the public—keeping a certain percentage and giving the rest to the British government.

Security Force

For their protection and to deal with rebels—both from among the public and other influential families—they had guards and forces of armed men called sipahi (soldiers). They fought in the field and did so on various occasions. This occurred during my childhood. They were not the aggressors but got involved for the right cause. They always succeeded.

Village Court

There was an established village court called Kachahri to deal with disputes and crime. The head of my family would hold the court, but the public had their representatives to deal with cases there.

Amenities and Others

From their ancestors on, they kept acquiring land, property, and wealth. There was an orchard of mangoes and various other fruits, land for crops, and a river for fishing. They had elephants, horses, and cattle. They rode elephants to hunt for tigers, leopards, and other feared animals. My father hunted a leopard that had strayed into the area. He went on foot as the period of elephants had passed. Munshi Ismail, a very loyal manager for the family, accompanied him.

Eid Gah

There was also an Eid Gah (place for Eid), where the family of Mahammadia Estate and the public offered prayers of Eid al-Fitr and Eid al-Adha. People came from far away—a radius of eight-and-a-half kilometres—to offer the prayer. It still exists (2016), but the geographic area is reduced because of land given to migrant Santalis in the late 1940s and early 1950s.

These Santalis were an indigenous community, probably from the state of Assam. The Santali lived on hunted animal food. The government (Congress) declared that it would leave as much of the area for the prayer gathering as was required. The rest would take over to be distributed to the migrants. We do not know if the government paid any compensation to my family.

Establishments of Facilities

My family established a masjid, madrasa, graveyard, weekly market, bridge, road, and dispensary:

Rahmatullah built the masjid. He also built the first madrasa. Its remains are just west of the existing madrasa. A pedestrian road passes between them, joining Harahi and Mahammadia. Ameer Bakhsh built the latest madrasa to its west.

They established the Hichcha Moti Hat (weekly marketplace). Ameer Bakhsh built an iron bridge across the Bhesna River on the road to Hichcha Moti Hat. Mahammadia Estate established the market for articles of day-to-day use, as well as for the sale of meat and cattle weekly. Other small bridges were also built elsewhere. A dispensary was established. The physician during my time was Dr. Manzoor Alam.

Parts of the property were named in a waqf to maintain the facilities mentioned above. This was particularly so for the bridge, masjid, madrasa, and dispensary. Ameer Bakhsh established this waqf. A paid mutawalli, as stated in the will of Ameer Bakhsh, was to look after these. Ameer Bakhsh was the first mutawalli, and his eldest daughter, Tahir un Nisa, was to be the one after him. Other members of the families were to follow.

Palatial Buildings

They also built palatial buildings, particularly the family residence. They were built in a fashion that saw each family with its own unit surrounding a compound.

Services

In order to have services, they also housed the families of a barber, oil maker, washer man, gardener, and fisherman. They served the family and earned their own bread.

Annual Function

There was an annual function called Punha. During this, representatives from various villages would come to give their taxes and bring gifts in any form that they liked or were able to afford. These generally consisted of fruits, vegetables, fish, goats, and sweets. The family of Mahammadia Estate presented these gifts to these representatives. Generally, the Hindus would get dhoti[24], and the Muslims, lungi. Some were also given traditional shirts. The Punha was chaired by the head of the family. I recall sitting with my father during these events. Traditionally, these representatives also gave gifts to us, often in the form of money.

Departure of British

After the British left India in 1947 and India became a democracy, things changed for these families all across India. There was no more Kingship, Zamindaris, Rajas, or Nawabs. They were given compensation for the land and public-utility places such as rivers and markets. They also could not keep large areas of land and were spared only what their families needed and what they could use for the cultivation of their day-to-day life. Subsequently, the members of the Mahammadia Estate family, as it was all across the nation, paid more attention to education and became professionals—e.g., lawyers, doctors, and professors. They also participated in politics and provided leadership for the public in their areas.

The following members of the family participated in politics as Members of the Legislative Assembly (MLAs), Members of Parliament (MPs), minister during the period of Independent India after 1947, and MLA of Bihar: Zia Ur Rahman from Chanderdai and his son Moid Ur Rahman. Both served as MLAs. Zia Ur Rahman was a maternal uncle of my father.

My uncle Hasib Ur Rahman, a lawyer, served as an MLA from the Perja Socialist Party and changed to Congress. He served as a minister in the government of Bihar. He then was elected as MP in the central government of India. Jamil Ur Rahman, a lawyer by profession and a son of Bhola Babu[25] of Chanderdai, became an MP and served in the central government. He was a maternal cousin of my father.

---

[24] Dhoti and lungi are traditional men's garments that resemble a sarong.

Abul Kalam completed his BA, Hafiz Ur Rahman completed his B. Comm, and Abdus Salaam was the first to become a doctor in the family. In the 1950s, I was the second doctor.

Mahammadia Post Office

It was established in early 1950 by two brothers, Wahid Ur Rahman and Hafiz Ur Rahman, who walked door to door to get signatures for government approval to open a post office. I was very young then and accompanied them from time to time. They were my uncles. Wahid Ur Rahman subsequently served as postmaster for many years.

Abul Kalam High School

It was established by Abul Kalam in 1974. It was recognized by the Bihar government in 1978.

Abul Kalam High School.

[25]Playing cricket on the field at Abul Kalam High School.

---

[25] Babu is like "Esquire," a term of respect toward men.

Kalam Chowk (Market)

Kalam Chowk (market) was established by Abul Kalam in 1973.
This market is within walking distance of the family residence.

Open markets are held on certain days of the week. There are shops that are open daily.

Mahammadia Welfare Society (sign in Urdu).

Mahammadia Welfare Society

The family embarked on establishing the Mahammadia Welfare Society. In the winter of 2016, the society distributed 500 blankets to the needy in the region.

My Home—A Recent Visit

Naushaba and I last visited India in January 2013. Prior to that, we visited two other times but had not been there for fifteen years. We would like to go more often, but we have difficulty getting visas thanks to the India and Pakistan problems. This reminds us of our past and brings us to the present. We saw all the familiar places of my childhood where I grew up. Father's planted mango trees in his orchard have grown into giant trees. My brother Mahboob Ur Rahman lives there. When Naushaba and I settled in Canada, I gave my share to him. On our 2013 trip, we went from Delhi to Bogdohra Airport in Darjeeling and then to Mahammadia by car. It is just over two hours drive from the airport to Mahammadia.

The following scenes are presented during our drive till we reached our home.

Bogdohra Airport in Darjeeling

Tea garden. Darjeeling is a renowned exporter of fine teas
to the world, and the place is a superb and unmatched resort.

Muslim missionary.

Girls with loads of wood for fuel.

My brother's house: from oxen cart to SUV.

Naiyer Habib and brother Mahboob Ur Rahman at our house.

(2013)
Brothers with wife: Naiyer Habib, Mahlaqa Naushaba Habib,
Halima Khatoon, Mahboob Ur Rahman.

Village chef with a special meal

Naushaba with Mahboob, in mango orchard

Mahboob and Naiyer on farm

Our father planted over a hundred mango trees of different varieties.

Then came the time for our departure.

Farewell on our departure.

A see-off on the train at Katihar Junction, my nephews in the centre.
On the left, Danish Mahboob; on the right, Nazish Rahman, flanked by their friends.

My Father, Habib Ur Rahman

Habib Ur Rahman was born in 1908 in Mahammadia, Purnea, India, and passed away on November 26, 1974, in Karachi, Pakistan. He was from the family of Zamindars of Mahammadia.

Habib Ur Rahman.

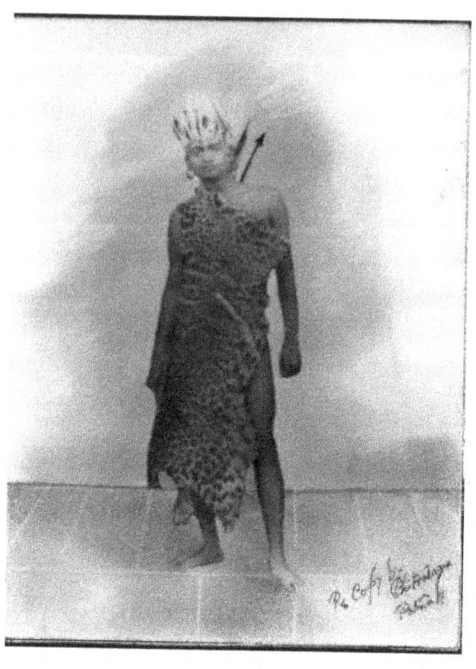

Participating in Fancy Dress at school.

Habib Ur Rahman in the 1990s

<u>High School</u>

My father studied at Purnea Zila School but was sent to Munger, Bihar, for high school.

Student at the Aligarh Muslim University

He was then sent with his brother to the Aligarh Muslim University (AMU).

He entered the AMU in 1929 and is described as having been a good, hard-working individual with excellent behaviour. He was active in social and other extracurricular activities of the university, and held positions in student leadership. He was likeable and was a popular person among his fellow students. He was a member of the cabinet of the Muslim University Union. The union was a very important organization of the university, representing the students at various levels. Elections were held in a very elaborate fashion. One of the important functions of this student union was to welcome dignitaries in an exemplary manner.

Importantly, he was the secretary of the Curzon Geographical Society. When I went for my education at AMU, he showed me his name on the board, which was in the department of geography, along with the names of others.

After Intermediate Arts, he started working toward a bachelor of arts degree for the years 3 and 4 classes but did not succeed in the examination. Documents are added here, testifying to the above facts.

Raj Nazargunj,

Pumea City,

The 14th July, 1932

To whom it may concern.

This is to certify that Habibur Rahman Sheikh, son of Haji Sheikh Majidur Rahman, zemindar of Mohamdia is known to me. He comes of a very respectable Mohammadan family of this district. He has passed the intermediate Examination of the Aligarh University. He is an intelligent youngman with active habits.

So far i know he bears a good moral character.

i wish him every success in his endeavour.

, M.L,C.,

Raja of Nazargunj.

Warden.

SIR SYED HALL
MUSLIM UNIVERSITY,
ALIGARH.

I5th March, I932.

Mr. Habibur Rahman Shaikh of IV ~~th~~ Yr class joined the institution in I929 as a member of Osmania Hostel and since then he has been residing in the same boarding House. I have pleasure in saying that he is a man of very sweet and gentle disposition and possesses pleasant manners. He became popular amongst his fellow-students very soon and consequently was elected to the Select Committee of the Union in I930. He held another office of the Secretaryship of the Curzon Geographical Society in the same year. His general behaviour is ~~xxxxx~~ examplary and I am confident that he would make himself prominent in every walk of life, and I find him quite suitable to take up a post of responsibility and trust. I wish him success in his future career,

Syed Bashir Ali
M.Sc., ~~xxx~~ F.I.C.S.,
Warden, Osmania.

DEPARTMENT OF GEOGRAPHY
MUSLIM UNIVERSITY,
ALIGARH.

18th March 32

Mr. Habibur Rahman Sheikh is a student of this institution for the last several years. He is reading for his B. A. degree with Geography and history as optional subject. As a student of this department, he was the Secretary of the Curzon Geographical Society in 1930-31. He is a very calm and quiet student and is extremely well-behaved. I shall be glad to hear of his success in his future career. His character is excellent.

Yours faithfully

M. B. Litt
Lecturer in Geography

J. R. Khan
Chairman.
Department of Geography
M. U. ALIGARH.

72

He lived in Osmania Hostel of Sir Syed Hall.[26] Although he studied, he was very active in Aligarh Traditional Senior Class of Students with naughtiness. The seniors were well-known in Aligarh. They considered themselves as royal over the junior students. When the junior students were admitted at AMU, the seniors collected them in a place. These students and others would get homemade food, which the seniors would steal and eat. The seniors made jokes about the newcomers and teased them in a gathering of theirs. It was their principle that by doing this, these shy new students would become active and bold. He failed his final year of the Bachelor of Arts degree.

Family Responsibility

My grandfather passed away, so my father returned home to look after the property and family. He could not study any longer.

Headmastership

Later on, he became headmaster of a middle school and served in Baghdahra, Jigin, and then Belgachchi school in Purnea District. He had a teacher, his close friend by the name of Sachida Nand Sinha. This was when he was headmaster of the middle school. Sachida Nand Sinha was Hindu Rajput. He became my teacher in Kanharia Middle School.

---

[26] Aligarh Muslim University is a residential university with many hostels. A few hostels are combined inside a single hall—e.g., Osmania Hostel—and others under Sir Syed Hall, Morison Court and others under Aftab Hall, etc. The provost is the administrative head of the hall; the warden is the head of the hostel.

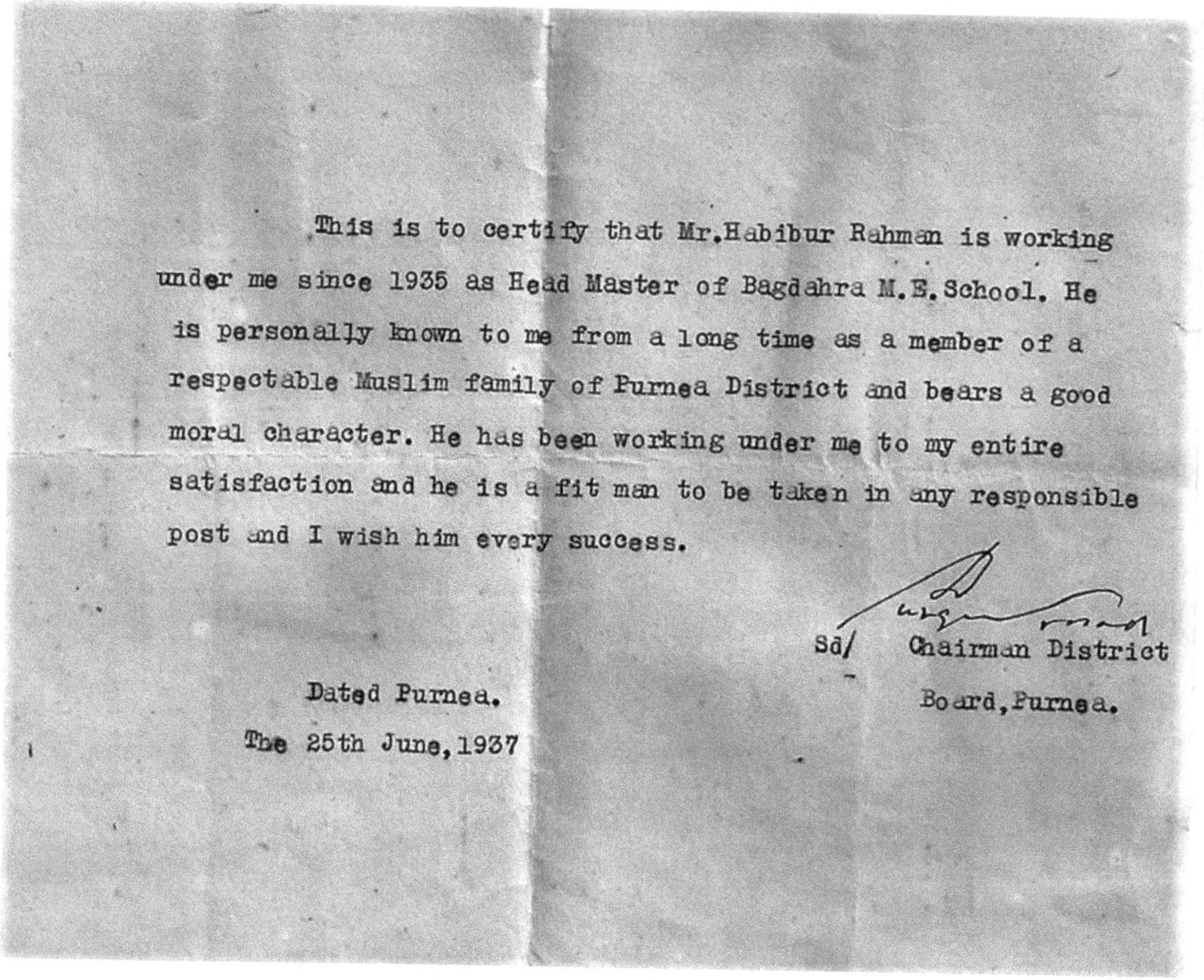

This is to certify that Mr.Habibur Rahman is working under me since 1935 as Head Master of Bagdahra M.E.School. He is personally known to me from a long time as a member of a respectable Muslim family of Purnea District and bears a good moral character. He has been working under me to my entire satisfaction and he is a fit man to be taken in any responsible post and I wish him every success.

Sd/   Chairman District

Board,Purnea.

Dated Purnea.

The 25th June,1937

His Marriages

My father first married Maimoona Saheba.[27] She was the sister of Shirf Ud Din Ahmad. My father had a daughter with her, by the name of Noor Jahan. Both mother and daughter passed away. Then he married my mother, Madina Khanam of Dinapore[28], Patna, Bihar, daughter of Dr. Ameer Ul Hussain Khan. This occurred likely in 1937. 3rd Marriage Mother of Mahbbob ur Rahman- Najmun Nisa Saheba.

---

[27] Saheba- Esq for women.

[28] Spelling variants of Dinapore, which is written on the plan of the house of our maternal grandfather, where it is also spelled as Dinapur and Danapur as well. We endeavour to use Dinapore.

My parents, Habib Ur Rahman and Madina Khanam (just married, 1937?).

My mother came from a city, and my father from a village. There were no connections of any kind, which begs the question of how this relationship was established. My mother's paternal uncle, Dr. Abdul Ghafoor Khan, was a renowned individual in Patna and the owner of Green Medical Hall, a well-known medical hall in Patna, Bihar. This Green Medical Hall was actually given to him by my maternal grandfather, Dr. Ameer Ul Hussain Khan, a generous man. My grandfather was married to his sister, Soghra Begum.[29] Dr. Abdul Ghafoor Khan was actually not a doctor; he received the title of doctor from the people. He was a compounding dispenser. He had a friendship with Bhola Babu of Chandardai village near Araria, in the Purnea district. He was the maternal uncle of my father. Thus, because of these two individuals' involvement, the marriage of my mother was solemnized with my father, with family consent.

---

[29] Begum is a respectful title for ladies.

During those days, my ancestral family did not encourage marriage outside the family or with city dwellers, and my mother faced that censure when she returned to the village as a bride. Fortunately, with her personality, she won the hearts and minds of not only the family but of the entire village and of the neighbouring villages.

He married his third wife, Bibi[30] Najmun Nisa, in Bharatpura, Bihar. She was a teacher.

My maternal uncle (husband of my mother's elder sister, Bibi Zaitoon), Dr. Abdul Wahab Khan, was a doctor in the Bharatpura Dispensary. My stepmother's father was a compounding pharmacist there. I visited Bharatpura Dispensary and was there with my uncle for a week. I used to visit my stepmother's family before her marriage to my father. They were very nice to me. I played with her sister, Tahira. Her father was a very nice person. I also met Salah Ud Din Sahib,[31] who was her brother-in-law.

We did not know then that my father would be married to her. The marriage was negotiated and settled by my uncle, Dr. Abdul Wahab Khan. My father gave my mother's health and her permission as the reasons for this marriage.

The eldest son—my brother from my third mother—was Mahboob Ur Rahman. He was attached to me from the beginning. The second son from my third mother, Rizwan Ur Rahman, a practicing cardiologist with the highest Indian qualification of DM, entered medical school at Banaras Hindu University. He also developed an attachment to us, particularly with Naushaba. We did what we could, even during my studentship, for Mahboob and continued that attention later for his settlement in Mahammadia. We offered the same care to Rizwan Ur Rahman for a short period of time during his education. Ultimately, I was very pleased that we could be of assistance to them on behalf of my father. He built his honourable status in the area. We are pleased that he maintained the dynasty by settling in Mahammadia.

My father had an average-medium build. He was approachable and kind-hearted to all. He was caring and just. He mixed with people of any status, young and old. He was particularly fond of children. He cracked jokes with them and made them laugh by making faces. He would call the children passing by.

Usually, in summer, he would sit on his easy chair under a mango tree, smoking his hookah (Hubble Bubble). When I grew up and became a medical doctor, I asked him not to smoke. He stopped smoking in front of me but continued doing it while hiding in the toilet room. I have tears rolling from my eyes as I type this.

He knew how to play chess. I learned from him. My father did not play chess regularly, but we played occasionally. He had neither the partner nor the time to play this game regularly.

He enjoyed hunting, but not innocent animals. Once, he killed a leopard that had strayed into our area. He was generous. A Hindu Sadhu,[32] hearing that my father had killed a leopard, asked if he could have the skin. My father loved the skin, but he gave it to him. He also killed many jackals that attacked our goats and other pet animals,

---

[30] Bibi is a title for respect for a woman.

[31] Sahib (or Saheeb) is a title of respect for men.

[32] Hindu monk.

especially hens, roosters, and their families. And he killed a renowned dangerous jungle hog. When he was going to kill the leopard and the hog, I could see the worry on my mother's face, but she accepted it for the benefit of the public.

He loved horses and riding them. He owned a cart to be pulled by a horse and trained the horse to pull the cart. He bought a small, maroon-coloured horse for me to ride.

He loved motorcycle riding. He had an accident in which one side of his leg burned in contact with the hot engine of the motorcycle. Once, he was going to buy a motorcycle in Calcutta. He had IR 2000 hidden under his T-shirt, in his waistband. We were on the train, and he was staying awake. Seeing him this way, I kept requesting him to sleep, reassuring him that I would be watchful. He ultimately went to take a nap. I dozed off, too, which I should not have. A pickpocket took his money away. My father woke up to find this out, as did I. It was a surprise and produced some sad moments. It was a dark night. Nothing could be done. My father was not upset with me, but I sat with guilt.

We went to Calcutta and enjoyed our holiday with sadness in both of us, but he never expressed it. He especially took me to various restaurants, introducing me to his chosen recipe menu. He loved food and knew various famous restaurants in Calcutta, Bengal. He loved shopping and travelling from Mahammadia to Calcutta, a one-day journey on the train.

Although he came from a Zamindar family, he never sounded off about his status. He helped the needy. He was humble in receiving guests, especially his friends and my mother's side of the family. He affectionately loved my mother's younger sister and her husband, as well as her family. Later, I was married to their daughter. My uncle, Fazal Ur Rehman Khan, who became my father-in-law, was posted as a medical officer in the nearby village of Amor. My father approached his brother-in-law, Maulvi Mohammad Tahir, who was an elected member of the council of the Purnea district, to have my uncle, Fazal Ur Rehman, transferred to our village clinic. He did not receive any response. My father's request was not honoured.

He used to be very upset with the prevailing politics. One time, he stood in the election for MLA or counsellor, I am not sure. He did not agree to spend extravagant amounts of money for a campaign. He travelled on his bullock cart from village to village. He did not win.

He performed Hajj at an early age, in his fifties. My mother chose not to go with him. On his return from Hajj, he did ablution and gave me his cap as a gift. He supplicated for me that God would give me the opportunity to perform Hajj.

He attempted to move to Pakistan in the early days. My mother did not approve of it, so he stayed in India.

His Sadness on Our Departure to Canada

My father looked very sad when Naushaba and I told him of our plans to migrate to Canada. This was natural. He also uttered that it was not bad there. He had always told me in India that I should educate myself and go to London to live, as it was not a good situation in our home country after Partition. It was very strange to me to hear this from him. I was sitting with him, and I assured him that I would get him to Canada. He came to the airport to say goodbye, and he had tears in his eyes—most unexpected from him. I questioned my decision but reassured myself that I would get him to Canada, which never happened. While I am typing this, I had to stop to let my tears from my eyes and heart flow—the most heartfelt and everlasting sadness of my life.

His Passing Away

My father passed away suddenly from a heart attack on November 26, 1974. My brother claims he passed away on November 11. According to him, our father wrote a letter to him and passed away the next day. There is a chance of error in registering death. So, the date remains disputed. I was a cardiologist, but I was of no assistance to him. He passed away rather suddenly.

I also admit that I was of no financial assistance to him, which he did not need. However, I have felt guilty of this all my life as a son. I felt grateful to do what I could do for his children, but I often feel that I could have done something for him. However, he maintained his dignified and comfortable life till his last day. On that last day, he was going shopping and asked my mother if she needed anything. He went on the bus. He debussed himself on reaching the market area in Liaqatabad and sat on a charpai (cot) in a store. Eventually, he lay down on it, and he never woke up. Neither I nor my family could attend his funeral. Such were the circumstances for me, having so recently arrived in Canada on a minister's permit.

We attended his grave later and supplicated for him. He was buried in the cemetery of Sakhi Hassan in Karachi. The grave was identifiable for a few years, but it isn't anymore. His grave also met the same fate as my mother's and at the same time. We go into the compound of the cemetery and offer our prayers.

I consoled myself by concluding that the grave would have met the same fate after me, as no one would have visited it.

Grave of Habib Ur Rahman
March 7, 1908 – November 26, 1974

My Mother, Madina Khanam

Mother

Zaitoona, Maimoona, Madina (Naiyer's mother), and Safina
(Naushaba's mother) Khanam, 1990s.

Madina Khanam was my mother. She was born in 1914, probably in Dinapore, Bihar. She passed away on March 15, 1993, in Regina, Saskatchewan, Canada. Madina Khanam was one of the seven children of Dr. Ameer Ul Hussain Khan. She had two brothers and four sisters. She was born in her father's house, and she was educated at home. She was very inquisitive in learning. She developed skills in Urdu, Persian, Islam, and Quranic Arabic reading. She watched her father practicing medicine and became interested in that subject, but she did not have the opportunity to go to medical school.

She always lived in the city, and then she married my father, who was from a rural area. Traditionally, the trend of our family was not to bring in a wife from a different family or locality. Therefore, on her arrival, people in the family did not welcome her, but they did not outwardly criticize her, either.

She as a Person

My mother was a very intelligent person. She was, overall, a housewife, a mother for her children, and a daughter-in-law who respected and loved all members of the family, be they senior or junior. She paid due respect according to what they all deserved.

With her etiquette, humbleness, and caring nature, she won the hearts and minds of the members of the family—and not only them but the villagers and the people in adjoining villages. She became a lady whom we call Har Dil Aziz in Urdu, meaning thereby beloved for all hearts. She helped the villagers in the area in a lot of ways, including with medical help.

My Teacher

She taught me up to fifth grade. My father had studied the Quran in his youth, but I guess he had lost track of it. I saw him reading it and asking my mother to listen for any needed corrections.

Disciplining and Caring Mom

She was never hesitant in disciplining her children. She made me understand and never scolded me if I wanted to avoid studying, particularly Quran, but she would not hesitate to beat me up for my naughtiness. I was not a less naughty boy than others. When we grew up and talked about the past, she would smile and say, "When I used to beat him, he would not go away, and he would not cry, and I would wish that somebody would come to take him away." It was my uncle, Wahid Ur Rahman, who used to come to pick me up while my mother was beating me, and you know what? I would scratch him and resist being taken away. I would stand there and receive all the beating that my mom would give me.

My Attachment

I, as a boy, would not like my mom to be out of my sight. If she would go to see a relative, even just next door or a few furlongs away, I would go with her. If it was a new place, I would sit with her. One day, after I'd grown up a bit, she got sick and had a high fever. It was hot weather. She did not have a blouse of fine light cloth, so I sewed her a blouse without any training under her supervision. No one was available to prepare a blouse for her.

Her Arrival in Canada

We brought my mother to Canada, and she lived with us here for thirteen years. She immigrated to Canada on September 13, 1980, as a landed immigrant and received her Canadian citizenship on July 24, 1985. She started receiving old age security from December 1992 but did not survive to receive the next instalment, due in December 1993.

She travelled from Karachi to Frankfurt on Lufthansa and from Frankfurt to Regina on Air Canada. Before this, she had never travelled on an airplane. She could understand some English but could not speak it. We had faith that the airlines would look after such a traveller. We sent all the details about her and asked that she wears it around her neck with her travel documents. She was told to show these to the airline crew, whom she would recognize by their uniform if she had any problems. In Frankfurt, she was found wandering in the airport by Dr. Vijay Kapadia of Australia. Being of East Indian origin, he approached her and talked to her. He handed her over to Air Canada and kindly called me to give me the details and reassure us. We were so grateful for this human touch. I called her through Air Canada, who assured us that all of our arrangements were in place; otherwise, I planned to fly to Frankfurt. She came to Regina via Calgary. We tried to contact Dr. Kapadia in Australia at the address he'd provided, but he was not available. We lost contact with him. He had given his business card to my mom. We still have it today as I write this book (2016). We should maintain our human touch, always looking around to see if we can offer any help to anyone.

I had a busy life, and while I did give some time, it wasn't enough, in my judgment. I would be busy in the main area of the house, having returned from work after dinner. She would come down and I would have a few words with her, then I would get busy. After a while, she would say, "I am going, son," and I would say, "OK."

We must love our parents and converse with them wholeheartedly with kindness to avoid this disappointment that I now experience!

Her Hajj

She wanted to visit our kith and kin in India and Pakistan. Naushaba asked me to take her for Hajj. We went to perform Hajj at Mecca and Medina on visas granted by the government of Saudi Arabia on July 18, 1986. This was the best thing we did for her. Had Naushaba not asked me, it might have been missed.

My Mother's Last Days of Life

My mother lived with us. Near the end of her life, she was visiting my sister Yasmin, who had also immigrated to Canada and lived in Edmonton. There, she fell in the bathroom in an attempt to do ablution for prayer and broke her hip. She was hospitalized. The doctor was not willing to operate on her. I brought her back to our home in Regina. We kept her at home, but it was difficult to handle her, and she insisted that she should go to the hospital. We arranged for her to go to the Wascana Rehab Centre. She stayed there and started to get sicker. There was an infection in her hip, and she needed acute care. We brought her to the Plains Health Centre, Room 834, on Level 8. I was practicing in the hospital. The physicians involved in her care included orthopedic surgeon Dr. Bachynski, internist Dr. Gerald Sinclair, plastic surgeon Dr. Al-Varez, Dr. Jim Carter, and, lastly, general surgeon Dr. Cuddington.

Naushaba always attended to her and kept at her bedside. I attended her from time to time. She started to become silent and to keep her eyes closed. Her hip was considered to be incurable. She was not eating. Dr. Cuddington put a gastrostomy tube to feed her. She was deteriorating. I talked to my mother about her condition, which I feel I should not have, but I guess, in the end, I concluded that it was the right thing to do. I explained that things were not good and that there was not much that could be done medically. I told her that if her heart stopped, we should not attempt to restart it because it would be more suffering for her. She listened silently with her eyes closed, as usual.

The next morning, she passed away. Naushaba and I were present at her bedside. We both embraced and held each other for a while. God bless her.

Many of our patients, friends, and colleagues sent messages of sympathy to us on her death. A patient of mine laminated the news of her death on a card with her prayer from the bible and mailed it to us. Her card and greeting letter got lost in the piles of mail. We could not identify her.

> HABIB FAMILY—Mother of Dr. N. Habib passed away at the age of 73 on March 15, 1993 at Plains Health Centre. The family wishes to thank all those who called, sent cards and flowers. Friends so wishing may make contributions to the Heart and Stroke Foundation of Saskatchewan, in lieu of flowers. The family wishes to thank all staff and physicians of the Wascana Rehabilitation Centre, Plains Health Centre and Total Nursing Care Service for their excellent care, also Speers Funeral Chapel for all funeral arrangements. A Muslim Funeral Prayer will be held at 8:00 p.m. on Thursday, March 18, 1993 at Speers Funeral Chapel, 2136 College Avenue. People of other faiths are more than welcome at the same time.

Naiyer Habib & Mahlaqa Naushaba Habib

My mother had wished to be buried in the graveyard in Pakistan, and we arranged for her body to go there. I accompanied her by air on Singapore Airlines, touching down in Singapore and heading to Karachi. The prayer of Janaza (funeral prayer) was offered, and she was buried peacefully on the same day of our arrival. She was buried in Karachi, in the cemetery of Sakhi Hasan.

For a few years, we would visit her grave and offer prayers for salvation. More recently, I was informed that her grave no longer exists and that another lady was buried in the same grave[33]. They had built a marble covering. I had meant to have the graveyard fully cemented, but a nephew of mine was of the very firm mind, from the point of view of religion, that there was some controversial prohibition with such cementing. He had taken the responsibility of looking after the grave, so I gave in. My first reaction was to take legal steps, but ultimately, by seeing what happened, I accepted it—very disheartened—and did not take any further steps. I saw that the relatives of my relatives who are buried there do not seem to care for their graves, and that would have been the ultimate fate of her grave, too. So be it as it may, we pray for her.

Grave of Madina Khanam
January 31, 1914 - March 15, 1993
Her name is inscribed in Urdu.

---

[33] Islamically, after ten years, another person may be buried in the same grave in which someone is already buried, after covering the remains.

Sacrifice of Love of Our Parents—A Tragedy of Our Lives

When our parents passed away, I started to think about how they could send their son to live in a hostel from grade five, given how attached I was, especially to my mom. Until I became a full-fledged doctor, I continued to stay away from them. Not only that, but after a full education, I went on to marry, at their request, a pre-arranged girl, alone because of the situation that existed between India and Pakistan. I had to return alone to go to a foreign land for education. I lived with my arranged bride for five-and-a-half years and, ultimately, settled in a foreign land, but of course, I only did so after a sincere attempt to return and settle with our parents. The circumstances did not permit that. Naushaba left after marriage, leaving her mom and three sisters.

This is a tragedy of our life, to look back and see what our parents might have felt with us being away, and me, the only son of my mother over the years. My success was their wish that they always kept in view!

Naushaba shares the same sadness as me. She led a life of difficulties and became educated to support the family, then got married and faced the same goods and bads, happiness and sadness, being away from the family.

We supported our families together and remained close in touch.

OUR HAJJ AND UMRAH

We are also presenting some accounts of our Hajj, including some pertinent points of Hajj, with my mother.

The first Hajj I did was with my mother. My wife told me that I should accompany her for Hajj. She was getting older and wondered whether another such opportunity would come. So did I! I am thankful to Naushaba, and may Allah reward her for this advice. Had I not gone, I could not imagine if my mother could have performed Hajj. And I might have regretted it for all my life.

It was a hard journey. The arrangements we made through the travel agency were poor. It was a quick decision to go, so I picked up a travel agent randomly. We resolved the problems his shoddy work presented as we faced them.

The first was the accommodation. We were taken to a building by a government bus. A Saudi official was in charge. He took our passports and assigned us accommodation. He allotted us a room where there was another family. This family was cooking in the same room, and I could not imagine that I, and especially my mother, could live there. We didn't know what to do. Meanwhile, a Pakistani family in the next room was watching us. They asked us to come and stay in their room with them. I was hesitant, but I could not refuse the offer. They insisted. They provided us with a mattress and space in the same room in which they were also staying on mattresses on the floor. It was a nice setup with the family. God bless them.

Then I faced another problem—a very worrisome one. To complete another part of Hajj, we were to stay in tents in the city of Mina. From the tent where my mom was, I went out for a little walk and lost my way back. I tried to return for an hour or two, and it got more complicated. I was so worried that my mother was alone in the tent, and the next morning, we were to depart on a bus for another place. I joined up with a couple who had also lost their way. The Saudi officials were of no help. One problem was the language barrier, but they could not put things together to get us any help. They were also very rude. Then, lo and behold, a young man in Arabic dress appeared. He saw that we were very worried and reassured us after learning about our problem. A bus arrived, and he asked us to ride in it with him. He took me to my tent, exactly where my mother was, and in spite of the fact that I had no knowledge of the address. How did he do that?! I thanked him and God, having concluded that his appearance was a gift from God. His was an example of our belief that God's help comes in various ways.

I went with my family to Hajj for a second time. This was according to a Saudi visa of July 12, 1988. This Hajj was arranged through an agency. As such, we had no problems and were able to perform the Hajj fairly easily.

Then, later on, because of a desire of my wife, we went for Umrah[34], which is considered a smaller Hajj. This was according to a visa of February 21, 2011. As this expedition was also arranged through an agency, there were no difficulties other than hot weather. We performed Umrah and visited the various sites of Islamic history, going back to the Prophet's time.

I have attempted to cite all the pictures that we took of those historic sites. In the early years, there was a prohibition around taking pictures. Now, it is permitted. We thought to include these. Since then, almost all the important sites have been demolished to expand the Kaaba Mosque and Medina Mosque areas to accommodate more people. They did not leave even a sign of the existence of the demolished historic places. We were fortunate that we could see those before they were demolished. It seems to me that the Taliban destroyed the Buddhist places in Afghanistan, and the Muslims destroyed the Islamic places in Syria and Iraq, particularly Baghdad. We Muslims do not pray to these sites. We just like to see our historic sites. Performing the pilgrimage: Another difference between Hajj and Umrah is that Hajj is strictly performed in the designated months of Shawwal, Dhul-Hijjah (Zul Hijjah), and Dhul-Qadah only, whereas Umrah can be performed at any time of the year.

Naiyer with mother in Karachi, coming from Hajj, 1986.

---

[34] Umrah – Search Google to learn it

Naiyer and Naushaba in Hajj at Arafat, 1988.

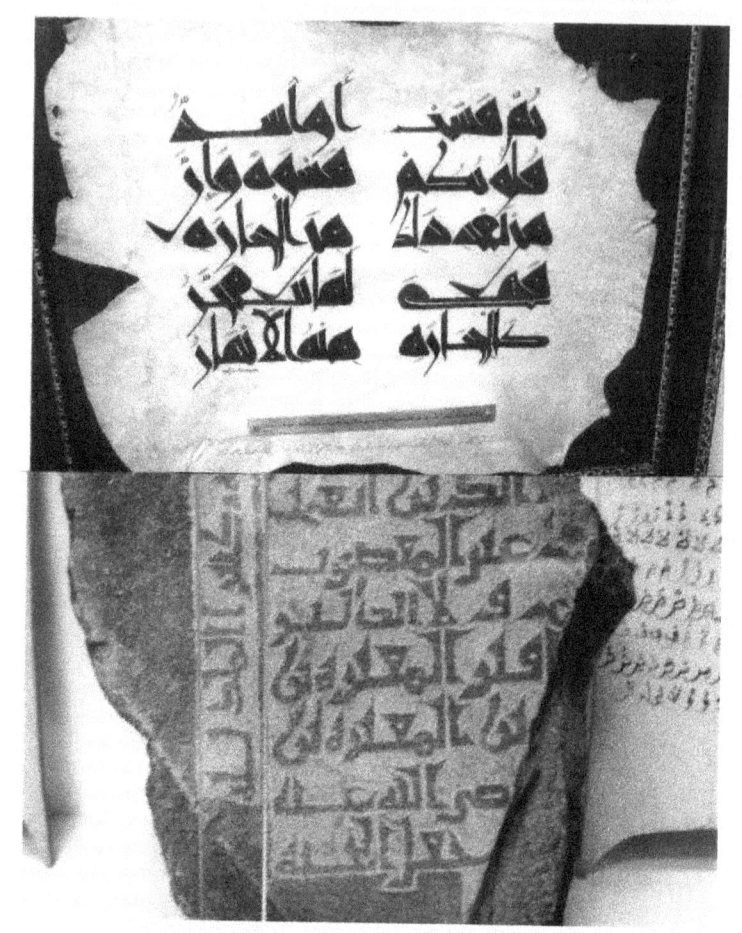

Copy of complete Quran compiled by Uthman bin Afan, the third caliph (period of governance 644-656), from the collection of memorized Quran by people from the time of the Prophet, written on leaf, skin, stone in the order as arranged by the Prophet, Mohammad, Peace be upon him. The original is kept in Istanbul, Turkey (2011 visit).

Mosque of the Prophet at the site where he lived, preached
and is buried with Abu Bakr and Umar by his side.

Inside view of the Prophet's Mosque, with people waiting for congregation prayer.

The site in Prophet's Mosque where the Prophet offered, led prayer and preached.

L: The hole points to the Prophet's grave inside. R: 1ST Prophet's, 2nd Abu Bak Siddique, 3rd Umar.

Masjid Quba, built by the Prophet and others with mud and brick

Mosque of Abu Bakr, built where he lived, now demolished for expansion. Naushaba in front.

Mosque in Madina of Umar, who governed as Caliph from 717-720.
Demolished by the Saudi government for expansion.

Masjid Ghannam, where the Prophet prayed for rain in the extreme hot weather.
Rain followed. This has also been demolished now.

Mosque of Ali in Madina, demolished by the Saudi government for expansion.

Masjid Qiblatain in Madina. Muslims all over the world face the same direction to offer prayer.
Here, Allah commanded the Prophet to change from facing Masjid Al Aqsa to facing Kaaba during prayer,
which has been done ever since.

Jannate Baqai across the Prophet's Mosque (graveyards of people including the Prophet's son Ibrahim). This is now closed to the public and may be demolished.

Ritual of Safa-Marwa (Saee), running seven times between the two mountains on each end.

Kaaba, built by Ibrahim and his son Ismael.
Muslims perform a ritual of circumventing it.
Naushaba in front.
Women wear modest, loose dresses with covered heads,
and only their hands and faces are open.

Naiyer Habib
Men wear two pieces of clothing, as shown.

Naiyer and Naushaba at one and the other end of the residue of the mountain.

Prophet Ibrahim had to leave his son, Ismail, and his wife, Hajra, on command from God in the wilderness near the site where Kaaba is. There was no food or water. Days after, Ismail was about to die with no water and his mother's milk having dried up. She ran between Safa and Marwa Mountains to find someone or water. It is said that where Ismail struck the ground, water started to come out. Later, settlement developed there. So, the Muslims in Hajj complete their journey by running between Safa and Marwa seven times, a one-way distance of 450 metres. Since the big mountain has shrunk, it is preserved in the background where we stand.

Graveyard of the Martyrs of the Badr-Ist war, where 313 ill-equipped Muslims defeated 1,000 well-equipped Quraish who waged war against them.

Naiyer and Naushaba at the site of the Battle of Badr.

The graves of martyrs from the first battle between 313 ill-equipped Muslims and 1,000 wellarmed Quraish of Mecca. Muslims won the battle. They were reassured by God of a win.

Here, fathers and brothers were on one side and sons and brothers on the other.

Names of some of the martyrs of war at the battle of Badr.

Historic Mountain Ohod

Ohod[35] Mountain, site of the second battle between the Quraish (Meccan)
and Muslims from Madina. Naiyer & Naushaba.

Khalid Bin Walid was the army chief who led the Quraishi army. He converted to Islam and led the Muslim army in many battles and was a renowned army chief. Here, renowned army chief Hamza was killed by the hired slave of Hinda, the wife of Abu Sufyan, whose father was killed by Hamza in the Battle of Badr. Later, the slave converted to Islam. Hinda had vowed to chew the liver of Hamza, which she did.

---

[35] Most commonly known as Mount Uhud.

موقع غزوة أُحد

يقع جبل أُحد على بُعد (٤كم) شمال المسجد النبوي وفي محيطه دارت أحداث معركة أُحد الشهيرة ودفن بمحيطه سبعين من أصحاب رسول الله صلى الله عليه وسلم الذين استشهدوا في المعركة، وفي مقدمتهم حمزة بن عبد المطلب رضي الله عنه وعنهم عم رسول الله صلى الله عليه وسلم، وكان الرسول صلى الله عليه وسلم يتعهدهم بالزيارة بين الحين والآخر.

Ohod's Battle site

Ohod mountain is located 4 km north of the prophet's mosque, where one of the most famous battles happened, seventy of the prophet's companions Peace be upon him martyred in that battle, one of them was Hamza Bin Abdulmottalib who was the prophet's uncle may Allah be pleased with him, the prophet promised to visit them every now and then.

مركز الاتصال السياحي
Tourism Contact Center
800 755 0000
www.scta.gov.sa
www.mas.gov.sa
www.sauditourism.com.sa

الهيئة العامة للسياحة والآثار
Saudi Commission for Tourism & Antiquities

Grave of Hamza

This is a site where the caravan of the Prophet wanted to rest,
but the Prophet was inspired by God not to, for some ominous reason.

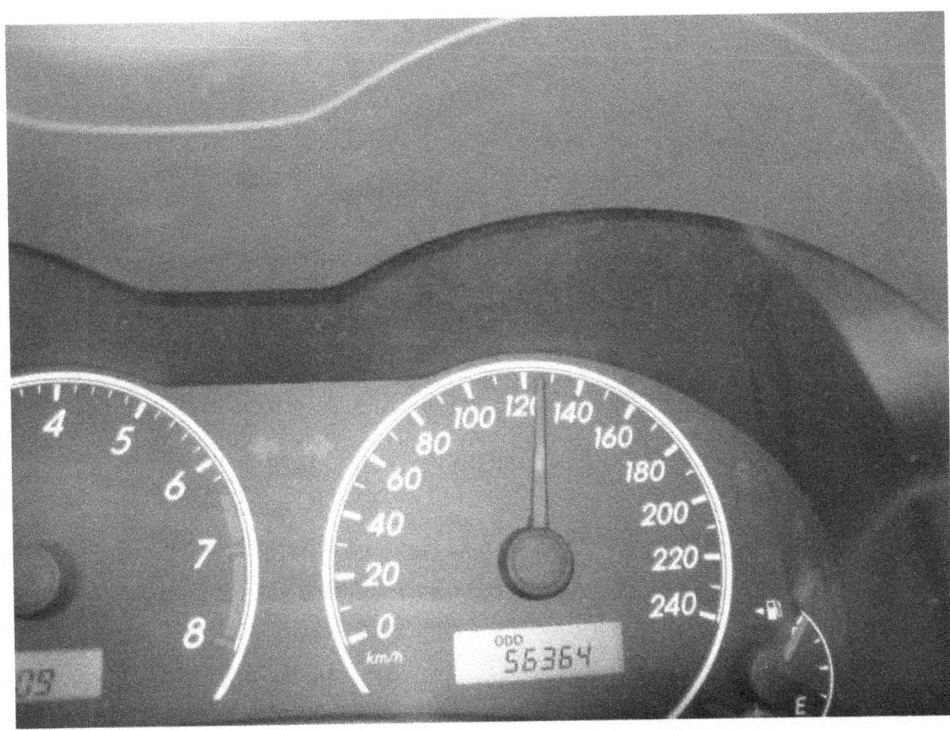

Here, our taxi ran fast without using an accelerator,
as confirmed by the speedometer's 125 km/hour readout.

The top of Mount Arafat, where the Prophet delivered his last sermon during Hajj.
The Pilgrims are required to go there for prayers for the completion of Hajj. Us.

Camel rides for tourists.

Masjid Jinn, where Jinn listened to the Prophet read the Quran.

On the top of Jabal al-Nour Mountain is the Cave of Hira,
where the Prophet received the first message of God.

The library at the site where the Prophet is supposed to have been born, now demolished.

Graveyard where the Prophet's wife, Khadija, is buried.

BUA: A Personality to be Grateful For!

Her name was Bibi Soghra. Bibi is a title placed as a prefix to demonstrate respect and affection in our home culture. Bibi Soghra lived with my maternal grandmother as a helping hand. Her daughter had passed away, leaving her with no other relatives but a son-in-law who had respect and love for her. His name was Kaloot, and he used to visit her. What an exemplary example of a son-in-law! According to family tradition, where possible, the mother of the bride will traditionally send someone as a helping hand with her daughter. She accompanied my mother. She lived all her life with her raising me, my sisters, and the children of my sister, Nilofar. She took her last breath at around age seventy. She did all this as a member of the family, with no wage earned. I had moved away, and our children were born abroad.

Do you know what she ate all her life and survived? A few cups of tea, using the same pack of tea time and again, and maybe a piece of bread daily. She used to cook some special food for me to my liking and beckon me to come. I would run to her to enjoy my cherished food.

During play, I made a little arrow and bow and fitted a nail in the arrow. Bua was in the kitchen. One day, I went to the kitchen window and pointed the arrow at her, and told her I was going to shoot her to scare her. While I was telling her this, the arrow left the bow and went straight into her temple, sparing her eye. I ran and removed the arrow. Her advice, with a smile, was that no one should play with dangerous things. Her image, love, and affection are always with me! These are lessons in life.

MY THIRD Mother, Najmun Nisa, and OUR SIBLING

Najmun Nisa was the third wife of my father. She was the daughter of Liaquat Hussain from the village of Asthawan in Bihar. He was a compounding pharmacist at a hospital in Bharatpura. The marriage was solemnized with my mother's permission. She welcomed her into the family. She was a teacher by profession. Because of some family circumstances, she passed through a difficult time and wanted to educate children. She achieved this goal. With her, my father had a daughter and three sons. One of them passed away in infancy. The eldest son was Mahboob Ur Rahman, and the son after him was Rizwan Ur Rahman.

Najmun Nisa, 1990s.

Siblings from my Mother, Madina Khanam

I had one full brother and two full sisters from my mother.

Najam Habib, brother

I am told that I had a brother by the name of Najam who passed away immediately after birth, or probably he was born dead. I was born next after him.

Nilofar Habib, sister

My sister Nilofar Habib, whose nickname was Kausar, was next after me, approximately four years younger. She studied at home and subsequently also attended Harahi Primary School in our village. A tutor by the name of Abdul Jabbar taught her at home.

She married Saeed Akhter of Serwaily, a village four or five miles from our home. The father of Saeed Akhter was a very influential person in that area. His name was Abdul Haque. He ultimately passed away when he went to Hajj. Nilofar had five sons and one daughter.

Yasmin Habib, sister

Yasmin was my second sister. She was approximately fourteen years younger than me. She also moved to Pakistan with our mother. She had studied at home and some in a local school. She married Shamim Ahmed in Regina. She immigrated to Regina, sponsored by me, and Shamim Ahmad followed. They had a daughter, Madeeha Ahmed. Yasmin was very much attached to her daughter. Yasmin was born in 1950 and passed away at a young age on December 10, 2000. She is buried in the cemetery in Edmonton.

Yasmin was very close to me. She came to visit us and stayed for over a week in Regina when the end of her life was imminent. Her death has left another vacuum in my life.

I personally asked Shamim to remarry. He had a lot of respect for me. I felt he might be hesitant to remarry after the death of his wife, who was my sister. This feeling is inherent in our culture. I wanted to remove this inhibition from him. He was reluctant but remarried.

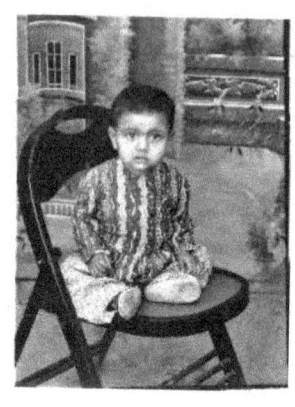 

Yasmin   Nilofar

Yasmin   Nilofar

Yasmin's grave.
(Note: year of birth is 1950. 1957 is an error)

108

Siblings from my Third Mother, Najmun Nisa

I had three brothers and one sister from my third mother. A brother passed away tragically in childhood.

Sanober Habib, sister

Sanober was the eldest. She is married and is living in Patna with her family. She raised her children with her caring husband without any helping hand. She was still educating them when we visited in 2013.

Mahboob Ur Rahman, brother

My older brother was attached to me and used to visit me when I was in medical school.

Mahboob started a bachelor of arts program but could not complete it. Subsequently, he settled in our ancestral home, representing my father. He looks more like our father than any of us. After some hardship, by his own efforts, he is now doing very well, by the grace of God, and looking after the family property. He acquired a fair amount of property and built a nice house. He established himself, and he is one of the best members of the Mahammadia family. He has the respect and affection of the people around the area. People also trust him.

I tried to support him. I considered this to be my duty after the passing of our father. I left my share of the property to Mahboob. We have remained close.

Mahboob married Halima Khatoon in the Siwan Chhapra area. They are parents to three boys: Danish Mahboob, Tabish, and Nazish Rahman. They also have three daughters: Shahla Afreen, Sana Rahman, and Sadaf Rahman. The eldest son is just married and has a baby daughter. Shahla Afreen is married to Mohammad Zainul Abdin and has two sons. Sana Rahman is married and has two children. Sadaf Rahman is pursuing her education. We have visited Mahboob about three times since we moved and settled in Canada.

Rizwan Ur Rahman, brother

My second brother is Rizwan Ur Rahman. He completed his Doctorate of Science in medicine after earning his MD from the Banaras Hindu University. After living and working in Saudi Arabia for several years, he is now in New Delhi. Fortunately, he has acquired a large amount of property and is doing very well financially. He married Tasneem in Kashmir, who is also a doctor. They have two daughters and one son. The names of his children by birth order are: daughter Nausheen, son Hamad, and the youngest, daughter Hiba. After Rizwan settled into public life, I was able to visit his family in 2013. We also visited him in 2011 in Jeddah when we went for Umrah.

BACK, L to R: Naushaba, Sana Rahman, Shahla, Afreen, Danish Mahboob.
MIDDLE, L to R: Naiyer, Mohammad Zainul Abdin, Mahboob, and Halima Khatoon with Shala's children,
Mohammad Azmat Hussain, Nazish Rahman,
Front: Two sons of Shahla Afreen and Zainul Abdin.

Tabish

L to R: Rizwan, Nausheen, Hiba, Rizwan's wife Tasneem, Hamad.

CHILDHOOD OF NAIYER HABIB

by

Naiyer Habib

I was born at the house of my maternal grandfather, Dr. Ameer Ul Hussain Khan, in Dinapore, a subdivision of Patna District of the state of Bihar, India.[36]

Naiyer as a baby on his father's lap.

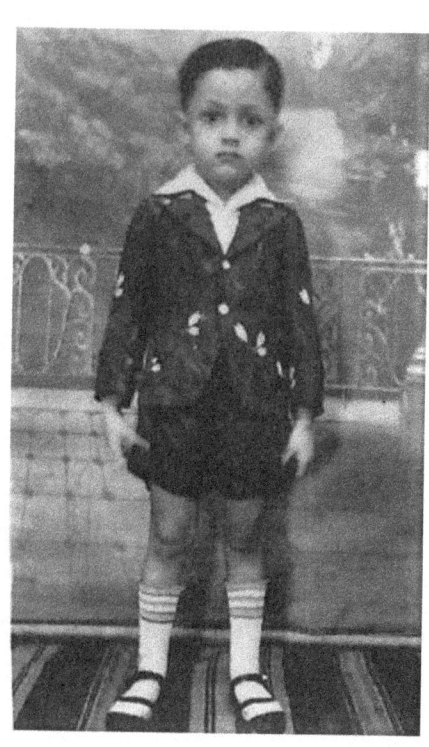

Naiyer at four-and-a-half years of age.

---

[36] My wife was also born in the house of our maternal grandfather.

My maternal grandfather's house, where both Naushaba and I were born.

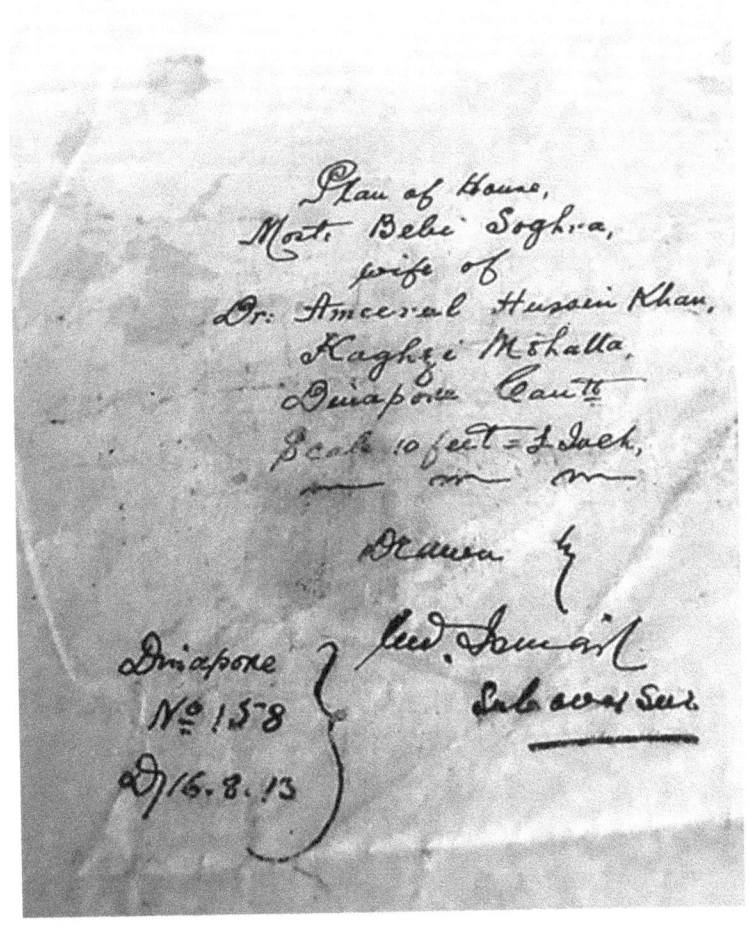

Detail of the house.

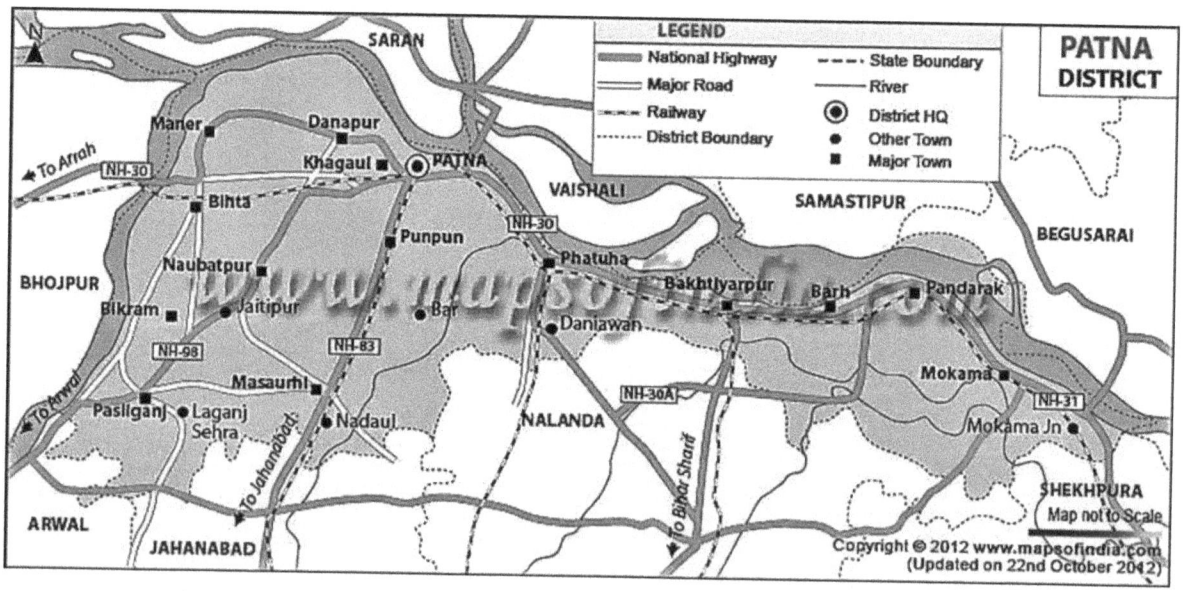

House Plan.

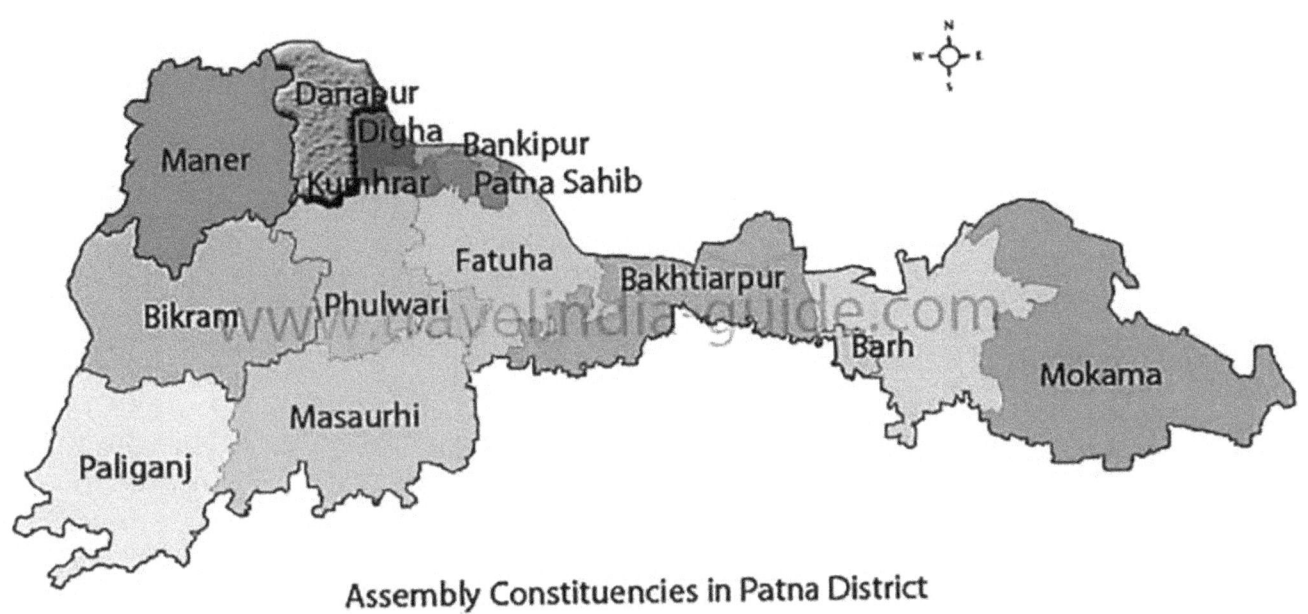

Assembly Constituencies in Patna District

Dinapore/Danapur[37]

Gol Ghar (Round House): a large building in Patna built to store grain in 1786 for the famine; now a site for visitors.

Dinapore is a satellite town of Patna in the Bihar state of India. It is part of the Patna Metropolitan Region. It was constituted as a municipality in 1887. Dinapore is also a shelter and hatchery for migrating Siberian cranes, locally called "janhgil." They visit every year during the monsoon season for breeding and leave this place before the start of the winter season.

---

[37] With permission from Maps of India.

Flagstaff ghat[38] on the Ganges at Dinapore, Patna, 1859 is one of the oldest ghats. Gurdwara Handi Sahib, a gurdwara of Guru Tegh Bahadur, is a pilgrimage place for Sikhs. The Naulakha temple, along with various historical buildings of British rule, are places of interest.

I stayed there with my mother, though I do not recall for how long, before going to the paternal side of my family.

Maternal Grandfather (Nana In Urdu Language), Dr. Ameer Ul Hussain Khan

As our mothers were sisters, Naushaba and I shared the same maternal grandfather. He was the most important person in my life.

He had a horse-driven carriage that he used to take on house calls to see patients. Most times, I would go with him. The street children would jump on a little platform attached to the back of his carriage and would be mischievous. The carriage driver would threaten these mischievous children by splashing his whip on them, but they would only run away briefly before returning to ride again. It was fun. His house was by the side of the Ganges River. At times, he would cross the river on the man-driven riverboat to see patients. I would sometimes accompany him to the bank of the river and return home.

My Nana had a liking for pigeons. They were of different varieties. He used to feed them. The pigeons sang in their language and danced. There was a birdhouse on the veranda where he used to sit.

At 5:17 p.m., on January 30, 1948, our leader, Mahatma Mohan Das Karam Chand Gandhi, was shot dead at Birla House (now Gandhi Smriti) in New Delhi, India. The opinion of the public was that the assassin was most likely Muslim. It was evening, and our house was the only Muslim house in the whole neighbourhood. It was on the second major road of the city. All traffic was closed. Hindus were walking and gossiping with one another with swords and other tools of assassination, which we could see through our split window viewer. There was no male member in our house other than my grandfather, who had become a disabled person because of filariasis swelling the lower half of his body. We were scared, but he was calm. My aunt Maimoona Khanam, the second daughter of my grandfather, was an active lady in the house. She asked him to have the gun with him and to face the attackers if any situation requiring it arose. She put the gun, filled with cartridges, by his side. He looked as if he couldn't care less. He kept on with his religious recitations on his religious beads. I was cuddled up with my mother. Eventually, news came that the assassin was Nathuram Godse, a member of the Hindu Mahasabha party. This allayed our fears.

---

[38] Ghat: series of steps, leading to water, here from a high level, down to a steamer/ship in the water.

His Influence

My grandfather influenced me a great deal. He was a practicing physician. His method of practice and being a physician had an influence on my life. I was born in his house and raised there until I started to remember the details of my life. I do not recall if I was there from my birth to this period continuously or if I visited or stayed with my paternal family before I started remembering my childhood.

His Passing Away

One day, my beloved, honourable, respected Nana fell ill. My mother and Naushaba's mother came to visit him with her family. He was mostly in bed. After a few days, my mother and the family were to return home. Naushaba's mother and her family stayed.

It was nighttime. My Nana was on his bed, and I sat beside him. He held me and placed me on his chest. He cried with tears rolling continuously from his eyes. Tears roll from my eyes now as I recall this incident of my life. We then parted and parted forever. His kindness and his character as a physician inspired me to be a physician. I have said that I would have been the poorest physician here if I were to collect a fee from patients.

Maternal Grandmother, Soghra Begum

She was Bibi Soghra. She was Naushaba's maternal grandmother, as was mine. She was a very calm and quiet housewife who was always seen to be busy in the kitchen with her maids, whom she treated as members of the family. They lived in the house with her children. I did not see any daughter giving her a helping hand. I could not say if it was the daughters or her not wanting to get help from them. I saw her looking after my grandfather, who was fairly disabled because of filariasis. She used to help him with toiletry, bathing, and getting dressed. There was a room next to his room with these facilities for him.

Eventually, Bibi got sick. I could not tell you much about the nature of her illness. I recall her lying in a bed in the centre of the hall of the house. All the relatives were also in the hall. She passed away in peace. The burial took place in the graveyard at Shahtoli, Dinapore. I attended the funeral with my Nana.

My Settlement

I do not recall when I went to my paternal side of the family. I do remember waiting at my Nana's house for my father to come. My mother told me that he was coming, so I remained excited till his arrival. This is what I remember from my remote past.

Then, the entire family went to my paternal family in Mahammadia, Purnea. I was very excited. I was told that I had grandfathers. These were my grandfather's stepbrothers. My own grandfather had already passed away before my birth. When I met them, I did not feel the warmth and affection that I was used to receiving from my Nana. I was disappointed and went to my mother. She tried to console me, but it did not matter.

I was now living in a village area. I was not accustomed to that. I heard people speaking in the rural language. There were gardens and farms and trees all around. Time passed.

My Childhood Life

I had a younger uncle who was around my age. We used to run around in the garden and orchard, here and there. We were full of naughtiness. We had a cousin, Safia, who was the daughter of my father's sister. She was a simple girl. My uncle/friend and I decided to be naughty with her. We told her that we would make a picture of her. She got excited. We made her sit on a chair, with my uncle/friend acting as a photographer. After she did as she was told, Uncle said sitting was not very good and that she should stand up. He asked me to "adjust" the chair, an "adjustment" that was actually pulling the chair away from her without her noticing. I did that. Then my uncle told her, "That is very good. Now you can sit down, and I will take your picture." The poor girl sat and, as there was no chair, she fell flat on the floor. She cried, and my mom heard. She knew what was happening. We both ran away. We met Safia when we visited in 2013 and I reminded her of this incident, and we laughed.

In childhood, when I was at home, my Uncle Mojib Ur Rahman and I would fight, and we would love each other. We would exchange gifts, and then when we fought, we would ask each other to return the gifts. We would go out to catch birds and even take the eggs from birds' nests, which I would never encourage anybody to do now, the way I am. We also used to pretend to shoot each other. One of us would discharge the gun, and the other would fall down, and so on. One day, my father was watching, and we saw him smiling.

Tricking My Father

My father used to have my sister and me with him to sleep at noon because of the heat outside. When he fell asleep, and we would hear his snoring, both of us would stealthily leave the bed, take our shoes, and run away. Our father never reprimanded us.

My Sister's Doll

As a youngster, I would often imitate being a doctor. I would pick up one of my maternal grandfather's used syringes and, using ink, inject my sister's doll. Not only that, but I would operate on her doll by cutting its arm. Of course, this would be done in secret. You could imagine her anger . . . and what happened to me when my mom received her complaint. Naushaba used to play with my sister. She would have an angry look with silence.

I Got a Pony

My father bought me a beautiful pony. Its colour was shiny maroon. This horse was of a short breed. He also purchased a leather saddle. I used to ride on it with my nice dress jacket and pants made by my mother. It was strange to note that if I was riding, the horse would be very well-behaved. One day, my sister wanted to ride on it, and sat on the leather saddle. This horse misbehaved with her. She fell off his back. This horse used to disappear and wander to faraway places and then come back. My father was fond of horses. He used to have a horse at home, and I enjoyed riding the horse. I still miss riding the horse while we live here. I still miss it and wish I could have a horse here to ride.

EDUCATION OF NAIYER HABIB

by
Naiyer Habib

INITIAL SCHOOLING

My mother was my first teacher, and she taught me at home to the standard that I was admitted to grade five in school.

I started to go to a madrasa in the neighbourhood. My great-grandfather—my paternal grandfather's uncle, Ameer Bakhsh—had established this madrasa. This was primarily for learning the Quran and Islam. My mother had started teaching me the Quran at home. At the madrasa, I noticed students sitting on mats on the floor of the hall in a line. The teacher was also sitting on the floor, on one side in the front corner. He had a huge stick by his side. I realized that it was to beat the students for not behaving as he expected, be it in study or discipline. On my return home, I rebelled and told the story to my mother. She arranged for a Hafiz[39] who came to my home to teach the Quran in the evening.

I found the Quran study to be hard, and was not interested, likely because I was reading without understanding. I would start arguing with my mother long before the respected Hafiz was scheduled to come. She would try to make me understand its importance but would never get upset or scold me. Sometimes, she would promise that she would send someone to give me an early break. I would go and await the relief. My mother would indeed send someone who would tell the respected Hafiz that I was not feeling well and ask if he could relieve me. That would happen, but the respected Hafiz would sometimes smile and understand that it was a made-up excuse.

I finished reading the Quran up to fourteen parts before I was sent away to school. I completed the Quran a long time later, at the end of my medical career, when we moved to our home at Wascana Mews in Regina. My mother

---

[39] Learned person who memorizes the Quran.

was a housewife and busy, but she taught me lots of subjects, including English, in the morning hours. When my uncles came home from school during the holidays, my mother would ask them to teach me mathematics and English. Time passed.

KANHARIA MIDDLE SCHOOL

At last, it was time for me to move my education to school, with courses recommended by the board of education. It had so happened that when I was born, my father had gone with his friend Sri[40] Sachida Nand Sinha to Dinapore. They had stayed at my maternal grandfather's house. At that time, Sri S. N. Sinha was the head of the Kanharia Middle School. He told my father that when I grew up, he would like to teach me. My father promised that he would. So it was that the preparation for me to go to school started.

Kanharia Middle School was upgraded to middle school from primary. Sri Sachida Nand Sinha was a well-known headmaster of middle schools. He was renowned for maintaining excellent teaching standards and had a reputation for upgrading and improving schools. As such, he would regularly be sent to schools that needed improvement, either in response to a public demand or a decision by the government in consultation with him.

I went to Kanharia Middle School from grades five to seven. Kanharia is a village about nine or ten kilometres away from my own village, Mahammadia. It is thirty-seven kilometres east of the district town of Purnea and 307 kilometres from Patna, the provincial capital of Bihar. Kanharia is a village like any typical village in India, and its setting was not different from that of Mahammadia. Floods affected roads and farmland bloomed with crops in season. Scenes of farmers working in the field were appealing to the eyes. There was no electricity. Farmers ploughed the land with oxen. Communication there was similar to that in any village in India. There would be a village market once a week.

Map data ©2016 Google

---

[40] Hindi word used with respect, such as "honourable."

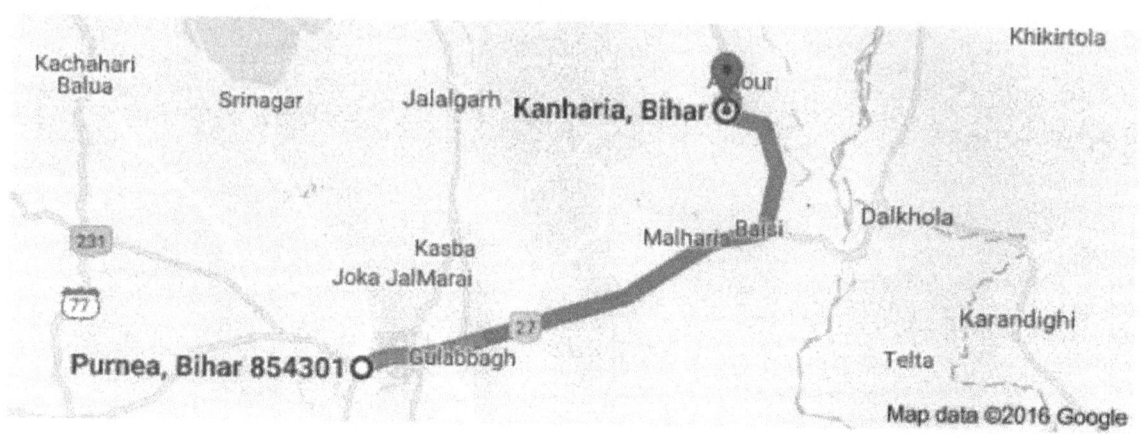

The majority of the population in and around Mahammadia was made up of Muslims. The majority of the population of Kanharia was made up of Hindus. They all lived in a friendly, cooperative, and accommodating manner.

Of course, I was reluctant to go away from home. I was to stay in a hostel at the school. A helper was to accompany me, to look after me and help me there, including preparing food. We had to go on a bullock cart. It took about four hours for us to get there. I arrived there in the afternoon after starting in the morning hours. My father accompanied me.

Sri Sachida Nand Sinha was called Panditji[41] . He was away when we arrived and was to come in a few days. My family was very influential, as we were Zamindars. Therefore, I was placed in the room where Panditji normally stayed. It was a half office-half bedroom, with a little barrier between.

Given that this was such a drastic change in my life and that I was only eight years old, I felt shy about facing new people. I confined myself in the room for a few days. I had been given a place in the room of the Panditji. This was a small building office-cum-Panditji's residence! I realized this offer was an expression of great affection and honour for me.

There was another student by the name of Mati Ur Rahman. He came to meet me in the room and took me out. We became familiar with each other. He was in a more senior class than mine.

When Panditji returned, I was admitted into grade five. I was given a place to sleep like everybody else, in the classroom after class, from the evening to the morning. My helper looked after this.

When Panditji arrived, there was no hostel for the students. They slept in the classroom at night and then packed their stuff for the classes to start at 10. Panditji was, as I said, a great person to bring improvement and prosperity. Under his direction and plan, a hostel was built. This building was divided into multiple rooms to accommodate the students. The entire construction was made of bamboo and special grass, with a foundation of mud and pillars

---

[41] Panditji –a scholar of Hindi language and Religion

of bamboo. That was the way the buildings were built then. Classes were held in the rooms and also outside in the sun.

Panditji would get up early in the morning and, after his wash, shower, and prayer, would teach the senior students, preparing them for the competitive examination of the district for scholarship awards. As an exception, and because of his commitment to my father, he taught me regularly. Then, he would collect all the students after supper, including me, to teach. All of this teaching was undertaken by him on a voluntary basis.

There was an annual test. Some of my classmates would whisper to help each other, and I did it, too. The invigilator, who was the examiner for that subject, noticed. He came over to me, and on my examination paper, he wrote to deduct a certain percentage of my mark. I was very upset by this because I had been doing very well in my class, always standing first or second or third. It was my naughtiness that inspired me to pour ink on the invigilator's writing. He saw this and remembered me. He called me and asked me what it was. I was ashamed, but other than warning me, he did not do anything.

It was expected that the examination might require drawing a diagram of the state. Someone made a copy and hid it at the examination site. As it turned out, a diagram was required, so this copy was thrown from one student to the next to trace it on their exam paper. The invigilator noticed but could not identify who was behind it. Some had already been traced, but not others. Those old days!

One of the subjects for the examination was singing. I would not do that. I was too shy to sing. I was asked by my teacher, Munshi Rahman, to at least read a song as prose. Apparently, I did that, so I got a passing mark in this subject.

I recall these memories and smile, comparing those days with the days now.

There was a Brahmin cook who cooked for everybody. All the Hindu students sat inside the room attached to the kitchen on a mat on the floor, and he served them. This would be a vegetarian meal. However, a few Muslim students would stand outside with their utensils, and he would pour the food into their containers, which they would take to their rooms.

The Muslims and students of lower caste were not allowed to enter the kitchen area. There were no lower-caste students with us there at that time. The Muslims were considered to be the people who ate beef, which is highly prohibited in the Hindu religion. The Hindus have a lot of respect for the cow. So, this was one of the main problems, that they were considered to be untouchable from those points of view. My helper usually cooked my food, but he would go home to bring stuff, and during that period, I would stand in the same line to collect my food. I had developed a friendship with a senior student, Mati Ur Rahman, whom I had met when I was staying in the room in Panditji's office. He helped me and would generally compel me not to stand in the line, assuring me that he would get the food for me.

Friday Prayer is a weekly prayer for Muslims in the congregation. We went to the masjid for Friday Prayer. Sometimes, when the flood season came, we had to walk through water, which was flowing all over, about thigh height, to go to the masjid. Looking back today, I am amazed at how I could go through that water when today, even a slight encounter with anything dirty forces me to take a shower and clean myself.

There was also a weekly market. We went there because that was one of the ways to entertain ourselves. During the flood season, we had to go through the flooded area to reach the marketplace. There was another short market right near the school on a weekly basis, as well. A class friend of mine, Sohan, had a stall from his father's store. We would visit him.

During holidays, we would go home. Sometimes, in coming back from home, there would be a flood. The bullock cart would not be able to go on the road, and one time, the road had broken. In this instance, my helper carried me on his shoulders through the water and put me on the other side, and then he carried all his stuff across.

I liked to play soccer. My position was right out. One day, I sprained my ankle, and my helper told my mother when he visited her. When I returned home for my holiday, my mother asked me not to play the game because I was the only son. She made me understand that I should just pay attention to my studies because I had to make my future bright. If I injured myself, I would neglect my studies and not get good grades. I understood and respected that. That was the end of my career in any sport, although I occasionally played badminton.

I stayed at Kanharia Middle School, other than my trips home on holiday, for three years. I completed my seventh grade there with high marks. I stood first in my class but was considered to stand third, as two students—Rudra Pandey and Saeed Ur Rahman—were sent for a district scholarship test and were successful. On my completion of middle school, all my teachers were invited to our home and were given gifts of dress, to pay respect to them. All my teachers were Hindu, except one Muslim. This is how we lived as Muslims and Hindus.

PURNEA ZILA HIGH SCHOOL

Now was the time for me to go to high school. I was registered at the Purnea Zila School. My father had also studied there. I completed my matriculation (grade 11) and studied four years in Purnea Zila School. The Purnea Zila School year of recognition was 1853. It was about twelve kilometres from my village home and located in the town of Purnea.

I was given a leading role for the Muslim students to celebrate religious functions. A student was killed by police in a riot in Patna, the capital of the State of Bihar. There was an uproar all across the state. He was Deena Nath. I do not recall the reason for the student protests. I was picked as the representative of Purnea Zila School to make the strike successful. Finally, things settled down with hard negotiation. Shahab Ud Din took the provincial leadership for the students.

I stayed in the hostel of the Purnea Zila School. There was a wing for Muslim students, with a designated room for our prayer. There were strict rules in the hostel to maintain discipline. The hostel warden inspected in the evening to see that everybody was studying and in the hostel. Of course, we were people with naughtiness. We wanted to watch movies, and we had permission to go to movies at fixed intervals. Sometimes, the movies wouldn't have finished by the time we were due back, so some of us would go to watch movies outside in the movie hall, and others would ensure that we were protected. I put here my own example for this mischief:

I would leave a book open and the light on and then disappear from my seat with a couple of friends. The warden would make his inspecting visit. Friends would change the book and even close it, giving the impression that I had only temporarily left my seat. We would come back only after ensuring that everything was calm and quiet. We successfully crossed over the iron fence with the locked gate. This was our strange naughtiness, and when I remember it, it makes me smile. I moved out of the hostel later on and stayed in private lodging in Line Bazaar.

I should mention that I studied English with Man Mohan Babu. He was a brilliant Bengali teacher who had also taught my father. A high school friend of mine named Jugraj Bothra was another student studying with me. We were close friends in Purnea Zila School. We used to go to restaurants at lunch break to have a snack. He was the son of a businessman, and ultimately started doing business with his father and also opened a pharmacy. We visited him on our trip in 1993. I completed my matriculation in first division with high marks in 1956.

Purnea Zila School.

Purnea Zila School Hostel.

L to R: 3rd Naushaba Habib, wife of Jugraj, Naiyer Habib, Jugraj Bothra, all others their children.

UNIVERSITY AND CHOOSING A CAREER

Now was the time to go to a university and to decide which branch I would pick up. I was very interested in becoming a doctor after having seen my maternal grandfather, Dr. Ameer Ul Hussain Khan. He was a very noble man. When I was a little child, I would go with him whenever he went to see his patients on call. He was very charitable in his clinic, which he ran from his home. Patients would bring a rupee or two, fruit, fish, vegetables, or eggs. I noticed that he gave most of these things to other patients who were needy and poor. He never demanded a fee from his patients. This influenced me to become a doctor. As I mentioned before, when I became a doctor, I said that if I were to collect money from the patients, I would be a poor doctor compared to others. This was when I started practicing in Canada.

Anyway, there were some decisions to be made about my career. Man Mohan Babu told my father that I should be studying arts and that I would be a brilliant leader. My father said that there was discrimination in India against Muslims. He was not sure whether I would be admitted to high-grade institutions, and even if I succeeded in those, whether I would have a job. He felt strongly that I should study medicine. He offered an illustration of why, saying that even if I did not have a job, if I just opened my dispensary at home, this man (pointing at a walking man) would come and give me a couple of rupees for treatment, and so on, and that I would earn my living without having to depend on others. This was an appealing view.

My uncle, Dr. Abdus Salaam, who was also studying medicine, advised my father that he should send me for engineering because I was good at mathematics and the state was flooded with doctors.

Then came the choice of which college and university I should attend. I felt strongly about going to Patna and studying there at colleges under Patna University. My father had studied at Aligarh Muslim University (AMU). He wanted me to have exposure to the tradition and discipline of the university that he loved, admired, and enjoyed as a student. I did not want to go there because I had an impression that the majority of the people who were running the various institutions did not have a good view of AMU. They discriminated against the students from this institution. I had an apprehension that medical schools may not take me because I had studied at Aligarh Muslim University. I was reluctant, and my mother favoured this, but this opposition could not sustain. Father noted that Darbhanga Medical College had medical students who had studied at Aligarh and that they continued to admit students from AMU. This gave me some consolation. Thus, it was decided that I should complete my intermediate science at Aligarh Muslim University prior to admission into medical college. It was 1958. I was anxious about going far away from my home, about an eighteen- or twenty-hour journey on the train.

ALIGARH MUSLIM UNIVERSITY

The main campus of AMU is located in the city of Aligarh. Spread over 467.6 hectares, AMU offers more than 300 courses in both traditional and modern branches of education. In addition to this, it has three off-campus centres—at Malappuram (Kerala), Murshidabad (West Bengal), and Kishanganj (Bihar). The university population is comprised of all castes, creeds, religions, and genders, and the school is an Institute of National Importance provided under the Seventh Schedule of the Constitution at its commencement[42].

We have added a chapter on the Aligarh Muslim University and its founder, Sir Syed Ahmed Khan, towards the end of this book because of its important association with the awakening movement for the education of Muslims of India who were falling behind in education.

Aligarh Muslim University is a residential university. Discipline is maintained on the campus, which was observed more strictly when I was there in the 1950s than it is today. Sherwani is worn by male students of the university. This is a nice dress for men, extending from the neck to below the knee, and it is a traditional attire for the university. It is required to be worn during official programs. The university provides Sherwani at a subsidized price. Sherwani is a unique tradition of AMU.

I arrived at AMU in 1956. We stayed with a friend of my father, Mukhtar Sahib, who was a geography professor and was also the proctor of the university. The proctor was to look after the security of the entire campus. The next day, accompanied by my father, I went to the university to be admitted. It was required that we all wear Sherwani. I did not have this for my size yet. My father gave me his, but it was much too large for me. However, I had no choice, and I had not learned to oppose my father. Thus, wearing that loose Sherwani, I went around and around on the university campus, stopping at various places feeling shy but knowing I had no alternative. Meanwhile, my father ordered a Sherwani to be made for me, and of course, it took a day or two before I could get it. I was relieved.

My father had been a student at AMU in the 1930s, and he took me around to visit all the places in the university compound, pointing out specific spots with which he was associated. He had been a student secretary in the Department of Geography, and he showed me his name on the board in that department. There were three halls, where there were various hostels—Sir Syed Hall, Aftab Hall, and Viqarul Mulk Hall. He had lived in the hostel of Sir Syed Hall. Most of the senior students lived in Sir Syed Hall Hostels.

I lived in Morison Court Hostel in Aftab Hall—my father's choice. For managing purposes, three or four hostels were placed under one name. Aftab Hall was one of them. The head of the hall was called the provost, and the head of the hostel was a warden. This hostel was called a stable by the students, because it looked like a place where horses lived. It did look like it, with its rooms in a row in a compound. However, the feature of this hostel was that the students were studious, and they were paying much more attention to their studies compared to students

---

[42] Source: Wikipedia (edited).

living in other hostels. As a result, the students of this hostel were far better than the students elsewhere. This was why my father chose it for me. Again, I did not have a choice, and I did stay.

All students were required to be in the uniform of a black Sherwani. Some students also wore caps. We were required to move around in a disciplined manner in the university compound with no loitering. There were proctors to watch and ensure discipline.

Each hostel had an attached place for prayer. Morison Court had common baths, whereas some hostels in some halls had attached baths, but their toilet was in a central place in the hall, outside the room.

Breakfast, lunch, and supper were served to students. On Fridays, they got dessert. The food was not of the standard that the students would have liked, but it was not bad either. A siren would sound in the morning, indicating that we should wake up and have Fajr (before dawn) Prayer, and then again at night to say that all outside activity should cease and that everyone should be in the hostel.

There were all sorts of sports and other activities on the university campus. There was a student union building. The election of the university union members was very well organized and done with great enthusiasm. Many of the students who were elected president entered into high positions in politics in due course. The union building had photographs of various individuals who had played roles in the independence of India, and there was no discrimination here: Mohammad Ali Jinnah, Jawaharlal Nehru, Gandhiji. Sir Ahmad Khan had a large portrait in the centre of the building. Portraits of Rabindranath Tagore and others whom I do not recall are on a wall in the main hall of the union building.

The poet Majaz wrote "The Tarana," a classical Urdu musical poem. Dignitaries sat on the central stage of the student union building. At the end of Tarana, flowers and their petals would be showered from the ceiling onto the dignitaries. It was a very sombre and pleasant sight and sound. The Tarana with music was very impressive and was available on the university website.

I liked the university and the entire setting. My mother gave me a new bicycle, because I had to travel from one department to another, and they were located far apart. I had only one jacket throughout my stay there, which was damaged by acid in the chemistry laboratory. I had it repaired and continued to wear it. However, for classes, I wore a Sherwani and pajamas. I was interested in biology because I was pursuing a career in medicine.

Aligarh Muslim University was open for admission to all, but there was a higher percentage of reserved seats for Muslim students than anyone else. My youngest brother studied medicine at Banaras Hindu University, where he qualified for a DSc, the highest medical degree in India now. Both institutions continue to run successfully.

I studied at Aligarh Muslim University between 1956 and 1958. I completed intermediate science in 1958, in the first division. There were three terminal examinations a year. In the first year, despite being a biology student, I stood second in order of merit among the 300 students of intermediate science. I received recognition for this, as noted below:

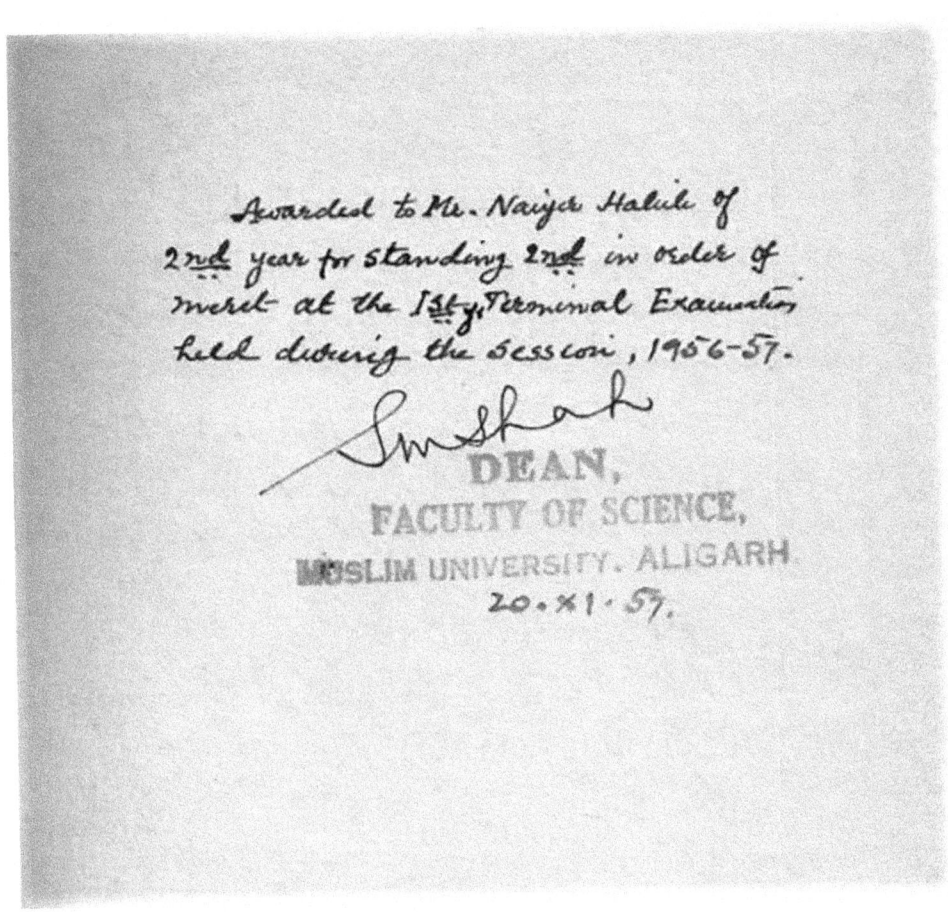

Awarded to Mr. Naiyer Habib of
2nd year for standing 2nd in order of
merit at the 1st y. Terminal Examination
held during the session, 1956-57.

DEAN,
FACULTY OF SCIENCE,
MUSLIM UNIVERSITY. ALIGARH.
20.XI.57.

However, in the final examination, I could not achieve this honour and was placed in seventh position. I also received a university monthly scholarship of IRS (Indian rupees) thirty, based on my high school achievement. It was a big help, as the economic situation at home was not very good.

In the first biology class, I met Professor Zahoor Qasim. He was a tall, handsome, British-looking individual from the family of Nawab of Rampur. This was the first zoology class. I sat in the front row. He asked us to come along to visit the laboratory, and we all did. As usual, I was in the front. He asked the lab boy to bring a frog. I had a sort of repulsion to frogs, lizards, earthworms, and cockroaches. When the lab boy showed up with the frog, I thought he was just going to show it to us. But it turned out it was not a question of simply showing us this creature but touching it. He told us that many of us would not like touching it but reminded us that this was the animal we would be experimenting on often. Oh my God, I thought. What would I do? As I said, I was always a front-row student. Professor Qasim looked around and focused on me. He asked me to open the jar and touch the frog. Well, I was to be a doctor, and that was my aim, so putting myself under a lot of stress, I touched it, and my whole body shivered as I did. So that was the experience of that day. Then we used to dissect frogs, and we were even asked to practice this at our hostel. We got a dish in which we froze melted wax. We tagged the frog on that and dissected it. We also had to dissect earthworms and to dissect cockroaches and isolate the brain. With my growing experience, I began dissecting animals very well. I got the highest marks in the practical part of zoology because my dissections were among the best and complete.

We were taught by the biochemistry professor Shahab Ud Din Sahib[43]. He had a habit of asking questions in class. He also had a habit of humiliating the students, as a joke, who failed to answer his questions. When everyone would fail, he would smile and say you all leave this responsibility to Naiyer Habib to answer your question. He would ask me the question, and—fortunately—I would be able to answer it. He was very fond of me, and I had a lot of respect for him.

There was a professor of English, B. N. Khan. He behaved like an English person. One day in class, he said, "I was unfortunate to be born in India." He was a very dark-complexioned person. After the class, when he was not around, we all started saying to ourselves in his accent, "Black Englishman." It was a fun day.

While I was at Aligarh Muslim University, I met a challenge of racial conflict that arose in the city. I do not recall exactly, but it had something to do with Gitangli[44], a religious book of the majority Hindu. Whether some Muslim insulted the book or made some incendiary remark, I do not recall, but it led to a riot all across India. The students of AMU were supposed to have been attacked, but this was fortunately averted.

Dr. Zakir Hussain was the vice-chancellor of the university at that time. He became the governor of the state of Bihar, whence I came, and then the president of India. He established an institution called Jamia Millia Islamia in Delhi, which is a very progressive university that is open to all.

In an address to the students in the union, he pointed out that we all had to live with caution and that any step we took must be cautious. He said that there are people around who, if you pointed your finger at someone just for recognition, would interpret it that you were pointing your finger to poke in that individual's eye.

I visited Aligarh Muslim University in February 2013, and Naushaba accompanied me. It was my wish to see the institution again and to show it to Naushaba. It was not the same. The environment was similar to any university in India or elsewhere. A dress code is observed at all of the university's events. It shows a disciplined group in graceful attire.

Iftikhar Ali Khan was a very close friend of mine. He stayed in Sir Syed Hall, and I stayed in Morison Court. We had a connecting gate between our hostels. He was a national football (soccer in the West) goalkeeper from Hyderabad and was on the university team that participated nationally. Generally, we met in a café called Café-Defus. We used to alternate in payment. We loved namakpara, tea, and burfee (an Indian snack). Sometimes, we would go to the restaurant in Sir Syed Hall. Sir Syed Hall and Strechy Hall had very nice restaurants in the compound of the hostels. We would walk around and revise our teaching as we did. This was a routine.

We both went to visit Agra, a historic city of Mughal time, by bus. We visited the historic places, including the Taj Mahal. We took a lot of pictures, but the roll of film was bumped out of my trousers' side pocket due to the vibration of the bus while driving. Its loss is a sadness I endure. I visited the city with Naushaba in later years and took pictures, but those lost pictures with my best friend when we visited together were gone forever.

---

[43] Saheb (or Sahib) is a title of respect for men.
[44] A collection of poems by the Bengali poet Rabindranath Tagore.

132

We completed our intermediate science, and Iftikhar went to study forestry while I went to study medicine. We parted each other's company but continued to communicate. As situations changed, though, we lost contact. After establishing myself in the West, I visited Pakistan in 1972, and I found out that Iftikhar was also in Pakistan, so I put an advertisement in the paper, and thus, the contact was re-established. We were very happy to meet. Meanwhile, Naushaba and I had decided to go to Canada along with our family. I did not have much money. He offered me money without my asking him. I promised to repay it as soon as I reached Canada, as I had left some money in the United States. Iftikhar was more sacrificing to me than I assessed myself, but I did not have the opportunity to show my sincerity to him. We met again in 1993. He came to the marriage ceremony function of our older son. Our families visited one another.

Time went by, and he passed away. After several years, his son Imran contacted me after an internet search. I was so pleased. When we returned to visit Pakistan, we contacted him and socialized. We met a second time, and although we contacted him, we did not succeed in meeting his family. This was one of my greatest disappointments.

I had a few other close friends at the Aligarh Muslim University. There was Riaz Meshak, from Endomen Nikobar Island; Habibullah, originally of Tibbat Nativity; Rizwan Ur Rahman and Shafiq Ur Rahman of Kursail, Purnea; and Abrar of Bihar Sharif. Shafiq Ur Rahman has passed away.

As recently as the fall of 2016, I had contact with Rizwan Ur Rahman. His daughter had found me through Facebook. We were so pleased to be in touch. Since November 2016, I have lost contact with him. I have been calling and emailing but have not gotten a response. I am worried and sad.

The association of their memory brings the sadness of missing them but also happiness for the time we had together. Their pictures from that time, 1956-58, are posted here.

With best wishes to my
Loving friend Nayier Habib on
his visit to Calcutta on 13th June.

Riaz Meshack
19/6/61

Rizwan Ur Rahman

Iftikhar

Naiyer Habib and Habib Ul Allah

Naiyer Habib wearing Sherwani (1957), the Aligarh Muslim University uniform.

Some pictures of our lives and others of reminders when we visited in 2013.

Sir Syed Ahmad Khan

His grave is in the compound of the AMU Mosque

Victoria Gate of AMU

Naushaba and Naiyer at Strechy Hall of AMU, 2013 visit.

AMU Mosque (a portion seen). On the right, Strechy Hall.

AMU Mosque with Sir Syed's grave on the extreme right.

Viqarul Mulk Hall Gate (student residence hall).

Naushaba and Mona Abid at the historic student union building, 2013.

Naiyer, Naushaba, and Mona Abid, 2013, a visit to Morison Court Hostel, where I stayed from 1956-58.

My room in the Morison Court Hostel (2013 visit)
—outside on the L; inside on the R.

The dining room that we used in 1956-58.
They served me a meal and asked, "Is it the same?" I replied, "Yes!"

School students at the campus, 2013.

Delhi to Aligarh 2013—Roadside Scenes

We have incorporated the pictures of us visiting the Aligarh Muslim University above, but here we are presenting what we saw on our way from Delhi to Aligarh as we drove on the road. It reflects the culture, living, business, and transportation of the area—splendid scenes not seen in the West:

Roadside trading shop.

Trader passing through.

Transportation of loads by buffalo, camel, and ox trucks, still in 2013.

Fuel made of cow dung, stacked under cover.

Monkeys enjoying their freedom.

Caravan of goats.

PRINCE OF WALES MEDICAL COLLEGE

After I completed my intermediate science at Aligarh Muslim University in 1958, it was time for me to enter medical school. This had been my dream since childhood. I joined the Prince of Wales Medical College, Patna University, Bihar, in 1958.

Patna is the capital and largest city in Bihar. The city of Patna is situated on the southern bank of the Ganges River and has a very rich history. I completed my education in medicine, living in this city from 1958 to 1966.

As mentioned, I was influenced by my maternal grandfather to be a physician. My father, mother and I finally chose a medical career for me, considering this profession to be the best for me, particularly because I could be in this profession and not depend on someone else for a job.

The Prince of Wales Medical College was a reputable institution. The alternative was Darbhanga Medical College in the district of Darbhanga in Bihar. The Prince of Wales Medical College's admission criteria were based on a competitive written examination and an interview, whereas Darbhanga Medical College admitted students on the basis of their marks and an interview. I applied for both. I started preparing for the competitive examination. Instead of staying at home, I went to Patna. My cousin Shamim Ahmad Khan lived in Phulwari Sharif. He was working with a pharmaceutical medical store. He arranged a room in the business building of the company for my stay.

Curiosity

I was curious when I was a young student (and I still am). There was a wire showing from the electrical panel in the room where I was staying and studying. I always looked at it with curiosity and suspected strongly that it might be a hot wire. One evening, I decided that I would touch it to see how it felt. I had been told that electricity jerks the whole body. Despite that, I attempted it. The whole left side of my arm and shoulder were shocked with electricity, but fortunately, nothing happened to me. I laughed it off. Of course, it was foolish, but it was because of my curious nature. Watch it!

The Darbhanga Medical College admission process was finalized with a selection of students. I was among them and appeared in the interview. I got the impression that I had qualified to be admitted to this institution. The interviewers were high officials—the professors—of the medical college. They apparently already had the list of candidates who had been successful in the examination. I was asked whether I had appeared for the competition of that institution. I replied in affirmation. They further asked, "If you are to be selected for admission at the Patna Medical College, will you go there, or will you stay here?" I was in a dilemma. I was thinking that if I said yes, they might not admit me. But if I said no and then left, it would not be a good idea. Walking on the path of honesty, I affirmed that, yes, if I was selected there, I would go. Afterward, I became depressed and started to get worried that, in case I wasn't selected there and didn't accept an offer of admission here, I would be in trouble. I told them that I didn't know what the situation of my selection at Patna Medical College would be and that, if it was possible to leave this option open for me, I would be thankful. I did not get a positive answer, but they gave me the impression that they would try, so that was over for then.

Patna Medical College was established as Temple Medical School in 1874. The Temple Medical School was shifted to Darbhanga and replaced by the medical college known as Prince of Wales Medical College, Patna.

The formal inauguration of this medical college was on February 25, 1925. The first batch of thirty-five M.B.B. students was trained clinically at Calcutta Medical College and then transferred to the Prince of Wales Medical College, Patna. This was affiliated with the Patna University. Patna University was the first university in Bihar, established in 1917. The postgraduate teaching in medicine, surgery, physiology, obstetrics, and gynecology was first started in this institution in undivided India[45].

The results of the Prince of Wales Medical College competition were eventually released, and we were called to appear for medical evaluation, which lasted a whole day for all of us. There was no direct interview, but questions were asked at each stage of the medical examination. Fortunately, I was selected. One of the first people I met was Dr. Abid Hussain. He had a colourful T-shirt and trousers, whereas I was wearing pajamas and a bush shirt. He came to me, and we chatted for a few minutes. He was also a smoker. I was not much impressed with him, and tried to avoid him. Lo and behold, he became one of my best friends during medical school and remains so to this day. The second person I met was Rehan. He and I chatted a bit and then departed. So it was that I entered medical school at my cherished institution for my cherished career in medicine.

The first class I attended at medical school was anatomy, where human bodies were dissected by the students. It was a hard time for me, and worse than touching the frog at Aligarh Muslim University. However, there was no way out. Gloves were not provided. We had to dissect the human body with our bare hands. My hands smelled for a few days. I had a hard time eating after that. I tried to eat with a spoon. There was no custom then for the average hotel—and we were eating in hotels—to have forks or knives. I stayed a few days in the Taj Hotel in Patna, near the medical college. I started to wonder whether I would be able to carry on this dissection. However, it was my dream to be a doctor, and I could not have left it. Things started rolling after that.

We all started participating in the various subjects. We were to study the non-clinical subjects of anatomy, physiology, and biochemistry, as well as pharmacy, in the first two years. The next three years were to be clinical: medicine, surgery, and pathology. I was poor at making diagrams and scored low in anatomy. People who had the practice of doing excellent diagrams got excellent marks in that course. I wondered whether the handmade art of body structure was more important or if knowledge was. I thought it was a poor way of assessing students. Be that as it may, things passed.

I suffered from infectious hepatitis soon after admission. I was admitted to the special ward, which was reserved for medical students, who sometimes would pose as patients, in order to be admitted for good food and rest. It was a somewhat luxurious place for the medical students. It was at the top of the administrative building of the Cottage Hospital, which was for VIPs and paying rich people. Anyway, I stayed there for a few weeks with my infectious hepatitis, and when I was released, it was a great relief to me.

---

[45] Ref:https://en.wikipedia.org/wiki/Patna Medical_College and_Hospital.

148

Muslim students celebrated their functions. They used to celebrate the birthday of the Prophet, and I took an active part in this celebration by arranging and running it, along with some other active students, particularly Abid Hussain and Helal Ahmad Siddiqui. Others were also involved. We made no discrimination of having isolated functions for Muslims only; they were open for all. The idea was to know one another in a country with a mixed population based on culture and religion. The Hindu students celebrated their Hindu functions, and we Muslims were invited.

Some Hindus and some Muslims across the country would not participate in each other's religious celebrations, considering this to be against their religions. Many have divergent views within their own religions.

We were not provided with accommodation in the first two years. We lived outside, renting places. Abid and I stayed together. When we entered the third year, we were given accommodation in the medical hostel outside the college, Dharhara Hostel. Then we gradually moved from that to a new hostel by the side of Khuda Bakhsh Library and then into the "Old Boys' Hostel," which was the main hostel in the compound of the college.

I used to study regularly on time and to sleep on time. Abid was the kind of person who would go around here and there, watch movies, and come late to rest and sleep. However, when it was examination time, he would study almost the whole night. I resented that, and Abid understood. In a way, I behaved like a guardian. If I stayed awake and he returned to our place, he could guess from my facial expression what I was thinking about him. Time passed, and now we remember these, and we laugh. One time, I was sleeping when Abid came in late. There was a plate on the floor, and his foot fell on it as he navigated his way in the darkness. This was a plate of Tamcheen (ceramic-coated tin) and as soon as he put his shoe on it, it started to jump, and its coating started to break and make noises, one after the other. I got up and exclaimed, "So you came, sir!" He said, "Yes, Yar."[46] It was late. That was it. We recall this incident whenever we meet, including as recently as in February 2013, when we were visiting him at Siwan. This shows our respect and care for each other. Abid passed away in 2017. It has left us in sadness.

Mohammad Shahab Ud Din was a careless guy among us, never looking after his hair, dress, shoes, or bed. Abid and I would tease him and used to go after him for these habits. He was an avid user of paan[47]. He, Abid, and I were roommates when we moved to the hostel. He would go in a lungi to get paan from the paan stall across the road from our hostel. I told Abid to run after him and pull his lungi. He ran away.

Later on, Shabab helped me by arranging my residency at the Watts Hospital in Durham, North Carolina, where he had moved earlier. He is a pediatrician in Boston to this day. Other friends included Hashvardhan, Satya Prakash, Hafiz Ur Rahman, Arun Kumar, Helal Ahmad Siddiqui, Jai Prakash, Devender Singh, Sachida Nand Sinha, Rehan, Mukherjee, and Ramesh.

---

46 Urdu nickname for a close friend.

47 Paan is a preparation combining betel leaf with areca nuts and sometimes with tobacco. It is chewed for its stimulant and psychoactive effects.

Naiyer, Abid, and Shahab, in our medical school's Old Boys' Hostel.

BACK: L to R- Naiyer, Satya Prakash, Abid.
CENTRE: Mukherji.

FRONT: Ramesh,

in a boat on the Ganges River.

Naiyer Habib and Mumtaz Ud Din Haider

This is my friend, Dr. Mumtaz Ud Din Haider. He completed his master of surgery, and I my doctorate of medicine in 1966. After that, we did not know about each other till 2013, when we met in Karachi, getting a lead from a friend.

MB, BS, Prince of Wales Medical College alumni 1963 graduate list.

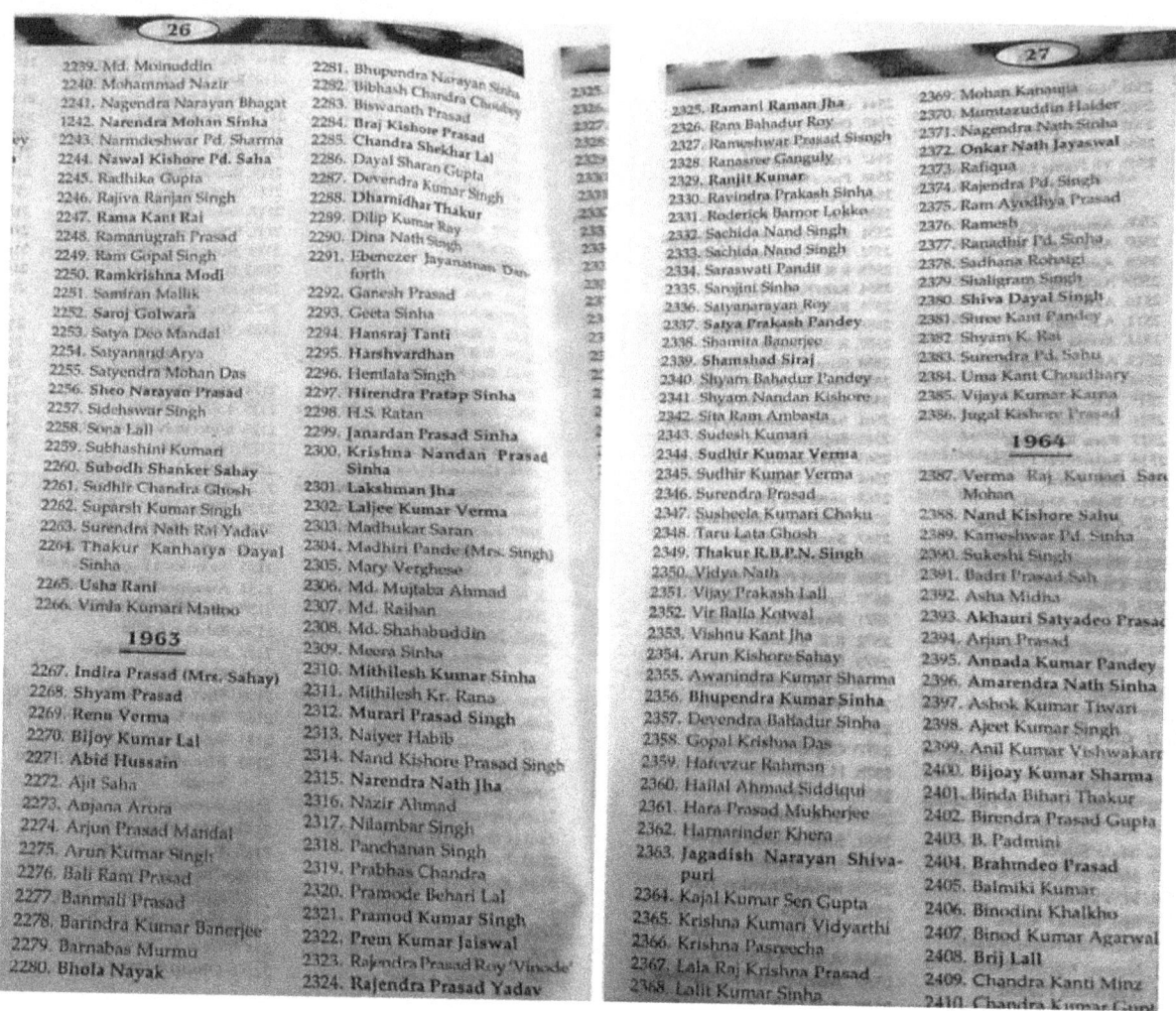

26

2239. Md. Moinuddin
2240. Mohammad Nazir
2241. Nagendra Narayan Bhagat
1242. Narendra Mohan Sinha
2243. Narmdeshwar Pd. Sharma
2244. Nawal Kishore Pd. Saha
2245. Radhika Gupta
2246. Rajiva Ranjan Singh
2247. Rama Kant Rai
2248. Ramanugrah Prasad
2249. Ram Gopal Singh
2250. Ramkrishna Modi
2251. Samiran Mallik
2252. Saroj Golwara
2253. Satya Deo Mandal
2254. Satyanand Arya
2255. Satyendra Mohan Das
2256. Sheo Narayan Prasad
2257. Sidehswar Singh
2258. Sona Lall
2259. Subhashini Kumari
2260. Subodh Shanker Sahay
2261. Sudhir Chandra Ghosh
2262. Suparsh Kumar Singh
2263. Surendra Nath Rai Yadav
2264. Thakur Kanhaiya Dayal Sinha
2265. Usha Rani
2266. Vimla Kumari Matloo

1963

2267. Indira Prasad (Mrs. Sahay)
2268. Shyam Prasad
2269. Renu Verma
2270. Bijoy Kumar Lal
2271. Abid Hussain
2272. Ajit Saha
2273. Anjana Arora
2274. Arjun Prasad Mandal
2275. Arun Kumar Singh
2276. Bali Ram Prasad
2277. Banmali Prasad
2278. Barindra Kumar Banerjee
2279. Barnabas Murmu
2280. Bhola Nayak

2281. Bhupendra Narayan Sinha
2282. Bibhash Chandra Choubey
2283. Biswanath Prasad
2284. Braj Kishore Prasad
2285. Chandra Shekhar Lal
2286. Dayal Sharan Gupta
2287. Devendra Kumar Singh
2288. Dharnidhar Thakur
2289. Dilip Kumar Roy
2290. Dina Nath Singh
2291. Ebenezer Jayanatnas Danforth
2292. Ganesh Prasad
2293. Geeta Sinha
2294. Hansraj Tanti
2295. Harshvardhan
2296. Hemlata Singh
2297. Hirendra Pratap Sinha
2298. H.S. Ratan
2299. Janardan Prasad Sinha
2300. Krishna Nandan Prasad Sinha
2301. Lakshman Jha
2302. Laljee Kumar Verma
2303. Madhukar Saran
2304. Madhiri Pande (Mrs. Singh)
2305. Mary Verghese
2306. Md. Mujtaba Ahmad
2307. Md. Raihan
2308. Md. Shahabuddin
2309. Meera Sinha
2310. Mithilesh Kumar Sinha
2311. Mithilesh Kr. Rana
2312. Murari Prasad Singh
2313. Naiyer Habib
2314. Nand Kishore Prasad Singh
2315. Narendra Nath Jha
2316. Nazir Ahmad
2317. Nilambar Singh
2318. Panchanan Singh
2319. Prabhas Chandra
2320. Pramode Behari Lal
2321. Pramod Kumar Singh
2322. Prem Kumar Jaiswal
2323. Rajendra Prasad Roy 'Vinode'
2324. Rajendra Prasad Yadav

27

2325. Ramani Raman Jha
2326. Ram Bahadur Roy
2327. Rameshwar Prasad Sisngh
2328. Ranasree Ganguly
2329. Ranjit Kumar
2330. Ravindra Prakash Sinha
2331. Roderick Barnor Lokke
2332. Sachida Nand Singh
2333. Sachida Nand Singh
2334. Saraswati Pandit
2335. Sarojini Sinha
2336. Satyanarayan Roy
2337. Satya Prakash Pandey
2338. Shamita Banerjee
2339. Shamshad Siraj
2340. Shyam Bahadur Pandey
2341. Shyam Nandan Kishore
2342. Sita Ram Ambasta
2343. Sudesh Kumari
2344. Sudhir Kumar Verma
2345. Sudhir Kumar Verma
2346. Surendra Prasad
2347. Susheela Kumari Chaku
2348. Taru Lata Ghosh
2349. Thakur R.B.P.N. Singh
2350. Vidya Nath
2351. Vijay Prakash Lall
2352. Vir Balla Kotwal
2353. Vishnu Kant Jha
2354. Arun Kishore Sahay
2355. Awanindra Kumar Sharma
2356. Bhupendra Kumar Sinha
2357. Devendra Bahadur Sinha
2358. Gopal Krishna Das
2359. Hafezur Rahman
2360. Hailal Ahmad Siddiqui
2361. Hara Prasad Mukherjee
2362. Harnarinder Khera
2363. Jagadish Narayan Shivapuri
2364. Kajal Kumar Sen Gupta
2365. Krishna Kumari Vidyarthi
2366. Krishna Pasreecha
2367. Lala Raj Krishna Prasad
2368. Lalit Kumar Sinha

2369. Mohan Kanaujia
2370. Mumtazuddin Haider
2371. Nagendra Nath Sinha
2372. Onkar Nath Jayaswal
2373. Rafiqua
2374. Rajendra Pd. Singh
2375. Ram Ayodhya Prasad
2376. Ramesh
2377. Ranadhir Pd. Sinha
2378. Sadhana Rohatgi
2379. Shaligram Singh
2380. Shiva Dayal Singh
2381. Shree Kant Pandey
2382. Shyam K. Rai
2383. Surendra Pd. Sahu
2384. Uma Kant Choudhary
2385. Vijaya Kumar Kajra
2386. Jugal Kishore Prasad

1964

2387. Verma Raj Kumari Sam Mohan
2388. Nand Kishore Sahu
2389. Kameshwar Pd. Sinha
2390. Sukeshi Singh
2391. Badri Prasad Sah
2392. Asha Midha
2393. Akhauri Satyadeo Prasad
2394. Arjun Prasad
2395. Annada Kumar Pandey
2396. Amarendra Nath Sinha
2397. Ashok Kumar Tiwari
2398. Ajeet Kumar Singh
2399. Anil Kumar Vishwakarma
2400. Bijoay Kumar Sharma
2401. Binda Bihari Thakur
2402. Birendra Prasad Gupta
2403. B. Padmini
2404. Brahmdeo Prasad
2405. Balmiki Kumar
2406. Binodini Khalkho
2407. Binod Kumar Agarwal
2408. Brij Lall
2409. Chandra Kanti Minz
2410. Chandra Kumar Guru

1   2

Mischief by Fellow Students

Now, getting back to some of the mischief engaged in by my fellow students: When our dermatology professor would enter the class, the majority of students used to crack a joke of one sort or another, and he would get upset. He was a man with a really good heart. A fellow friend came from the hostel wrapped up in a quilt, from head to leg, and sat in the back. The professor saw him and asked him why he was doing this foolish thing. He stood up and said, "Sir, I do not feel good, and I am feeling so cold." Everybody laughed, and he sat back down. One time, some of these students brought a donkey into the class when the dermatology professor was to take class. He came in and saw the donkey and got very upset. Ultimately, the donkey was removed. So these were those days of laughter. Of course, I was a non-participant in these.

Anniversary of the College

We celebrated an anniversary of our medical school with an exhibit and procession in fancy dress on the campus. Our professors and director general of health also took part in the fancy dress.

153

Naiyer

154

Prince of Wales Medical College, Patna

Office of the principal.

Lecture theatre—many memories!

Our Old Boys' Hostel.

Entering for MD and House Physicianship

An MD was the highest post-graduate degree in medicine in India (later, the DSc was added). Dr. Madhusudan Das was head of the University Department of Medicine and the MD program. He was a man of principle. We would not see him smiling, ever. He was a very just and fair person. I wanted to do this MD under him and was thrilled to be assigned to Professor Das for my MD.

Dr. Das and Me

While the process of my admission to MD was active, I had to do a housemanship. Accordingly, as discussed above, I was honoured to complete my junior (July 1963-December 1964) and senior (January 1965-June 1965) housemanship under Dr. Das in the Patna Medical College Professorial Unit Hospital.

The senior house physician made rounds with Professor Das. He came on time. His car would stop in the portico of the Hathwa Ward, and the senior house physician would get into the back and go with him, first to make rounds in the Cottage Hospital, which was a special ward for VIPs. There was also a special ward for medical students there. The majority of the time, I was not late in my duty, but sometimes, I would miss Professor Das by a few minutes. If I wasn't at the point of pick-up for the special VIP ward round, he would drive away. I would walk fast and sometimes run through a shortcut, and by the time Professor Das would enter the Cottage Ward, I would be there. These are the times to remember and smile. However, he was never upset about this—or at least I did not perceive him to be.

157

I and others respected Professor Das for his honesty, sense of justice, and respect for others. These were the principles I had followed in my life, and I intended to continue to do so. This association with Professor Das further empowered my conviction with this. One time, the ward was full, and a patient who was related to a political VIP was admitted. If all the beds were full, new patients were to be placed on the floor. If there were more serious patients, the beds were to be given to them, and lesser ill patients would be placed on the floor. This young man had a fever and was brought into the ward. A VIP patient arrived at the same time. As the young man was very ill, the VIP was given a place on the floor, which did not suit him. He told the nurse and the people who were carrying the patients on stretchers that he should not be on the floor but on the bed. He was directed to talk to me, and I told him that there were more seriously ill patients who were already in the beds and that I could not give him a bed, being less ill than others. He started to show off, but I continued to tell him that I couldn't do anything for him. I told him that he could talk to Professor Das or the superintendent of the hospital to get better accommodation but that Dr. Das was not currently in town. As expected, he threatened some actions to be taken against me, but I did not give him a bed.

When Professor Das came the next day, the matter was placed before him. He supported what I had done and went to speak to the superintendent of the hospital. The matter was resolved, and my dignity was maintained. I had followed the principles of dignity, honesty, being outspoken, and not trying to please people for any self-gain. It is difficult to impossible for people in my home country to survive without sacrificing these things. I thought to mention this because this was the principle on which I have based my life, and it was one of the factors that did not permit me to stay in my home country. (It was not, however, the only factor.)

Some of the medical graduates got jobs in the hospital, in the medical college compound, and I was appointed a medical block development medical officer in a village, even though I had high grades in medical school. It was political discrimination, and I did not accept it. Then, there was a job to be a demonstrator in biochemistry. The head of biochemistry was Dr. Awadesh Sharan. He was a very nice gentleman, and he behaved like an Englishman.

I applied for the biochemistry demonstrator job and was selected. I talked to the then-registrar of Dr. Das, Dr. Chandeshwar Prasad Thakur, who is now (2016) a member of parliament and is on the political scene with the present Indian government of Bhartia Janta Party. He asked me just to go ahead and accept and said they would not let Dr. Das know. It appeared so far so good. The vice chancellor, Dr. Jacob, was in the interview and was impressed with me.

One day, we were making medical rounds in the Hathwa Ward—the ward where Dr. Das admitted patients and taught on those patients—Dr. Jacob, the Vice Chancellor, came in to meet Dr. Das. They chatted for a few minutes. I was standing there because I was making rounds as Dr. Das's senior house physician. Dr. Jacob saw me and smilingly congratulated me for having been selected as the demonstrator. I could not say what happened to me. I was just cold and frozen. Immediately after the rounds, Dr. Das held a class in his chamber. Dr. Thakur was also there. As soon as I entered the classroom, Dr. Das asked me, "So you will be a demonstrator, or do you want to do the MD?" I did not know what to answer. I did tell him, "Sir, if it will interfere with my MD, I will resign from being the demonstrator." Dr. Thakur also smilingly nodded in affirmation. So that was over.

MD Result

The MD exam was a tough one, and we all studied hard, as much as we could. The day of the exam came. My theory was very good in my own assessment. Next was an oral examination. After that, Dr. Thakur came out and said, "Dr. Habib, you did very well. You did excellent. The external examiner was very pleased with you." I felt good about it. I did get an MD, and I was told by Dr. Thakur that I had scored the highest grade. However, there was no grading announcement for the successful MD candidate, that being the highest degree in India at that time and for a period to follow. With this over, I could not attend the convocation of my doctorate of medicine degree because I was out of the country by then (though I did attend my convocation of MB, BS). Dr. Abid Hussain arranged to send my degree to the United States, where I had gone after my marriage. I completed my MD in 1966 and then went to Pakistan to get married. Because of the conflict between India and Pakistan, we quickly decided to go to the US and figure out what our next step might be. This rapid succession of events in my life did not permit me to attend my doctorate of medicine convocation, a milestone in my life.

This degree required researching and writing a thesis. Below is a copy of the front page of my thesis and the result from the newspaper.

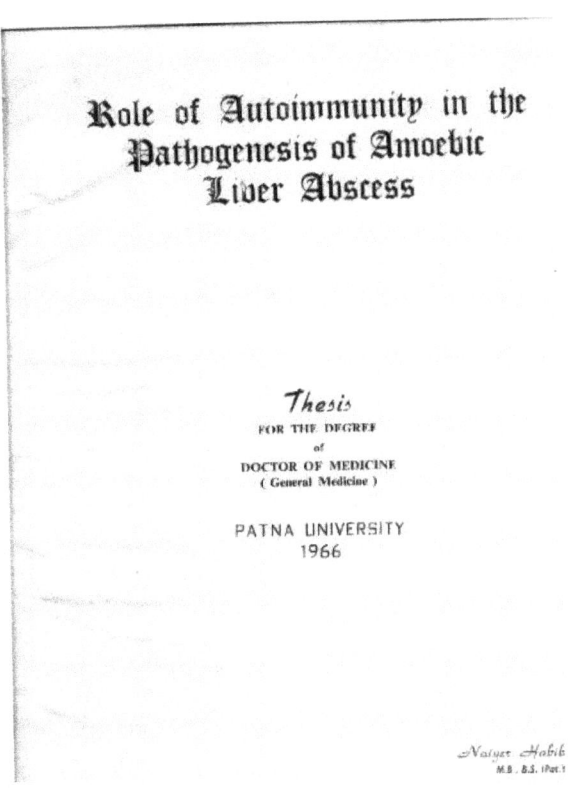

Role of Autoimmunity in the Pathogenesis of Amoebic Liver Abscess

Thesis
FOR THE DEGREE
of
DOCTOR OF MEDICINE
(General Medicine)

PATNA UNIVERSITY
1966

Naiyer Habib
M.B . B.S. IPart 1

Patna Varsity Results

DOCTOR OF MEDICINE

M.D BRANCH I, GENERAL MEDICINE

Naiyer Habib, Arun Kumar Sinha, Duryodhan Sahoo, Raghu Bansh Shukla, Ramanand Jayaswal, A.V Subrahamanian.

BRANCH IV. FORENSIC MEDICINE

Upendra Prasad Varma.

BRANCH V. PAEDIATRICS

Sheela Khan, Anil Kumar Sinha, Ganesh Prasad Sinha, Sankara Ayyar K, Shamsad Ali

BRANCH IX DERMATOLOGY

P.P. Pally.

BRANCH X (RADIOLOGY)

Surendra Prasad Jaiswal.

BRANCH XI. BIO-CHEMISTRY

Kameshwar Prasad Sinha, Nirmal Prakash.

N.B: The results of the unregistered candidates have been held up.

MASTER OF SURGERY

BRANCH I. GENERAL SURGERY

Krishna Kumar Saraogi, Lakshman Jha, Mumtazuddin Havier, Narendra Nath Jha, Shyam Prasad, Arjun Prasad, Dipak Midha, Rameshwar Singh, Surendra Narain Sinha, Shailendra Pratap Singh, Suresh Prasad Sharma, Ananta Prasad Panda, Debendra Kumar Behera, Satyendra Narayan Panda, Nawal Kishore Narayan Sinh Nazir Ahmad, Ram Chandra Sinha, Sukhdeo Chand Lodha, Raghavendra Sharma, Sardul Singh, Abid Husain, Shree Kumar Narayan, Krishna Chandra Sinha, Janardan Prasad Sinha, Shyam K. Rai, Jang Bahadur Singh, Hirendra Pratap Sinha. Md Haider Imam Ansari, Shamshul Hassan, Dhaneshwar Prasad Sharma.

M.S BRANCH II. OFHTHALMOLOGY

Chhaya Aikat (Mrs Pandeya) Hamida, Makeshwar Prasad.

M.S. BRANCH III. OTORHINOLARYNGOLOGY

Framode Bihari Lal, Thakur Kanhaiya Dayal Sinha.

M.S BRANCH IV, ORTHOPAEDIC SURGERY

Darbari Singh, Krishna Mohan Palhi, Ran Vijay Prasad Singh, Ramendra Prasad Sinha, Ranjit Bose, Satish Chandra Agrawal, Rabindra Kumar Srivastava, Venov Shrivastava, Jamuna Prasad.

M.S. BRANCH VI. OBSTETRICS AND GYANAECOLOGY

Devendra Bahadur Singh, Nirmala Verma (Mrs Saxena), Vijaya Nath, Mohini Verma, Indrani Gupta, Sandhya Das, Prem Lata Ckhandiar (Mrs. Sinha), Sharda Swarnkar.

M.S. BRANCH VII. ANAESTHESIOLOGY

Bal Krishna Golash, Mahesh Chandra Tayal

M.S. BRANCH VIII, PLASTIC SURGERY

Balwant Singh Chandalia, Sinha Hari Roy Prasad, Appu Kuttan P.K.

N.B. Results of unregistered candidates are held up.

yan Singh, 5. Jai Narayan Singh, 6. Bal Binod Sharma, Bachaspati Dwivedi.

SECOND CLASS (IN ORDER OF MERIT)

1. Janardan Prasad Sinha, 2. Lal Keshwar Singh, 3. Rameshwar Prasad Sinha, 4. Jogesh Narain Roy, 5. Birendra Kumar Singh, 6. Diwakar Sahu. 7. To be published later, 8. Tara Upadhyaya, 9. Awadh Bihari Prasad, 10. Sachindra Nath Dwivedi, 11. Suresh Kumar Roy; 12. Dinesh Prasad Singh, 13. Vidya Sinha, Veena Singh, 15. Promca Datta, 16. Gunesh Jha, 17. Suresh Kumar Singh 'Survdeo' Subhash Chandra, 19. Lalan Prasad Singh, 20. Amarendra Kumar Sinha, 21. Shree Niwas Tiwary, 22 Rama Shankar Prasad, 23. Bimla Kumari Sinna. Jai Krishna Singh. 25. Madnesh war Narayan Yadav, 26. Pushpalata Agrawal, 27. Arjun Prasad Veer, Ram Krit Prasad Singh 29. Bandana Ghosh Dastidar Jai Nath Singh 31 Renuka Rani Kansyakar 32 Ranila'a 33 Bishwanath Pandey 34 Shakti Kumar Sharma 35 Chandradeo Singh 36 Nand Kumar Singh, Shradha Nand Sharma 38 Alind Prasad Singh Madhuri Kumari Satya Narayan Pandey 41 Umesh Narain Pandey 42 Ashok Kumar Pandey, 43 Shridama Singh 44 Ram Ayodhya, Urmila Sinha, 46 Urmila Devi (Mrs. Rai).

THIRD CLASS (IN ORDER OF MERIT)

1. Anuradha Singh, 2. Sita Ram Prasad Sinha, 3. Satya Samavrita Singh, 4. Rani Sagar Singh, 5. Damodar Prasad, 6. Davinder Kaur Saini, 7. Prabha Rani, 8. Urmila Sharma, 9. Beni Prasad Singh, 10. Pratima Saxena, 11. Mahendra Prasad Sinha.

N.B: Result of unregistered candidate has been held up.

LABOUR & SOCIAL WELFARE (M. A.)

FIRST CLASS (IN ORDER OF MERIT)

Birendra Kumar.

SECOND CLASS (IN ORDER OF MERIT)

1. Radha Kant Saran, 2. Jang Bahadur Roy, 3. Dadan Prasad 4. Bipin Kumar Sinha, 5. Kamta Prasad Singh, 6. Rameshwar Prasad Singh, 7. Mohd Shaban Wani, 8. Uma Shankar Pd. Srivastava, 9. Narendra Narain Singh, 10. Suresh Prasad, 11. Jagdish Prasad Gupta, Tapan Kumar Srivastava, 13. Chougthan Norendra Singh, 14. Jagdish Narayan Singh, 15. To be published later. 16. Purushottam Jha, 17. Raj Kishore Prasad Singh, 18. Pratipal Kaur Bhatia, Sushila Rani.

THIRD CLASS (IN ORDER OF MERIT)

1. Raj Kumar Singh, 2. S. Arif Hassan, 3. Awadh Bihari Pandey.

N.B: The result of unregistered candidate is held up.

ROYAL COLLEGE OF PHYSICIANS AND SURGEONS OF CANADA—SPECIALTY

After completing my training in the US, I was eligible to take the specialty examination of the Royal College of Physicians and Surgeons of Canada. I completed the certification for CRCP in November 1971, and in March 1972, I completed a fellowship of the Royal College of Physicians and Surgeons of Canada (FRCPC).

Summary of My Education

1. Childhood to 1949: Home education by my mother to the standard of grade 5.

2. 1949 to 1952: Grades 5 through 7 at Kanharia Middle School, Kanharia, India.

3. 1952 to 1956: Grades 8 through 11 at Purnea Zila School, Bihar, India.

4. 1956 to 1958: Intermediate Science, Aligarh Muslim University, Aligarh, India.

5. July 1958 to April 1963: MB, BS, Prince of Wales Medical College, Patna University, Patna, Bihar, India.

6. 1964 to 1966: Doctorate in Medicine (MD) with thesis, faculty of medicine, Patna University.

7. November 30, 1971: CRCP Royal College of Physicians and Surgeons of Canada.

8. March 16, 1972: FRCPC Royal College of Physicians and Surgeons of Canada.

Certificates and Degrees

Matriculation certificate in Hindi, 1956. Succeeded in the First Division.

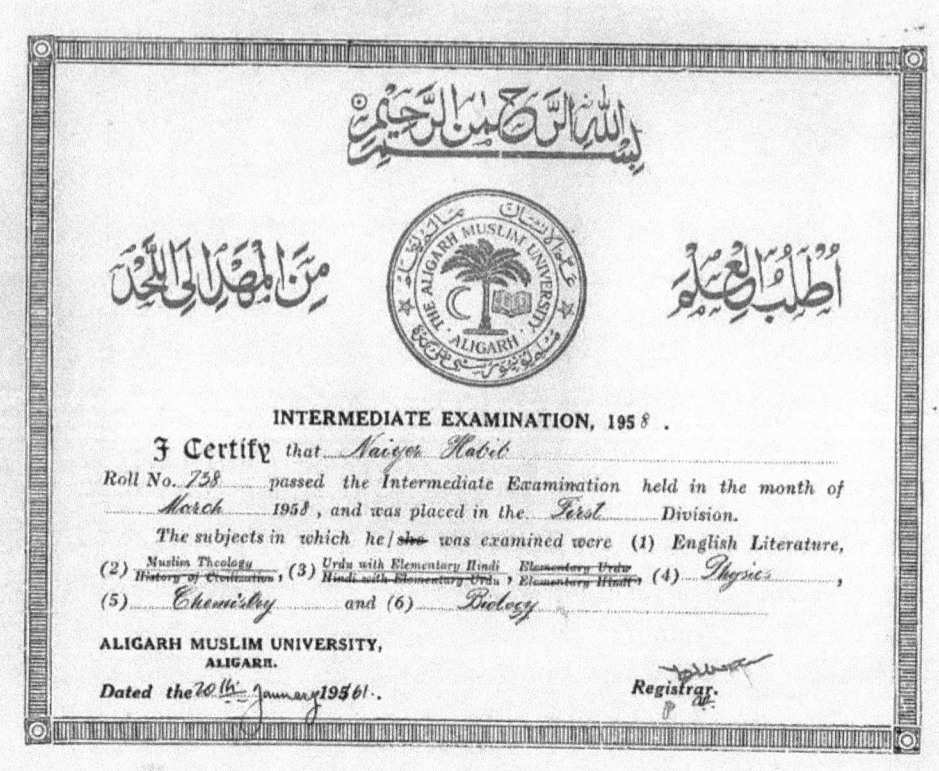

Intermediate Science, First Division, 1958.

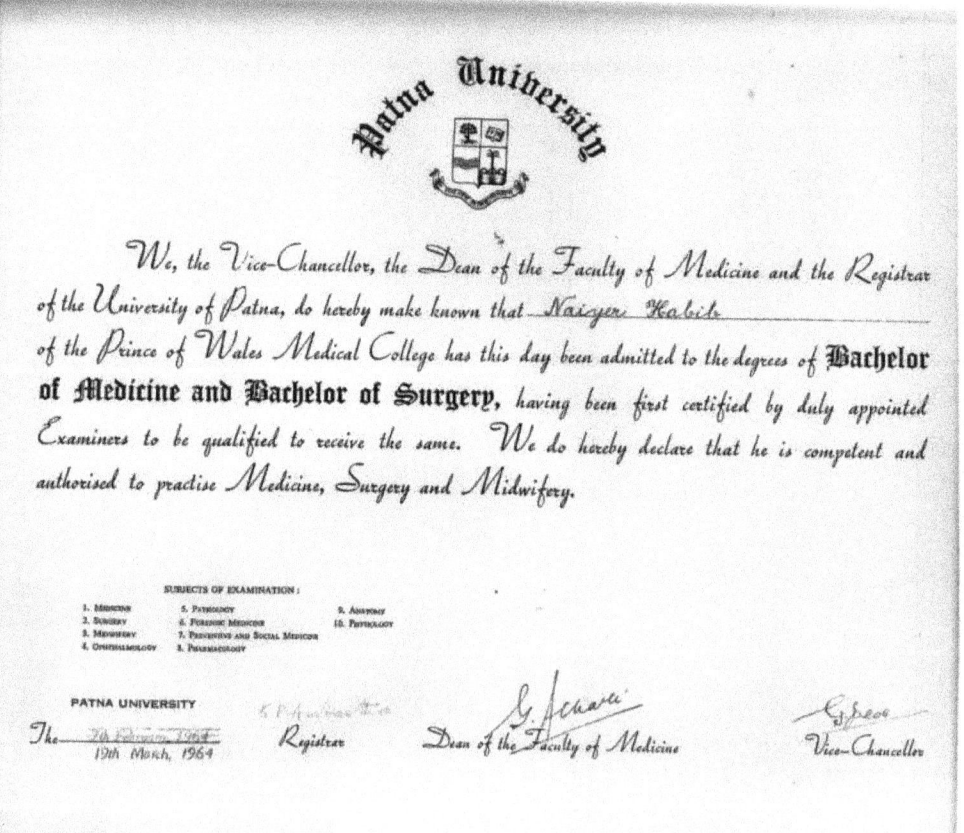

MB, BS, Patna University, 1963.

PATNA UNIVERSITY

We, the Vice-Chancellor, the Dean of the

Faculty of Medicine and the Registrar of the

University of Patna,

do hereby make known that

Naiyer Habib

has this day been admitted to the degree of

Doctor of Medicine (General Medicine).

having been first certified by duly appointed Examiners

to be qualified to receive the same.

Patna University

The 18th March, 1967

Vice-Chancellor

Dean of the Faculty of Medicine

Registrar

Doctorate in Medicine with Thesis, Patna University, 1966.

The Royal College of Physicians and Surgeons of Canada under authority granted to it by the Parliament of Canada has issued this **Specialist Certificate** to

Le Collège Royal des Médecins et Chirurgiens du Canada en vertu de l'autorité qui lui est conférée par le Parlement du Canada a émis ce **Certificat de Spécialiste** à

Naiyer Habib

who has given evidence of proficiency in the Specialty of

qui a fait preuve de compétence dans la Spécialité de

Internal Medicine

Médecine interne

In witness whereof we have hereunto set our signatures.

En foi de quoi nous avons ici apposé nos signatures.

November 30, 1971

2430

CRCP.

Collegium Regale Medicorum et Chirurgorum Canadense

Regnante Praeside, Sociisque annuentibus, decrevit

Naiyer Habib

virum doctum,

Medicinae

peritum examine rite probatum in Societatem suam in partitionem e Medicinae adsciscere, omniamque honorum atque privilegiorum, quibus Socii eiusdem Collegii fruuntur, participem facere.

Cuius rei nos, qui litteris hisce Collegii sigillo munitis nomina subscripsimus, testes et auctores sumus.

Datum, die XVI mensis III anno MCMLXXII

PRAESES

VICE-PRAESES

SECRETARIUS

FRCPC.

164

Registration to Practice Medicine

I qualified for full registration to practice Medicine in the following places and practiced for months to years there, depending on where we lived. I had educational licenses for training at places where I received training.

1. Bihar, India.

2. United Kingdom, General Medical Council of Britain.

3. Pakistan, Medical Council of Pakistan.

4. Canada, Medical Council of Canada:

   a. College of Physicians and Surgeons of Saskatchewan;

   b. College of Physicians and Surgeons of British Columbia.

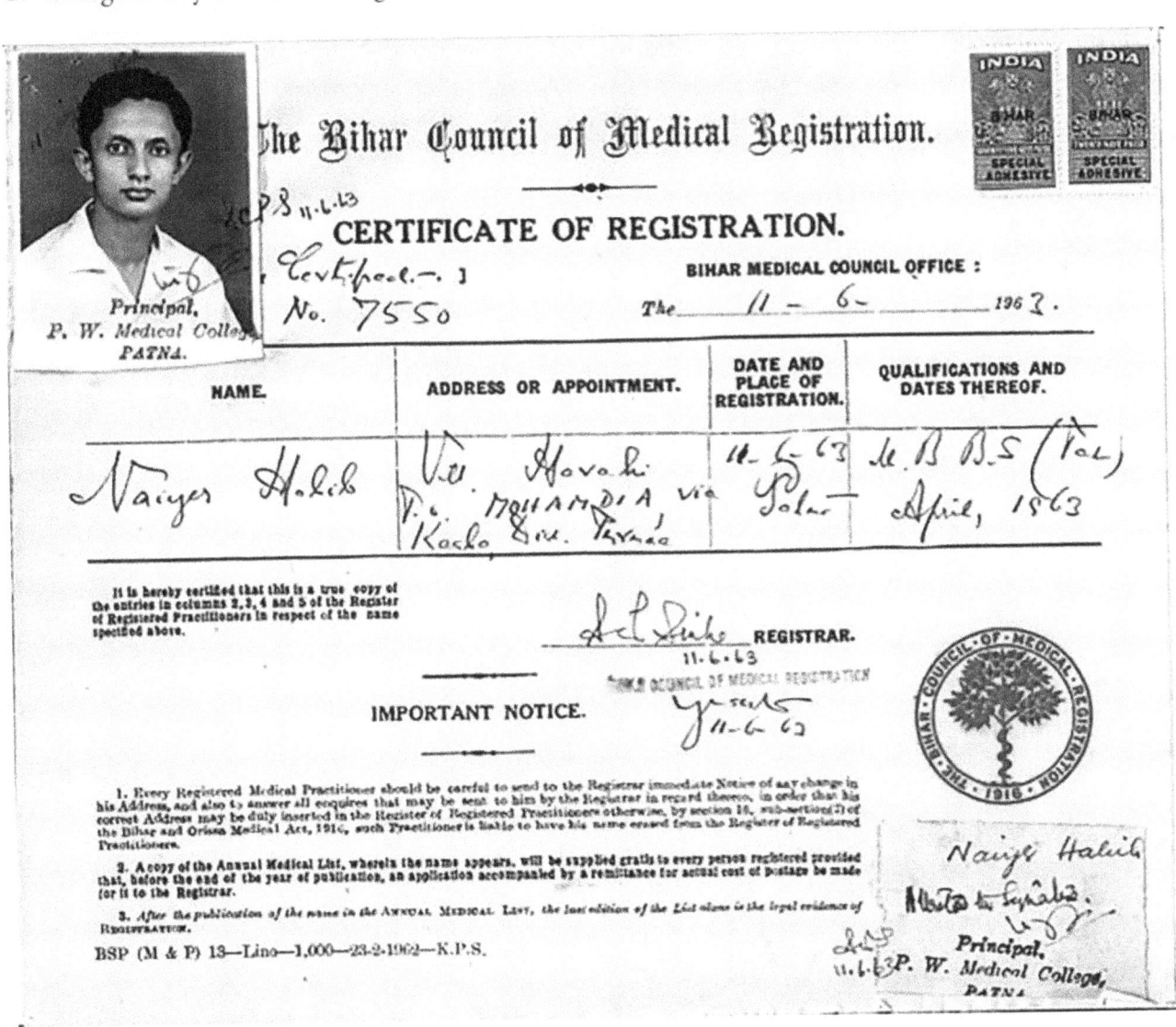

GENERAL MEDICAL COUNCIL
44 HALLAM STREET, LONDON, W1N 6AE

MEDICAL ACTS 1956-1969

CERTIFICATE OF FULL REGISTRATION
AS A MEDICAL PRACTITIONER
(PRINCIPAL LIST)

Registration No.:   Date of Certificate:

1589647   1 Feb 1973

I HEREBY CERTIFY that the person named below has to-day been fully registered under the Medical Acts in the Principal List of the Register of Medical Practitioners:—

HABIB, Naiyer 70 North Hill, London N6 MB BS 1964, MD 1967 Patna	1 Feb 1973	C

The particulars shown above comprise the name, date of full registration, address, and qualifications of the practitioner to whom this certificate relates. If two dates are shown, the first date (distinguished by an asterisk) is that of *provisional* registration.

A letter E after the date of registration indicates that the practitioner was registered by the Registrar of the Branch Council for England and Wales. C or F indicates that the practitioner was registered as a Commonwealth or as a foreign practitioner, as the case may be.

MRDrafal

REGISTRAR

NOTE

This certificate affords evidence of registration in the Principal List on the date stated. Evidence that the practitioner continues to be registered in the Principal List in subsequent years will be afforded by the inclusion of the practitioner's name as fully registered in the Medical Register which is published annually by the Council, and reference should thereafter be made to the CURRENT Medical Register for evidence of the continued registration of the practitioner in the Principal List.

William Clowes & Son Ltd., Printers to the General Medical Council, London /Colchester, and Beccles.

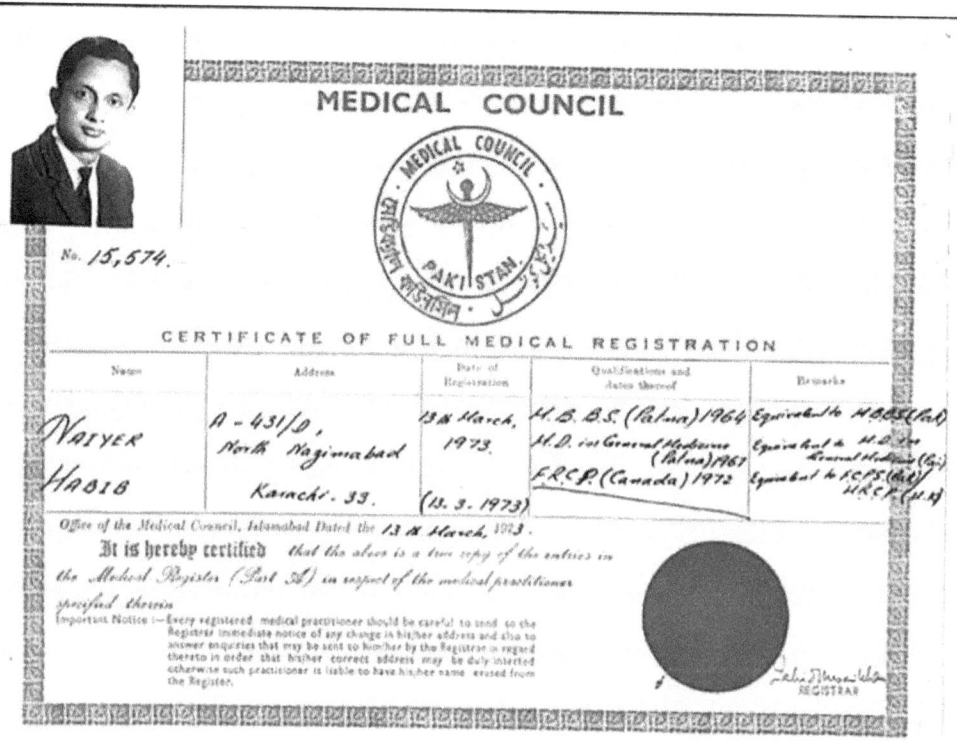

The Medical Council of Canada

We, the Medical Council of Canada, by virtue of the authority given under the Canada Medical Act (1-2 George V) do hereby admit

Naiyer Habib.

A Licentiate of THE MEDICAL COUNCIL OF CANADA, and have caused his name to be entered in the Canadian Medical Register.

In Witness Whereof the President and Registrar have this day set their Signatures and the Seal of the Council.

Given at Ottawa this _____ day of July 1974

Number
37,405

_____ Burse
PRESIDENT

_____
REGISTRAR

Signature of Licentiate

_____

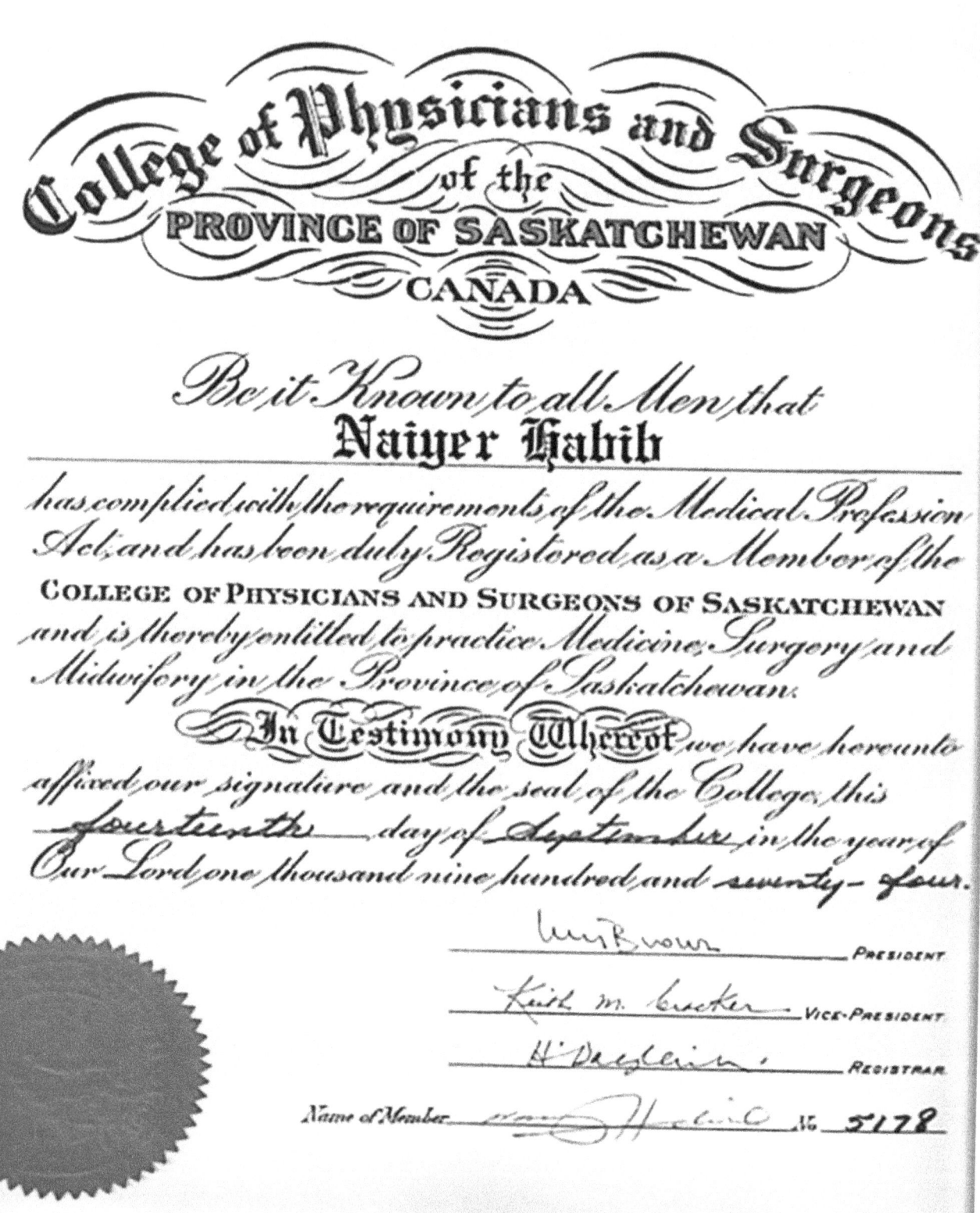

College of Physicians and Surgeons
of the
PROVINCE OF SASKATCHEWAN
CANADA

Be it Known to all Men that

Naiyer Habib

has complied with the requirements of the Medical Profession Act, and has been duly Registered as a Member of the COLLEGE OF PHYSICIANS AND SURGEONS OF SASKATCHEWAN *and is thereby entitled to practice Medicine, Surgery and Midwifery in the Province of Saskatchewan.*

In Testimony Whereof we have hereunto affixed our signature and the seal of the College, this fourteenth *day of* September *in the year of Our Lord one thousand nine hundred and* seventy-four.

_____ PRESIDENT

_____ VICE-PRESIDENT

_____ REGISTRAR

Name of Member _____ No. 5178

College of Physicians and Surgeons

INCORPORATED 1886

VIRTUTE ET VERITATE

British Columbia

This is to Certify that

Naiyer Habib

was registered on the ___28th___ day of ___October___ A.D. 2004

as a Member of the College of Physicians and Surgeons of

British Columbia and is entitled to practise Medicine,

Surgery and Midwifery, within the said Province.

Registration Number ___17537___

REGISTRAR

PRESIDENT

ANCESTRY OF MAHLAQA NAUSHABA KHANAM

by

Mahlaqa Naushaba Habib

I was born in the house of our maternal grandfather, Dr. Ameer Ul Hussain Khan, in 1944. My parents were also married in the same house. I was only three or four years old when we moved to East Pakistan as refugees.

My father passed away when I was eleven years of age. I was determined to be educated to support my family: my mother and three very young sisters. To do so, circumstances demanded that I stay with one of our close relatives as an orphan, facing all that an orphan may face in general. I remained determined to get my education, so I accepted all the miseries.

My uncle returned from East Pakistan after the death of my father in 1956. Still, I stayed with my relative till I completed grade nine. Then I moved to my uncle's, where my mother and sisters were living.

Finally, I completed my master of arts degree in political science. I worked as a private tutor to support my education.

I married Naiyer Habib on December 25, 1966. We moved to the US. Both sides of our families lived together, and we looked after them.

Naushaba, at 10, holding baby: the only picture of her childhood.

Sisters Noor Afza, Mahlaqa Naushaba, Naheed, Nikhat Pervin, 1960/61.

History Of Ancestors

It is believed that my ancestry is descendent from Usuf Zai Pathan from Afghanistan. They settled in Delhi at the time of Emperor Akbar, who ruled India from 1556 to 1605 AD. After some time, the period is unknown, as are the names of the members of the family who settled at or near Nagpur, India. One brother (name unknown) married and settled at Amnour in Chhapra district of the state of Bihar, and the second brother (name unknown) married and settled at Kona Sarai in Bihar Sharif of Bihar. After several generations, two members of the family, Asghar Khan and Chand Khan, were known. It is not known where these two were living or who their parents were. Another member of the family, Daulat Khan, was known to settle in Nathupur near Patna on the advice of Irshad, who was a worshipper. Nathupur was the final place of my family's settlement.

Descendants from Daulat Khan to Haji Abdul Rahim Khan are unknown. Haji Abdul Rahim Khan was a descendant of Daulat Khan.Haji Abdul Rahim Khan had two sons-Abdul Ghafur Khan,Peshkar and Dr. Mohammad Zainuddin Khan. Their descendants are noted in Ancestry Charts # 1 and #2. Our family descends from Abdul Ghafur Kan. Abdul Ghafur Khan is my paternal grandfather.

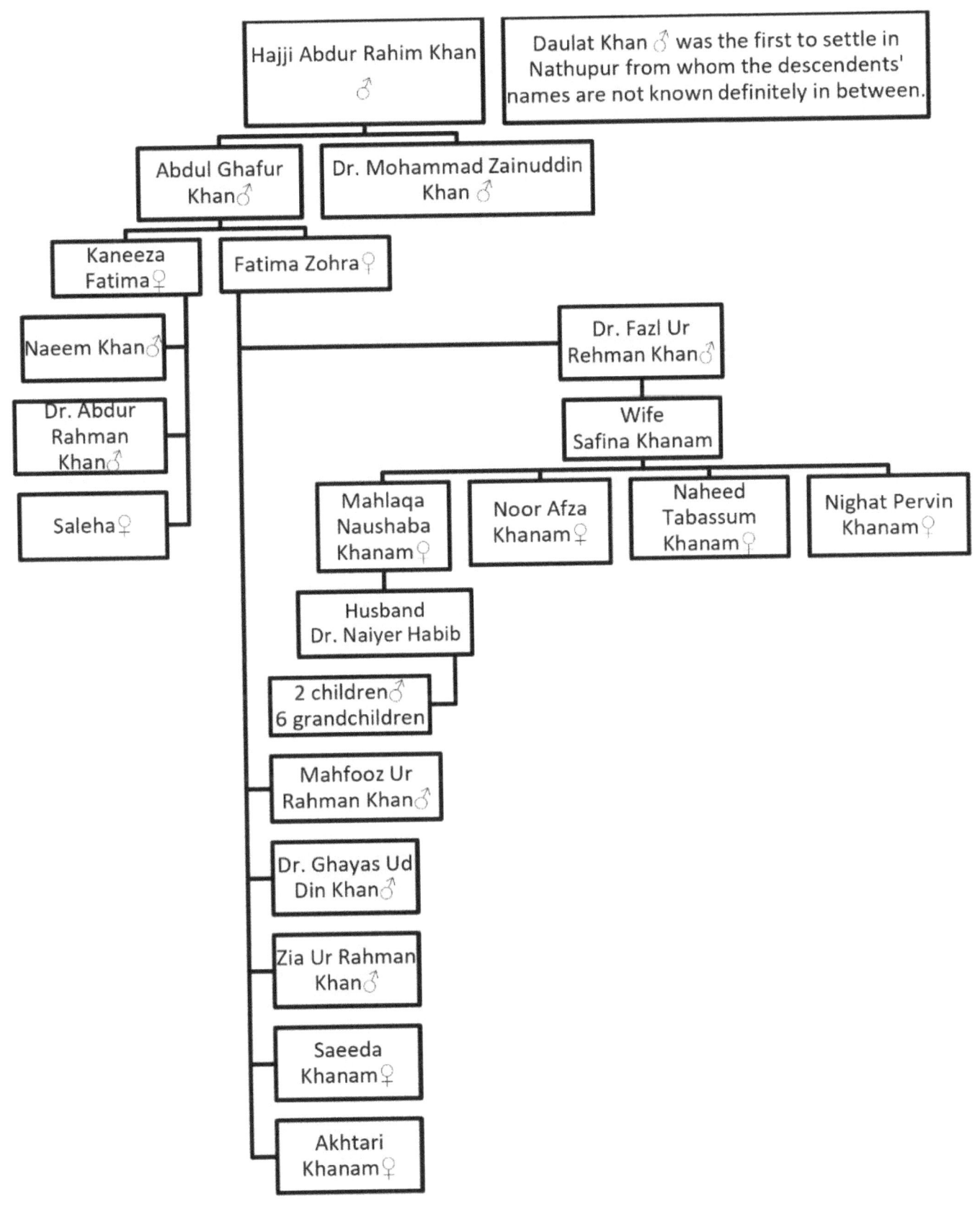

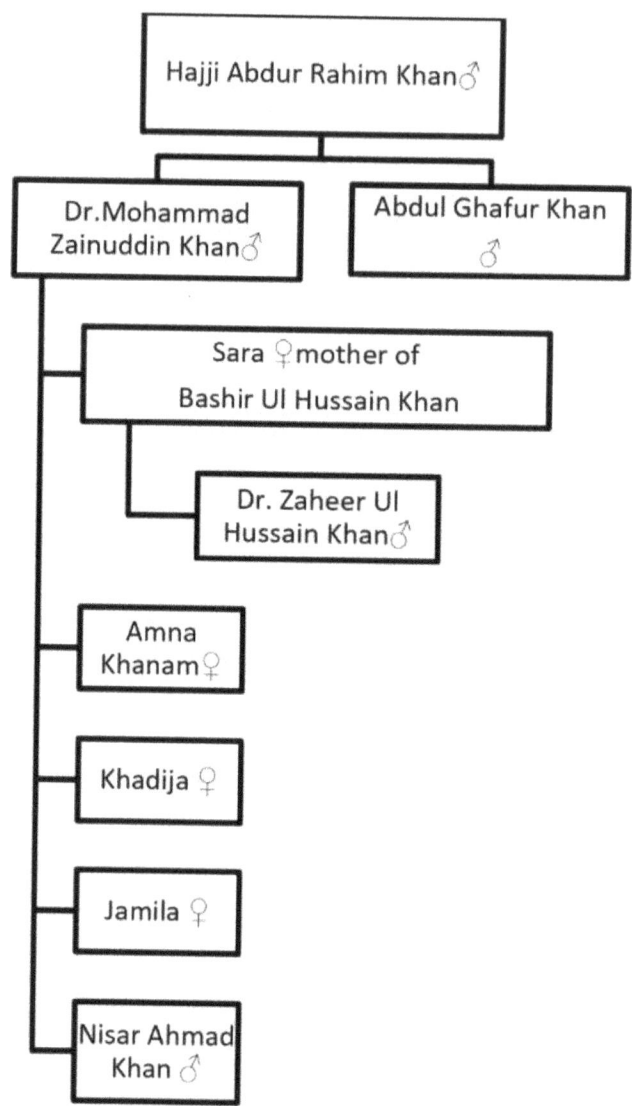

NOTE: After review with our relatives and from our own knowledge, we can say that the grandparents of our paternal grandfather, Abdul Ghafur Khan, and my maternal grandfather, Ameer ul Hussain Khan, had the same grandparents. We could not establish the link from the ancestry information available to us.

Nathupur is a village about fourteen kilometres away from Patna in the state of Bihar. According to the 2009 census, Nathupur had a population of 7,813 people.

Daulat Khan settled in the village of Nathupur. My paternal grandfather was Abdul Ghaffur Khan, son of Hajji[48] Abdur Rahman Khan. My paternal grandfather was married to Fatima Zohra.

My paternal grandmother, Fatima Zohra.

We are unable to establish a link between Hajji Abdur Rahman Khan and anyone. My grandfather, Abdul Ghaffur Khan, used to pass through the area of Nathupur. One day, a respected elderly gentleman told him that he should settle in this area and that he would flourish. It was on the strength of that that he decided to settle in that area. Life was passing happily, and his children were getting educated.

My grandfather was very much interested in the education of his children, so they all received higher education. My grandfather was a peshkar, which is equivalent to a modern-day lawyer. His work was mainly to have the papers of cases arranged and then place them in the court.

---

[48] Hajji (or Haji) is a title to a person who performs Hajj.

My grandfather acquired a fair amount of property. He and his first wife, Kaneeza Fatima, had two sons and a daughter. Their two sons were Naeem Khan and Dr. Abdur Rahman Khan, and their daughter was Saleha. After a while, his first wife passed away. He then married a second wife. Her name was Fatima Zohra. She had four sons and two daughters. The sons were Dr. Fazal Ur Rehman Khan, Mahfooz Ur Rahman Khan, Dr. Ghayas Ud Din Khan, and Zia Ur Rahman Khan, and the daughters were Saeeda Khanam and Akhtari Khanam. My father was Dr. Fazal Ur Rehman Khan.

Establishments Built By My Ancestors

On our recent visit in 2013, we saw some ruins of old establishments. One building, Baharistan, was built by Nisar Ahmad Khan in 1938. Other buildings seem to have been built by my paternal grandfather.

Status Of My Village After 1947 Riot And Abandoned By Family

On our visit to Nathupur in 2013, we viewed the ruins with emotion, thinking about our ancestors and how it had come to this! The pictures reflecting the past appear below. It includes the house of our grandfather and the house of Uncle Nisar Ahmed. The municipal government has put a sign on the ruins, but we did not pursue it.

The mosque was in ruins but has been renovated, and prayer started after it had been abandoned for sixty-six years, since 1947. The local Hindus have been occupying it, using it to keep their cattle. The cattle would die. A Hindu priest was visiting, and he forbade them from mistreating the mosque. The death of their cattle was an action of God! A lady told us, pointing at her husband, that he had become disabled. He could no longer walk. She went to the door of the mosque and prayed, "Data (giver), cure my husband. I shall look after the mosque." She confirmed that her husband's disability had disappeared and that he had started walking and working. She used to keep the mosque clean till the Muslims from the surrounding area renovated and started the prayer, likely in 2011. These ruins reflect how a noble family was affected by the Partition of India.

The mosque built by our ancestor; Naushaba is on the right (2013 visit).

Site inside the mosque where the imam stands to lead the prayer.

The ruins.

My grandfather's house (2014 visit).

Baharistan: Home built in 1938 by Uncle Nisar Ahmad Khan.

Naiyer and Naushaba are standing on the veranda of Baharistan, built in 1938 (2013 visit).

My Parents

Dr. Fazal Ur Rehman Khan, son of Abdul Ghaffur Khan and Fatima Zohra, was my father. He was born in approximately 1916. He was a physician. My mother was Safina Khanam, a daughter of Dr. Ameer Ul Hussain Khan, a World War I returned veteran physician. She was the youngest child of our maternal grandparents. She was born in approximately 1920.

My parents were married at our maternal grandfather's house in Dinapore. That could have been in 1940—not sure. They were first cousins.

He practiced medicine, likely in Chapra[49], Bihar, for a short period in the village of Amour, Purnea, Bihar, near the family of my husband, Naiyer. He was in Calcutta before moving to East Pakistan, in Jessore. He was a doctor for the railway in the town of Padidan, in Sindh province, Pakistan, after his final move to West Pakistan. He passed away suddenly in Padidan on Sunday, Ramadan 17*th*, 1374, according to the Islamic Calendar (April 10, 1955).

My mother was considered to be the noblest person in the family, with a nice, quiet, most gentle nature. She was devastated after the passing away of her husband (my father). She was a young widow with four daughters. I was the oldest, at eleven years. We passed through a period of miseries. Finally, I completed my master of arts in political science with the objective of supporting the family. Naiyer and I got married and moved to the US. Together, we looked after, and still look after, both sides of our families.

My Mother Passes Away

On my visit to see my mom in 1982, she passed away leaning on me while we were together in a taxi in North Nazimabad, Karachi, on Wednesday 29*th* of Ramadan 1402 (July 21, 1982). The next day was the Eid. We perceived the scene of peace all around us. God bless her in Heaven. She was buried in Karachi in the cemetery of Sakhi Hassan. We go there to offer prayer for her salvation when we visit Karachi.

My Mother's Grave (Safina Khanam)

---

[49] Also spelled Chhapra.

Dr. Fazal Ur Rehman Khan and wife, Safina Khanam, in the early1940s.

Safina Khanam, 1972.

Departure From India As Refugees & Move To Pakistan

There were Hindu-Muslim riots in India, all across the country. This resulted because of the Partition of India. The Partition was finalized in a haphazard manner, according to various authorities. The internet and books are filled with various opinions, but ultimately, Muslims wanted their homeland. A line was drawn by Sir Cyril Radcliffe, who was appointed by the British to divide the country based on majority Hindu and Muslim populations. It is noted that even a residence was split by that line, dividing India and Pakistan. It is known as the Radcliffe Line. The Hindu majority felt that Muslims should go to Pakistan, and the Muslim majority felt that the division was unjust—hence, the communal riots. A search online or at the library will bring the factors regarding the conflicts between Hindus and Muslims in India into light; the subject is beyond the scope of this book. The history of riots between these two communities goes back to the 1920s, and there was perhaps resentment even before that. Both are to be blamed for the hate that took root and, alas, continues to this day.

My father went to Calcutta and opened his clinic in 1946-1947. The clinic was burned down during the riots, and my father disappeared. It was unknown where he went or what happened to him. Our family was living in Nathupur. There were Hindu inhabitants living around this graceful Muslim family, and there was a plan to attack it by the Hindus. A known loyal Hindu lady who used to work for the family informed them about the impending attack. It was unbelievable to expect this from neighbours who were so closely knit. This was also happening elsewhere. There was no protection for the family. The ladies decided to jump into the well to commit suicide to save their honour. Nisar Ahmad Khan, first cousin of my father, an advocate, was a magistrate. He learned about the situation while he was on the road in a Jeep. He was not on duty. On the way, he noticed two police officers. He took them with him, and under their guard, he took the entire family—men, women, and children—under protection, on foot. As they were walking, the Hindus remarked, "Here are these women walking without parda" (the Muslim way of not exposing women to strangers). This was a very traditional and honourable family that lived in respectful friendship with Hindus in the area. They went to Patna and stayed in Anjuman Islamia Hall. Subsequently, our maternal grandfather, Dr. Ameer Ul Hussain Khan, took us to his home in Dinapore. Some other relatives also moved there.

Nisar Ahmad Khan was charged for what he did to have the family escorted to safety, as he had no authority to do so. A warrant was issued, so he took refuge and returned after a few years when his case was fought, and the charge was dismissed. He practiced law in Patna with dignity and honour.

After about six months, my father came to our maternal grandfather's house from somewhere. We were thankful to God and too overwhelmed with emotion to explore the details. On arrival, he decided that we had to go to Pakistan. Thus, we, along with our paternal grandmother, my younger aunt Akhtari, Uncle Ghayas Ud Din Khan, Uncle Mahfooz Ur Rahman Khan, and Uncle Zia Ur Rahman Khan, with all his family, moved to the city of Jessore in East Pakistan, in 1947-48.

Life in East Pakistan

Thus, the carriage of life existing in this horrible situation restarted. I was about three years old. Right in the beginning, we lived in the airport hangar at Jessore. We lived on one side, separated by a curtain; on the other side was Dr. Ghaffar Khan's family, friends of my father's. Then, we stayed in the doctors' residence of the Sadar Hospital at the Dortana location in Jessore. Finally, we went to stay with our uncle, Dr. Ghayas Khan, in Comilla, where he had moved from Barisal before moving to Karachi, West Pakistan.

After a few months, the Pakistani government announced that they needed professional doctors, engineers, professors, and teachers. Therefore, my older auntie, Saeeda Khanam, with her husband, Professor Anis Khan, and my youngest uncle, Zia Ur Rahman Khan, went to Karachi. Uncle Zia Ur Rahman Khan was still studying and needed to complete his education. He was a gold medalist in applied chemistry and nuclear physics, having achieved a double master of science. He had applied for medical school.

We stayed in Jessore. My uncle, Dr. Ghayas, was appointed a doctor for a jail. He moved with his family to Barisal. He then moved to Comilla.

My father, Auntie Akhtari, the second uncle Mahfooz Ur Rahman Khan, with his wife, Shakeela (they had no children), and my paternal grandmother stayed in Jessore. My father opened a medical clinic, but he could not pay much attention to this. The reason was that he noted the condition of the Muslims who came from India and were still coming, bringing nothing with them. He saw that the train was coming full of dead bodies. People who had survived the train trip were placed in the camp. My father and a few other professionals involved themselves in this settlement. With the government's help, they had land and houses allotted to them. The places that are more prominently known are Chamchampur and Basepara, formerly in East Pakistan.

My father's companion, Dr. Ghaffar Khan, an engineer and a magistrate by profession, occupied an empty house, but my father did not procure anything for himself. I remember that thousands of blankets arrived at the camp. They used to be distributed among the refugees. My father did not allow even a single blanket to be kept at our house.

Even though I was young, I remember that when our clothes were torn.

During this period of life, we moved from the airport hangar to a small house. In this house, my Aunt Shakeela passed away. My family was shocked.

I recall that one evening, the members of my family were sitting with sadness. I learned that a member of my family had put 30,000 rupees cash in the bank and that the bank had failed.

This was another tragedy that my family faced. However, we had to put ourselves together and gather strength from within ourselves.

Thus, life kept on passing. We did not go to any school, but we studied at home. Uncle Mahfooz remarried Auntie Rabia, from whom are Jawaid, RukhSana Rahman, Surayya, and Perwaiz. After the birth of Perwaiz, Auntie Rabia passed away. Uncle Mahfooz had an accident and lost his memory. All of a sudden, after I came to the US, he disappeared and could not be traced.

My father was running his clinic, but along with this, he was busy with the affairs of the refugees. My family in Karachi suggested to my father that we all move to Karachi so that all members of the family could stay together. My father decided to go to Karachi in the latter part of 1954.

Move to West Pakistan

When people learned that my father was leaving, they were very sad. They lined up, asking him not to go, and on the day of departure, they were present in very large numbers along the whole route from home to the airport. He could not change his decision. He decided that he would go alone to start and then that all the others would follow. Thus, my father went to Karachi.

Dr. Fazal Ur Rehman, with close friends, leaving for Karachi.

Farewell gathering, starred with garland. Dr. Fazal Ur Rehman with Afza daughter, in front.
Red dot in the picture represents Afza

My father, leaving for Karachi.

Subsequently, we went to Karachi in 1955 by ship, along with my grandmother and Auntie Akhtari. Uncle Mahfooz and Uncle Ghyas still stayed in East Pakistan.

While my father was in Karachi, West Pakistan, he was appointed as a railway physician. He lived in Mirpur Khas, and then he was transferred to Padidan.

When we came to Karachi, he came from Padidan. On the second day after we arrived in Karachi, he fainted in the bathroom. He recovered, and no diagnosis was made of this event. So, after a few days, we all went to Padidan. It was very hot in Padidan, and it was difficult to tolerate. My parents wished that I would be admitted to a school, but there were no good schools in Padidan. Therefore, it was decided that, after Eid, I would go to Mirpur Khas to study and stay with my maternal uncle, Dr. Safirul Hussain Khan. Since I was to stay at my uncle's, my father was planning to send pure ghee[50] and wheat for flour. He had acquired some land in Sindh, a state of Pakistan, adjacent to India.

---

[50] Clarified butter, prepared heating butter to remove solid milk and water used for cooking.

My Father Passes Away and Our Family Status

My father went by train from Padidan to another railway station to see some patients. After attending to the patients, he returned to the railway station to get the train for Padidan. He was waiting in the waiting room when he passed away suddenly on Sunday, 17th of Ramadan, 1374, according to the Islamic Calendar (April 10, 1955). The unexpected death of my father changed our lives forever.

As my family, which had high status at home in profession and education, was affected by the Partition of India, we started to wonder which was worse: the partition or the sudden death of my father. We had to leave Padidan because our house was provided by the hospital. It was decided that we all should go to Mirpur Khas, to my maternal uncle, till my paternal uncle, Dr. Ghayas, came to Karachi from East Pakistan. I knew life would be hard ahead of us. At eleven, I was the eldest daughter. I knew my father had high dreams for our education, which fell apart, but we were determined to get an education. Education was very important to us because my father used to say, "Look, we lost our home, land, and wealth. The only thing that is with us is education." According to my father, our grandfather would not compromise on education. He used to say, "Get an education, even if I have to sell my house brick by brick." I was admitted in grade seven, and I stayed with my maternal uncle till grade nine. My mother and sisters went to the house of my other Uncle Abdul Samad Khan, my father's cousin, for a few months, then to Karachi to the house of my cousin brother, Bashir Ul Hussain Khan, for a few months while waiting for the arrival of my uncle, Dr. Ghayas Ud Din Khan, from East Pakistan. Uncle Abdul Samad Khan was an engineer and was a director at the Water and Power Development Authority (WAPDA), the nuclear centre of Pakistan. He was a most caring individual and had respect for my parents. Our uncle, Dr. Ghayasuddin on arrival at Karachi, took my mother and sisters with him. Then, his children and my sisters started school there.

He wanted me to go to Karachi with him, so we all could be together, but I was thinking that I would ease the burden of my uncle by staying in Mirpur Khas.

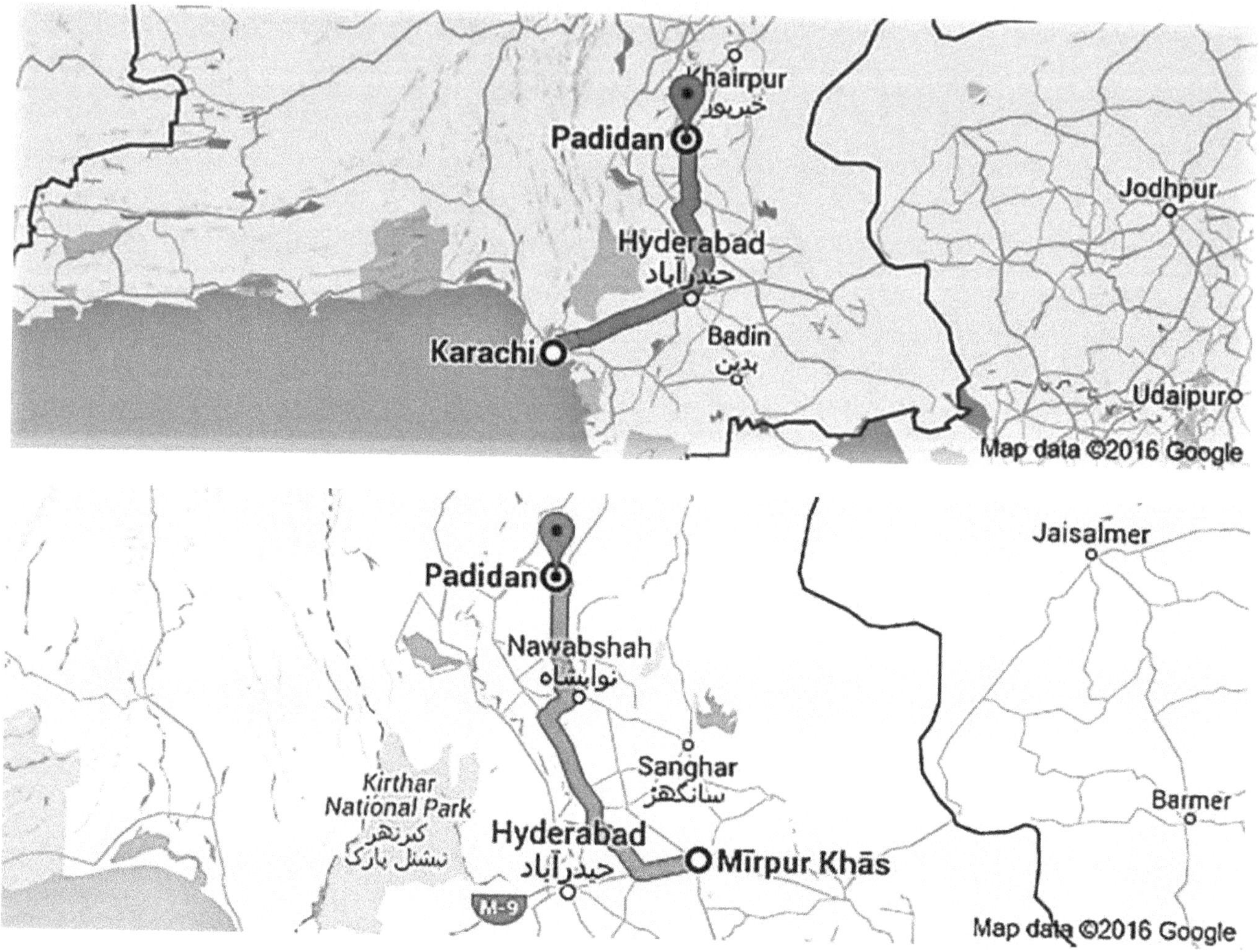

Maps Padidan: Karachi and Mirpur Khas.

L to R: Safir Ul Hussain Khan, Abdus Samad Din Khan.

I was still in Mirpur Khas. My mother kept Khan, Ghayas Ud insisting that I also come back.

Living as an orphan is not easy when staying with somebody. You live in fear and apprehension that anything you do, even unintentionally, will not suit the host. You may have the desire for some food and drink or to live or dress in a certain way, yet you suppress it or leave it unfulfilled. I was thankful to my relatives to live with them for my education.

Finally, after my grade nine examination and summer holiday, I came home to see my mother, and, as usual, she asked me not to go. I decided I would not go back to my uncle's place and admitted myself into grade ten at Raunaq-e-Islam Girls School in Karachi. Now, my small family was joined together under one roof. When I was in grade eleven, I received a scholarship of 5,000 rupees. This money helped me to get admitted into a bachelor of arts program at the Sir Syed Government Girls College. I met a good friend of mine there, Qamar Jahan, and we stayed together.

I completed my BA at Sir Syed Government Girls College and, there, developed a very good friendship with Feroza—a friendship that endures to this day. We visited her in 2016 while we were there. Feroza's family considered me and my family as their own.

Feroza and Naushaba (1965).

After my BA, I intended to do an MA at the University of Karachi. I had some money from my scholarship, and I had saved some money from tutoring. On top of that, my youngest uncle, Zia Ur Rehman, used to sometimes give me pocket expenses. With these savings, I got myself admitted into an MA program at the University of Karachi in political science. After completing that, I wanted to study international law.

During this, I was introduced to Kishwar Ghani. We became very close friends. After attending university, I used to go to her home often—or I should say that Kishwar Ghani used to tell me to come and stay. Then we would study at her home together. Upon seeing me, Kishwar's mother and father used to say, "Naushaba has come! Serve her a meal." At times, we used to stop by the elder sister of Kishwar. She cooked good food and fed us well. Sometimes, when there was a delay in our studies at Kishwar's home, Kishwar would go with me to the bus stop. She would ask me, "Are you taking the bus?" and I would say, "Yes" (it was the cheapest ride). Then, she would quietly give money to a rickshaw driver and ask him to take me home. She used to tell me that she did not consider me to be separate from her own family. Since then, we have shared all of our moments of happiness and sadness. Luckily, she is also in Canada now.

Naushaba and Kishwar (1965).

Uncle Mahfooz arrived in Karachi with his four children after the death of his wife. With this development, our family was large and saddled with economic strain. This brought tension into the family. Time passed and, while I waited for my MA results, I started teaching at White Hall English School. I taught the junior class in the morning, and then I was offered to teach the middle-class students in the afternoon after my lunch break. I decided to tutor one child. I was earning a fair amount of money. My mother was complaining that I had been working too hard and that there was no need to do this.

Finally, I achieved my goal of education by receiving my Master of Arts by the grace of God. I intended to study international law next. I got married in the same year that I completed my MA degree and subsequently moved to the US with my husband.

EDUCATION OF MAHLAQA NAUSHABA KHANAM

by

Mahlaqa Naushaba Habib

Primary Education

I studied at home till grade six. When we arrived at Karachi and moved to Padidan with my father, a teacher came to teach us the Quran, Urdu, English, and Math.

My parents started thinking that I should be admitted to grade seven in Mirpur Khas, in the Dar-un-Niswan Girls School. My cousin studied there, and the plan was that I would stay at her house. I was supposed to leave after Eid. My father passed away in the month of Ramadan, preceding Eid. After that, I went to the Dar-un-Niswan Girls School in Mirpur Khas and studied there for three years.

Thereafter, I moved to Karachi. I was admitted at Raunaq-e-Islam Girls School and completed my matriculation from there. At that time, matriculation included grade eleven.

Thereafter, I was admitted to Sir Syed Girls College for my Bachelor of Arts. I completed that, and then I took my admission for Master of Arts in Political Science at Karachi University.

While I was studying for my BA, I started teaching small children. After appearing in the examination for my MA, I started teaching again at White Hall School. In addition to that, I taught children during the lunch hour. Thus, these periods passed, by the grace of God, under good and bad circumstances. Being the eldest daughter of the family, I was determined to complete my education so that I would be able to support my family.

In Canada, I attended medical office management courses to manage my husband's medical office.

This is a horse-driven tanga. We used to ride to school on it (though we went to university by bus).

Summary of My Education

1. To Grade 9, 1957: Dar-un-Niswan Girls School in Mirpur Khas.

2. Board of Secondary High School, 1960: Raunaq-e-Islam Girls School in Karachi.

3. Intermediate arts degree, 1962: Sir Syed Girls College in Karachi.

4. Bachelor of arts degree, 1964: Sir Syed Girls College, in Karachi.

5. Master of arts in political science degree, 1966: University of Karachi, in Karachi.

6. Typing 1970: Bliss College, Columbus, Ohio.

7. Innovative patient scheduling, July 1988: Practice Management Resource Centre, Ottawa, Ontario.

8. Mastering patient communication, July 1988: Practice Management Resource Centre, Ottawa, Ontario.

RAUNAQ-E-ISLAM GIRLS SCHOOL, KARACHI

This school was founded in 1948 for girls and included Islamic studies.

Naushaba

SIR SYED GIRLS COLLEGE

This is one of the premier educational institutions for girls in Karachi. The school was founded by Syed Altaf Ali Barelvi in 1954 with the sole intention of providing higher education to girls. The college was named Sir Syed Girls College after the leader, Sir Syed Ahmad Khan, who established the Aligarh Muslim University. The present building of the college was completed in 1963. In September 1972, the college was nationalized, and they named it Sir Syed Government Girls College.

UNIVERSITY OF KARACHI

This public research university, located in Karachi, Sindh, Pakistan, is one of the oldest universities in Pakistan, having been established as a federal university in 1951 under the leadership of Oxford-trained Muslim League activist and political scientist, Dr. Ahmad Haleem.

At the time of the establishment of Pakistan as a sovereign state in 1947, the means for higher education and research were negligible and diminished in the country. Responding to the impending requirement for higher learning, the Pakistan government started establishing relevant educational institutions of higher learning and research and thus underwent rapid modernization under a policy guided by Prime Minister Liaquat Ali Khan. After heavy political lobbying backed by the residents of Karachi, the University of Karachi was established through parliamentary authorization as a "federal university" in 1951. On October 23, 1950, the Karachi University Act was authorized, and after an amendment in 1951, it was enacted by Prime Minister Liaquat Ali Khan. Dr. Haleem was the first vice-chancellor.

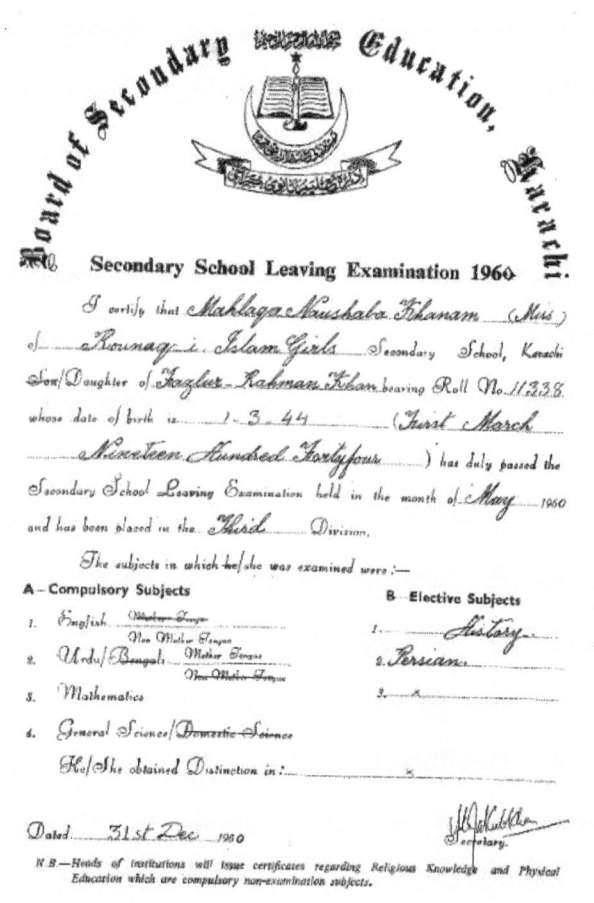

194

University of Karachi

Bachelor of Arts (Pass)

Whereas *Mahlaqa Naushaba Khanam*

has pursued a course of study prescribed by this University for the Degree of Bachelor of Arts (Pass) in the Faculty of Arts and has passed the requisite examinations held in *May* 1964, having been placed in *Second* class.

It is hereby certified that he/she has this day been duly admitted to the degree of Bachelor of Arts (Pass) in this University at the Convocation of 1965.

I. H. Qureshi
Vice-Chancellor

Registrar

Dated Karachi, the 15th May 1965.

Note :- Detailed transcripts of examination results have been issued separately.

University of Karachi

FACULTY OF ARTS
Master of Arts

Whereas MAHLAQA NAUSHABA KHANAM D/O FAZLUR REHMAN KHAN

has pursued a course of study prescribed by this University for the Degree of Master of Arts in POLITICAL SCIENCE in the Faculty of Arts and has passed the requisite examination, held in 19.. having been placed in SECOND class.

It is hereby certified that he/she has this day been duly admitted to the degree of **Master of Arts** in this University at the Convocation of 19..

I. H. Qureshi
Vice-Chancellor

Registrar

Dated Karachi, the 17th MAY 19..

Note :- Detailed transcripts of examination results have been issued separately.

195

Convocation

Naushaba

Kishwar

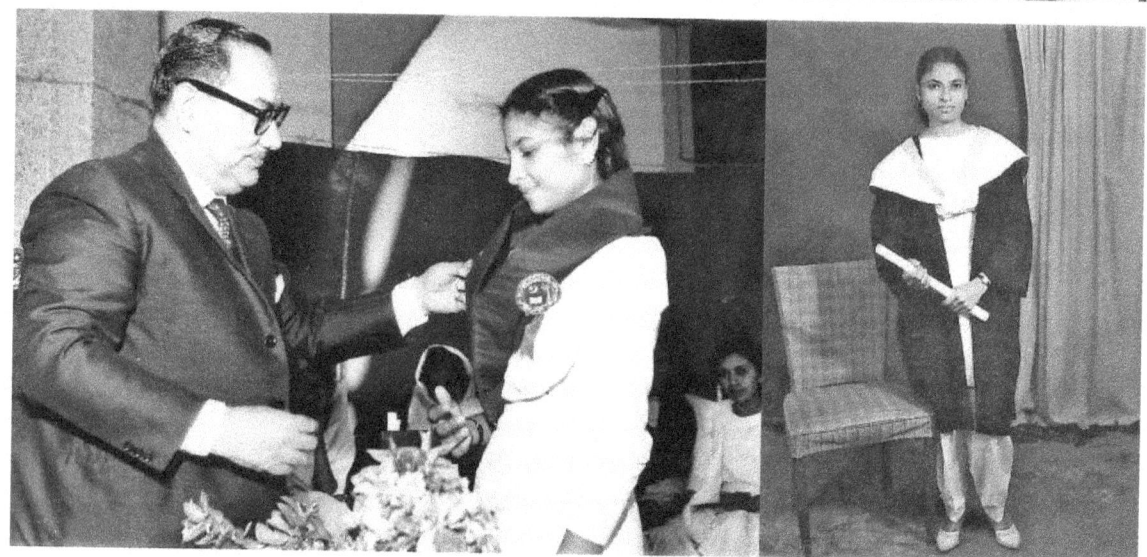

196

Recollection Of Some Memories During Education

Student

When I tutored students, one family asked me to teach their seven-year-old daughter, who was not able to speak but, according to the parents, was very intelligent and good at following instructions. They wished to get an education for her. I accepted their request and started teaching. I was amazed to see how eager she was to learn and follow instructions. She continued writing and practicing what I was teaching. Unfortunately, I could not teach her for long, despite my wish. My uncle did not want me to go to somebody's house to teach, which I had to do in teaching her.

Teacher

When I was choosing subjects for my BA, I was interested in political science and home economics. Home economics is the field of study that deals with the economics and management of the home. I took the course. The teacher, whose name I have unfortunately forgotten, was very strict. We never saw her smiling. She said that cooking was an art and that it should not be taken casually. She proved that during her teaching. She was very skillful and well-organised, and she wanted us to be, too. We tried hard, but she was so strict she used to say that we would never pass the examination. We were so afraid. My friends made jokes about her non-smiling face. We did pass. We missed her very much.

My political science teacher was Mrs. Shah. Later, she became the principal of Sir Syed Girls College. She was a very pleasant and smiling person. She was never annoyed by students asking repeated questions, and she was always willing to help with a smile. I felt it important for me to study political science. Mrs. Shah taught and explained very well. It was this that also attracted me to political science, the systematic study of government politics and political behaviour. It was also about how a society governs at all levels.

Girls Marching for Education

At my time, girls accounted for about 25% of the university's population. With the march of girls for education, it is now expected that there will be Karachi Girls University in Karachi.

Teacher Grade 7 Fairy Folk School, Karachi, 1964-1966

FAIRY FOLK SCHOOL

(ENGLISH MEDIUM)

North Nazimabad D Block, Near Barkat-e-Hadiry Bus Stop

Ref: ________ Karachi 8. 8. 1966

8 AUG 1966

This is to certify, that Miss Mah-e-Laqna Naushaba Khanam is working under me, as a class Teacher of class VII since 1964.

She is drawing a monthly salary of Rs 150/- (One Hundred & Fifty) only.

Principal,
FAIRY FOLK SCHOOL
Ahmad Hasan
Sulemani
8.8.1966.

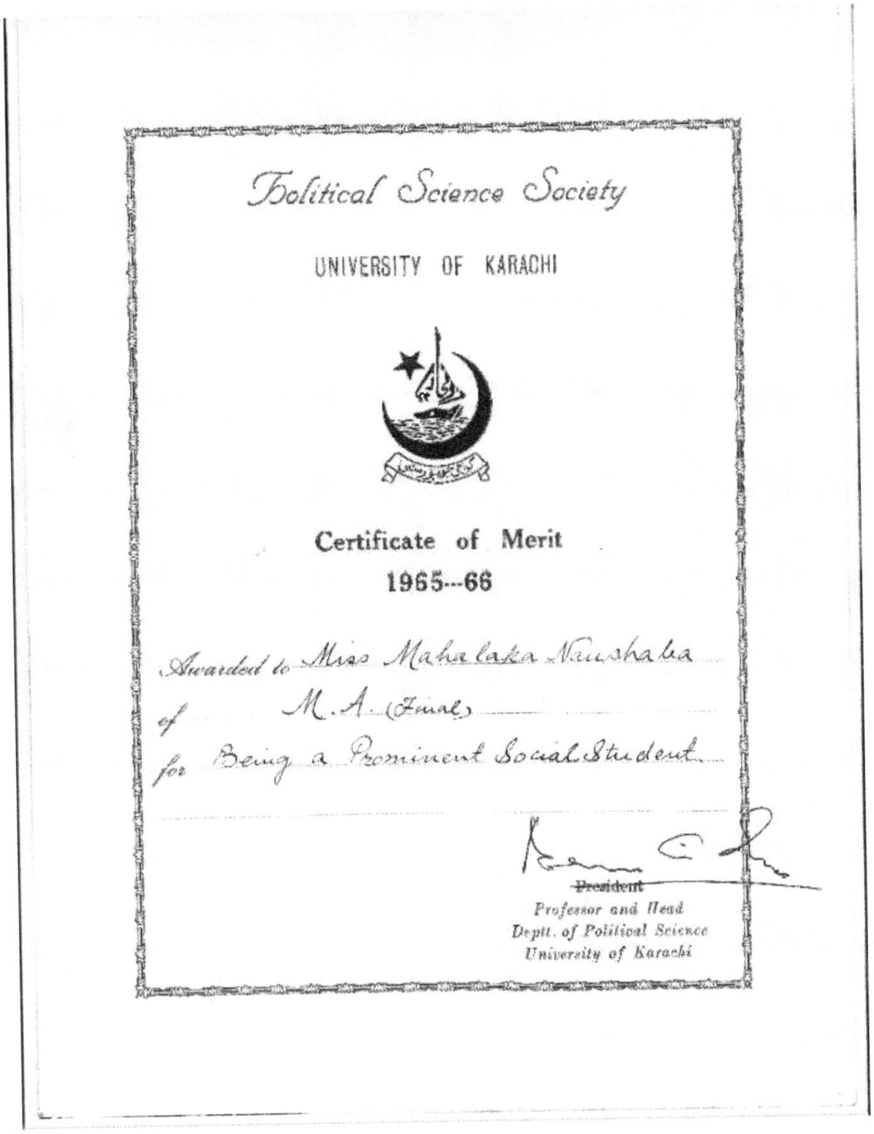

Political Science Society

UNIVERSITY OF KARACHI

Certificate of Merit
1965---66

Awarded to Miss Mahalaka Naushaba
of M.A. (Final)
for Being a Prominent Social Student

President
Professor and Head
Deptt. of Political Science
University of Karachi

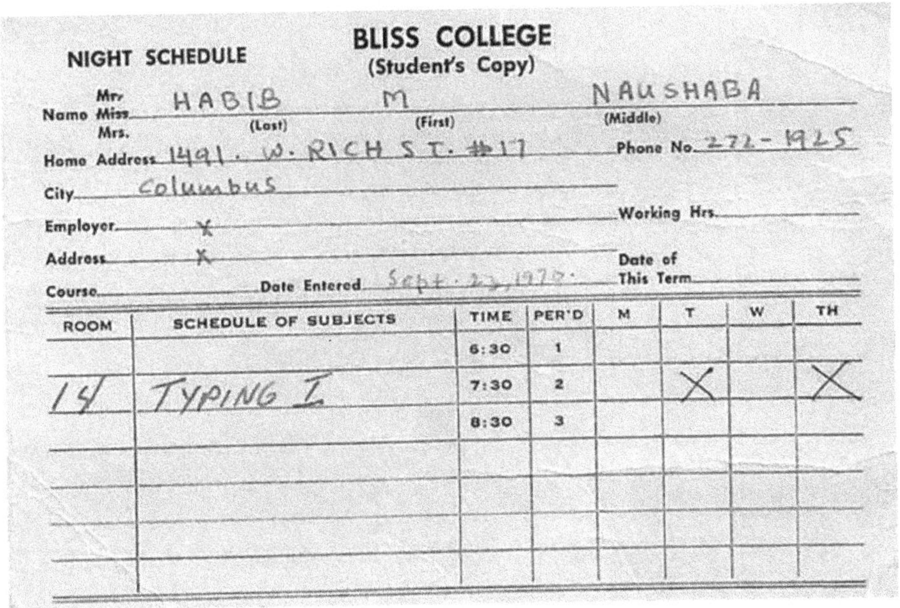

BLISS COLLEGE
(Student's Copy)

NIGHT SCHEDULE

Name: Mr. Miss Mrs. HABIB (Last) M (First) NAUSHABA (Middle)

Home Address: 1491. W. RICH ST. #17   Phone No. 272-1925

City: Columbus

Employer: X   Working Hrs.

Address: X

Course: Date Entered: Sept. 22, 1970.   Date of This Term:

ROOM	SCHEDULE OF SUBJECTS	TIME	PER'D	M	T	W	TH
		6:30	1				
14	TYPING I	7:30	2		X		X
		8:30	3				

PMRC PRACTICE MANAGEMENT RESOURCE CENTRE
A Division Of Don Price
And Associates Inc.
POST OFFICE BOX 4892 STATION E OTTAWA, ONTARIO K1S 5J1 (613) 523-4937

This is to certify that: MRS. N. HABIB

has successfully completed the following Practice Management Course

MASTERING PATIENT COMMUNICATION

Dated at Ottawa

JULY 29, 1988

PRESIDENT

PMRC PRACTICE MANAGEMENT RESOURCE CENTRE
A Division Of Don Price
And Associates Inc.
POST OFFICE BOX 4892 STATION E OTTAWA, ONTARIO K1S 5J1 (613) 523-4937

This is to certify that: MRS. N. HABIB

has successfully completed the following Practice Management Course

INNOVATIVE PATIENT SCHEDULING

Dated at Ottawa

JULY 29, 1988

PRESIDENT

RESEARCH

I was a research associate with my husband, Dr. Naiyer Habib. I was co-author of the HOPE TRIAL, published in *The New England Journal of Medicine*, Appendix—Saskatchewan investigator.

The New England Journal of Medicine

Established in 1812 as THE NEW ENGLAND JOURNAL OF MEDICINE AND SURGERY

VOLUME 342   JANUARY 20, 2000   NUMBER 3

The New England Journal of Medicine

We are indebted to N. Bender, B. Rangoonwala, A. Ljunggren, G. Olsson, W. Whitehill, J.C. Dairon, J. Ghadiali, B. Carter, J.P. St. Pierre, W. Schulz, M. Jensen, L. Rios-Nogales, M. Bravo, J. Bourgouin, C. Vint-Reed, and F. Schutze for support and to Karin Dearness for secretarial help.

APPENDIX

The following persons participated in the Heart Outcomes Prevention Evaluation Study: **International Steering Committee:** S. Yusuf, P. Sleight, G. Dagenais, T. Montague, J. Bosch, J. Pogue, W. Taylor, L. Sardo; **Canada:** M. Arnold, R. Baigrie, R. Davies, H. Gerstein, P. Jha, D. Johnstone, C. Joyner, R. Kuritzky, E. Lonn, B. Mitchell, A. Morris, B. Sussex, K. Teo, R. Tsuyuki, B. Zinman; **United States:** J. Probstfield, J. Young; **Argentina:** R. Diaz, E. Paolasso; **Brazil:** A. Avezum, L. Piegas; **Europe:** J. Mann, B. Wolffenbuttel, J. Ostergren; **Mexico:** E. Meaney; **Canadian Regional Coordinators:** M. Aprile, D. Bedard, J. Cossett, G. Ewart, L. Harris, J. Kellen, D. LaForge, A. Magi, J. Skanes, P. Squires, K. Stevens; **Coordination:** J. Bosch, F. Cherian, I. Holadyk-Gris, P. Kalkbrenner, E. Lonn, F. Mazur, M. McQueen, M. Micks, S. Monti, J. Pogue, L. Sardo, K. Thompson, L. Westfall, S. Yusuf, L. Richardson, N. Raw, M. Genisans, R. Diaz, E. Paolasso, A. Avezum, L. Piegas; **Diabetic Subcommittee:** H. Gerstein, B. Zinman; **Events Adjudication Committee:** G. Dagenais, M. Arnold, P. Auger, A. Avezum, I. Bata, V. Bernstein, M. Bourassa, R. Diaz, B. Fisher, J. Grover, C. Gun, M. Gupta, C. Held, R. Hoeschen, S. Kouz, E. Lonn, J. Mann, J. Mathew, E. Meaney, D. Meldrum, C. Pilon, R. Ramos, R. Roccaforte, R. Starra, M. Trivi; **Substudies–Publication Committee:** R. Davies, D. Johnstone, E. Lonn, J. Probstfield, M. McQueen; **Data Safety and Monitoring Board:** D. Sackett, R. Collins, E. Davis, C. Furberg, C. Hennekens, B. Pitt, R. Turner; **Investigators: Argentina:** J. Braver, C. Cuneo, M. Diaz, C. Dizeo, L. Guzman, S. Lipshitz, S. Llanos, J. Lopez, A. Lorenzatti, R. Machado, C. Mackey, M. Mancini, M. Marino, F. Martinez, A. Matrone, R. Nordaby, A. Orlandini, G. Romero, M. Ruiz, M. Rusculleda, S. Saavedra, J. San Damaso, J. Serra, F. Tuero, G. Zapata, A. Zavala;

Lent, P. Liu, H. Lochnan, M. Lovell, D. Lowe, T. Mabb, S. Maclean, K. Man, L. Marois, D. Massel, E. Matthews, R. McManus, E. McPhee, M. McQueen, J. McSherry, D. Millar, F. Miller, L. Miners, J. Misterski, G. Moe, C. Mulaisho, C. Munoz, S. Nawaz, C. Noseworthy, H. O'Keefe, L. Oosterveld, A. Panju, H. Paquette, M. Parkovnick, R. Paterson, P. Pflugfelder, S. Powers, T. Rebane, A. Redda, E. Reeves, J. Ricci, Z. Sasson, M. Sayles, M. Scott, M. Sibbick, N. Singh, R. Southern, D. Spence, L. Sternberg, J. Stewart, S. Styling, B. Sullivan, H. Sullivan, M. Sullivan, J. Swan, J. Taichman, K. Tan, P. Tanser, C. Tartaglia, K. Taylor, D. Thomson, M. Turek, T. Vakani, A. vanWalraven, M. Varey, R. Vexler, J. Walters, A. Weeks, M. Weingert, S. Wetmore, P. Whitsitt, J. Willing, C. Wilson, J. Wilson, G. Wisenberg, M. Wolfe, B. Wolter, L. Yao; **Prince Edward Island:** G. Costain, E. Hickey, E. MacMillan; **Quebec:** N. Aris-Jilwan, P. Auger, P. Banville, J. Beaudoin, A. Belanger, N. Belanger, L. Belleville, N. Bilodeau, P. Bogaty, M. Boulianne, M. Bourassa, J. Brophy, M. Brouillette, J. Buithieu, C. Calve, J. Campeau, P. Carmichael, S. Carrier, J. Chiasson, B. Coutu, D. Coutu, S. Croteau, G. D'Amours, N. Dagenais, F. Delage, J. Deschamps, D. Dion, Y. Douville, F. Dumont, R. Dupuis, L. Frechette, S. Gauthier, P. Gervais, G. Giguere, R. Giroux, D. Gossard, G. Gosselin, G. Goulet, F. Grondin, J. Halle, L. Henri, G. Houde, M. Joyal, N. Kandalaft, A. Karabatsos, G. Kiwan, S. Kouz, R. Labbe, M. Langlais, C. Lauzon, M. LeBlanc, J. Lenis, S. Leroux, R. Loisel, K. MacLellan, A. Morissette, H. Noel, F. Ouimet, L. Pedneault, J. Piche, C. Pilon, P. Plourde, C. Poirier, D. Poisson, L. Primeau, G. Pruneau, C. Remillard, B. Roberge, M. Robert, M. Rodrique, C. Roy, L. Roy, M. Ruel, M. Samson, D. Saulnier, D. Savard, A. Serpa, F. Sestier, M. Smilovitch, R. Starra, R. St.-Hilaire, P. Theroux, A. Toupin-Halle, J. Tremblay, H. Truchon, J. Turcotte, S. Vachon, R. Vienneau, P. Wilson; **Saskatchewan:** M. Habib, N. Habib, S. Ahmed, M. Hart, J. Walker, M. Walker, G. Thomasse, L. Meunier, Z. Sayeed, J. Lopez; **Denmark:** H. Juhl, K. Kolendorf; **Finland:** T. Hamalainen; **France:** H. Gin, V. Rigellau; **Germany:** M. Bohm, E. Erdmann, A. Gordalla, R. Hampel, C. Hartmann, G. Hasslacher, H. Henrichs, J. Hensen, R. Hopf, E. Kromer, T. Martin, J. Maus, B. Mayer, S. Miedlich, A. Moeller, H. Nast, R. Oehmen-Britsch, R. Paschke, R. Brehn, G. Riegger, R. Riel, C. Rozak

Hope

This certificate recognizes the outstanding participation
and commitment to the

Heart Outcomes & Prevention Evaluation (HOPE) Study

HOPE Centre: Regina General Hospital

Study Personnel: Mrs. Naushaba Habib

Your commitment to quality in the study is greatly appreciated
and has helped us to answer questions that will affect positively,
the health of many.

Dr. S. Yusuf
Study Chair

Dr. G. Dagenais
Study Co-Chair

Dr. P. Sleight
Study Co-Chair

Dr. H. Friesen
MRC President

Centre No: 123

OUR MARRIAGE

Arrangement and Fulfillment

The next step was our marriage. This was after completion of my MD, a postgraduate degree (after MB, BS), while Naushaba had completed her master's degree(MA) in political science at the University of Karachi. It was 1966.

Our marriage was arranged between our parents. My mother and Naushaba's mother were sisters. Naushaba's mother was married after I was born. My parents had a lot of affection and respect for Naushaba's parents. She had her first daughter, Mahlaqa Naushaba Khanam. I might have been four or five years of age when Naushaba was born. My father was excited and wanted me to be married to Naushaba. My father talked to his sister-in-law and established the relationship then. As time went by, this came to be the reality by the grace of God, and our marriage took place.

Arranged marriages are frowned upon in the west, although they still take place even in the west in our cultural type of families. How they are conducted depends on the family. Usually, the parents start looking for a bride or groom when their son or daughter reaches marriageable age. In other circumstances, the parents have eyes on the girl or the boy as children, and they would eventually like them to marry. When the time comes, they get their children's consent, giving the option to accept or reject this on discussion. They arrange for the couple to meet. This meeting is only to get to know each other's compatibility.

In some other circumstances, the boy or the girl may express their choice to their parents directly or through a friend or relative. Living together before marriage and dating, as practiced in the west, is forbidden.

If the couple agrees, the parents on both sides start negotiations to finalize the marriage. It is understood that the parents, with their experience, may be better guides in such a selection. This is the Islamic guideline that is followed by our family.

On the other hand, there can also be horror when marriages are arranged. These horrors are divorce, murder, runaways, and abuse. These calamities take place if parents force their sons or daughters to marry against their will or even if they decide on their own in the so-called love marriage without taking it seriously as a lifelong commitment.

The above is applicable to other classes of religion and cultures in people of our nationality, even in the West. Western culture is also spreading in our society and culture, here in Canada and back in our former home. By this, I am referring to culture, and I do not mean any religion. It is a mix of liberated ideas in marriage that we are focusing on. The majority of Westerners have given up the moral teaching of their religion, which is also spreading in the Eastern culture.

An example that follows here demonstrates the importance of being obedient to parents and accepting parents' decisions without question. Naushaba's uncle, Ghayas Ud Din Khan, was studying engineering. His father, Naushaba's paternal grandfather, called him and told him, "You have to study medicine, and you have to get married"—and it was done without argument or questioning. Ghayas Ud Din was a successful doctor, and he and his wife led a happy married life.

Our case may be unbelievable, if not to all but to many. It may be surprisingly unique. Naushaba left India and moved to East Pakistan when she was four or five years old. We had no contact with each other thereafter. We never saw each other, talked, wrote, or even glanced at each other's pictures from then till we got married until we met on the night of our marriage. People wanted to see her picture. My mom's response was that I would see her at our wedding. I respected that and never raised a word to anyone about our marriage. I did start to get feelings for her, even at the age of ten, when I was in middle school, but I never expressed them to anyone. My father was very vocal about this when he talked to people, praising Naushaba. It is sad that I had to go alone to get married where Naushaba was living in Pakistan, with none of my relatives on my father's side participating because of the Partition of India and the strain between the two countries. There were still murders of military and civilians being committed at the border of India and Pakistan in November 2016 while we were visiting Pakistan from our beloved adopted country, Canada.

The question started to arise about the marriage date. My parents thought that we should get married after I completed my medical degree. I completed my MBBS in 1963 and then a one-year compulsory internship by the end of 1964. Unfortunately, the War of 1965 occurred between India and Pakistan, and the plans for our wedding had to be deferred.

Eventually, people in Pakistan started to get suspicious about whether this marriage would even go on. At this point in time, I would like to quote my respected professor of medicine, Dr. Das. He had become aware that I was making preparations to go to Pakistan for my marriage. In the elevator one day, he asked me, "So your marriage is withheld?" I answered in affirmation. This comment showed his affection for me; it was a fine example of how a man of solitude could express his sympathy!

Naushaba had graduated in Karachi from the Sir Syed Girls College, and now, because of our delayed marriage, she entered the master's program in political science while I entered my doctor of medicine program. She completed her master's degree in Pakistan while I completed my doctor of medicine degree in India, the highest postgraduate degree from India at that time.

I attempted then to go to Pakistan for our marriage celebration in December 1966 but encountered difficulty obtaining a passport. My friend and former college roommate, Dr. Abid Hussain, took over the responsibility of sorting through my problems with the staff in the passport office. Abid was a man who had time to deal with such a situation, and he pushed things so that I could get the passport.

Because of the bad relationship between India and Pakistan, which continues today as it was then, I had to go alone. I was the only son of my mother and a cherished son of my father. They endured because of their commitment, which became mandatory in order to see this wedding succeed.

So, I departed by train from Purnea to Karachi, Pakistan, travelling in the cheapest third class because of economic strain. Ultimately, I crossed the border. There was a customs check at the Wagah border. This went through OK, but I was very apprehensive. When I crossed there, approximately thirty-five kilometres from Lahore after all formalities, I wandered into the shop area that was primarily full of tea shops and so on. People learned that I had come from India, and they all gathered around me. They looked after me very affectionately and offered tea and snacks. It was the time when Ayub Khan was the president of Pakistan. I was very much impressed with the treatment I received and being in the land of Pakistan. Everything was very good during that period in Pakistan.

I rode on the train from Lahore to Karachi and arrived at the house of my cousin, Bashir Ul Hussain Khan, in North Nazimabad Karachi in D-Block by taxi from the railway station. Bashir was the oldest brother on our maternal side and son of our older maternal uncle, Dr. Zahir Ul Hussain Khan. He was also the son-in-law of our second maternal uncle, Dr. Safir Ul Hussain Khan.

It was arranged that I would stay with Bashir, with whom there had been some prior financial arrangement made with my mother, for conducting my marriage.

Now was the time to meet the families and make a decision about the marriage date. Ramadan was to begin, so in the family meeting, it was proposed that we defer the marriage during the month of Ramadan and have it done in Eid. Ramadan is the month of devotion to God and fasting rather than celebrating marriage. Because of the visa granted to me for a month, I did not want to take the risk. Naushaba's Uncle Samad Khan supported my concern. Thus, the marriage was arranged and held in the month of Ramadan, on Sunday, December 25, 1966, or Ramadan 12th, 1386.

The marriage was celebrated according to tradition and religion. Its details are not within the scope of the book, but suffice it to say that, under oath, the couple publicly agrees to the marriage and to lead a responsible life. All attendees pray for the success of the marriage on its completion. We had never talked or written to each other all our lives, till the day of our marriage. I had not even seen Naushaba or her picture since she was about seven or eight years old.

After our wedding, we met and visited family members. Now the question was what to do? I could not stay in Pakistan, leaving my whole people in India and just finishing my doctorate degree. I could not take Naushaba to India because of the conflict between the two countries. There were uncertainties for her permanent settlement in India, so there was an expected delay.

Naiyer and Naushaba at their marriage, December 25, 1966.
Naiyer and Naushaba.

Groom arrives and is received at the bride's house, December 25, 1966.

Post-marriage visit.

Naiyer and Naushaba with Naushaba's mother and sisters.

PLAN FOR LIFE IN THE US

We decided that I should go to the United States for training and bring Naushaba with me. For this, I sought the assistance of my friend, Dr. Mohammad Shahab Ud Din, another of my medical school roommates, who was in pediatric training in the United States at Watts Hospital, Durham, North Carolina. This hospital does not exist anymore. Thus, through correspondence, I was appointed as a first-year resident with a salary of $425 per month. They advanced me money to pay for my fare and Naushaba's.

Now, it was time for me to return to India, the country of my birth, to process the official papers for my departure to the United States. I left from the Karachi railway station. I was overwhelmed with feelings about departing alone and leaving Naushaba in Pakistan. Fortunately, however, things were looking good for us to reunite in the United States.

Uncle Noor Alam, Naushaba, and Naiyer at Karachi Railway Station,
January 1967.

I returned to India by train in January 1967 to have my visa processed from my country of citizenship. I had various feelings: the feelings of leaving my new wife in Pakistan, leaving my parents in India, and getting married without my parents' participation to fulfil their desire and commitment. Now, we were to leave them in India, although with a plan that I would return to them in due course. It was a long journey for me, having had no such experience in life, to a country with an entirely new culture.

Immigration vs Exchange Visitor Visa

On returning to India, I went to Calcutta and met with some officials of the United States in the American Consulate. All formalities, including a medical assessment, were finalized. I met the immigration officer, and he asked what kind of visa I wanted. I did not know. He explained to me about immigration and education. I did not wish to settle in the US, so I obtained an exchange visitor J visa for the United States. It was very easy to get an immigrant visa if I wanted, and I could have gotten it then. In retrospect, I realize it was a mistake for me not to have done that. I used to hear from people that the majority of sons and daughters who left India for foreign countries would stay there, leaving their parents behind. I made sure that I compelled myself not to stay in the United States and to return home. And I came back home.

Departure to the US

On obtaining the visa for the US, I went to Calcutta. It was February 1967. My friend Dr. Abid Hussain, with his wife, my brother-in-law, sisters, and my parents, came to see me off. It was my first experience flying on a plane. It was a Pan American flight to Heathrow. I stayed in a hotel near the airport, likely named Skyway, after all official formalities. The experience of the stay and the use of its facilities, particularly the room, was all new to me: air conditioning, toilet, shower, and TV. I got over them, except spilled water on the bathroom floor. I did not know that the shower curtain was supposed to be inside the bathtub, not out. Anyway, I wiped the floor with a towel.

DURHAM, NORTH CAROLINA

Arrival in Durham

The next day, I flew to John F. Kennedy Airport in New York, to Durham, where I met Dr. Shahab Ud Din, and stayed at the Watts Hospital.

Ultimately, everything materialized. I arrived at Durham on February 27, 1967. Naushaba joined me in May 1967. Like me, she had never travelled to a foreign country or been on a plane, so I was naturally quite worried. I got ready to go and receive her in New York.

She was to arrive at the John F. Kennedy Airport, knowing no one and not being familiar with the procedures and surroundings of the airport, and I was to receive her there. I was very excited. The night before her arrival, I wanted to make sure that I did not miss anything. I booked my flight from Durham to arrive in New York in the morning. I did not trust an alarm clock to wake me up. Instead of staying in my room in the hospital, I stayed at Jack Tar Hotel. The idea was that the hotel operator would wake me up. So, from Jack Tar Hotel, I went to the airport and flew from there to New York. There, I anxiously awaited the moment of her arrival.

John F Kennedy Airport, 1967.

Roof of the airport, where I waited for the arrival of Naushaba's plane.

I went to the airport well in advance of Naushaba's anticipated arrival. I found where the host was to be, to receive an arriving passenger. After my anxious wait, the plane landed, and passengers started coming out and assembling in the immigration area. She arrived by Pan Am. The passengers were being checked by the immigration officials as to their luggage and documents. I kept watching Naushaba. She passed through nicely and came out to the area where I was supposed to receive her. Accompanying Naushaba with her luggage, we went to a hotel and stayed overnight.

Naushaba, bound for Durham from New York.   Naiyer picking up Naushaba at New York.

The next morning, we went to the airport again and flew from there to Durham, North Carolina. We were received at the airport in Durham by our landlady, Jacque, and we went to our rented place to settle. All my worries, anxieties, and excitement were ended in happiness, peace, and calmness.

And so began our life in the US. We were in Durham for just over a year before we moved to Orlando, Florida, to join the Orange Memorial Hospital on March 1, 1968. Durham's population in 1970 was 100,768. The most recent data show the city's population to be 251,893 as of July 1, 2014. The Eno and Occoneechee Indian tribes, related to the Sioux and the Shakori, lived and farmed in the area that became Durham. During the mid-1700s, Scots, Irish, and English colonists settled on land granted by King Charles I.

Durham went through various twists and turns of history. It was incorporated by an act of the North Carolina General Assembly on April 10, 1869. It was named Durham for Dr. Bartlet Durham. He had provided the land on which the Durham Station was built before its incorporation as a city[51]. It is the home of the world-renowned Duke University.

Naiyer and Naushaba on the Duke University Campus, Durham, NC.

Watts Hospital, now (2016) NCSS&M[52].

---

[51] Wikipedia

[52] Photo used with permission of the North Carolina School of Science and Mathematics (NCSS&M), Lisa Watts, communications director, Open Durham and Preservation Durham, courtesy of Diane.

My Appointment at Watts Hospital

With the help of my friend Dr. Mohammad Shahab Ud Din, I received an appointment as a first-year resident at the Watts Hospital. Letters addressed by Dr. Hubert Royster, the program director of the Watts Hospital, to me and subsequently to Naushaba are self-explanatory and noted below. These letters reflect the caring attitude of Dr. Royster for me and for us both, having come from a foreign country. We were moved by such a kind attitude, which was not expected. It is rare for someone in such a position to go out of the way to help someone in our position.

Dr. Royster and his administrative assistant, Mary, took extra responsibility for ensuring that all matters regarding my arrival at Durham were arranged efficiently, including securing documents for my visa and arranging the advance payment of my salary for airline tickets. They arranged my ticket on Pan American Airlines through a travel agent in Durham. He detailed every direction from my point of departure to my arrival at the Watts Hospital. They arranged to send Dr. Shahab Ud Din and Dr. Rao to receive me at the airport and settle me in at Watts Hospital. He wrote a letter to Naushaba to facilitate her arrival, which was after mine.

Naiyer Habib, M. D.
vill. Harahi
P. O. Mahmadia via Kasba
Dist. Purnea (BIHAR)
I N D I A

Dear Dr. Habib:

Your letter addressed to me and sent in care of Dr. Shahabuddin with your wife's address at the bottom has now been read, and I will attempt to answer it.

Enclosed is a letter which you may use if it will be of any assistance to you in obtaining a visa for your wife. As stated to you previously, the hospital will take care of your air travel through a loan. However, we are not in a position to do this for any one but house officers. Therefor, our policy on this would be that if you wish to get a loan for transportation for your wife to come over, you would have to find another source from which to get these funds. We would be unable to do this.

Since the time is growing short for you, you would be wise at this time to plan to come by yourself and make arrangements for your wife to join you in the not too distant future. However, if you are able to arrange for the the funds for her transportation and can get her passport and visa, we certainly would be happy for you to bring her and more than glad to look for a place for the two of you to stay.

On a separate sheet of paper we have enclosed the Pan American Airline schedule as given to us by the Triangle Travel Agency here in Durham. Please let us know immediately if this satisfactory, so that we may make reservations for you, after receiving your acceptance form. The agency here can mail the tickets directly to you, if that is what you wish. After receiving the tickets if you should want to make any change, you may do this through the Pan American office there.

We suggest the date of departure for you as Saturday, February 25 so that you will have enough time to get to the hospital to become oriented to your surroundings before going to work. You will need to appear before the State Board of Medical Examiners in Raleigh which is not far from Durham, although you will not need to take an examination, before going to work.

If you have any questions about the above, please let us know. Looking forward to hearing from you very soon, I am

Sincerely,

Hubert A. Royster, Jr., M. D.
Director of Medical Education

HAR:mcm
enclosures - 2

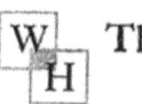

The WATTS HOSPITAL

CLUB BOULEVARD AT BROAD STREET
DURHAM, NORTH CAROLINA, 27705
U. S. A.
February 13, 1967

Naiyer Habib, M. D.
vill. Harahi
P. O. Mahmadia via Kasba
Dist. Purnea (BIHAR)
INDIA

Dear Dr. Habib:

Your acceptance, uniform measurements and informative letter were received this morning. We are delighted that you are coming and, according to your letter, will expect you about February 26th. Unless you just want to, it will probably not be necessary for you to cable us about your arrangements, as the Triangle Travel Agency, Inc., Durham, by our instructions this morning, are sending by teletype a prepaid ticket to the Pan American Airlines in Calcutta for you with a stop in Karachi. We decided this would be the easiest way to handle things, as you said you would make your own travel arrangements. Therefore, instead of a ticket sent to you, a prepaid ticket is being sent to Pan American Airlines, and you are to deal directly with them for your flight time. You will pick up your ticket there.

If you have time by letter you may inform us of the decision that you made as to flight time, but Triangle Travel Agency has told us they can get this information from Pan American and notify us so that we can meet you. As far as we know, there will be some one to meet you, whether it will be myself or another representative. However, if you are not met at the airport, please come to Durham by limousine to the Jack Tar Hotel and from the Jack Tar by taxi to Watts Hospital main entrance, and ask at the information desk for Mr. Lane Leslie, our housekeeper, or if it is on a Monday through Friday this office will be open until 4:30 p.m. and you can come on up here, and we will see you to your room. If something should happen that you do not arrive until after 10 P.M., the main entrance of the hospital will be closed, and you will have the taxi driver take you to the Emergency Entrance, where you will have a nurse call the operator to contact Mr. Leslie. This is explained only in the event you are not met at the airport.

We were hoping to hear from you sooner but realize that your delay in answering was unavoidable. We have ordered your uniforms. It generally takes about six weeks to get these, and they will probably not be here when you arrive, but perhaps there are some in stock that will fit you, at least white coats.

The Board of Medical Examiners for the State of North Carolina requires that you present them certain documents in order to obtain a license in this state. I will probably take you over to Raleigh shortly after you arrive. Your files here contain almost all the documents necessary, but you are required by the Board to have 3 letters of recommendation to be addressed as follows:

-1-

214

Joseph J. Combs, M. D.
Secretary
North Carolina Board Medical Examiners
716 Professional Building
Raleigh, North Carolina
U. S. A.

Dr. Shahabuddin will have one letter ready for you so you will need to bring only two letters of recommendation, or else have the two sent directly to Dr. Combs. Please stress to your references that it is necessary that this be done immediately so they will be here by the time you arrive, or else bring them with you.

We assume you received our letter dated January 31 regarding a travel agency as a possible sponsor for a travel loan for your wife. However, we believe you will have enough out of your stipend in a short period of time to make it possible for her travel over here to be financed.

If you need our help for any reason or regarding travel, please let us know.

We are certainly looking forward to having you with us and are informing Dr. Shahabuddin today that you are coming.

Sincerely,

Hubert A. Royster, Jr., M. D.
Director of Medical Education

HAR:mcm

U. S. A.
February 28, 1967

Mahlaqa Naushaba
A/85/9 Dastagir Society
Karachi, W. PAKISTAN

Dear Mrs. Habib:

Dr. Habib arrived safely and on time Sunday evening at 11:03. Dr. Shahabuddin and Dr. Rao met him at the airport. We are very pleased to have Dr. Habib with us.

Your husband's stipend will be $425 a month. When you come to this country, he will be granted $50 a month living out allowance, for we do not have quarters for married residents whose families are with them.

It has been approved by our hospital director, Mr. John Moulton, to advance Dr. Habib $600 on his salary to pay for your air passage from Karachi to Raleigh-Durham Airport.

It will be necessary for Dr. Habib to find a place for you to live before you can come over. We will help him in any way we can. We would not want you to come to America without a place to live. Since you will need an already furnished apartment and one within walking distance of the hospital, it will be a little difficult to find. We therefore feel that you should go ahead and get your visa and passport and then notify Mr. Habib when you have done this. Dr. Habib can then try to find an apartment or house. As soon as he finds a suitable place for both of you, the hospital will give him a check for $600 to present to the travel agency here for your ticket. He will talk to the travel agency in Durham regarding flight times. He will advise you the most economical and fastest connections from Karachi to Durham. You should also consult the Pan American Airlines in Karachi and arrange your exact flight time with them. When you know just when you will come, the travel agency here would send Pan American Airlines a prepaid ticket for you, either directly to you or to Pan American, whichever you wish.

With every good wish, I am,

Sincerely,

Hubert A. Royster, Jr., M. D.
Director of Medical Education

Our Housing

Mary arranged our housing before Naushaba's arrival at 2811 Hillsborough Road, a property belonging to Jacque Thomas. We moved there when Naushaba arrived and lived there from February 1967 to February 29, 1968. Jacque had arranged our household necessities, and she became our mother from all points of view of life.

Us at our first home, 2811 Hillsborough Road, Durham.

My Work at Watts Hospital

I joined as a first-year resident at Watts Hospital and started my work in February 1967. I stayed in the hospital in the assigned room until Naushaba arrived, and we moved to our rented duplex.

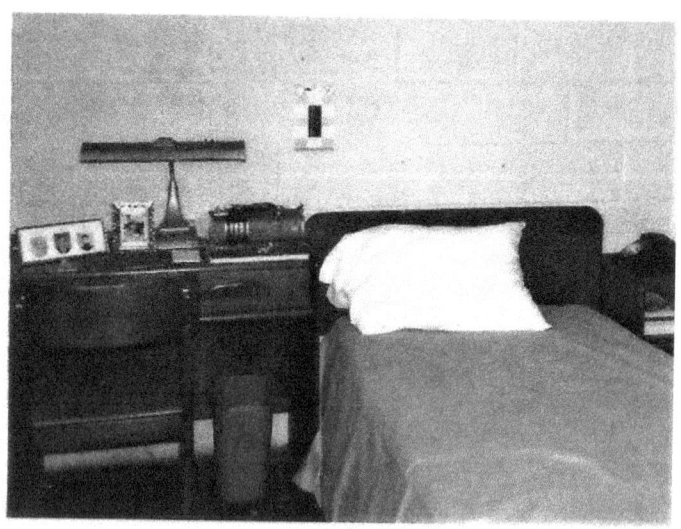

My room at Watts Hospital.

Dr. Habib at work in the hospital.

In the lobby of Watts Hospital with Dr. Shahabuddin on my left and my wife,
Naushaba, on my right (1967).

I worked in the hospital for almost thirty-six hours straight and would return home for twelve hours before going back to work. Naushaba would stay home. She spent her time there socializing with Jacque and Jacque's friends. They were living in the same house in the next duplex.

My work was appreciated. I received awards as a resident for my academic achievement, as well as a sense of appreciation from Dr. Royster.

Watts Hospital

Durham   North Carolina

This is to certify that

Naiyer Habib, M.B., B.S., M.D.

has served in this Hospital in the capacity of

First Year Resident in Medicine

and has performed all duties pertaining to that office to the satisfaction
of the Board of Trustees and Staff from

March 1, 1967 to February 29, 1968

Given at Durham, North Carolina, February 29, 1968

Joseph C McCracken M.D.
Chief of Medical Service

John F. Moulton
Director

Hal S. ____
President

1967 House Staff in trainig @Watts Hospital L to R-Siripun, Rao, N.Habib, M.Shahabuddin,?,?Lee,?,?,?

THE WATTS HOSPITAL
CLUB BOULEVARD AT BROAD STREET
DURHAM, NORTH CAROLINA 27705

DEPARTMENT OF RADIOLOGY

JOHN F. SHERRILL, JR., M.D.   DONALD M. MONSON, M.D.
GUY W. SCHLASEMAN, M.D.   MORRIS A. JONES, JR., M.D.

June 10, 1968

Dr. Naiyer Habib
Orange Memorial Hospital
Orlando, Florida

Dear Dr. Habib:

As the Watts Hospital staff physicians, house
staff, and guests gather tonight at Turnage's
for their annual house staff party, we have a
particular reason to remember you. Your participation in the X-Ray Case of the Week has been
outstanding, and you have won the house staff
competition for 1967-68.

Enclosed you will find a small token of our
remembrance as "House Staff Radiologic Diagnos-
tician of the Year."

Yours very truly,

Morris A. Jones, Jr., M.D.

MAJ/jc

Shower Party And Our First Son, 1967

Jacque and her friends arranged a surprise shower party for Naushaba for the birth of our first baby. It is a custom in Western society that friends and relatives get together and bring gifts for an expected baby. That is what she arranged; she asked me not to let Naushaba know.

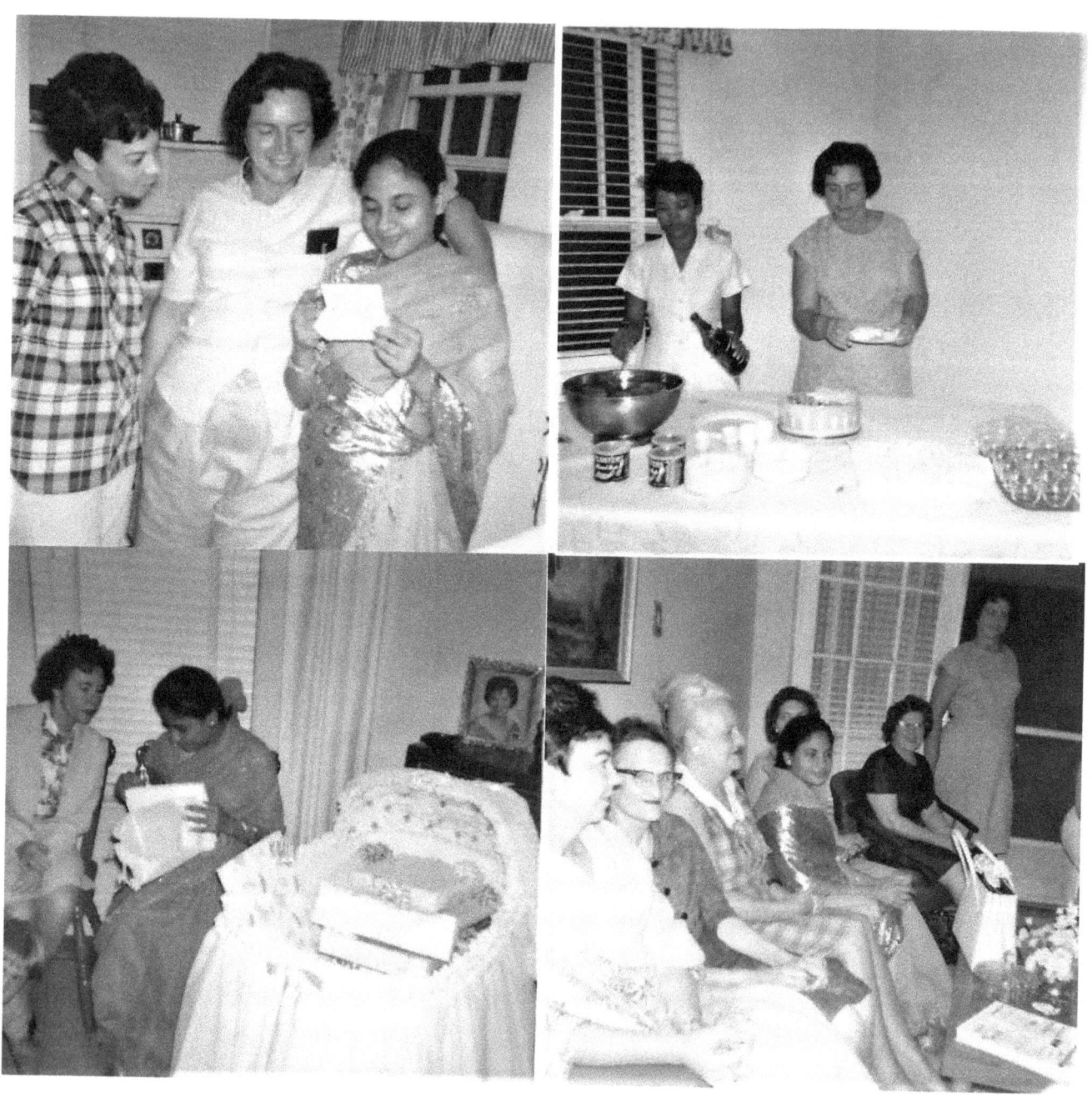

Top left, L to R: Jean, Jacque, Naushaba. Top right: Jacque with helper
Bottom left: Mary Meyer and Naushaba.
Bottom Right Jean is on the left and Jacque is on the right standing.

Delivery

After Naushaba's delivery at Watts Hospital, Jacque, Jean, and Jean's daughter Robin brought Naushaba home. Jacque took time off to look after Naushaba and the baby. She also brought food for Naushaba while she was in the hospital. Naushaba dressed in the sari of my mother's wedding to come home with our first child. This shows a respect for, and affection for, my mother, culturally.

Illness

Meanwhile, Naushaba got sick and was hospitalized. Jacque took time off from her nursing duties at the Duke Hospital to look after her. I kept working in the hospital and attending her from time to time.

Jacque was a respectful mother to us. She loved us as her children. She never lost sight of this. We were so grateful.

Robin, Jean's daughter, watching while I clean my first car
while at Jacque's house, a Ford Falcon 1960.

Mazhar Ali Khan's Visit

Mazhar Ali Khan, a first cousin of Naushaba's and a second cousin of mine, came to visit in 1968. He was my best man for our marriage. He came to Detroit for higher education and visited us in Durham. He still lives in Detroit, and we still visit him.

Mazhar Ali Khan with Naiyer.

Jacque and My Driving

I purchased a 1960 Ford Falcon for $300 soon after Naushaba's arrival, around May 1967. That was our first car, and I learned to drive it under supervision. She was such a caring person that she made me use chains on my tires to drive in the snow in Durham's winter. I was driving well. One of the lessons she taught me was to look to the curb on my right in the face of an oncoming car at night so that my eyes would not be blinded with light. I still remember this instruction and follow it to this day.

I was a very nervous guy taking the driving test. I drove a bit but then committed some error at a stop sign and failed. When I went again, and the instructor asked me to make a turn, I went uphill. I failed again. I came home and told Jacque that I could not get the license and that I would not go for another test. Jacque just smiled. She called a driving test officer in the nearby city of Hillsborough. She told him about me, that I drove very well, and that she had trained me, but that I was very nervous when it came to road tests. The officer asked her to take me there. He was a very nice gentleman. He asked me to drive one block. We came back, and he issued me the driver's license. I had no problem driving thereafter.

Departure from Durham

I was to go to Orlando to join the Orange Memorial Hospital in March 1968. There was disappointment and sadness in leaving Jacque in Durham. We promised to be in touch. Jean's daughter Robin visited us in Orlando for a few days, and Jacque visited us whenever she was passing through.

Jacque, Lost and Found

After our stay in Columbus, Ohio, we went to Pakistan. A few years passed, and we returned to Canada in 1973. We wanted to re-establish our connection with Jacque, but we could not find her. It was a very, very sad experience. We wished to bring her to Canada. This wish was never fulfilled, even upon finding her. This disappointment will stay with Naushaba and me.

We tried to get in touch with her. I wrote a letter to Catherine, who had been our next-door neighbour, but the letter was returned. I wrote to the post office in Durham to see if there was any forwarding address for Catherine. They said no, so we left things alone with sadness. Then, I thought while I was working in Regina that I should write a letter to the address of the house at 2811 Hillsboro. I did this. The person who was living in the house took my letter to the grocery store where we used to shop, and the owner of the store knew Jacque. She forwarded the letter to her. We cannot express the happiness we felt when Naushaba received Jacque's letter in the office and brought it to me. We immediately called her.

PLAINS HEALTH CENTRE
4500 WASCANA PARKWAY
REGINA, SASK., CANADA
S4S 5W9
TEL: (306) 584-6707

June 29, 1993

Resident
2811 Hillsborough Road
Durham, North Carolina
USA

Dear Sir/Madame:

The land lady who used to own this house was Mrs. J.P. Thomas. This was in 1960's. She was as our mother. I have been trying to locate her through various sources but I have failed. I know it has been so long and that the owner of this house might have changed from time to time that it is difficult to keep track of her. However, I shall be most grateful if you know anything about her, where she is and how she could be contacted. You may drop a note to the above address. Our family will be most grateful to you.

There used to be a neighbour in the left side if you face the road. They used to know her very well but I am sure they may not be there at all. Thus, if you know anything about her please drop me a note. If you don't know anything disregard the letter.

Thank you for your attention to this matter.

With kind regards.

Yours truly,

Dr. Naiyer Habib
FACP,FRCP(C),FACC

NH:bm

Jacqueline P. Thomas
1220-4th St. South
Safety Harbor, Fla.
34695

PM
20 JUL
1993

Dr. Naiyer Habib
FACP, FRCP(C), FACC
4500 Wascana Parkway
Regina, Sask, Canada
S4S 5W9

Plains Health Centre

1220 - 4th St. S.
Safety Harbor, Fla.
34695
July 19, 1993

Dear Naiyer, Nashaba, and boys,

I was very surprised when Edna Ray called me from Durham, N.C. and read the letter from you.

First of all, I moved to Florida in Oct. 1978. Lucile's husband died and I came to live with her —

Second — I still own the house in Durham but am in the process of getting it sold. That will be a relief when this is completed —

It has been so long since I heard from you and I have wondered about all of you often — The two boys are grown now and I am sure I would not even reconize Adnon now. How are they doing and what profession are they in?

Lee's two girls are in college now at the University of S.C. Rebecca will be a senior This fall and Stephanie will be a sophmore - They have Turned out real well -

Sure wish you could come down to visit us - Lucile will be 84 y.o. This December and I will be 70 in April 1994. Time really passes fast.

We are planning to go to S.C. and I will go up to Durham for a few days during the time I am up There - We hope To leave the latter part of August and stay until the last of ~~Sept.~~ Give every one a big hug for me and send me some pictures of the family -

I love all of you,
Jacqueline

Phone #
1-813-726-6600

We planned to see Jacque, who by then was living in Florida. There was a cardiology conference in Miami, and we both went there. It might have been in the late 1980s. We took a taxi to see her in Tampa after the conference. We couldn't express our excitement when we arrived at Jacque.

Some people have aversions to certain things—e.g., lizards, cockroaches, etc. For me, it's dogs. Jacque owned a big dog. He was standing beside her when we arrived. We avoid dogs. I have a habit of changing my whole dress if a dog touches me or if I go to a place where there is a dog, even washing my shoes and taking a shower. Besides, the Islamic religion we follow advises having no contact with a dog's saliva or fur if the dog is wet. I had gone too far with add-on aversion. Here it was, Jacque's house, and here was this big dog there. Jacque was unaware of the situation with me. We could not leave the house and go stay in a hotel. It had been years since we'd seen each other, and we'd put in such efforts to find her. She was such a respectful mother to us. We had to spend time together, and we decided to stay. So the dog was there, and we were there. The dog even came to our room and lay near the foot of our bed. Accepting the dog loved by Jacque, despite my aversion, was a show of respect for Jacque, whom we loved and respected so much. Remember my frog story in my class!

The dog notwithstanding, we had a good time. We went shopping, drove around the city, and so on. When we were leaving, Jacque gave us pictures of our family from Durham. She returned them to us, saying, "Naushaba, I do not know how long I shall be alive, and I do not know what will happen to these pictures. Please take them with you." She also gave us her own portrait. We adore it, treasure it, and remember her. All these were very sentimental for us both!

Jacque was our mother and the grandmother of our son. How much she cared for and loved us is difficult to imagine, but we value it so much. It was not written for us to live with our birth mothers. We met, and circumstances kept parting us. God bless our mother and mother of each of us from the bottom of our hearts.

The Mother.
(1996)

Jacque Passes Away

Ultimately, we were informed by Jacque's son, who is a doctor, Dr. Lee Thomas, in South Carolina, that she passed away on November 12, 1998, at 4:30 in the morning, in her sleep. God bless her soul. Her son found my address in her notebook and informed me that she had passed away. We had correspondence initially, and he gave me some details of her children and family. Subsequently, we had no contact. I attempted to get in touch once or twice, but I never heard from him. So it was that this all settled in one way or another. This is the cycle of life that we all go through.

From:	Dr. N. Habib [nhabib@cableregina.com]
Sent:	Thursday, November 19, 1998 10:24 PM
To:	'William Lee Thomas'
Subject:	RE: Jacqueline Thomas

Dear Lee
I just received your E Mail

It was one of the greatest shock for us all.
we join in prayer and we pray for blessings from God to her to rest her sole in peace.

Jackie was a mother to us all as well. We do not have words to express our feelings for her.

We had lost her for a few years. Our untiring effort to find her was successful.
We visited her in Clear water. She showed picture of you all with great admiration and love affection. I thought we will have opportunity to meet you all some time as family. That did not happen. We hope to meet you all sometime but it will not be the same without her.

We learnt from Jeanne (Phoenix) that she was sick and she did not know where she was. My wife called Jackie but did not find. We did not know what to do next. We got your address from her but we did not find where it was.

Adnan , my son to whom she was grandma was to see her but it is too late!

Our prayers for her and for you all.

Please stay in touch at least once a while if not frequently.

Wishing you and your family all the best!

Please E Mail your address and phone number if you do not mind. We shall be grateful. (He sent)

Naiyer Habib

-----Original Message-----
From:	William Lee Thomas [SMTP:Wilthomas@InfoAve.Net]
Sent:	Monday, November 16, 1998 10:39 AM
To:	nhabib@cableregina.com
Subject:	Jacqueline Thomas

Dr. Habib, we have heard Jacqueline talk about you and your family over the years, and we found your card in her address book. We wanted to let you know that she died during her sleep around 4:30 am, Nov. 12. She had been transferred from the nursing home to Clearwater hospital for IVs. Her nausea had caused her to stop eating, and then was drinking so little she was getting dehydrated.
Her funeral was Saturday in Safety Harbor, and her church family was very supportive--while she was in the nursing home and then in attendance at her funeral. We are glad she is free from pain, and has a new body with Christ.
Hoping you and your family are doing well.
Lee and Lou C. Thomas

ORLANDO, FLORIDA

We lived in Orlando, Florida, from March 1968 to July 1970.

Before European settlers arrived in 1536, Orlando was sparsely populated by the Creek and other Native American tribes. Prior to being known by its current name, Orlando was known as Jernigan. This originates from the first permanent settler, Aaron Jernigan, a cattleman who acquired land. Jernigan became Orlando in 1857. Various versions of history are cited in Wikipedia for the name Orlando. It was incorporated as a town on July 31, 1875[53].

Now the city, which was more of a rural small city, has grown to be one of the largest cities in the US. In 1970, the year we left, its population was 99,006. As of 2016, Orlando is home to 2,387,138 people, according to US Census Bureau figures, making it the twenty-fourth largest metropolitan area in the United States[54].

Orlando's Disney World is one of the biggest international attractions for visitors. Its opening was being finalized when we were there. It opened on October 1, 1971, just after we had left.

Life In Orlando

I had completed my first year of residency in Durham, North Carolina, and it was time for me to go for a higher grade of residency. This led to my appointment as an internal medicine resident at Orange Memorial Hospital in Orlando. Orlando was a beautiful, small city. It is a hub for citrus fruit. The orange blossom fragrance was a soul-reviving experience for us, even in the city. The orange orchards were in the outlying areas of the city, and they emitted a beautiful scent when they were in season. This city was also called a city of lakes. There were small-to-moderate-sized lakes all over the city that offered beautiful water scenes, along with the water birds in them. There were many parks full of flowers where we walked.

Naushaba at Eola Park in Orlando, Florida.

---

53 https://en.wikipedia.org/wiki/Orlando,_Florida.

54 Wikipedia.

Naiyer at Eola Fountain in the park.

We arrived in Orlando and stayed in a house with one upstairs bedroom. We did not stay there too long. We moved to another house that belonged to Mr. Horn and was nearer the hospital, at 107 Sturtevant Street, on March 1, 1968, and then moved to 723 Lucerne Terrace, from June 30, 1970, to June 30, 1971, before moving to Columbus, Ohio.

107 Sturtevant Street, Orlando, our residence at Mr. Horn's rented house.

Orlando was a centrally located city in Florida, from which it was easy to visit various places of entertainment. We enjoyed going on trips or staying in the area. We visited Busch Gardens, Daytona Beach, Miami Beach, West Palm Beach, Tampa, Sunken Gardens, Rainbow Springs, Marineland, Lion Country, Everglades, and NASA Space Center. We took memorable pictures. Orlando itself had many attractive places that we enjoyed.

Alligator Garden

There were many alligators of different sizes, from baby to adult, at this large alligator garden that we used to visit. When Jean's daughter Robin visited us, we took her there.

Winter Park

There was a nearby small city, Winter Park, that was very popular with peacocks. Many peacocks walked around and danced in the garden. We used to visit and enjoyed seeing the peacocks' activities.

Armstrong's Landing on The Moon

On July 20, 1969, we watched Neil Armstrong's landing on the moon on our TV. It was such a historic event.

Only Muslim Family

We were the only Muslim family in the area, except for one Lebanese Muslim family, who had assimilated into Western culture. There was also one Hindu family. We, two Muslim families and the Hindu family together, became very good family friends. They also had small children. The Muslim population in Orlando in 2010 was 27,939. We could not find any earlier count of the Muslim population.

Religious Activities

I never had any problem observing my religious duty as a resident anywhere during my stay in the United States. They respected me and were prepared to accommodate me as to time for work.

Food Problem / Disney World

We ran into a problem with the availability of Halal food (meat from Islamically slaughtered goats, chickens, cows, along with other food free from pork and alcohol ingredients). We mainly ate vegetables and fish. Ultimately, we gave up by consulting my father and taking the advice of others to eat them and say, Bismillah[55]. It was also indicated that, as long as they have bled the animal on killing or slaughtering, saying Bismillah should be OK. We were very tired of eating only fish and vegetables, and only limited kinds of fish were available there. Kosher[56] food was permissible but also very limited there in those days.

Disney World Planning

When we were there, the plan for Disney World had started. Since its launch, the city has become one of the largest in the United States, with highways and big roads, and most of the lakes have disappeared. We did visit Disney World after a few years of its establishment and enjoyed it.

---

[55] In the name of God to bless what you are doing, beginning with Allah's name.
[56] Prepared in the Jewish way.

Orange Memorial Hospital[57].

History Of Orange Memorial Hospital

Orange General Hospital was opened in 1918. In 1946, its name was changed to Orange Memorial Hospital. In 1951, Orange Memorial became approved as a teaching hospital, one of the first in Florida. It was affiliated with the University of South Florida.

I was in Orlando and received my training in internal medicine and cardiology from July 1968 to July 1970. The hospital was upgraded. Since 2008, other hospitals have joined with Orange Memorial Hospital to become consolidated Orlando Health.

My Work and Training at Orange Memorial Hospital

I joined Orange Memorial Hospital as a second-year junior resident in internal medicine and progressed to clinical cardiology/senior resident in my final year of the training program. I was eventually named the chief resident.

Dr. Freeman Cary was the program director for education at Orange Memorial Hospital. I used to take calls and attend to patients. I rotated through various attending physicians in various specialties during my training. Physicians whose patients were under me had gained confidence in my looking after their patients and trusted me.

---

[57] Courtesy of Helen Galloway of the Orlando Health Foundation and systems librarian Aidybert Silva-Ortiz.

I was looking after some patients with complicated problems requiring complete care even though I may not be on call to learn the disease process fully. I followed these patients myself for their full management. I especially wanted to manage my own diabetic patients who had challenging issues to make sure that they got proper treatment. Adjusting the treatment of such patients is required on an hour-to-hour and day-to-day basis. I did not want to give that up. I also looked after patients with difficult-to-treat heart failure in this way. I learned all aspects of these diseases, as it was showing their changing life history, requiring timely, appropriate treatment. This experience was very helpful in my own practice. I emphasized this way of management and care of patients to my medical students and trainees.

Educational Activities

We attended teaching hospital rounds led by Dr. Cary. There were conferences on various subjects in the hospital. Teaching physicians from the Emory University School of Medicine, such as Dr. Willis Hurst, cardiologist Dr. Nanette Wenger, gastroenterologist Dr. Gambro, and others came as visiting professors.

Dr. Freeman Cary, teaching the doctors in training, 1969.

Residents were required to prepare a project to present annually, and I never got behind. Indeed, I have always won the award for excellence.

234

There was a tradition of an annual paper-writing competition for the residents in training. I was fortunate to be a recipient of the award from the department of medicine in both years of my training.

Dr. Naiyer Habib, presenting a paper.

ORANGE MEMORIAL HOSPITAL
A Teaching Hospital

COLLEGE OF MEDICINE
UNIVERSITY OF SOUTH FLORIDA

PRESENTS

8TH ANNUAL RESIDENTS' DAY

SATURDAY, JUNE 21, 1969   NEW TEACHING AUDITORIUM

9:30   HEPATIC NECROSIS RELATED TO HALOTHANE - CASE REPORT
        AND BRIEF REVIEW
        NAIYER HABIB, M.D.* - MEDICINE

9:45   PRESENTATION OF A CASE OF STROMAL LUTEINIZATION ASSOCI-
        ATED WITH MASCULINIZATION OR HYPERTHECOSIS SYNDROME
        JACKIE G. FAUP, M.D.* - OB-GYN

10:00   TRANSFER OF POSTERIOR TIBIALIS TENDON - LOCAL
        EXPERIENCE AND A REVIEW OF LITERATURE
        HARRY TUCKER, M.D.* - ORTHOPEDICS

10:15   THE HISTOPATHOLOGY OF CHORDOMA
        CESAR BARO, M.D.* ** - PATHOLOGY

10:30   CASE PRESENTATION OF MASSIVE FACIAL TRAUMA
        ROY WILSON, M.D.* - PLASTIC SURGERY

10:45   AMPUTATION IN THE SEVERELY BURNED PATIENT
        ROBERT C. HOWARD, M.D.* - SURGERY

11:00   CYTOLOGY OF THE URINARY TRACT
        MARIO RIVERON, M.D.* - UROLOGY

11:15   JUDGING

        DR. MORTON LEVY - MEDICINE
        DR. REX BLEAKNEY - OB-GYN
        DR. W. R. WILLIS - ORTHOPEDICS
        DR. CECIL BUTT - PATHOLOGY
        DR. JOE O'MALLEY - PLASTIC SURGERY
        DR. DON WEEKS - SURGERY
        DR. TRUETT FRAZIER - UROLOGY

*   WINNERS OF DEPARTMENTAL RESIDENTS' DAY
** PREVIOUS RESIDENTS' DAY WINNER, 1967

FHC/LJ
6-13-69

ORANGE MEMORIAL HOSPITAL
A TEACHING HOSPITAL

COLLEGE OF MEDICINE
UNIVERSITY OF SOUTH FLORIDA

PRESENTS

NINTH ANNUAL RESIDENTS' DAY

SATURDAY, JUNE 20, 1970   NEW TEACHING AUDITORIUM

9:00 A.M.   SYNCHRONIZED DIRECT CURRENT CARDIOVERSION IN
             DIGITALIZED PATIENTS
             NAYIER HABIB, M.D.* - MEDICINE

9:15 A.M.   PHYSIOLOGY OF MENSTRUATION
             ALBERT B. CORZO, M.D.* - OB-GYN

9:30 A.M.   FIBROSARCOMA AS A CAUSE OF PERONEAL SPASTIC FLATFOOT
             JAMES JOHNSON, M.D.* - ORTHOPEDICS

9:45 A.M.   DISSECTING ANEURYSM
             ROBERT HOWARD, M.D.* - SURGERY

10:00 A.M.   SECONDARY TUMORS OF THE KIDNEY
             MARIO RIVERON, M.D.** - UROLOGY

10:15 A.M.   SPONTANEOUS RUPTURE OF THE SPLEEN
             GUILLERMO RUIZ, M.D.* - PATHOLOGY

10:30 A.M.   MENINGOCOCCAL MENINGITIS AND D.I.C. AT THE
             ORANGE MEMORIAL HOSPITAL
             DOMINGO ALVAREZ, M.D.* - PEDIATRICS

10:45   PIERRE ROBIN SYNDROME
             JAMES BAKER, M.D.* - PLASTIC SURGERY

11:00   JUDGING

*DEPARTMENTAL RESIDENTS' DAY WINNERS
**PREVIOUS RESIDENTS' DAY WINNER

JUDGES: DR. MORTON LEVY - MEDICINE
          DR. REX BLEAKNEY - OB-GYN
          DR. W. R. WILLIS - ORTHOPEDICS
          DR. D. L. WEEKS - SURGERY
          DR. M. W. THOMLEY - UROLOGY
          DR. BEN WILLARD - PATHOLOGY
          DR. GILBERT WALKER - PEDIATRICS
          DR. JOE O'MALLEY - PLASTIC SURGERY

In my third year, I was appointed chief resident, bypassing some senior residents who were not very happy to see me upgraded to this position. This was the director of education's decision, apparently with input from other physicians. My administrative work was fair, and in my dealings with the house officers[58] and my communication with the nurses, I gained respect in the institution. None of these people had any concerns about consulting me or communicating with me for any problem. This was true for the nurses, the house officer staff, and the house officers regarding the nurses or the administration.

---

[58] Doctors in training

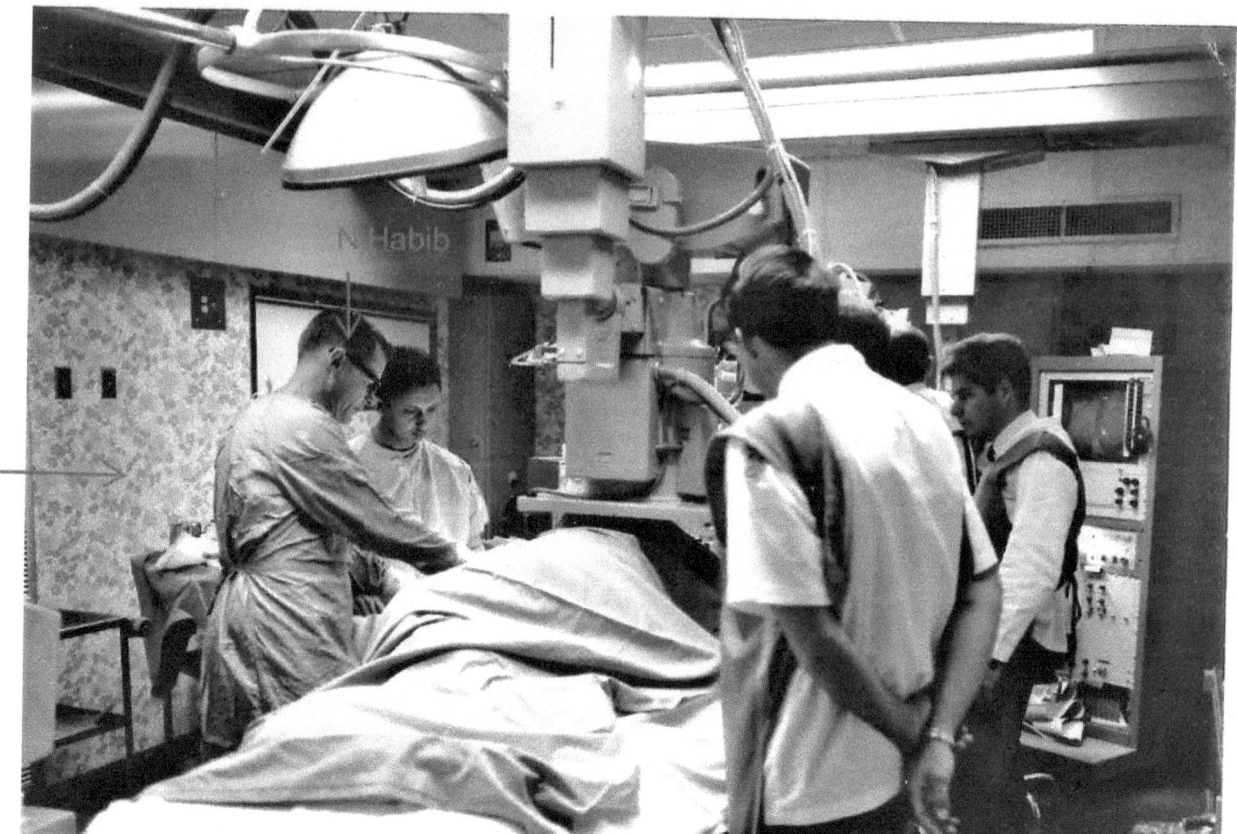

Dr.Gilbert

N.Habib

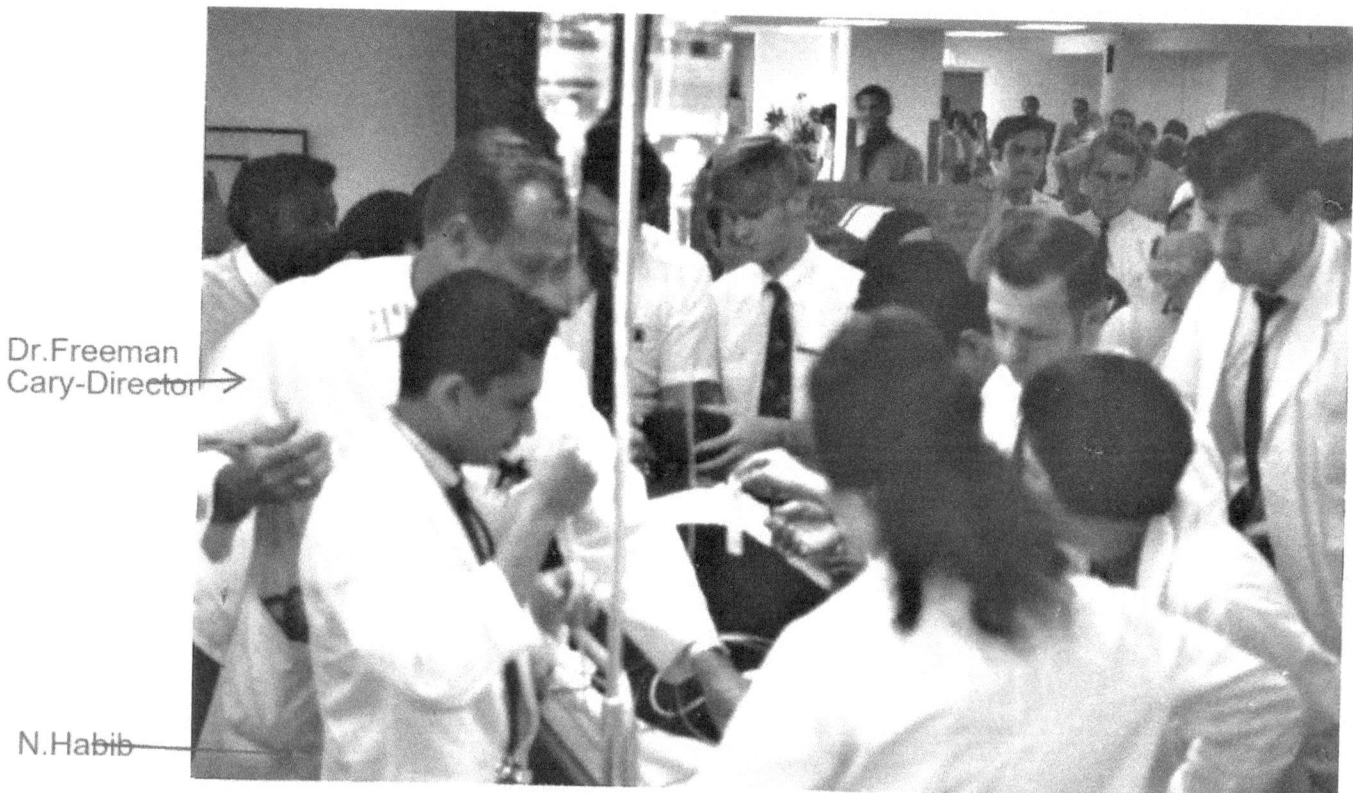

Dr.Freeman
Cary-Director

N.Habib

Top: Cardiac catheterization laboratory.
I am participating in a cardiac catheterization with Dr. Clarence Gilbert.
Bottom: I am heading cardiopulmonary resuscitation
in the hallway of the hospital, with Dr. Freeman Cary.

Physicians Who Trained Me

Dr. Morton Levy was the chief of medicine. He admired us and invited Naushaba and me to his house for dinner, where he presented a memorable gift to us. Dr. Jonathan Partain also invited us for dinner. In my final year in Orlando, Dr. Freeman Cary presented me with a briefcase as a token of his appreciation on behalf of the medical staff. Dr. Clarence Gilbert gave us a beautiful shell, which stands in our house as a memory of Orlando and Dr. Gilbert.

Drs. Partain and Gilbert were the cardiology trainers, and I learned a lot about cardiac catheterization and coronary angiography from them. Dr. Allen Holcomb helped me learn nephrology, including getting involved in the dialysis program.

Dr. Frank C. Bone was a gastroenterologist, and I learned about endoscopy, intestinal biopsy, and liver biopsy from him.

Some Friends to Remember in Orlando

Dr. Laxamana, Dr. Cruz, Dr. Fernandez, and Dr. Cortez were our colleagues who worked at the institution as residents. Dr. Fagnou was also a very senior person. He had joined the residency after entering family practice, to become a specialist of internal medicine. I had respect for him. There were others, too, whose names I do not recall anymore.

Dr. P. L. Puri*, with his wife, Santosh, and baby daughter, Perneeta, were very close friends of ours. We used to go to Daytona Beach together. We associated with each other as family. They moved to Philadelphia for his further training in surgery. We visited them when we took a car trip to New York and Washington. They visited us when we were in Columbus. They had another younger son. With our moves to various places, we lost contact with them, even to this day, despite our efforts. We miss them very much. Santosh was also a physician, and she ultimately upgraded her training. Apparently, they moved to India. We tried to establish contact there but we failed.

I located him after 2 decades of searching in Massachusetts practicing surgery. He refused to recognize me. I gave him all our references. We were shocked. He may have some reasons!

Dr. P. L. Puri, wife, Santosh, and baby Perneeta.

Dr. S. N. Tiwari was a physician from India. His father was a minister in the Bihar government or an MP in the central government. He came to the United Kingdom to get a UK degree and got involved in research. He had done the original research on the medication propranolol. His scientific research paper was published in the prestigious *British Medical Journal* and was well received. He also had other publications. Unfortunately, however, Dr. Tiwari could not pass the MRCP examination to fulfil his objective of attaining a medical degree from the UK. The feeling was that the consultant physician had probably wanted to keep him doing research and writing papers. He ultimately gave up and applied to go to the United States. It so happened that he was accepted for an internship at the Orange Memorial Hospital, where I was chief resident. The administrative secretary of the medical education of the hospital, Mrs. Oman, talked to me about him and, when he arrived, introduced me to him. He was very happy to have found us. He started work, but being a senior physician who'd done research, working as an intern was sort of a menial thing on call. He used to call me to express his frustrations. I would pacify him as much as I could. I spoke to Dr. Cary, who upgraded him to a first-year resident, which somewhat alleviated his situation. And then, lo and behold, Dr. Gamborg, a gastroenterologist of high status from Emory University, came to give the teaching round and lectures at Orange Memorial. Dr. Tiwari had written a paper on gastroenterology while he was in the United Kingdom. I again spoke to Dr. Cary, and we introduced Dr. Tiwari to Dr. Gamborg. They had a conversation, and on the strength of Dr. Tiwari's work, Dr. Gamborg accepted him to the gastroenterological program at Emory University. He went there for training and returned to Orange Memorial Hospital as a gastroenterologist when he was done. I had left by that time.

He was attached to our family, and he visited us as well as invited us to his place to serve us dinner. He cooked himself. We went to visit the NASA Space Center with him at Cape Kennedy, near Orlando.

In Orlando, I finished my training as a third-year senior medical resi

dent and clinical cardiology fellow. It was time for us to move on.

Summary of Training at Orange Memorial Hospital,
University of South Florida
Junior resident, March-June 1968.
Senior assistant resident, July 1968-June 1969.
Chief senior resident, July 1968-June 1969.
Fellow in cardiology, July 1969-June 1970.

Orange Memorial Hospital

Orlando, Florida

A Teaching Hospital

College of Medicine, University of South Florida

This is to Certify that

Naiyer Habib, M.D.

has satisfactorily completed   Four   months service as

Junior Resident in Medicine
March 1, 1968 to June 30, 1968

PRESIDENT, MEDICAL STAFF   PRESIDENT, BOARD OF GOVERNORS

DIRECTOR OF MEDICAL EDUCATION   HOSPITAL DIRECTOR

CHIEF OF SERVICE   SECRETARY, BOARD OF GOVERNORS

SEAL

Orange Memorial Hospital

Orlando, Florida

A Teaching Hospital

College of Medicine, University of South Florida

This is to Certify that

Naiyer Habib, M.D.

has satisfactorily completed   twelve   months service as

Senior Assistant Resident in Medicine
July 1, 1968 to June 30, 1969

PRESIDENT, MEDICAL STAFF   PRESIDENT, BOARD OF GOVERNORS

DIRECTOR OF MEDICAL EDUCATION   HOSPITAL DIRECTOR

CHIEF OF SERVICE   SECRETARY, BOARD OF GOVERNORS

SEAL

242

Orange Memorial Hospital

Orlando, Florida

A Teaching Hospital

College of Medicine, University of South Florida

This is to Certify that

Naiyer Habib, M.D.

has satisfactorily completed **twelve** months service as

Senior Resident in Medicine

July 1, 1969 to June 30, 1970

_____
PRESIDENT, MEDICAL STAFF

_____
DIRECTOR OF MEDICAL EDUCATION

_____
CHIEF OF SERVICE

_____
PRESIDENT, BOARD OF GOVERNORS

_____
HOSPITAL DIRECTOR

_____
SECRETARY, BOARD OF GOVERNORS

Orange Memorial Hospital

Orlando, Florida

A Teaching Hospital

College of Medicine, University of South Florida

This is to Certify that

Naiyer Habib, M.D.

has satisfactorily completed **twelve** months service as

Fellow in Clinical Cardiology

July 1, 1969 to June 30, 1970

_____
PRESIDENT, MEDICAL STAFF

_____
DIRECTOR OF MEDICAL EDUCATION

_____
CHIEF OF SERVICE

_____
PRESIDENT, BOARD OF GOVERNORS

_____
HOSPITAL DIRECTOR

_____
SECRETARY, BOARD OF GOVERNORS

Loss Of My Application at The British Consulate

In Pakistan and India, we had very high regard for degrees and diplomas from the United Kingdom. I wanted to go to the United Kingdom to do my MRCP (Member of the Royal College of Physicians), and I applied for this at the British Consulate. I kept waiting and did not receive any response. When I contacted them, I found out that they had misplaced my application. I tried to see whether I could still get this to go to the United Kingdom. Meanwhile, the year was ending. My visa was renewable upon finding a job in training. This became a very complex problem for us as time was passing.

COLUMBUS, OHIO

I completed my fellowship in cardiology at the Hawkes Hospital of Mount Carmel in Columbus, Ohio. We were there from July 1970 to December 1971.

History of Columbus and Hawkes Mount Carmel Hospital

Columbus is the capital of the state of Ohio and was named for the explorer, Christopher Columbus. The city was founded in 1812 at the confluence of the Scioto and Olentangy Rivers and assumed the function of state capital in 1816. Its population was 539,677 in 1970 when we were there, and it had grown to 835,957 by 2014[59].

Hawkes Hospital of Mount Carmel (793 W. State St., Columbus, Ohio) was founded by Dr. W. B. Hawkes in 1885. Now, it is Mount Carmel West, one of the four hospitals of Mount Carmel Health. It is affiliated with Ohio State University. I attended weekly cardiology conferences at Ohio State University from this hospital.

---

[59] Wikipedia.

Mount Carmel Hospital, Columbus, Ohio[60]

Steps To Acquire The Position Of Fellowship Of Cardiology

I saw an advertisement for a vacancy in the cardiology program for a fellowship at the Hawkes Hospital in May 1970. Dr. Ralph D. Lach was the program director. He was one of my mentors. I applied for the position. I also had applied at one other hospital, but Mount Carmel was a better choice. I wanted to make a quick decision about my appointment, so I wrote to Dr. Lach that I needed a timely decision because of my visa requirements. Dr. Lach contacted me and asked me to come to visit the institution and meet them. He offered to pay all the expenses. What else could I have expected! I immediately went there.

[60] Courtesy of Kristin Rodgers, curator, and Judith Wiener, Ohio State University.

May 26, 1970

Naiyer Habib, M.D.
107 West Sturtevant Street
Orlando, Florida   32806

Dear Doctor Habib:

Thank you for your interest in the Cardiology Fellowship at
Mount Carmel Hospital. We appreciate your request for further information and an application is enclosed. You may be interested
in more information about Mount Carmel.

Mount Carmel Hospital is situated in Columbus, Ohio, which is
the capital of the state and home of four universities, including
Ohio State University and its College of Medicine.

Mount Carmel Hospital is an institution of 500 beds. All the
major specialties and subspecialties are represented well in its
medical staff of 450 physicians.

A very active teaching program has been the tradition and the
backbone of Mount Carmel Hospital for many years. The internship is
traditionally filled, with the majority of the students being graduates of the Ohio State University College of Medicine. Other medical schools are frequently represented, and the class beginning July
1, 1970, will have two graduates of the University of Missouri, in
addition to 17 graduates of the Ohio State University. This is the
only hospital in the area that fills its internship quota consistently.
Mount Carmel has active medical student and externship rotations, with
over 200 students of the College of Medicine rotating through the various services at Mount Carmel in a given year. All members of the
teaching faculty are Board Qualified or Board Certified.

An active Outpatient Department, with clinics in all the major
specialties and subspecialties of medicine and surgery, is incorporated into the training program for the interns and residents. The
Department of Medicine has from eight to twelve residents, distributed
throughout a three year fully accredited program, and the Cardiology
Fellowship has been in existance for over three years. The hospital
has had a Coronary Care Unit for five years and has just opened a new
twelve bed coronary care facility, in addition to a nine bed Medical-
Surgical Intensive Care Unit. Closed cardiac surgery is performed in
the hospital, and there are plans to expand this capability to include
open heart procedures, utilizing a team of well-trained cardiovascular
and thoracic surgeons, who work together as a three man partnership.

The catheterization facilities include two rooms of the X-Ray
Department, both of which have television monitored image intensifi-
cation systems. One room is equipped with biplane Schoenander rapid
serial film changers, and the other has a 35 mm. cineangiographic ap-
paratus, with a six inch tube and a magnifier. An automatic rotating
patient cradle is used for the cardiac catheterization.

246

Cardiac catheter pacemaking and cardioversion are, of course, a part of the activities.

Mount Carmel Hospital has a very active Vectorcardiographic Laboratory, in addition to the electrocardiographic activities. Fifty to seventy-five VCGs are performed each month. Noninvasive cardiovascular studies, such as phonocardiogram, apex cardiogram and carotid pulse tracings, are also available. A full-time technician is assigned to the Cardiovascular Service, which includes the noninvasive studies and cardiac catheterization.

The duties of the Cardiology Fellow are as follows:

1) Supervision of the care of patients in the Cardiac Care Unit.

2) Assistance at cardiac catheterization and angiography.

3) Assistance or performance at all special cardiac procedures.

4) Supervision of the Cardiopulmonary Clinic.

5) Preparation and moderating of the weekly Clinical Cardiology Conference.

6) Moderating a weekly advanced electrocardiography "drill session", for the resident staff. (The Fellow may also be invited to participate in the basic EKG course for interns and students).

7) Participation in the cardiovascular aspect of routine autopsies performed by the hospital pathologists.

8) Informal teaching of members of the House Staff at rounds and conferences, as well as in the bedside setting.

9) Acting as cardiologic consultant to the Inpatient Clinical Service.

10) Presenting cardiologic subjects for discussion at the Department of Medicine Journal Club.

The stipend for the position of Cardiology Fellow is $8,250 if single and $9,000 if married. Many apartment facilities are available in the vicinity of the hospital or at a greater distance. Free meals while on duty and professional laundry are provided in addition to the stipend. Malpractice insurance will be provided.

The position is open to individuals who have completed at least two, and preferably, three years in Internal Medicine in an approved training program. Graduates of medical schools outside the United States must have their ECFMG certificate. Mount Carmel Hospital will pay up to $500 for moving expenses.

If this program appears to interest you further, please complete the enclosed application form and return it to me at the following address:

Ralph D. Lach, M.D.
Office of Medical Education
Mount Carmel Hospital
793 West State Street
Columbus, Ohio   43222

I again thank you for your correspondence and hope that you sustain an interest in the postgraduate program at Mount Carmel Hospital.

Sincerely yours,

Ralph D. Lach, M.D.
Director
Cardiac Care Unit

We met, saw, and praised their program. I promised to accept the position. So here I was appointed a fellow in cardiology under Dr. Lach, effective July 1, 1970, through December 31, 1971. It was the help from God, for which I was thankful.

My Work And Training At The Hawkes Hospital Of Mount Carmel

So it was that I joined the hospital. Here, I did not have to take night calls as a fellow in cardiology. However, I was given the responsibility of holding cardiology conferences at the institution. My presentations and the arrangements for conducting the conferences were very much liked by Dr. Lach, the house staff, and the medical staff.

The house staff held a family picnic, along with the medical staff, annually. We all participated. The event was celebrated with an invitation to the families of all members of the house and medical staff, with an offer of gifts for the house staff and their families.

There was also an annual function to recognize the house staff and give them awards and certificates for completing their training. I also received a certificate and a book autographed by Dr. Lach and with his comments, which I still have in my possession.

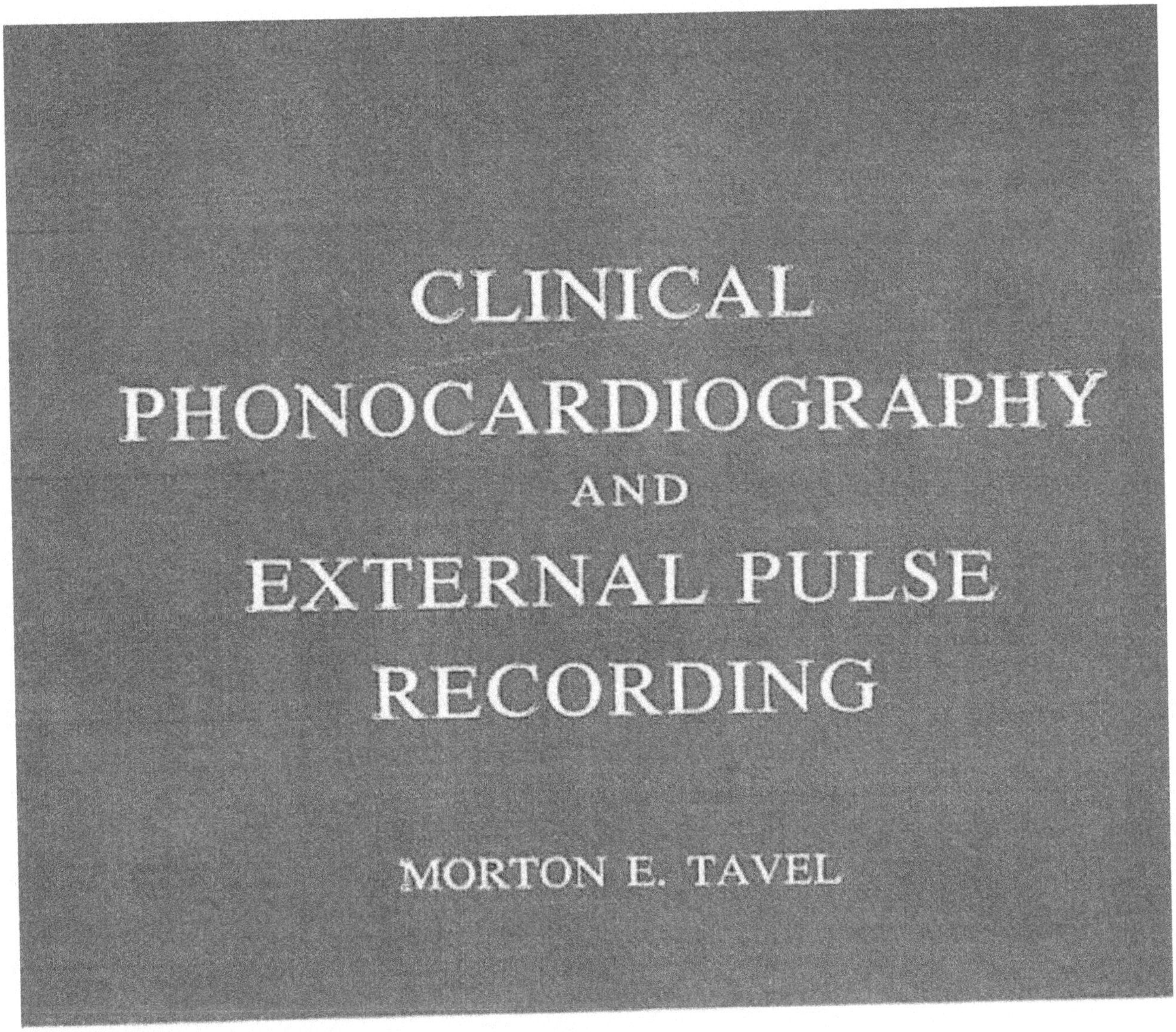

CLINICAL
PHONOCARDIOGRAPHY
AND
EXTERNAL PULSE
RECORDING
MORTON E. TAVEL

To Dr Naiyer Habib
with best wishes for
a successful career.

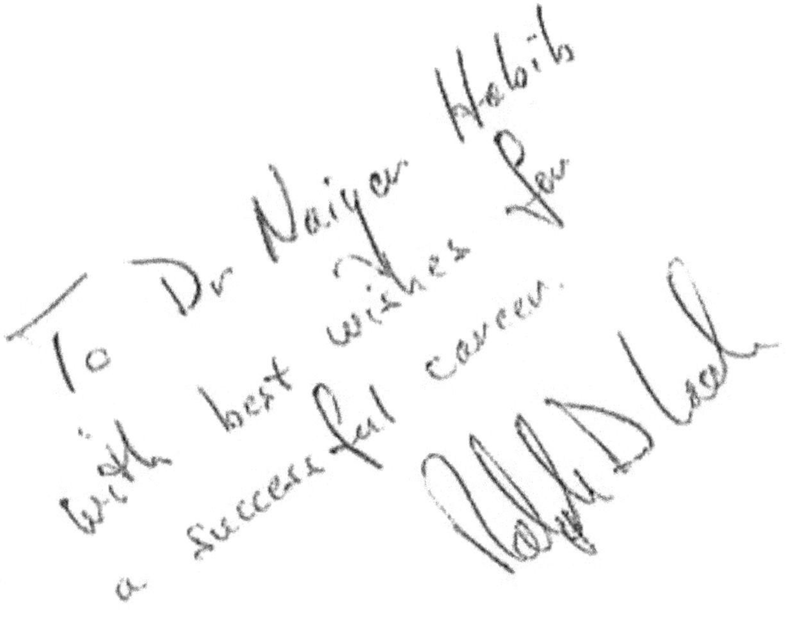

This Certifies That

Naiyer Habib, M.D.

Having honorably and with proficiency served this Hospital as

Fellow in Cardiology

from July 1, 1970   to December 31, 1971

is awarded this

Certificate

To which has been affixed the Corporate Seal

We rented an apartment at 17-1491 W. Rich Street in Columbus. It had one bedroom. We purchased a used crib for our son. The apartment was furnished, and the seats of the sofa were old. Naushaba sewed covers for the seats with new cloth.

Our apartment at 1491 W. Rich Street.

MY MENTORS

A mentor is a trusted and experienced advisor. A person with some quality of his own finds encouragement from a mentor, whose association helps this quality to flourish. This association migrates the better qualities from the mentor and eliminates the unwanted ones. A passive individual in association with a mentor may not gain much. My mentors helped me in both ways.

Some documents in the form of letters to me of their own initiative or to others for my reference as required for my seeking a position, reflect their opinions of me. These were written in the last days of my association with them. They were not written on my request. The intent to include them in this book is for my progeny to know who their forefather/mother were, how we were respected, and how we respected and valued our associations with such respectable individuals. I am not inserting these for our praise, as it is the end of our lives, and we have nothing to gain in publicity from them.

Honesty, the possession of a competitive mind that we could exercise without harming others; selflessness, the definition and achievement of our goals with no discrimination; and the mindful performance of our duties were our principles of life, nurtured under Quranic guidance and that of our mentors.

The Quran

It was our mentor, as guided by our parents, and stays with us. It was the mentor of our parents and forefathers. It is a book to guide us all as Muslims in our day-to-day life. Some of its guiding principles are illustrated here.

A word of caution: The Quran was written in the Arabic language. Its translation may cause misunderstandings, depending on the specific words used, e.g., the word "kafir" means "ungrateful" as well as "infidel." Which word is more reasonable or fitting? One could read the book *The Sublime Quran* by Laleh Bakhtiar[61]. There are spurious translations by those who want to falsify the religion of Islam. So, when in doubt, I suggest reading translations and explanations by a range of interpreting writers. For a detailed study, you can go to the Quran, Tafheemul Quran, at http: www.tafheem.net/tafheem.html. More recently written in English only, " The Meaning of the Holy Qur'an in Today's English by Yahiya Emerick (Amazon.com) highly recommended dealing with various controversies with evidence.

The Quran is divided into thirty parts. It has 114 surahs (chapters) divided into ayas (verses). E.g., 2:62 means surah (chapter) 2 and aya (verse) 62.

(2:62) VERILY, those who have attained to faith [in this divine writ], as well as those who follow the Jewish faith, and the Christians, and the Sabians—all who believe in God and the Last Day and do righteous deeds—shall have their reward with their Sustainer; and no fear need they have, and neither shall they grieve (Asad)[62].

---

[61] English translation of the Quran, available at Amazon.com.
[62] Names of translators within brackets.

(4:112) But he who commits a fault or a sin and then throws the blame therefore on an innocent person burdens himself with the guilt of calumny and [yet another] flagrant sin. (Asad).

(60:8) Allah forbids you not, with regard to those who fight you not for (your) Faith nor drive you out of your homes, from dealing kindly and justly with them: for Allah loveth those who are just (Y. Ali).

(60:9) Allah only forbids you, with regard to those who fight you for (your) Faith, and drive you out of your homes, and support (others) in driving you out, from turning to them (for friendship and protection). It is such as turn to them (in these circumstances) that do wrong.

(Y. Ali).

(49:12) O you who have attained to faith! Avoid most guesswork [about one another] for, behold, some of [such] guesswork is [in itself] a sin; and do not spy upon one another, and neither allow yourselves to speak ill of one another behind your backs. Would any of you like to eat the flesh of his dead brother? Nay, you would loathe it! And be conscious of God. Verily, God is an acceptor of repentance, a dispenser of grace! (Asad).

(4:135) O YOU who have attained to faith! Be ever steadfast in upholding equity, bearing witness to the truth for the sake of God, even though it be against your own selves or your parents and kinsfolk. Whether the person concerned be rich or poor, God's claim takes precedence over [the claims of] either of them. Do not, then, follow your own desires, lest you swerve from justice: for if you distort [the truth], behold, God is indeed aware of all that you do! (Asad).

4:86 But when you are greeted with a greeting [of peace], answer with an even better greeting, or [at least] with the like thereof. Verily, God keeps count indeed of all things (Asad).

So, who can guide us better?

We as a Couple

Similar was the situation with my life partner. We avoided the influence of others who were not compatible with our principles of life. We learned from each other **and modified our own patterns of living accordingly.**

Our Parents

Of course, our parents were our first mentors from birth till their last breaths—monitoring, modifying, and advising us to adopt them into our lives.

Our Maternal Grandfather

Dr. Ameer Ul Hussain Khan, a World War II veteran physician, influenced me to be a physician. He was a kind, religious, very caring, and charitable physician. He never demanded fees from his patients, irrespective of caste, creed, religion, or status. I was around him when he saw his patients and even went with him on his horse-driven carriage when he attended to his patients in their homes. I was only about five years of age.

Then comes my association with the following respectable individuals during my education and career, whom I consider my mentors. Their ways of life had a significant overall influence on me (not only educational), irrespective of race or religion.

Sachida Nand Sinha.

Respected Sachida Nand Sinha

His mentorship lesson was a live example of discipline, religious devotion, unbiased living, selflessness, and fulfillment of commitment. He was very affectionate but a man of principle in dealing with all. Who could be a better mentor? He was a devoted Hindu Rajput who followed his religion very passionately. He was a teacher when my father was a headmaster, and they were close friends. He visited me with my father at my maternal grandfather's house, travelling on the train and crossing the Ganges River on a steamer, which took between fourteen and eighteen hours from Purnea to Dinapore, or Patna in those days. They came to see me the first time I started recollecting about things. He asked my father there if he could teach me when I grew up. My father followed that through. He was a well-known headmaster of a middle school after my father retired. He used to be sent to schools that needed their programs upgraded.

Panditjti's[63] daily routine would be to get up early in the morning before sunrise and walk through the veranda of the hostel, calling us to wake up. Panditji would return after his call to nature, which, like all of us, he offered in the field, hiding behind the bush. Afterward, he would take a shower in the open, in the compound of the school, with the help of a student. The student-operated the handle of the tube well to bring out the water for him. Whether it was summer or winter, he would always shower with natural water, which was cold. After that, he would face the sun and say his prayer before returning to his room, which was also his office.

Meanwhile, all the students of higher grades would be in the open. Panditji would teach them for an hour or so with no fee before the regular classes of the school. His ongoing teaching was aimed at winning scholarships and awards in the district competition that the students attended annually. His students always received these awards.

I was not in the higher grades. I was in fifth grade. But he would include me in his teaching, as I was special to him because of his commitment to my father, his friend, and my father's commitment to him, as noted earlier. So I also used to be called to take a desk and sit, and he would teach me. This continued for the next three years for me, along with others. Does anybody see a Hindu-Muslim problem!!!? Alas!

In the evening, the students from the higher classes would gather around Panditji. He would teach while some of the students rotated in, giving him a massage. This was a show of respect to our teacher, Guru Dakshina[64]. This tradition is one of acknowledgment, respect, and thanks. It is a form of reciprocity and exchange between student and teacher. The repayment is not exclusively monetary and maybe a special task the teacher wants the student to accomplish. I was not allowed to do massage, perhaps because of my provenance with such a high family. We also had a Brahmin student of a higher caste than our Panditji, and he didn't perform massage on the teacher, either. Our Panditji was of the Rajput class of family.

Occasionally, students who didn't answer questions or answered them incorrectly would be caned, but not too heavily. I was a victim of this once by our respected Panditji. By this time, I was in the senior class. All failed to give the right answer or did not answer. I did not, also. Of course, it was an emotional day for me when I completed my middle school (from grade five to seven) and was to move to Purnea Zila High School.

Eventually, I left Purnea for higher education and to come to the West. When we returned many years later to visit the homeland, Naushaba and I went to see him. He had retired by then and was running a private school for children in Purnea Town. It must have been about fifteen years since I had seen him last, but he recognized me immediately and said, "Naiyer." We were all surprised. We both paid respect to him. He was having a lung problem with bronchitis. He told me about his health. I saw the medications that he was taking. I examined his chest with my ears on it as I had no stethoscope. I reassured him. It was very painful for me to think that I was not there around him. We stayed a bit and then left.

---

[63] *Pandit: A Hindu Scholar* learned in Sanskrit, Hindu religion, and philosophy. "ji," added as a term of respect.

[64] Guru dakshina in Hindu mythology refers to the tradition of repaying one's teacher or guru after a period of study or the completion of a course of formal education or spiritual guidance.

I am not hesitant to say that here, he was a devoted Hindu and was a friend of my father, a Muslim. He influenced me with his principle of fulfilling his promise to take me as his student, his selfless sacrifice of teaching students with no monetary gain, his religious devotion, and his routine of life. Was there any shadow of discrimination here?!

Professor Shahab Ud Din

Professor Shahab Ud Din was the biochemistry professor at the Aligarh Muslim University when I was in intermediate science. He was an excellent teacher. He always questioned the students and—no praise to me— when nobody could answer a question, he would direct them to me. Fortunately, I would answer him. He would taunt the other students thus: "Is it Naiyer who is responsible for you all?" So, this pressed me to be always better prepared in the subject. His style of teaching was inspiring. We, as a group, were invited to his house for tea after our final examination. It was a pleasure to have him as my teacher.

Dr. Das, taking Guard of Honour on the campus of the college
during the medical college's Jubilee celebration.

Dr. Madhusudan Das

Dr. Madhusudan Das was a just, strict man of principle, yet also a considerate mentor, which was rare in that part of the world. He was head of the university's department of medicine and a professor of medicine at the Prince of Wales Medical College and Patna Medical College Hospital. He taught medicine in my clinical classes. He was a man of few words who was rarely seen smiling and was very strict and punctual. He never expressed his anger toward anyone. He was a nondiscriminating, non-biased, very knowledgeable physician. These traits commanded respect from all who knew him. He never married but adopted a little girl, who passed away.

My association with Dr. Das was as a medical student, and then I was his house physician in the Hathwa Medical Ward at the Patna Medical College Hospital. Subsequently, I was a candidate for my doctorate in medicine (MD) (after my MB, BS) under him.

He drove his own Mercedes. He would come to the class on time. When he arrived, there would be silence in the class. No one would go to receive him or get near his car. That is why he was very different compared to other professors of medicine, who loved having the students surround their cars, showing welcome with praise when they arrived to teach near the entrance of the building.

I had a lot of respect for Dr. Das for the qualities that he possessed. I knew that he liked me without his expressing it. He never showed anger toward me; rather, he supported me all through. He wrote a letter of reference, which appears below, including a separate little note to me. Dr. Das has passed away. His memory is with me.

PATNA UNIVERSITY
DEPARTMENT OF MEDICINE :

Dr.M.DAS,F.R.C.P.,
Professor of Medicine &
Head of University Department of Medicine,
Patna University,Patna.
BIHAR (INDIA):

Dated Patna the.. 28/9/68.

Dr.Naiyer Habib has been a bright student and did uniformly well.He worked as one of my houseman in the Medical inpatient department for one year = July 1963 to June 1964.He evinced great interest in his work and performed his duties with great devotion.He worked under me on"The role of Autoimmunity in the Pathogenesis of Amoebic liver abscess" for his thesis for the degree of Doctorate of Medicine.His was well spoken of and he got M.D.in September 1966.He is full of promises.

(M.DAS),
Head of the Department of Medicine,
PATNA UNIVERSITY, PATNA.

Dear Dr Hobie,

I am enclosing a certificate
as desired. Hope this proves
useful. I am glad you
are doing well.

Wishing you every success

Yours sincerely

M...

28/9/68

Dr. Hubert Royster and his secretary, Mary.

Dr. Hubert Royster

Dr. Hubert Royster was the medical director for the educational program for the interns and residents at the Watts Hospital in Durham, North Carolina. Mary was his administrative assistant.

With the help of my friend Dr. Mohammad Shahab Ud Din, I received an appointment as a first-year resident at the Watts Hospital. Both were very helpful. It should be remembered that this appointment was arranged while I was in Karachi by contacting Dr. Shahab Ud Din. Dr. Royster took extra responsibility to ensure that all matters regarding my arrival at Durham were arranged efficiently, including the documents for my visa to the US, advance payment of my salary for airline tickets, and other things. He also arranged my ticket through a travel agent in Durham by Pan American Airlines and every direction from my point of departure to my arrival at the Watts Hospital. They arranged to send Dr. Shahab Ud Din and Dr. Rao to receive me at the airport and settle in at Watts Hospital. He also wrote a letter to Naushaba to facilitate her arrival, which was after my arrival here. This is called going out of the way for us. They were affectionate. Mary arranged our housing before Naushaba's arrival.

In order to have another residency position, which was a requirement for the extension of my exchange visitor program, I applied to some institutions. A head of the department of gastroenterology chatted with me and came to interview me in Durham from an institution in New York. He offered me a position in gastroenterology, which was not a subject of my choice at all. The time was nearing when I was supposed to apply for a visa. I had not received any other appointment. He was very nice in offering the position and various things. I accepted it. Soon after, I got a very good position offer from the Orange Memorial Hospital in internal medicine and cardiology. Now, I had a dilemma. I did not want to go to the gastroenterology program which I had just accepted, so I contacted the head of gastroenterology and told him that I would like to be excused from the position. I also contacted him by letter. In response, I received a threatening letter from him, indicating that I had signed a contract and that I was compelled to join; otherwise, he would take action against me.

I was truly in a bind. As was my habit, I wanted to explore my options for dealing with it. I met with Dr. Royster and explained the entire situation to him. He said he would look into it. He asked me to talk to Mary, and they corresponded with the individual, which relieved me. I am thankful to them.

Dr. Royster was happy with my work. There was some sadness. He gave me a handwritten note on the envelope for the completion of my work, showing appreciation and affection.

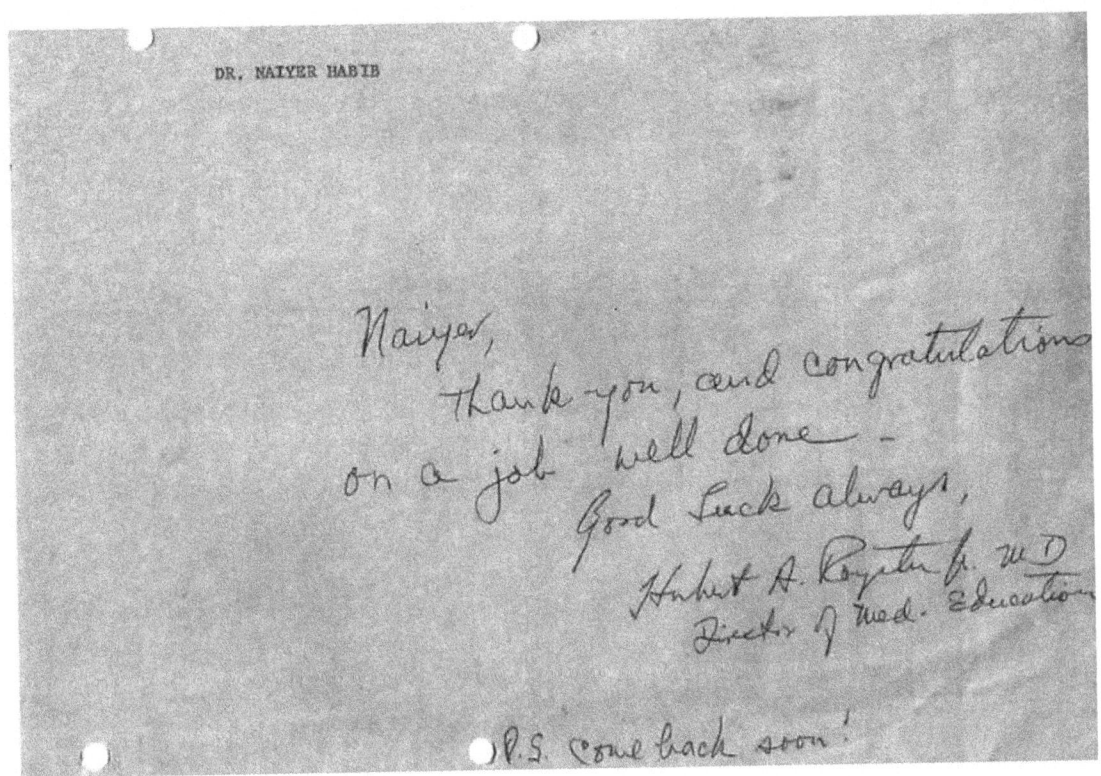

Naiyer,
thank you, and congratulations
on a job well done —
Good Luck always,
Hubert A. Royster Jr. MD
Director of Med. Education

P.S. come back soon!

Subsequent to my joining Orange Memorial Hospital, he wrote me a letter, which I have kept as a treasure to remind me of them.

Addressing someone with a first name is an expression of great American or Western affection. Besides, why a director of a program would write such a letter to a resident who completed training and was gone?! I respected his affection.

W   The WATTS HOSPITAL
H

July 16, 1969

Naiyer Habib, M. D.
Orange Memorial Hospital
Orlando, Florida 32806

Dear Naiyer:

    We were all delighted to hear from Mrs. Thomas that you have been doing such a good job in your residency, and that now you have a fellowship plus a cash prize. Congratulations!

    None of us had any doubts as to your ability, but it is nice to have conformation.

    Please write us and give us the news. All your old friends here are very much interested in your career.

    Mrs. Royster joins me in sending our best wishes to you and your family.

Sincerely yours,

Hubert A. Royster, Jr., M. D.
Director of Medical Education

HAR:mcm

259

Others in North Carolina

Dr. Peter Gabe

Dr. Peter Gabel was a fine gentleman and an excellent cardiology teacher at the Watts Hospital.

Dr. Yardley

Dr. Yardley was an excellent teacher. Like Dr. Gabel, he was a friendly teacher.

Dr. Macraken

Dr. Macraken was the chief of medicine at the Watts Hospital. He was a very gentle individual and a caring and excellent teacher. He gave me a hat as a gift when I was departing.

ORANGE MEMORIAL HOSPITAL
ORLANDO, FLORIDA 32806
A TEACHING HOSPITAL
COLLEGE OF MEDICINE, UNIVERSITY OF SOUTH FLORIDA

FREEMAN H. CARY, M.D.
DIRECTOR OF MEDICAL EDUCATION
AND
CLINICAL PROFESSOR OF MEDICAL EDUCATION

WITH APPRECIATION AND BEST WISHES FROM THE DEPARTMENT OF MEDICINE.

FREEMAN H. CARY, M.D. FOR DR. MORTON LEVY, CHIEF OF MEDICINE
9/28/70

Dr. Freeman Cary

Dr. Freeman Cary

The following is the opinion of a US senator that exemplifies Dr. Cary: *I have known Dr. Cary since I came to Washington in 1972. He was an extremely dedicated and capable public servant. His professional advice and personal friendship meant a great deal to me over the years. His fifteen years of service to the nation in the office of Attending Physician to the U.S. Capitol, earned him the deep respect of a great many senators and representatives*[65].

Dr. Cary was the program director for residency, fellowship, and internship at Orange Memorial Hospital, which was affiliated with the University of South Florida. I was appointed as a second-year resident in medicine and then carried on doing my cardiology at that institution. Dr. Cary was an individual who was very devoted to his job and was an excellent mentor for all of us. He used to make rounds at the bedside with all house staff, teaching them clinical medicine.

He oversaw the conferences. During my chief residency, I was involved with assisting him in arranging these conferences, and even in conducting them. He appointed me chief resident in my last year, although there were

---

[65] http://thomas.loc.gov/cgi-bin/query/z?r101:S19OC0-B1141.

other senior residents. He had developed a respectful and affectionate view of me. This is expressed in the following letter, as well as the note of the gift, as mentioned in the letter. The gift was a Samsonite briefcase, which I adore and still have.

ORANGE MEMORIAL HOSPITAL
ORLANDO, FLORIDA 32806
A TEACHING HOSPITAL
COLLEGE OF MEDICINE, UNIVERSITY OF SOUTH FLORIDA

FREEMAN H. CARY, M.D.
DIRECTOR OF MEDICAL EDUCATION
AND
CLINICAL PROFESSOR OF MEDICAL EDUCATION

13 July 1970

Dear Nayeri,

I hope that you are enjoying your new job and that your family is making a nice adjustment to Columbus.

It is difficult to put into words how much I appreciated the job you did as chief medical resident and cardiac fellow. I am sorry that time did not permit more personal contact with you. The Dept of medicine has been trying to decide for 6 weeks on an appropriate gift for you. I hope it will be on its way shortly.

The new house staff is adjusting very well and we have had some great cardiac cases — anomalous left coronary off the P.A., acute pneumo-coccal B.E. c̄ meningitis, infundibular pulmonic stenosis, tumor of mediastinum simulating aneurysm of P.A., etc.

The little table you gave me is very beautiful and occupies a choice spot in my room and heart. You were very thoughtful —

Most affectionately,
Freeman H. Cary md

Others in Orlando, Dr. Morton Levy

Dr. Morton Levy was the head of medicine, with a very pleasant personality, full of nobility.

261

Drs. Clarence Gilbert and Jonathan Partain

Drs. Clarence Gilbert and Jonathan Partain were the cardiologists with whom I was very closely associated in training in my last year. I learned cardiac catheterization and coronary angiography under them.

Dr. Frank C. Bone

(January 10, 1919-July 25, 2012)

Dr. Bone was a gastroenterologist. He was a very hardworking and nice individual. I was in rotation with him in gastroenterology. I learned endoscopy, intestinal biopsy, and liver biopsy under his supervision.

Dr. Allen Holcomb

Dr. Allen Holcomb was a nephrologist. I rotated with him for nephrology training. I was involved in the dialysis program and learned renal biopsy.

Dr. Michael Anthony

Dr. Michael Anthony was the overall program director of the residency program at Mount Carmel Hospital in Columbus. He was a very nice gentleman and an excellent teacher and administrator. He was a good listener to any concerns that the house staff had, which he would then resolve. He also wrote a letter of reference for me, which is included in the story of our departure to England.

Dr. Ralph D. Lach

Dr. Ralph D. Lach was the individual who appointed me a fellow in cardiology at Mount Carmel Hospital's teaching program. As time passed, he made me responsible for cardiology conferences. He trusted me fully with the management of cardiac patients. He trained me further in cardiac catheterization and coronary angiography. I had only been trained for the femoral approach, and I started doing brachial cut-down. He started leaving me alone to perform the cardiac catheterizations.

The first time he left me alone without warning, he told me to go ahead and start and that he would be there shortly. I had already made the incision for the catheter, and he had not returned. Now, the catheter was to be passed. I called him, and he said that I could do it and to proceed. Oh my God! So I proceeded, and the total time taken to complete the cardiac catheterization was only fifteen minutes, from the time of the incision to the completion of the procedure. He was very pleased. After that, he started to leave me alone in the cardiac catheterization laboratory.

Can you imagine this? We were doing a film recording of the coronary angiogram in one room and moving the patient with the catheter in the vessel to another room, placing the machine from the front and from the side of the patient's body and filming simultaneously on a large biplane film!

Dr. Lach invited us to his home for dinner and gave us a present, as well as to my son, who was little. We invited him and his wife for dinner at our apartment.

Dr. Ralph Lach and family (1970).

Dr. Ralph Lach and family (2009).

He founded the first community hospital catheterization laboratory in central Ohio in 1966. As his fellow, I later established the first cardiac catheterization laboratory in Regina, Saskatchewan. He met and learned balloon angioplasty from Dr. Andreas Gruentzig of Sweden, who conceived of and initiated the procedure. He was the first to perform coronary angioplasty in the north-central United States in 1979. Here, again, I, as his cardiology fellow, attended the course on coronary angioplasty by Dr. Gruentzig in 1984 when he moved to Emory University. Later, I performed the first angioplasty in Regina, or perhaps in the entire province of Saskatchewan.

In 2006, his residents and fellows recognized him. I sent a write-up, dated June 2, 2006, that expressed my tribute to him, and it was published in the memoir that was given to Dr. Lach.

DR. RALPH D. LACH

Summer 2006

.

Dear Dr. Lach,

Upon the occasion of your retirement, we are pleased to present you with this keepsake book, chronicling our many years spent working together. Please accept it as a token of our gratitude and respect for you as mentor, colleague, and friend. Your guidance and support has helped to shape and enhance the lives and careers of each of us in a multitude of ways. In appreciation for your integrity and professionalism, your generosity, warmth, and wit, we celebrate you today, and wish you countless blessings.

With fondness and admiration,
Your Mount Carmel Cardiology Fellows

Bruce Auerbach	Bobby (Feliciano) Delor	Nayee (Sayed) Husaini	Bharat H. Sangani
Maheswora Baidya	Denny Gabos	Dipak Mukherjee	Mukesh Shah
Stephen Baker	Raj Gaglani	J.R. Nelson	J Turk Tannabe
Wayne Beaver	Bruce Graham	Edwin Palileo	Pala Ashfaq
Wm. Boliek	Naiyer Habib	Rajendra Patel	
Alejendro Boza	Volney Wade Hash	Nandety Rao	
Howard Cheshire	J. Richard Hurt	Guru Reddy	

"HONORING DR. RALPH LACH AND BARBARA LACH –

We recently learned that Dr. Lach will be retiring, and that all of the Cardiology Fellows are gathering to give him a farewell. This letter is meant to express our affection and love for him and Barbara.

My wife and I recall the smiling face, short thick hair, and golden glasses of Dr. Lach. We felt so lively back then! We recall Barbara's affection and sweetness.

I was excited and pleased to join Mount Carmel Hospital in 1970. I took part in a period of training as a fellow under Dr. Lach. I have many wonderful memories of that time. We enjoyed every moment of it! I recall especially enjoying the Breakfast Meetings held at Mount Carmel, which were attended by resident fellows, medical students and others.

"I TOOK PART IN A PERIOD OF TRAINING AS A FELLOW UNDER DR. LACH. I HAVE MANY WONDERFUL MEMORIES OF THAT TIME. WE ENJOYED EVERY MOMENT OF IT!"

Dr. Lach was an exceptional educator and motivator. He trained us rigorously, always helping us to gain self-confidence. During cardiac catheterization, he would instruct us to begin the procedure ourselves, and explained that he would step in to observe from time to time, in case there were any problems. In actuality, we rarely saw him again until the catheterizations were completed. Fortunately, we did not have many catastrophes! I remember that we used to do Cine angiograms in one room, and then have to move patients to a second room to do filming on big X-ray film or Schonander. Back then, the patients would have to be moved with lines in the femoral artery or in the brachial.

I remember a story Dr. Lach told us about a Senior Physician he once knew. Each day before his rounds, the doctor would stop in a particular room, open a box, and read something from a piece of paper he kept inside the box. Some time later, this physician died. Those with whom he had worked were curious to see what was hidden in that box after all this time, so they opened it and looked. On the page was written 'Genu Valgus – knee bent outward,' and 'Genu Varus – knee bent inward.' I checked the dictionary, because I realized that I myself had forgotten which term was which. So you see, the Senior Physician was not the only one who benefited from a little reminder!

I would like to share a couple of incidents that I recall from my earliest days learning under Dr. Lach. The first one occurred when I was brand new and was not familiar with Dr. Lach's routines. He enjoyed conducting Saturday rounds as a group, and although it was not required that we attend, we knew he expected to see us there. Very early the first morning, I dropped my wife and 3-or-4-year old baby off at the drugstore, and told them I would be back very shortly, since Dr. Lach was only making morning rounds with a few of my patients. Little did I know that Dr. Lach was known to spend many hours (sometimes until late afternoon), on Saturday rounds! Not wanting to offend him or appear disinterested in learning from him, I said nothing. Meanwhile my wife and son, left without a car (and of course we had no cell phones in those days) waited for me in that small drugstore for many hours.

"WE BOTH FELT TREMENDOUS ADMIRATION AND GRATITUDE
TOWARD HIM, AND BARBARA TOO. WE STILL HAVE VIVID MEMORIES
OF THEIR KINDNESS AND HOSPITALITY. THEY GENEROUSLY GAVE
US SEVERAL GIFTS, WHICH WE STILL HAVE TODAY. THEY ARE VERY
SPECIAL TO US."

On another occasion, my family had planned a holiday getaway to Newark, OH to visit an old friend. Our intention was to leave Saturday morning, but by 1:00 in the afternoon, there I was at the hospital, still making rounds with Dr. Lach. The sky had grown dark with clouds, and a big storm was building. Once again, I did not tell Dr. Lach my plans, partly because it is a reflection of our Eastern culture to always respect one's teacher, but also because I did not want to give Dr. Lach the impression that I didn't value his exceptional teaching. We finally left quite late that day for Newark, arriving in my friend's darkened neighborhood only to discover that the area was very poorly marked, and had almost no street signs to direct us. We eventually managed to meet my friend, but not until well after midnight!

My reason for sharing these anecdotes is to say that we never had any ill feelings or unhappiness whatsoever towards Dr. Lach regarding such incidents. We only felt tremendous admiration and gratitude toward him, and Barbara too. We still have vivid memories of their kindness and hospitality. They generously gave us several gifts, which we still have today. They are very special to us.

Unfortunately, I was unable to find our photos of us together with Dr. Lach and Barbara from our Mount. Carmel days, but I have included some images of our children at one of the fellows' picnics. Perhaps they will bring back memories to Dr. Lach and others who attended. I wonder whether the tradition of the annual picnic has continued.

When it came time for me to leave Mt. Carmel and Dr. Lach, of course it was with much sadness. Dr. Lach surprised me at the Annual Function by presenting my family with gifts, and me with an award.

Under Dr. Lach's guidance and as his fellow, God blessed me with the ability to achieve much success as cardiologist, teacher, researcher and finally as the establisher of the Cardiology Program at the University of Saskatchewan, Regina. I headed the Cardiology Department from 1976 to 2001, stepping down when the health care system changed. Currently I am semi-retired, only doing office practice three days a week.

We as a family wish Dr. Lach and
Barbara Lach all the best for the future and
for their well-being.

So long! God bless you all, I send my regards
to the physicians and fellows who remember
us, and thank you for the opportunity to
contribute."

–Naiyer and Mahlaqa Naushaba Habib

RALPH D. LACH, M. D., F. A. C. C.
CARDIOLOGY

MAIN OFFICE
30 SOUTH DAVIS AVENUE
COLUMBUS, OHIO 43222
:LEPHONE: (614) 221-1728

ARLINGTON OFFICE
1800 ZOLLINGER ROAD
COLUMBUS, OHIO 43221
TELEPHONE: (614) 457-5359

November 22, 1971

The Royal College of Physicians of Edinburgh
9 Queen Street
Edinburgh, U.K.

Re: Naiyer Habib, M.D.

Dear Sir:

I am writing in support of the application of Dr. Naiyer Habib. Dr. Habib has had full training in Internal Medicine in this country in Durham, North Carolina and Orlando, Florida prior to starting his Fellowship in Cardiology under my direction at Mount Carmel Hospital in July, 1970. He will remain in this position until December 31, 1971.

During his Fellowship, Dr. Habib has had numerous responsibilities on the Cardiology Service. He has had considerable experience in both right and left cardiac catheterization, including selective cine coronary arteriography, primarily with the percutaneous Judkin's technique, but also somewhat with the Sone's technique. He has been responsible as a consultant to the House Staff in the Department of Medicine to assist them with problems in the twelve bed Cardiac Care Unit and nine bed Intensive Care Unit. He has had the total responsibility for the presentation of a weekly one and one-half hour Cardiology conference, consisting of clinical case presentation and analysis and an electrocardiography teaching session. He has had experience in Frank vectorcardiography and indirect recordings such as carotid pulse tracings and phonocardiography.

During his sixteen months at Mount Carmel, Dr. Habib has achieved a reputation as being an extremely diligent and complete physician, an excellent teacher and a fine person. He is deeply respected by his peers as well as his superiors and subordinates. He has always been extremely willing to undertake any task that is suggested and he reads avidly. His command of the English language is excellent, and I should mention here that, except for two other members of the House Staff, Dr. Habib has achieved all his excellent work in the setting of a

268

50 member Intern and Resident complement, all of whom are American born and American trained. Similarly, he has worked with the medical students from the Ohio State University College of Medicine who rotate through our institution. I have no reservation in giving Dr. Habib the highest recommendation for his entry into the clinical practice of medicine or further training in Cardiology.

If I can be of any more assistance to him in the future, I would be most happy to be apprised of the opportunity.

Sincerely yours,

Ralph D. Lach, M.D. F.A.C.C.

RDL:pp

On our return to Canada, we were in touch with the Lachs. He sent me a book written by a cardiologist in Columbus, who had included a write-up about him, recognizing him as one of the pioneers of cardiology in Columbus.

Dr. Lach developed Parkinsonism. We had talked to each other on the phone and expressed a desire to visit him. This would not come true. He passed away on January 22, 2016, at his home, peacefully.

ENGLAND

Meanwhile, my papers were processed for going to the United Kingdom by the General Medical Council of Great Britain. I received the registration from the council.

I applied to the Royal College for my MRCP examination. A required letter of reference by Dr. Michael Anthony—the residence training director at the Hawkes Hospital Mount Carmel—was submitted to the college.

Mount Carmel Hospital
790 WEST STATE STREET
Columbus Ohio 43222
November 22, 1971

Royal College of Physicians of Edinburgh
9 Queen Street
Edinburgh EH2 1JQ

Gentlemen:

Naiyer Habib, M.D. began a Fellowship in Cardiology in Mount Carmel Hospital July 1, 1970 and will complete this fellowship December 31, 1971.

Doctor Habib is a most welcome addition to our house staff by virtue of his enthusiasm, cooperation, and fund of knowledge. He is an extremely quiet young man, but a most capable physician. His fund of knowledge in the area of general internal medicine is good, and in the area of cardiology, much better than average.

In spite of the fact that Doctor Habib is not a graduate of an American school he is held in very high esteem by the American graduates junior to him, and by the members of the attending staff.

His assistance in the cardiac catheterization laboratory has been excellent. Doctor Habib was awarded favorable recognition of his paper presented before the Society of Internal Medicine of Columbus in the spring of 1971. This competition was open to all residents in Internal Medicine and fellows in medical subspecialties in the Columbus community. The paper "Pacemaker Click - a Clinical Diagnosis" has been accepted for publication in the Ohio State Medical Journal.

I heartily endorse Doctor Habib's application to sit for the examination for membership in the Royal College of Physicians of Edinburgh.

Sincerely,

Michael A. Anthony, M.D.
Director, Medical Education

MAA:MSL:tw

We departed for England. I prepared to take a course for six weeks to appear in the MRCP examination at the Hammersmith Hospital, a well-recognized institution.

I had not made enough preparation for the first part of the MRCP examination, and I did not qualify. This was the first failure in my life. So I planned to stay further.

We lived in a small attached type of dwelling at 70 North Hill, London, from January 1, 1972, to April 6, 1972, when we left for Karachi, Pakistan. We had to put coins in the water meter to get hot water. It was a good place to live. Time was passing.

270

Hammersmith Hospital

I would take the subway to Hammersmith Hospital to attend the courses. Drs. John Goodwin and Celia Oakley conducted them. Dr. Oakley had worked with the legendary and internationally known Dr. Paul Wood as his house physician. Dr. John F. Goodwin was a world-renowned academic cardiologist in England who was celebrated for his work on obstructive cardiomyopathy. I was fortunate to be taught by such personalities.

Trip To Canada For Frcp Examination

It was from here that I went for my fellow of the Royal College of Physicians of Canada examination to Montreal, Canada, where I had already been certified in internal medicine. I passed the examination.

Second Child

Naushaba was pregnant with our second child in early 1972. She attended the neonatal clinic in London, where she always saw nurses but no physicians.

They asked for a chest x-ray examination, considering her to be of Asian origin, where tuberculosis was common. Naushaba suggested that she would rather not have an x-ray and explained that she had not been back to India or Pakistan in the last five years. She had a discussion with the nurses, on my questioning, about why no physician had seen her and to inquire about who would conduct the delivery. The nurses informed her that nurses looked after all the expectant mothers, and if there were any concerns, a physician would be consulted. Delivery was also done by nurses unless the pregnancy was suspected to be complicated, in which case a doctor would be consulted.

Once I learned this, I got quite concerned. While we were in the US, a physician attended while nurses assisted. I did not want to run into any problems. I had already qualified for FRCP from Canada, and so I abandoned my plan to appear for the examination and stay in the United Kingdom for my MRCP. We decided to leave.

PAKISTAN

Reasons And Process

Because of the problem of Pakistan and India still being at arms, I approached the Pakistani consulate and found that my mother and father had both moved to Pakistan without consulting me. The consulate told me that they would be happy to grant me citizenship. They stamped our Indian passport with a visa and gave us documents for acquiring citizenship.

We went to Karachi, Pakistan, arriving on April 7, 1972. After studying the entire situation and what we had experienced, we were very happy to join our parents and family there.

Warning by a Relative

Lo and behold, a member of our family visited us the next morning. He told us that he came only to tell us that we should immediately go back to the US; otherwise, we would repent. He emphasized that he could have come to see us some other day but that it was too important for him to wait. It was a surprise that puzzled us. I told him, looking at his sincerity for us, that I would think about it.

Citizenship

Our next priority was to finalize our stay, immigration, citizenship, etc. I had no option but to accept the citizenship of Pakistan, which had already been promised to me while we were in the UK. This went through. They cancelled our Indian passports and took them away from us. I copied a few pages to keep, which I still have. I received citizenship in Pakistan on May 20, 1972.

Registration for Medical Practice

My Canadian and Indian qualifications were assessed. My FRCP was recognized as equivalent to a fellow of the College of Physicians and Surgeons Pakistan. I received registration from the Registrar of the Medical Council of Pakistan, Pakistan College of Physicians.

Disappointing Experiences In Pakistan Schooling Of Our Child

We looked for admission in a good school for our eldest child. Grammar school with English medium was recommended. He was evaluated and was told not to qualify because he was weak in spoken English, which was unbelievable. He was American-born with English at home and school. The prevailing situation there was that only children from families with close contact with the ministerial level and others, the very important personalities, were admitted. He was admitted to a Christian school with courtesy and manners. I could have taken issues with them, but such incidences had initiated our doubts about staying in such a country permanently.

Tehran Visit

Meanwhile, I was to go to Tehran, Iran, to appear for an examination for the American board. There was a rule of restriction for doctors to go out of Pakistan. I was not getting permission to leave Pakistan for Tehran. I was asked to prove that I had not been an East Pakistani. East Pakistan had just parted from the West to become Bangladesh. I showed the officials all the documents confirming my continuous residence in India, the US, England, and Karachi, but it didn't make any difference.

A suggestion came from someone to get proof from an official. My mother's second cousin was a deputy superintendent of police at the airport in Karachi. Noor Alam Saheb[66] certified that I had never been to East Pakistan (Bangladesh).

---

[66] Saheb is a title of courtesy, like "Esquire."

I was also having some problems with the State Bank in Pakistan. It was another requirement to obtain permission from the State Bank of Pakistan to visit abroad. A relative of ours, Nasim Ali Warsi, was in a high office there, and he took me to the department responsible for issuing permission from the state bank to go abroad. He introduced me to Masroor Siddiqui Saheb, who was a very fine gentleman to me. All the paperwork was completed.

I was eventually able to go to Tehran in 1972. I travelled via Lebanon, a beautiful country then; its township was along the shore. I walked around and then caught another plane to Tehran. I took my examination and then toured the beautiful cultural city. I purchased a portable baby carrier for our second son, like our first son's.

I failed the American board examination. I had no time to prepare for the examination because of the turmoil of my life from the US to the UK and to Pakistan. There was a limited time frame for accepting training to appear for the examination. It was my last chance to appear and the only one at which I had appeared.

Search For Professional Career

My other priority was to finalize my professional career. I did not have much expectation of Pakistan having a position according to my qualifications and experience. As in any developing country, Pakistan was a place where favouring one another was rampant. It was against my principles to use such resources. However, I was interested in having an academic role, such as a teacher, researcher, or consultant.

Anyway, I went to meet the principal of the Medical College of Karachi and presented my card. Although he was sitting alone and doing some work, he made me sit outside on the waiting chair like anybody else for a long time. Ultimately, he called me, and asked the reason for my visit. I explained that I had just come from the United States with my qualification in cardiology and said that if he had any position there to fit me, I would be thankful. Without any conversation, he told me right away that there was no such opportunity for me in his institution. After, I went to Jinnah Hospital and met the same end.

Language Riots

There was a movement to make Sindhi the official language instead of Urdu, the provincial language of Sindh. Discrimination between native Sindhi and the migrant population of Muslims from India as refugees had started to flare up. I had picked up a form for submission of my documents for reassessment of my qualifications. It was in Sindhi and English only. When the riots started to take shape, I heard the chief minister, Mr. Mumtaz Ali Bhutto, on the radio addressing the people, saying that the elimination of Urdu was wrong. What could I say about this, or what was my opinion about the affairs prevailing there, especially for those who were intending to make their home there?

My Practice in Karachi

I arranged for an office in the Ghafoor Chamber, a prestigious office place for medical professionals. I was to share an office with a psychiatrist. As expected in the beginning, there were no patients or only occasional patients. I did not have a vehicle. My brother-in-law was to bring me from North Nazimabad to an area of downtown Karachi, locally referred to as Saddar, to my office and back. His ferrying would cost me PKR 300 a month. I met Dr. Rahman, who had his own hospital with his wife in Haidri. It has become a large hospital compared to what it was in the 1970s. I sat there and started to see a few patients. I walked on foot, maybe for about half a kilometre, carrying my ECG machine in my hand. I did not like this unexpected beginning of my life, but it had to be accepted. Then, there was Dr. Siddiqui practicing on the road from Haidri to North Nazimabad. He met me and was very courteous. He offered me to sit there to practice, so I started to run my clinic there, as well[67]. I started practicing also at my home and saw a few patients there.

My Experience Related to Three of My Patients

I will recount here my experience related to three of my patients, which demonstrates honest relationships with people and the morality of prevailing medical practice by some medical professionals there. My name was spreading among the inhabitants of Karachi, but nails were piercing the coffin of my desire to settle in Pakistan.

One of my female patients had anxiety reactions and various anxiety symptoms. It was endogenous anxiety, more due to fear of heart trouble. Its diagnosis had been reached by a cardiologist, and she was being treated as a heart patient. She was visiting a physician considered to be a cardiologist and was on multiple drugs. I diagnosed her as not having any cardiac problems and advised her to stop all her medications. She was surprised to hear this from me, and we engaged in lengthy discussions and arguments in response. She told me that various cardiologists had diagnosed her with heart trouble, and now here I was, taking her off all these medications. Anyway, after further discussion, she started to gain confidence in me. I suggested that she had anxiety reactions and should go to see a psychiatrist. I referred her to the psychiatrist with whom I was sharing the office in the Ghafoor chamber. This patient returned to me and narrated a story about the psychiatrist talking about me very badly. He had questioned my experience and ability to diagnose and had told her that I was no good. She said, "So I did not stay there, and I talked back to him. I reminded him that you are such a nice man, that you reassured me about my heart, and that you had chosen him to see me for help. And now here he was talking against you." I smiled and reassured her. She was quite happy with my management and lived a normal life thereafter.

Another patient, who was a relative of my father's friend, arrived at my home office with acute pulmonary edema. He was quite short of breath, so I treated him with medication from the pharmacy. Within an hour or so, he settled down, and in the next hour, he became almost normal. This is the way these patients' problems are resolved on receiving proper treatment. I did not hospitalize him. I sent him home and prescribed medication. It was a surprise to him and to the entire family that he had been seemingly about to die and then had recovered so quickly without being hospitalized. I did not charge him the tremendous fee that they expected. This and the treatment of other patients was spreading my name and fame. More and more patients started coming to see me.

The third patient was the father of a very rich family. His sons had engaged cardiologists and other specialists of repute for the treatment of their billionaire father. They learned from some other people about me and so visited, requesting me to see their bedridden father. They took me to his home. He was a slim, ill-looking gentleman lying in bed. On my evaluation, I concluded that the profile of the management instituted was the cause of his

---

[67] It is so unfortunate that I heard a few years after settling in Canada, that he was actually not a doctor, and that he had generated some bogus certificates on the basis of which he was practicing.

bedridden status. It consisted of multiple costly drugs and various prohibitions of activities and diets. I asked them to stop all drugs and the prohibitions if they trusted me. I further asked for a gradual normalization of his activities and diet. They kept looking at me quizzically but humbly agreed to follow my advice. By the grace of God, they saw a very rapid improvement to recovery.

Experiencing what we did was a major blow to our plan to settle in Karachi with all our family. It was also a family conflict—nothing to do with parents or sisters. A very close relative tried to forge to collect money from me rather than asking for it.

Thus, looking at the entire situation related to the politics of the government, relatives, the medical profession, and our son's educational matters, it became apparent that it was not possible for us to live in Pakistan under such circumstances. I already had left my motherland (India).

I always recalled my relative, mentioned earlier, who had come on the second day of our arrival in Pakistan asking us to return whenever we were facing circumstances not acceptable to our conscience despite our attempt to console us initially that perhaps things may get better.

We thus decided to leave. Upon learning we were leaving, the sons of the billionaire patient came to see me to ask if I would stay. They offered to build a hospital for me in Karachi or Lahore, but the arrow of my decision had left the bow. We could not change the decision after facing all the circumstances. They were injuring our conscience. We could not adjust.

A Tragic Decision

This was a tragic decision for us to take. I was the one who had not wanted to live in the West and who wanted to live together with our entire family. This dream did not seem to come true. After all my arrangements were made to depart, my father said that Pakistan was not that bad. It was he who, while in India, had wanted to depart from India to Pakistan. While we were in India and I was being educated, he used to tell me that I should settle in England and not come back to India to face problems. It was he who was saying that Pakistan was not that bad when we were leaving Pakistan. In these last moments, I interpreted a father's wish to keep his son and the daughter-in-law whom he had adored since her childhood. I was the son who had lived away from his home for education since age nine.

Naushaba was leaving the family, as well, and with similar thoughts.

Of course, it was my parents' decision and sacrifice to send their only son away for his future to succeed in life. It was only now a chance for us to live together. Not a single cent was spent for the father by this son in the father's lifetime. He was not included in the support that I was providing to other members of our family. He was always a self-supporting person till his last breath. God saved him even in being obliged to anyone to get service for any disabling illness. At the airport, he had tears in his eyes. I reassured him that I would call him and that we would settle together. As I wrote and read this paragraph, tears kept flowing from my eyes.

Unfortunately, desires, decisions, and wishes don't always come true, and that was the case for us. I think about that and get overwhelmed with emotion, but I had no option. It was not my selfishness. The West accepted me, and I did my duty while I was there. We do not repent this decision, knowing what India is and what Pakistan is. The Partition has placed its permanent stamp of tragedy on countless families—on some much more and on some less. We were also victims of it: Naushaba, as a refugee from India in childhood, and I, being unable to settle in India or Pakistan.

Having perceived all this, we decided to leave Pakistan. No land is bad. It is the people who make a place livable or non-livable. Some have the option to leave, and others do not.

USA Consulate Initial Step

First, I wanted to return to the United States, but as previously mentioned, I originally had no intention of settling in the West. I had gone to that country on an exchange visa. American law required me to stay out of the US for two years before I could apply for immigration. I did not have much hope that they would accept my application.

There was not much time for me to decide to stay longer because of an impending restriction. The Pakistani government was going to decide not to allow doctors to leave the country. I feared being trapped in Pakistan.

CANADA

Canadian Visa and Departure from Pakistan

I looked toward Canada and found a position of fellowship in cardiology at the University Hospital in the University of Saskatchewan's medical college. I applied for it. The papers were being processed at the University Hospital. Meanwhile, I contacted the Canadian consulate in Islamabad (the capital of Pakistan) and submitted my application. On its receipt, Mr. Qazi, a Pakistani official of the embassy, called me. He told me that the processing of our applications for immigration might take time, but that we could try to get a minister's permit to leave Pakistan by contacting the University Hospital. With this, everything would be expedited to go, and immigration could be finalized in Canada. I had no choice.

I called the program director at the University Hospital, Dr. R. N. Beck. He was head of endocrinology, as well. I told him the entire circumstances. He was willing to help me and reassured me. He approached the Honourable Mr. Otto Lang, who was a minister in the renowned Prime Minister Pierre Elliott Trudeau's cabinet. (For interest, I note our beloved prime minister's full name, Joseph Philippe Pierre Yves Elliott Trudeau). I was able to get the minister's permit, and the consulate called me with permission for visas for the entire family. We went to the Canadian consulate in Islamabad, got medical clearance (as arranged by Mr. Qazi), and were interviewed by Mr. Gibson, a fine gentleman. All of this was completed in no time. We received the minister's permits with the reassurance that they would be converted to immigration visas and citizenship in due course.

While in Islamabad, we visited Murree, a resort hilly place for holidays. My mother was with me and my family. We spent a couple of days there. Then we visited Lahore, a historic city related to the Moghul dynasty. We finally returned to Karachi.

I ran into some shortage of finances. I had left some money in the United States, in Columbus, with a friend of ours. Iftikhar Ali Khan, a friend from Aligarh Muslim University, found out what was going on. He loaned me money without my asking him and despite my hesitation. I repaid this money on my return to Canada.

Thus, our decision to settle in Canada was made. It was painful for me not to settle in India, and it was painful for both of us to leave Pakistan. Of course, it had been painful for Naushaba's family when they had to leave India as refugees. We consider ourselves to be victims of the Partition of India. There were many families affected by this partition, and perhaps we escaped the major victimization that the majority of the people suffered from. The internet is full of stories of these tragedies and arguments for and against the Partition. Be that as it may, we sought to return to the US, but today, we feel that it was best that we settled in Canada.

We arrived at the Toronto International Airport as a family with two sons on July 14, 1973, and passed through immigration. The immigration officials were very nice to us all. We had landed on a minister's permit with the intention to apply for immigration and then acquire citizenship.

After going through immigration, we rushed to catch our connecting flight to Saskatoon, which was departing very shortly from Toronto. We checked our luggage and rushed to board the plane.

We went to the desk of the Air Canada agent. He was talking to an individual. We stood behind him. As his discussion dragged on, I waved, indicating that our plane would be leaving shortly. He even did not look at us and paid no attention. He continued his conversation till our plane did depart. I did not know whether he was a man of principle without any flexibility or a discriminator against us for being brown. The person with whom he had been talking did not have any documents. I concluded that he had been talking about something not related to boarding that plane. After he was through, he looked at us. I indicated that our plane had already departed. Anyway, we got the next plane and boarded. There were only two seats left. The air hostess accommodated us in the plane by opening their special seats. According to the rules of these days, they might not have permitted us to get onto the plane. Our luggage had already gone on the previous plane. We landed in Saskatoon at night and saw only our children's one small bag. The others were missing but came a couple of days later.

Saskatchewan And Its Two Cities: Saskatoon And Regina

We started our life in Saskatoon, one of the two main cities of the province of Saskatchewan. Both cities, Regina and Saskatoon, play a role in our lives. They are separated by 252 kilometres.

Saskatchewan is a western province of Canada. It is bordered on the west by the province of Alberta, on the north by the Northwest Territories, on the east by the province of Manitoba, and on the south by the United States— Montana and North Dakota.

We could not imagine that we made this province in Canada our beloved home. We lived there for over three decades and spent the prime time of our life here, from 1973 to 2004. We loved it no less than our motherland.

The story goes like this: We were in Columbus, Ohio, in 1970. A friend had visited Winnipeg, in the province of Manitoba, and was telling us the story of his visit. We learned that it was so cold that people had to connect their car engines to heaters. We were so surprised! We were watching TV while visiting Pakistan, and a scene came on of the city of North Battleford, about 100 kilometres from Saskatoon. We saw a storm with blowing snow. A sign board with the word "Saskatchewan" was blown by the wind in that storm. What a surprise that we lived there for three decades. One does not know what is in his fate. We recall this often, and it becomes a topic of discussion among friends and relatives.

The province's name was derived from the Saskatchewan River, named by the Cree, meaning "swift-flowing river." Its main economy is based on agriculture (wheat, canola) and mining (including uranium and potash). It has energy resources of crude oil and electricity.

Saskatchewan has more sunshine than any other province of Canada. It has very cold winters with heavy snow but bright sunshine. The temperature may drop to -40°C at times. Summer temperatures, meanwhile, may go up to 37°C. It is the second province in Canada to suffer tornados. It also gets flooded because of the melting of the large amount of snow that collects in the winter. Winter may last up to six months.

The population of Saskatchewan was 1,117,503 as of January 2014. It was 926, 242 in 1971, and we arrived in 1973. Regina is the capital city of Saskatchewan, and Saskatoon is regarded as an academic centre.

Saskatoon

Saskatoon is a beautiful, clean city. It is a university city, as it is called. The famous Southern Saskatchewan River flows by the side of the university and through the city.

Saskatoon is in the northern part of the province. It is about 256 kilometres from Regina, going north on Highway 11. Its population was 126,449 in 1971, close to our arrival in 1973. The latest estimated metropolitan population (as of 2015) is 305,000.

Legislative Building in Regina

Regina was named in 1882 after Queen Victoria Regina. It was designated the capital of Saskatchewan in 1906. The city has its own richness and history. Its population was 139,469 in 1970-1971, close to the period when we arrived. As of the 2006 census, the total population had grown to 179,246. Out of this, the followers of Islam, Hinduism, Buddhism, and Judaism made up 2.9 percent.

Life in Saskatoon

We lived in Saskatoon for three years, from July 1973 to August 1976.

Leaving the airport, we asked the taxi driver about hotels and were taken to the Bessborough Hotel. This hotel is situated on the border of the Saskatchewan River. It was a very palatial hotel to stay in. It belonged to the Baltzan family, one of the wealthiest families in Saskatoon. We could see the university from the window of our room. The next day, we had breakfast, and then I left the family to stroll around and then went to the University

Hospital. There, I met Dr. Beck and got a bird's-eye view of the existing facilities and buildings. The University Hospital was just within walking distance from the hotel. Our luggage had not arrived. We were worried. We moved to another hotel, Big T, as the Bessborough was too expensive for us.

Residence Rental

We found a place to rent at 1220 College Avenue, across the road from the University Hospital. We rented the upper floor with two bedrooms. It belonged to Mr. Stacey. He provided us with an additional crib and a high chair from his storage. He was very nice. We settled there and saw heavy snow for the first time from this dwelling.

Our first experience with snow (with University Hospital across the road).

University Hospital.

City of Saskatoon—the Bessborough Hotel at the extreme left.

We did not have a car, so we took the bus to shop and buy groceries. In the case of grocery shopping, we used to hire a taxi to return to our residence after a bus ride to the grocery store in the Midtown Plaza. We purchased a car after my one-year contract with the university was finished.

We had celebrations of the birthdays of our children and of the Eid festival, inviting our limited circle of friends.

We developed friendships with some local Muslim people—the family of Shamim and Nahid Ahmad, Drs. Rauf and Abeda Qureshi, and Professor Vakil—and a couple of people of Hindu faith, including Dr. Ninan, the Saxena family, and Dr. Juma and his wife, Belan. Belan brought stuff for us, including food, and was very caring, as if we were family. So we were multi-religious and multicultural, living together and socializing.

Community Eid at University Residence lobby in Saskatoon, 1975.

Islamic Association of Saskatchewan, Saskatoon

As we grew more familiar with the community, I was elected vice president of the Islamic Association of Saskatoon for a year in 1975. Naushaba started teaching Islam to the children because the existing volunteer was leaving for his home country. She started taking the weekly Islamic school classes with a few children at the university residence, in one of the towers meant for families.

University Hospital Saskatoon

I was appointed a resident in medicine in cardiology for a year, from July 1973 to June 1974. Fortunately, I did not have to take calls at night. I worked with Dr. Pepe Lopez and Dr. R. C. Hayton, who were cardiologists. I had already learned cardiac catheterization and coronary angiography, but I continued with them. Dr. Merriman was running an exercise program and testing treadmill exercises. I worked with them in rotation. I also had exposure to Dr. Louis Horlick, an excellent teacher and individual. He had given me the opportunity and respect of a level higher than I deserved. It was a pleasure working with them all. I completed the period of the appointment.

University Hospital
University of Saskatchewan
SASKATOON, CANADA

This Certifies That

Naiyer Habib

served this Hospital as

Resident in Medicine
(Cardiology)

July 1, 1973 - June 30, 1974

EXECUTIVE DIRECTOR

DEPARTMENT HEAD

With my Canadian qualification and the training I'd gotten in the States, I was qualified to do full practice even without my residency in Saskatchewan, which I had not realized before. I had applied for a residency fellowship at the University Hospital. However, I respected that and continued to work with that appointment for a year. I maintained my morality.

After completing my training position, I tried to apply for a cardiology position, but despite my qualifications and experience, I could not get one in either Toronto or Calgary, where there were vacancies. I learned that they took a British person for the cardiology position in Calgary, even though he was not trained or qualified according to Canadian standards. Maybe they had some exception, with all due respect.

Medical Practice

Meanwhile, I joined Dr. Edward Sommerville to practice internal medicine in his group, although I handled most of the cardiology patients. The group, along with me, practiced in the City Hospital with an office in the Medical Arts Building at Spadina Crescent.

Our House

We purchased a house at a cost of $35,000 when I had already started the practice and bought the car. We moved to the residence at 334 Elm Street.

Our house at 334 Elm Street, Saskatoon (Naushaba standing), 1973.

We rented a van and loaded what we had into it. We bought some used furniture, and a new sofa and a new mattress. We did some renovation ourselves.

I first thought this to be funny, but realized the difficult economic strain, a serious fact of our lives and many other things, some noted below. I had a new mattress but an old bed frame. We bought a headboard from the used furniture store, and we loaded it in the back of our car. As I drove away, it fell and broke into two pieces. I repaired it and used it as a headboard.

We renovated the bathroom with tiling and painting and then did the kitchen and the basement, including the kitchen cabinets. We both did it together, and we survived.

These stories offer a reflection of the finances that we had to accommodate back then. Can our progeny imagine these facts of our lives!?

Naushaba learned driving. Belan helped her. Susan, a nurse, also helped her. Susan lived in the next house when we were living in the rented house on College Avenue. Soon after Naushaba got her driving license, she got a ticket. She felt she had not made a mistake.

Immigration To Citizenship: Canada

We entered Canada on non-immigrant visas on a minister's permit issued on June 28, 1973, in Islamabad, with validity to December 20, 1973. We arrived at the Toronto International Airport on July 14, 1973. The non-immigrant visa was extended, and we received immigrant status on January 17, 1975.

The day came when we received the notification of the award of citizenship. We attended the citizenship celebration and we were now citizens of Canada. We received our citizenship on October 31, 1977, while in Regina. We thanked God and took a breath of relief.

Naushaba and Naiyer are taking the Oath of Citizenship.

Now Canadian citizens!

OTTAWA 1977

Mr. Naiyer Habib,
308 Habkirk Dr.,
REGINA, SASK. S4S 6A8

Dear Mr. Habib:

Now that you have received your certificate of Canadian citizenship, it is with a great deal of pleasure that I am able to send you my personal congratulations and on behalf of your government - warmest best wishes.

This is an important step you have taken - important for you and important for Canada. For you it means an opportunity to share fully in the blessings of this land and, equally important, a responsibility to play your part to preserve and strengthen the ideals upon which our country rests. For Canada it means that you have chosen this among all the nations of the world as the one which you want to call "home". We are honoured by your choice.

With the rights and privileges you have acquired as well as the obligations which your citizenship carries, you share with all Canadians the ancient liberties of a free people living together in harmony under a democratic government which recognizes the rights of all of its citizens.

Again my congratulations. May the future hold for you a full measure of the happiness which is Canada.

Yours sincerely,

John Roberts

 The Secretary of State of Canada   Le Secrétaire d'État du Canada

OTTAWA 1977

Mrs. Mahlaqa Naushaba Habib,
308 Habkirk Dr.,
REGINA, SASK. S4S 6A8

Dear Mrs. Habib:

Now that you have received your certificate of Canadian citizenship, it is with a great deal of pleasure that I am able to send you my personal congratulations and on behalf of your government - warmest best wishes.

This is an important step you have taken - important for you and important for Canada. For you it means an opportunity to share fully in the blessings of this land and, equally important, a responsibility to play your part to preserve and strengthen the ideals upon which our country rests. For Canada it means that you have chosen this among all the nations of the world as the one which you want to call "home". We are honoured by your choice.

With the rights and privileges you have acquired as well as the obligations which your citizenship carries, you share with all Canadians the ancient liberties of a free people living together in harmony under a democratic government which recognizes the rights of all of its citizens.

Again my congratulations. May the future hold for you a full measure of the happiness which is Canada.

Yours sincerely,

John Roberts

OUR FAILURE TO LIVE WITH FAMILY TOGETHER

My desire to stay with both sides of the family together failed, although we were able to look after them. This sadness of life will never leave us. We attempted to fulfill this goal with the result as follows.

Yes, my mother came and stayed with us, and she passed away here. She wanted to be buried in Pakistan. We fulfilled her desire. I took her body to Karachi. She was buried in Karachi in the cemetery of Sakhi Hassan.

We also sponsored my younger sister, and there was an urgency to have her sponsored because the age limit was soon to be exceeded.

We also tried to sponsor Naushaba's youngest sister, but this application was rejected on the plea that her English was weak. If some emergency happened, she would not be able to handle it. I had a lawyer dealing with the case. We heard some remarks from the immigration officer through the lawyer that I'm avoiding including in the book. To think he made a racial remark against a newly expected immigrant.

The rest of the family was so knit together that it would not have been appropriate to separate them. Naushaba's mother could not come because of the three unmarried daughters, and she passed before we could have tried.

CAREER IN CARDIOLOGY

by

Dr. Naiyer Habib

Joining Academic Career

It was the objective of my life to be an academic cardiologist. I had failed to stay in the United States; otherwise, I would have continued there in academic cardiology. However, some circumstances prevent an individual from pursuing his objective. Ultimately, it has proved to be the best for us to be in Canada.

After settling and completing my education and training, my work in cardiology consisted of evaluating patients, investigating and treating as needed, and using procedures such as stress-testing, echocardiography, cardiac catheterization, and coronary angiography leading to coronary angioplasty and stenting if indicated. When valvuloplasty[68] started to come into vogue, I wanted to have this program initiated, but I eventually abandoned this plan, thinking there may not be enough cases. I was content to provide total care to my patients, and not just cardiologic care.

I was not happy doing a practice of internal medicine and had attempted to apply to join cardiology at some places without success. I had decided to attempt to return to the United States and had just started correspondence about the opportunity.

Meanwhile, I saw an advertisement for a cardiologist position at the Plains Health Centre through the University of Saskatchewan to start a cardiology program for Southern Saskatchewan. I was excited, but I was not sure whether I would be selected. I applied and was called for an interview by Dr. Gerald Sinclair, who was the head of the department of medicine.

---

[68] Valvuloplasty is a procedure of replacing a diseased heart valve by using the same procedure as cardiac catheterization, without open-heart surgery in selected cases. It is now a standard procedure.

CARDIOLOGIST — The department of medicine, Plains Health Centre, Regina, Saskatchewan, seeks a full-time academic cardiologist, skilled in invasive and non-invasive procedures, to develop and supervise a cardiac investigational laboratory in this new 300-bed teaching hospital of the University of Saskatchewan. An active cardiac surgical service will be relocated to the Plains Health Centre in 1976. Academic rank and salary commensurate with training and experience. Forward applications accompanied by curriculum vitae and the names and addresses of three referees to: Dr. G.E. Sinclair, Professor and Head, Department of Medicine, Plains Health Centre, Regina, SK.

Following are representative letters of appointment. Others have been misplaced.

University of Saskatchewan

DEPARTMENT OF MEDICINE
Gerald E. Sinclair, M.D., F.R.C.P.(C)
Professor & Head

4500 Wascana Parkway
Regina, Saskatchewan
S4S 5W9
Tel. 584-6211 - Ext. 451

April 29, 1976

Dr. N. Habib
334 Elm St. East
SASKATOON, Saskatchewan
S7J OH1

Dear Dr. Habib:

I am pleased to offer you an appointment in the Department of Medicine at the Plains Health Centre, to develop and supervise the Cardiac Investigational Laboratory and carry on the functions of a Cardiologist within the institution.

The appointment would carry the rank of Assistant Professor with an initial salary of $36,000.00 plus pension and other usual benefits. Further information as to these benefits could be obtained from Mr. Kargut (at the University Hospital).

The appointment is contingent on your agreement to the following:

1. A willingness to become knowledgeable of the problem-oriented medical record, to utilize the problem-oriented system in your ambulatory practice as well as on the inpatient service, and to assist in teaching the system to students and House Staff.

2. While on full salary to undertake a further period of intensive involvement with invasive techniques at an agreed-to centre for two months, as well as a minimum period of not less than one month receiving instruction in Echocardiography.

Since we are most anxious to proceed with planning of the laboratory, your appointment would commence at the earliest opportunity consistent with any obligation you may have to Dr. Somerville. I would hope that you could give some consideration to equipping the laboratory, even prior to joining us so that unnecessary delays in obtaining equipment could be minimized. In speaking with Dr. Lopez, I was impressed by

2.....

his willingness to provide whatever assistance we might wish to take advantage of.

I have indicated the desirability of recruiting a second Cardiologist so that service in continuity can be provided to the community when the laboratory has opened.

I am enclosing an application form from the Plains Health Centre. There are many other details which we might discuss once your application is being processed.

Yours sincerely,

Gerald E. Sinclair M.D.
Head, Department of Medicine

GES/jj
encl.

UNIVERSITY OF SASKATCHEWAN

SASKATOON, CANADA
S7N 0W0

July 30th, 1976

Dr. N. Habib,
Department of Medicine
Plains Health Centre
4500 Wascana Parkway
REGINA, Sask.

Dear Dr. Habib:

The Board of Governors has approved your appointment as Assistant Professor of Medicine (Regina) at the rate of $37,000 a year, from August 15, 1976. (For purposes of calculation of fringe benefits your University Component will be at the floor of the range plus three increments.)

It is a pleasure to advise you of this appointment and I trust you will enjoy your association with the University of Saskatchewan.

Yours sincerely,

R.W. Begg

RWB:M
c.c. Dr. Baltzan
     Dr. Sinclair
     Dean Murray
     Mr. Fox
     Personnel Office

UNIVERSITY OF SASKATCHEWAN

THE PRESIDENT

SASKATOON, CANADA
S7N 0W0

April 5th, 1979

Dr. N. Habib,
Department of Medicine
Plains Health Centre
4500 Wascana Parkway
REGINA, Sask.

Dear Dr. Habib:

The Board of Governors has confirmed the recommendation of the University Review Committee that you be granted tenure effective July 1, 1979.

May I congratulate you on the achievement of tenure and express the hope that you will continue to have a productive academic life at the University of Saskatchewan.

Yours sincerely,

R.W. Begg

RWB:MB
c.c. Personnel Office
     Dean
     Department Head

Regina Health District

17 January 1994

Dr. N. Habib
Plains Health Centre
REGINA, Saskatchewan

Dear Dr. Habib:

I am pleased to advise that effective this date the Board of Directors of the Regina Health District approved your appointment as Head of the Section of Cardiology for a three year term.

Yours truly,

Linda Lee Nilson, M.D.
Vice President Medical Services

LLN/sd

c.c. Dr. R. McKay, Head, Department of Medicine

Regina Health District

12 May 1997

Dr. N. Habib
Plains Health Centre
REGINA, Saskatchewan

Dear Dr. Habib:

I am pleased to advise that effective this date the Board of Directors of the Regina Health District approved your appointment as Head of the Section of Cardiology for an additional three year term.

Yours truly,

Mr. Dick Chinn
Vice President Operations - Medical

c.c.   Dr. R. McKay, Head, Department of Medicine

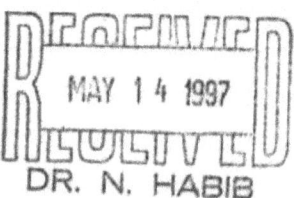
1440 – 14th Avenue, Regina, Saskatchewan S4P 0W5
(306) 766-4260   Fax (306) 766-4521

UNIVERSITY OF SASKATCHEWAN

College of Medicine

Health Sciences Building, 107 Wiggins Road
Saskatoon SK S7N 5E5 Canada
Faculty Affairs, Finance and Administration,
Research and Graduate Studies · Rm. B103
Phone: (306) 966-2673 Fax: (306) 966-6164
Admissions, Undergraduate, Postgraduate,
Medical Education · Rm. A204
Phone: (306) 966-6135 Fax: (306) 966-2601

July 14, 2008

Dr. N Habib
Midwest Medical Centre
2479 McCallum Road
Abbotsford BC V2S 3P8

Dear Dr. Habib,

I am pleased to inform you that on the recommendation of Dr. Tom Wilson, Head, Department of Medicine, your appointment as a Clinical Professor in the Department of Medicine, is being renewed until June 30, 2013.

On behalf of our students and residents, I thank you for your contributions to the teaching programs of the College of Medicine. Your participation is very much appreciated.

Sincerely,

William L. Albritton, MD, PhD, FRCP(C)
Dean of Medicine

WA/CZ/ssc

cc: Dr Tom Wilson, Head, Department of Medicine
cc: Dr Vern Hoeppner, Acting Head, Dept of medicine

299

Plains Health Centre

The renowned academic (teaching) hospital, Plains Health Centre.

The Plains Health Centre opened in 1974, serving as a tertiary referral and university training hospital for southern and eastern Saskatchewan from 1974 to 1998, during the well-known premiership of Honourable Allan Blakeney of the New Democratic Party. It was a splendid facility, with a design featuring single-bed rooms with attached toilet facilities for patients. It provided patient care in the branches of surgery and medicine, including an excellent cardiac science department that evolved during my period. It became a recognized training centre in those disciplines, as well as in family medicine. In 1987, the University of Saskatchewan decreased its support and/or discontinued most full-time professorships and teaching programs.

In 1998, the then-premier, Roy Romanow, also of the New Democratic Party, closed the Plains Health Centre to consolidate medical care, despite a hue and cry by the public and professionals. It was believed that there was political and personal interest of individuals at play. It was rather a blunder, in my assessment, that began to be realized with the passage of time. There had been a plan to build another tower linking to the existing one as an expansion for future needs, and there was an area for a helipad. After being closed as a hospital, the Plains Health Centre was converted into the Saskatchewan Institute of Applied Science and Technology. Now (2016), it seems that Saskatchewan's current government, led by Premier Brad Wall, may build a medical outpatient facility in the proximity of the former Plains Health Centre.

I had a real love for the institution. I was the establisher of the cardiology program there, and I worked as a physician, researcher, and professor there from 1974 until it closed in 1998. Once it was closed, I never put my foot into the building again. My mother passed away at this hospital, in room 834. Dr. Carter, Dr. Cuddington, Dr. Bachynski, and Dr. Sinclair looked after her. Dr. Alvarez was a consultant.

Our house at 9227 Wascana Mews was situated such that I could view the hospital from our back window. I used to say that Emperor Shah Jahan was placed by his son Aurangzeb in the Agra Fort Prison such that he could view the tomb, the Taj Mahal of his beloved wife, Mumtaz Mahal, from there. So it was with me and the Plains Health Centre.

I echo the sentiments of those people who wanted to keep that splendid facility active and progressive. When it went down the drain, it left a black mark on Premier Romanow and those who were involved in its demise.

Arrival in Regina

When we arrived in Regina, I dropped my family at the home of Dr. Chaudhry, whom I had met in Saskatoon. Dr. Sinclair and I met in the cafeteria of the Plains Health Centre. We chatted, and he took me around. We both seemed to be happy with each other. Subsequently, I received an appointment as a full-time assistant professor of medicine, with a tenured position at this institution, at a salary of $37,000 annually, in 1976.

My job was teaching and establishing the cardiology program at this institution, which had been built as an academic centre for Southern Saskatchewan. There was no academic activity in this part of Saskatchewan prior to this. Of course, residents and interns came to Regina for training at the Regina General Hospital.

I should like to mention that when I was desperate in Orlando and was trying to apply for a position, I did apply to the Regina General Hospital. They did not even respond to my letter. And now there I was, appointed an assistant professor of medicine in cardiology, with the responsibility of cardiology for all Southern Saskatchewan, at this very same institution.

Decision Error?

Was this decision right for me to achieve my academic goal? My academic goal was to do research and be recognized nationally and internationally as a cardiologist of academic repute. I accept that I achieved a reputation and achieved success, but I could not be an international speaker or researcher. In time, I realized that I was starting an institution and that that institution had to be established and grow to have its status recognized nationally and internationally. The prospect excited me, and I grabbed the first opportunity available to be in an academic position. But the decision was wrong! Be it as it may, this is a learning experience for others when choosing a career.

Cardiology Program

So it was that meetings and plans started regarding the establishment of a cardiology program at the Plains Health Centre. I received support from various sources and administrators. The amount of funding promised to me was very little, and so I refused to accept, emphasizing what minimum amount would be required for establishing the entire cardiology program, which would include the establishment of a cardiac catheterization laboratory for invasive and non-invasive procedures, to be supported by the non-invasive laboratories' equipment. On refusing, I also indicated a time frame that could not be delayed because, beyond it, I would have to seek other opportunities (which, at that point in time, I did not have). Certainly, I would have explored returning to the United States.

I was heard, and those in charge were convinced to provide me the funding. The planning began.

Meanwhile, I had been away from invasive procedures. In discussion with Dr. Sinclair, it was thought that I should refresh my cardiac catheterization skills. I had met Dr. Howard Zeft of Milwaukee (though I don't recall under what circumstances), and so I wrote to him. He asked me to come down to work with him and his group to refresh my invasive cardiology skills. At that time, there was no coronary angioplasty in Canada.

Meanwhile, everything required to initiate the cardiology program was in place. I went to Milwaukee for a period of three months, away from my family. It was very hard for me. The arrangement was made for me to stay as a paying guest in an elderly lady's house. She was a very nice person. She offered breakfast and gave me a room. I ate at St. Luke's Hospital, where I was attending the cardiac catheterization laboratory rotation with Drs. Zeft, Jack Manley, and James King. Dr. Zeft made me anxious, and it was difficult for me to do cardiac catheterization under his supervision. However, I managed.

I grew tired of eating in the hospital restaurant so much. When a room in the hospital became available, I moved to it. There was a kitchen outside the hospital's main building, and there was another doctor from India who had come for training under Dr. Dudley Johnson, a very eminent cardiac surgeon. We developed some friendly terms and, one day, decided to buy some utensils and have some chicken. We cooked our own food together in that kitchen, and it was the best food we'd had in our lifetime. *One acts when a limit to face the circumstance is reached unless the circumstance does not permit.* The three months of stay was completed, and although I visited Regina once during the three months for an important meeting on the establishment of cardiology, this was my final return.

A letter by Dr. Zeft about my involvement in refreshing my skills is cited below:

April 29, 1977

G. E. Sinclair, M.D., F.R.C.P.(C)
Professor & Head
Plains Health Centre,
4500 Wascana Parkway,
Regina, Saskatchewan.
S4S 5W9

Re: Naiyer Habib, M.D.

Dear Doctor Sinclair:

Dr. Naiyer Habib recently spent 3 months at St. Luke's Hospital in Milwaukee. He participated actively in our busy cardiology program. Doctor Habib arrived early in January of 1977 and remained with us until the end of March, 1977.

Doctor Habib was active in the cardiac catheterization program participating in one or two cardiac catheterization studies on most days. He also was busy with Doctor James King in his program of echocardiography. Furthermore, Doctor Habib was involved in the clinical side of things as well. He took part in the running of our busy Coronary Care Unit and in the care of various medical and cardiac clinical problems.

Doctor Habib was a very pleasant addition to our section for the three months that he spent with us. He is a dedicated and competent physician and Cardiologist. He is anxious to initiate a program of cardiac catheterization at your institution. With his three months in Milwaukee, I feel he has made a good start in this regard.

Sincerely your,

Howard J. Zeft, M.D., F.A.C.C.

HJZ/dm
cc: Naiyer Habib, M.D.

I never stopped keeping up with the pace of evolution in cardiology and bringing up-to-date practices to my cardiology program at the Plains Health Centre. The major development of Angioplasty is noted elsewhere in the book under that heading to the stage of performing multivessel stenting with Radial Approach.

PRECEPTORSHIP

- Invasive cardiology: January 6, 1977, to March 31, 1977, at St Luke's Hospital, University of Wisconsin (Milwaukee).

- Echo/Doppler colour (Dr. Ng Pandian): January 26/27, 1988 to February 1-5, 1988, at New England Medical Center, Tufts University (Boston, Massachusetts).

- Cardiac transplantation & endomyocardial biopsy (Dr. J.R. Burton): November 27-30, 1989, at the University of Alberta Hospital (Edmonton, Alberta).

- Radial approach for coronary Intervention and Catheterization – hands-on experience with eleven patients (Dr. G. Barbeau): April 18-19, 2000, at the University of Laval Hospital (Laval, Quebec).

START OF CARDIOLOGY PROGRAM AT THE PLAINS HEALTH CENTRE

Cardiac catheterization was performed by the radiologist Dr. Rodko and the cardiac surgeon Dr. Boyd in the department of radiology at the Regina General Hospital. Drs. Boyd and Edward Busse later performed cardiac surgery, too. But there was no cardiologist. One came and left after a short stay. Internists Drs. Gerald Sinclair, Ewing, and Kumar filled this need.

Furthermore, there was no stress testing, Holter monitor for arrhythmia, or 2-D echocardiograph (1970s) in Regina at all. I borrowed a bike from the physiotherapy department to be hooked up to an ECG machine to perform stress tests, which served the practical purpose for the time being. Cliff Beaton was very helpful to me. He was the main supervisor of the cardiac facility as it existed then. He was also the supervisor for the diagnostic facilities of neurology. Subsequently, a treadmill was purchased, and this was initiated after training the staff. There was only an M-mode echo (providing a 1-D view) on my arrival. Subsequently, 2-D echocardiography and Holter monitoring were purchased. It required several meetings with the administrative and ministerial staff to convince them of the need. At last, we had a well-established cardiology program. Things started to roll.

After my return from Milwaukee, I started cardiac catheterization at the Regina General Hospital, which was run by Dr. Rodko, who was a radiologist but not a cardiologist. Because of some conflict, I gave this up at the Regina General Hospital. We planned to do catheterization in the department of radiology at the Plains Health Centre. We did one procedure and faced a problem. We decided that we would wait for the laboratory to start, and the work of the cardiac catheterization laboratory had already begun.

I held the position of director of Cardiac Laboratory Investigations and, subsequently, head of cardiology. After visiting various institutions, I established one of the best cardiac catheterization laboratories in the nation. The equipment was biplane rotating, from Philips, the newest technology in cardiac catheterization.

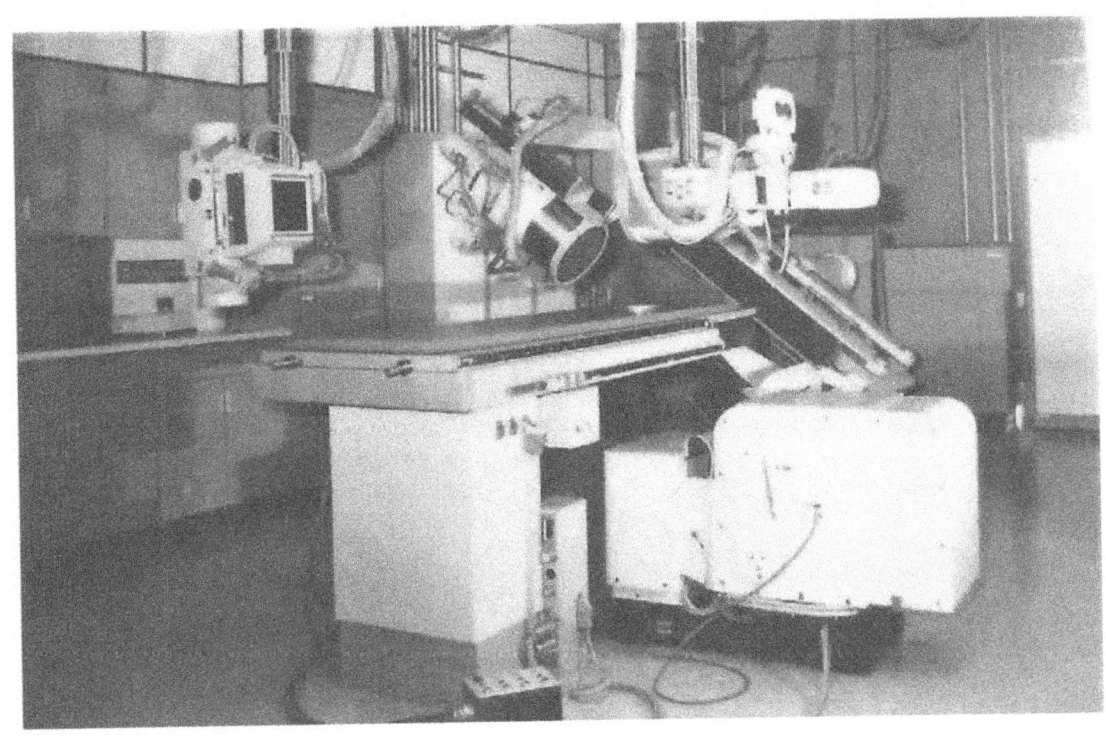

Cardiac Cath Laboratory, first established in 1979 by Dr. Habib.

Dr. N. Habib

Upgraded in 1993.

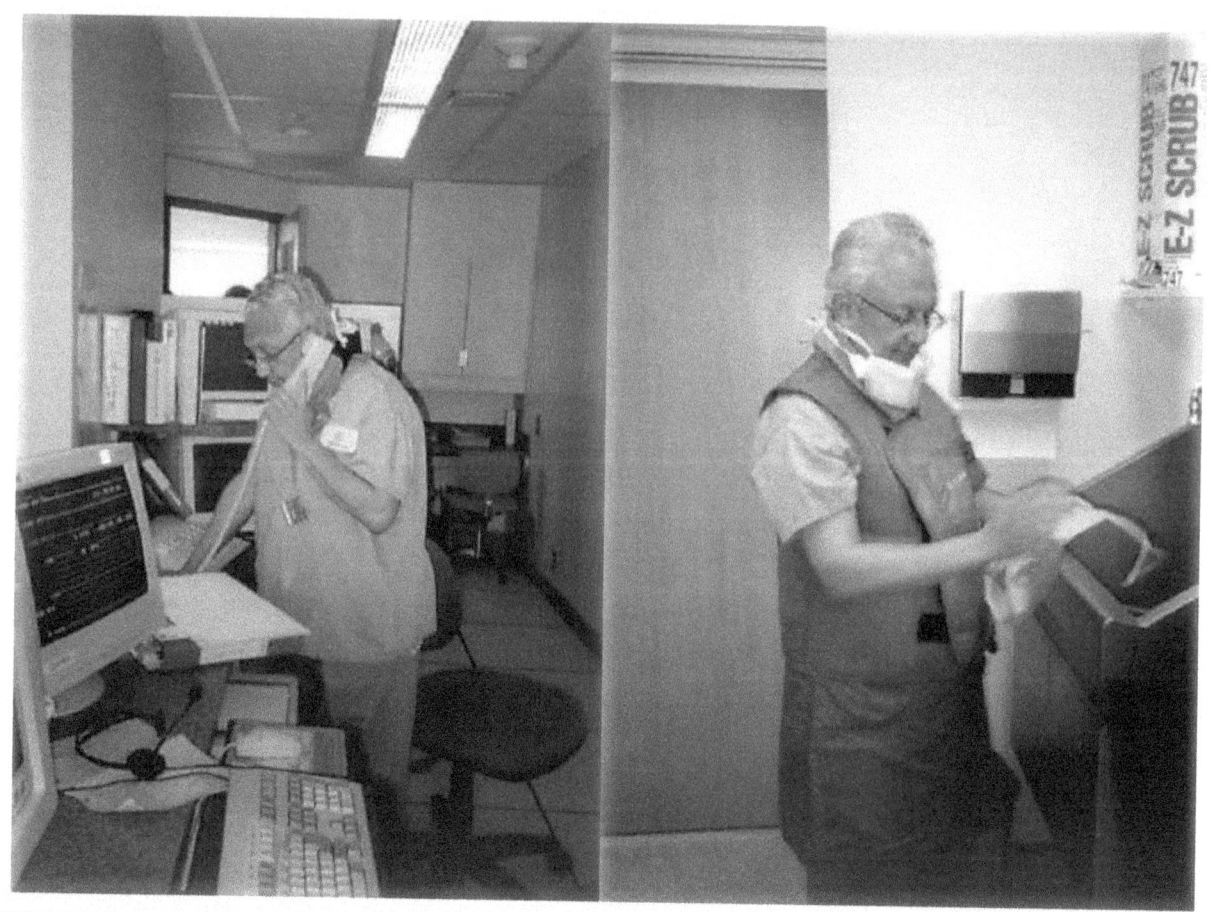

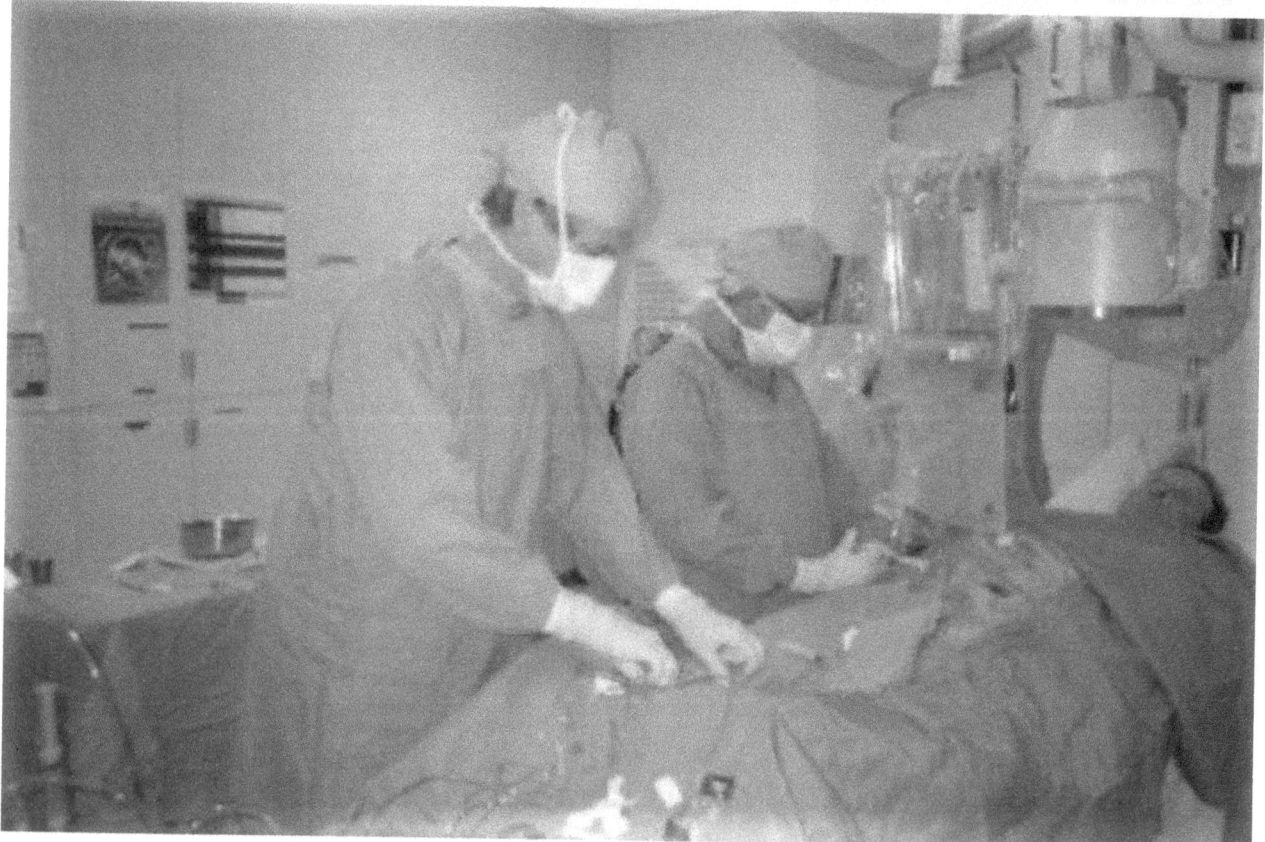

My day in the Cardiac Catheterization Laboratory for catheterization
and coronary intervention; Pat Lundy assisting.

A number of projects designed to improve the care of cardiac patients in the Regina Health District were embarked upon and established, including the initiation and establishment of cardiac investigation laboratories: Cardiac Catheterization Laboratory (April 1979) for diagnostic to therapeutic intervention, Exercise Laboratory (1978), Ambulatory Holter Monitoring (May 1982), upgrading echocardiography service to 2-D (November 1982), and a Pacemaker Clinic (October 28, 1983).

The cardiac care and cardiac surveillance units were modernized. I renamed these from the telemetry unit, borrowing the name from the Milwaukee General Hospital, where I had refreshed my cardiac catheterization skills.

I initiated and performed the first coronary angioplasty in Regina (and, possibly, Saskatchewan, unless Dr. Lopez did before me in Saskatoon) on April 27, 1983, at the Plains Health Centre, which was eventually followed by the coronary stenting program. I initiated intracoronary streptokinase thrombolysis treatment for acute myocardial infarction in June 1984. I wanted to initiate valvuloplasty, for which I had attended a course in Boston, but considering various situations I abandoned it. Angioplasty was in its initial phase worldwide.

I learned and performed coronary angioplasty and stenting as an interventional cardiologist, advancing from simple lesions to complex multi-vessel lesions with Radial Approach until I retired in 2004 from my active cardiology practice.

I was fortunate to learn from the grandfather of angioplasty, Dr. Andreas Gruentzig, by attending his demonstration course. He was the one to develop balloon angioplasty first in Switzerland, in September 1977. Dr. Gruentzig was born in Germany in 1939 and passed away in an airplane crash in 1985.

Dr. Andreas Roland Gruentzig

All work and stages of the cardiology program in Regina are confirmed in the following letter from Mr. Dick Chinn:

PLAINS HEALTH CENTRE

4500 WASCANA PARKWAY
REGINA • SASKATCHEWAN S4S 5W9
TELEPHONE (306) 584-6211
FAX (306) 584-6334

Administration FAX (306)584-6296

October 5, 1993

To Whom It May Concern:

RE: DR. NAIYER HABIB

This is to confirm that Dr. Habib was appointed to the Medical Staff of the Plains Health Centre on August 9, 1976. At that time he was also appointed Assistant Professor of Medicine, College of Medicine, University of Saskatchewan. He has been subsequently elevated to Clinical Professor of Medicine. He is also currently on the Active staff of the Regina Health District.

Since his appointment to staff in 1976, Dr. Habib has served on various hospital committees (ie. C.P.R. Committee, Health Records Committee) and in various administrative capacities. He has been the Head of the Section of Cardiology, Director of the Cardiac Catheterization Laboratory, and on the Executive of the General Medical Staff including the position of President. As a result of the latter roles, he has also served on the hospital's Medical Advisory Committee.

Dr. Habib was initially recruited to the Plains Health Centre primarily to develop and supervise the Cardiac Investigational Laboratory. Since that time he has not only been instrumental in that aspect of the hospital's cardiology program but has been involved in the following activities:

1.   Cardiovascular exercise laboratory - opened in 1978.

2.   Modern Cardiac Catheterization Laboratories with facilities of hemodynamics, cardiac catheterization and electrophysiological studies - April 1979.

3.   Echocardiography M and 2-Dimensional Modes - opened November 1981.

4.   Ambulatory Holter's monitoring - opened May 1982.

5. Modernized the Cardiac Care Unit with new computerized monitoring system and provision of hemodynamic facilities - opened January 1979.

6. Cardiac Surveillance Unit with facilities of eight bed telemetry system along with computerized arrhythmia monitoring system - opened October 1979.

7. Coronary angioplasty - first performed and established the facility April 27, 1983. Multi-vessel/multi-lesion angioplasty - 1989.

8. Pacemaker Clinic established October 28, 1983.

9. Intracoronary streptokinase thrombolysis treatment initiated and established June 1984.

Dr. Habib has been a very valuable member of the medical staff and the medical teaching program at the Plains Health Centre.

Yours sincerely,

Dick Chinn
Executive Director
Plains Health Centre.

Despite my pioneering work, I did not receive the Order of Saskatchewan. My answer to a question about this is noted in the About The Authors.

A second cardiologist, Dr. Jesus Hernandez, arrived and started working in the Regina General Hospital. He was also an interventional cardiologist who had trained in Edmonton, Alberta. Dr. Sinclair and I persuaded him to come to the Plains Health Centre. Thus, we were the two cardiologists on the team.

My Reputation Established

With the following case management, my reputation was established in Regina, and I earned respect:

1- Cardioversion with Theoretical Contraindication

A young girl was almost moribund in shock due to atrial fibrillation (chaotic beating of the heart) and very rapid heartbeat in the intensive care unit. She needed immediate cardioversion (electric shock treatment to the heart area of the chest) to reverse this rhythm to a normal heartbeat, so I was called. Her potassium (K) level was about 1.2 milliequivalent (mEq)—normal being 3.5, at the minimum. Cardioversion with such a K level was contraindicated. Potassium is given by intravenous drip at a rate which, if followed, means the patient might not have survived. So, I gave her a large bolus of potassium into her vein by calculating the amount that would normalize her potassium level. Then, I shocked her with cardioversion. With rectification of her heart rhythm, she recovered to a normal state within minutes and was out of danger. Of course, the surrounding personnel were staring at me with gestures of suspicion and of not accepting what I was doing. A physician with theoretical knowledge makes his judgement by facing the circumstance and modifying the prevailing guideline. That was what I did. This left a lasting impression and confidence in me. Dr. Rusnak, then head of surgery, was full of praise. The patient was in her post-gallbladder surgery in the intensive care unit.

We read and learn, but we face circumstances in which our own intelligence is challenged to achieve success. To that, I say guidance from God!

2- Foreign Body Removal from Pulmonary Artery with No Special Equipment Available in the Facility

An intravenous cannula[69] of about three inches floated from the inserted site of the vein, breaking loose from its hub into the right heart. Dr. McAlpine, head of anesthesiology, called me. We had already established the Cardiac Catheterization Laboratory but did not have any setup for removing a foreign object from the heart. The available setup was in the primitive stage in the '70s. So, I planned it in my own way. I placed an introducer in the right femoral vein and passed a pigtail catheter—a catheter with its end curved in the shape of a pig's tail—used for cardiac catheterization. The foreign body—the cannula—was in the pulmonary artery. I manipulated it in the heart to get the cannula twisted into the catheter loop under fluoroscopy. With some hard work, I was able to do it. I pulled it into the introducer as much as it could be. Feeling and seeing under fluoroscopy that it might have anchored in the introducer, I pulled the catheter out cautiously, leaving the cannula anchored in the introducer. Then, I removed the anchored cannula with some lung biopsy forceps. It required multiple attempts to trap the cannula in the heart and anchor it ultimately in the introducer.

Angioplasty

Angioplasty is a procedure to widen a narrowed or open obstructed artery of the heart by introducing a balloon over a wire.

The practice of cardiology was evolving. As mentioned above, coronary angioplasty was introduced by Dr. Andreas Gruentzig in Zurich, Switzerland, in 1979. Physicians from the United States started to go to observe him perform the procedure. He was persuaded to come to Emory University in Atlanta, Georgia, where he started giving courses on angioplasty. Dr. Hernandez and I attended the course in 1984, as we intended to start angioplasty at the Plains Health Centre. After that, I also went to the Montreal Heart Institute to observe the procedure with Dr. Paul David, who is well-known in Canada for this procedure. He had very elaborate arrangements for performing it. I reviewed many of his recorded video procedures on his patients, and they gave me significant know-how. I initiated the angioplasty at the Plains Health Centre, and I performed the first angioplasty in Regina.

---

[69] A thin tube inserted into a vein or body cavity to administer medicine, drain off fluid, or insert a surgical instrument.

Coronary stenting evolved using a wire over a balloon to be delivered at the site by opening the blocked artery with better results. I observed the procedure under Calgary's Dr. Merrill Knudtson, another renowned Canadian cardiologist. I observed his coronary stenting on eight simple to complex cases in his laboratory. Subsequently, Dr. Garbe, an associate, and I performed our first stenting in Regina under the supervision of Dr. Dean Traboulsi, an associate of Dr. Knudtson.

I would like to point out that I succeeded in these procedures without any hands-on training, which was not the norm then. In short order, I started doing coronary angioplasty and stenting through the small artery at the wrist, the radial approach, with hands-on experience for a week in April 2000 under a pioneer of this approach, Dr. G. Barbeau of the University of Laval, Quebec.

Health and Fitness

The Leader-Post   Regina, Saskatchewan   Thursday, April 19, 1984   A 13

Help for heart patients

By Coleen Dundas
of The Leader-Post

Patients with first stages of heart disease can now be treated surgically in Regina without having to undergo an open heart operation.

The new procedure, called coronary angioplasty, basically clears blocked coronary arteries by condensing the fatty matter into the artery walls with a tiny balloon, leaving a clear passage, explained cardiologist Dr. Nalyer Habib, head of the team that performed the procedure for the first time in Regina early this year.

The patient is awake during the two-hour procedure, said Habib, chief cardiologist at the Plains Health Centre.

Developed by a Swedish surgeon, the procedure has been in use since 1979 in some parts of the world. It has been performed in Saskatoon before this year, but the procedure is relatively new to Regina, he said.

The open-heart surgery team also stands ready for any emergency during the procedure rushed the first patient into the operating room for coronary bypass surgery, but since then the coronary angioplasty has been completely successful twice, Habib said.

The new procedure will be used for patients who have one or two of three main heart arteries blocked in a definite area, he said.

This is determined after several tests, including an angiogram, in which a dye visible to X-ray is inserted into the heart through a catheter, which is pushed along a major artery from the groin to the heart, Habib explained.

On an X-ray, the dye will not be seen through a blockage in an artery. Thus the blank area indicates the size and place of the blockage, called arterial sclerosis.

An angioplast is a similar procedure.

The groin area where the catheter will be inserted is anesthetized. Watching the procedure

on X-ray, the physician pushes the catheter up through the artery to the blocked part of the coronary blood vessel near the heart.

A wire, tipped with platinum that also can be easily seen on X-ray, is inserted through the catheter into the blockage. This wire holds the tiny balloon, which is about the circumference of a pen refill.

Using a syringe, the balloon is expanded with air as many times as it takes to compress the blockage into the artery walls, Habib said.

Coronary angioplasty is a favorable alternative to open heart surgery because only local anesthesia is used, the benefit is immediate, the procedure itself takes half as much time, and the patient is out of hospital in four or three days, compared with 10-14 days after open heart surgery.

But angioplasty is only an option for patients — usually the younger ones — whose coronary artery blockage is localized, Habib said.

In older patients, arterial sclerosis is usually spread throughout the coronary arteries, he said.

As with open-heart surgery, coronary angioplasty is a treatment not a cure for heart disease.

The coronary arteries become blocked again in about one of five cases that undergo angioplasty, Habib said.

If blockage does recur in angioplast patients, it will likely happen within the first six months following the procedure, Habib said. If it does, the angioplast can easily be repeated.

But in most patients, through a process called "healing fitness," the arteries strengthen to keep themselves clear, the cardiologist said.

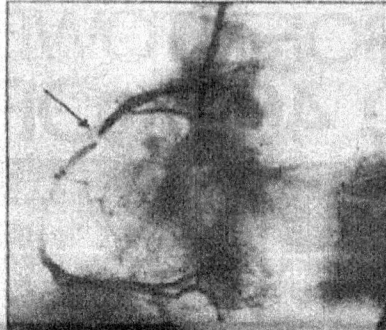

Arrow points to blockage in coronary artery

Dr. Nalyer Habib shows catheter used for coronary angioplasty

312

THE DEPARTMENTS OF MEDICINE (CARDIOLOGY)
and RADIOLOGY
EMORY UNIVERSITY SCHOOL OF MEDICINE
EMORY UNIVERSITY, ATLANTA, GEORGIA

DEMONSTRATIONS IN PERCUTANEOUS
TRANSLUMINAL CORONARY ANGIOPLASTY

ATLANTA, SEPTEMBER 16-20, 1984

CONFIRMATION

I confirm that

Dr. ~~Mrs.~~ *Naiyer Habib*

has attended the course of Demonstrations in Percutaneous Transluminal
Coronary Angioplasty XII in Atlanta. The scientific program lasted from
September 17-20, 1984, from 8:30 — 12:00 noon and 2:00 — 6:00 p.m.

A. Gruentzig, M.D.

313

PROGRAM

SUNDAY, SEPTEMBER 16, 1984

4:00 p.m. REGISTRATION
Woodruff Health Sciences Center
Administration Building

5:30-7:00 WELCOME PARTY
Woodruff Medical Center
Administration Building

MONDAY, SEPTEMBER 17, 1984

8:30 a.m. INTRODUCTION
J. Willis Hurst, M.D.

8:40 UP-TO-DATE RESULTS OF PTA

9:00 DEMONSTRATIONS OF ANGIOPLASTIES

11:00 Discussion

12:00 noon Lunch on your own

2:00 DEMONSTRATIONS OF ANGIOPLASTIES

4:00 Discussion and reports from other groups

6:00 Adjourn

TUESDAY, SEPTEMBER 18, 1984

8:30 a.m. DEMONSTRATIONS OF ANGIOPLASTIES

11:00 Discussion

12:00 noon Lunch on your own

2:00 DEMONSTRATIONS OF ANGIOPLASTIES

4:00 Discussion and reports from other groups

6:00 Adjourn

WEDNESDAY, SEPTEMBER 19, 1984

8:30 a.m. DEMONSTRATIONS OF ANGIOPLASTIES

11:00 Discussion

12:00 noon Lunch on your own

2:00 DEMONSTRATIONS OF ANGIOPLASTIES

4:00 Discussion and reports from other groups

6:00 Adjourn

THURSDAY, SEPTEMBER 20, 1984

8:30 a.m. DEMONSTRATIONS OF ANGIOPLASTIES

11:00 Discussion

1:00 p.m. Adjourn

2:30-10:30 Leave for recreational activities and
final party at Stone Mountain Park.

Emory University
School of Medicine

Demonstrations in Percutaneous Transluminal Angioplasty XII
by
ANDREAS GRUENTZIG

September 16-20, 1984
ATLANTA, GEORGIA

EMORY UNIVERSITY
SCHOOL OF MEDICINE

THE ROBERT W. WOODRUFF
HEALTH SCIENCES CENTER

Institut de Cardiologie de Montréal

5000 est, rue Bélanger, Montréal, Qué., H1T 1C8 — Tél.: 376-3330

Montreal, July 8, 1982.

RE: HABIB, Dr. Naiyer.

TO WHOM IT MAY CONCERN:

This letter is to certify that the above mentioned cardiologist
has spent one week beginning July 5 to 9, 1982 in the cardiac
laboratory of the Montreal Heart Institute in order to study a
percutaneous transluminal coronary angioplasty.

He was exposed to dilatations procedures as well as review a
videotapes of multiple procedures and controls realized in the
past 2 years.

Yours sincerely,

Paul Robert David, M.D.,
Cardiologist.

PRD/cg.

MERRIL L. KNUDTSON M.D.
1403 29th STREET N.W.
CALGARY, ALBERTA T2N 2T9
(403) 670-1559

95/6/29

To Whom It May Concern:

Please be advised that Dr. R. Habib spent three days at Foothills Hospital observing intracoronary stenting cases. During this time he witnessed 8 cases of complicated and simple cases.

If you have any questions about this experience, please call me at the above number.

Merril R. Knudtson, MD, FRCP(C)
Director
Cardiovascular Laboratories

I also attended a course in interventional cardiology by Dr. F. Mason Sones, who initiated the procedure of selective coronary angiography at the Cleveland Clinic in Ohio from June 11-13, 1997.

Thrombolysis

Thrombolysis is a process in which agents, Thrombolytic agents—such as streptokinase and, subsequently, others are used to prevent further damage to the heart muscle by dissolving blocking clots in the coronary artery to reestablish circulation. These agents were administered intravenously to the suffering patients with variable success.

It has now (2018) for some time been replaced by coronary angioplasty and stenting.

Medical Education Participation

Guest Speaker

I lectured as a guest speaker on various cardiology topics over the years in Regina and at various other places. I organized and chaired many continuing medical education conferences in Saskatchewan. I was the first to organize a cardiology conference in Regina, with guest speakers, in 1979. I was invited as a guest speaker by Dr. Garbe, my associate cardiologist and then a family physician, when he was opening a cardiac-care bed in the Estevan Hospital.

Teaching

I was teaching the medical students, interns, and residents. I was happy to hear their appreciation of my teaching, and I continued teaching till my last day when I moved from Regina.

I was happy if my residents (assigned to me for doctor training) told me that they chose cardiology as their career, especially interventional cardiology (cardiac catheterization and angioplasty). From time to time, this would come up in our conversation while waiting for classes or chatting after classes were over.

I once asked a very sharp resident what his choice would be. He smiled and told me he would specialize in catheterization. I queried him: just catheterization or interventional? He laughed and said urology, where a catheter is used for the urogenital system, as well. We laughed.

I had another excellent resident. She used to watch cardiology procedures when I performed angioplasties. I thought she would choose my specialty. I told her one day that she was very good and remarked that she seemed to be interested in what I did. She immediately responded, "No, I will do internal medicine." I asked why, and she replied, "I can't take it, Dr. Habib. It is stressful. Some patients may die or may not recover in my hands." I smiled and said, "Yes, it is true. Choose what you like."

The world runs, fulfilling its various needs by people of various interests as created by the Greatest Manager of all, God. We see these in our day-to-day life: farmers, labourers, firefighters, scientists, men and women, and on and on.

Teaching medical students, last session, 2004.

MEMORANDUM

Date_____ November 22, 1979

To: _____ DR. N. HABIB

From: _____ DR. G.E. SINCLAIR, HEAD, DEPARTMENT OF MEDICINE (REGINA)

Re: _____ TEACHING ACTIVITY AUDIT - ACADEMIC YEAR 1978-79

The following comments have been made by house staff attached to your service during the academic year ending June, 1979. The audit forms themselves are available for your scrutiny at any time upon request.

1. The rotation is excellent and Dr. Habib makes it his duty to teach residents. It is just a pity that residents have to spend a lot of valuable time getting patients transferred out of CCU and CSU because their own physicians are reluctant to do so themselves. Also being tied up with critically ill patients in CCU often prevents residents from attending to other matters of educational interest such as assisting and performing of procedures, exercise testing, out-patient clinics and seeing consults.

2. Very good rotation. Teaching good. Difficulty with the Catheterization Lab not being open and somewhat lacked the experience. Good to have CCU rotation. Full control and backup adequate.

3. CCU rotation was very helpful in learning procedures that is CVP, Swan Ganz, temporary pacemakers. The workload was ideal. Dr. Habib was excellent in presenting the principals in treatment of cardiac conditions.

4. I felt I could benefit from Dr. Habib's knowledge and especially as I had not done a rotation in cardiology previously. He is very pleasant and eager to help when called upon.

Dr. G.E. Sinclair, Head
Department of Medicine (Regina)

Medical Research And Publication

From a letter written by Linda Picot, secretary of research, from a research application (CHSRF-Research) clinical research and development program, Regina:

"Research projects as co-investigator included the internationally recognized study: DIG (Digitalis Investigation Group) Trial, HOPE (Heart Outcome Prevention Evaluation), HOPE-2, Resolved study (Randomized Evaluation Strategies of Left Ventricular Dysfunction), ALIVE (Azimilide post-Infarct Survival Evaluation trial), Assent (Assessment of the Safety and Efficacy of New Thrombolytic Agent), Symphony TriAl (Sibrafiban Versus Aspirin to Yield Maximum Protection from Ischemic Heart Disease Events Post-Acute Coronary Syndrome),

319

OASIS 2 (Organization to Assess Strategies for Ischemic Syndrome), Cure (Clopidogrel in Unstable Angina to Prevent Recurrent Ischemic Events), second symphony, React (Review of Education on ACE Inhibitors in Congestive Heart Failure Treatment), Overture (Omapatrilat Versus Enalapril Randomized Trial of Utility in Reducing Events), Sportif 5, efficacy and safety study of the oral direct thrombin inhibitor H376/95 compared with dose-adjusted warfarin (Coumadin) in the prevention of stroke and systemic embolic events in patients with atrial fibrillation)."

Other medical publications dating back to 1966:

Reprinted from the Journal of the Association of Physicians of India,
July 1966, Vol. 14, No. 7.

EVALUATION OF ROUTINE USE OF CORTICOSTEROIDS IN THE TREATMENT OF ENTERIC FEVER

A Comparative Study of 300 Cases:

C. P. Thakur, Naiyer Habib and Prof. M. Das

North Carolina Medical Journal

OWNED AND PUBLISHED BY
THE MEDICAL SOCIETY OF THE STATE OF NORTH CAROLINA

Reprinted from the NORTH CAROLINA MEDICAL
JOURNAL, Vol. 30, No. 8. August, 1969, Copyright
1969 Medical Society of the State of North Carolina.

Coronary Artery Aneurysm

Report of a Case

TAKEY CRIST, M.D.,* AND NAIYER HABIB, M.D.**

Pacemaker Click
A Clinical Diagnosis

Naiyer Habib, M.D., and Ralph D. Lach, M.D.

The Ohio State Medical Journal, January 1972

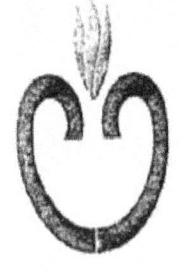

ANNUAL MEETING — CANADIAN CARDIOVASCULAR SOCIETY

OCTOBER 29, 30, 31 — NOVEMBER 1, 1986

OTTAWA, ONTARIO

OFFER OF PAPER FOR SCIENTIFIC PROGRAM

THE IMPORTANCE OF ATRIOVENTRICULAR SYNCHRONY IN [E]
INFERIOR MYOCARDIAL INFARCTION WITH RIGHT
VENTRICULAR DYSFUNCTION. M. Matangi*, G. Garbe,
N. Habib, J. Hernandez. Plains Health Centre,
Regina, Sask.

IMPORTANT

THE CANADIAN JOURNAL OF
CARDIOLOGY

May 1989   Volume 5 Number 4

Atenolol for the prevention of arrhythmias following coronary artery   229
bypass grafting

Murray F. Matangi, Judee Strickland, George J. Garbe, Naiyer Habib, Asish K. Basu, John J. Burgess, Andrew Maitland, Edward F.G. Busse

Supraventricular nonsinus tachycardia occurs in the immediate postoperative period
in 20 to 40% of patients following coronary artery bypass surgery. A double-blind, randomized,
placebo controlled trial of 70 patients undergoing this procedure indicates that atenolol is
extremely effective in preventing such arrhythmias

Contents continued on page V

Academic Membership And Fellowship Award

(From a letter by the secretary of research for a research application):

"Dr. Habib is a member of numerous local, provincial, national, and international medical associations. He is a fellow of the Royal College of Physicians and Surgeons of Canada (FRCPC), the American College of Cardiology (FACC), the American College of Physicians (FACP), and the College of Chest Physicians (FCCP). He is a member of the Canadian Medical Association, the Canadian Association of Interventional Cardiologists, the

Canadian Cardiovascular Society, and the Canadian Medical Protective Association. He is also a member of the American Heart Association. He was a member of the Saskatchewan Medical Association and now of the British Columbia Medical Association. He was a founder and past president of the Regina Cardiac Society and was a member of the Saskatchewan Heart Foundation. He served on committees with the Saskatchewan Medical Association, the Saskatchewan Heart Foundation, and the College of Physicians and Surgeons of Saskatchewan."

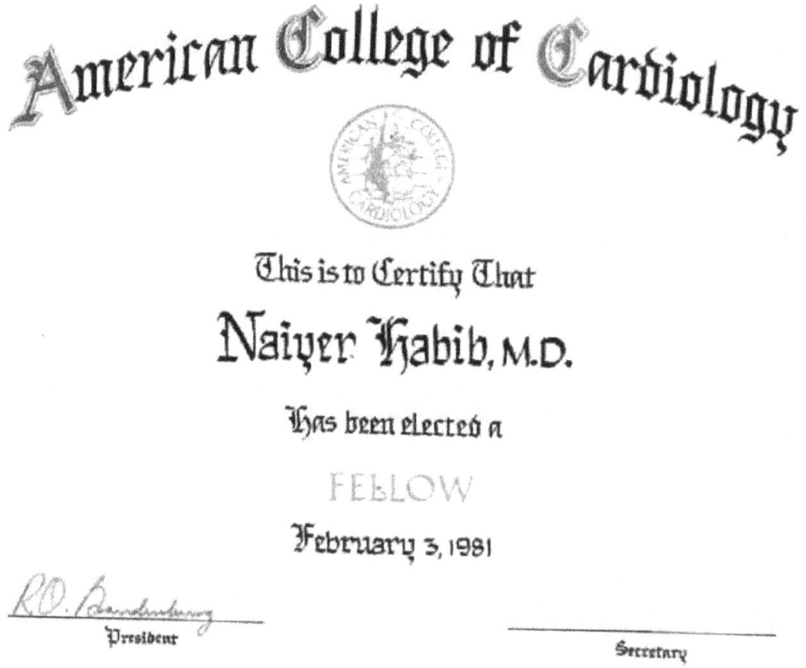

American College of Cardiology

This is to Certify That

Naiyer Habib, M.D.

Has been elected a

FELLOW

February 3, 1981

R.O. Brandenburg
President

_____
Secretary

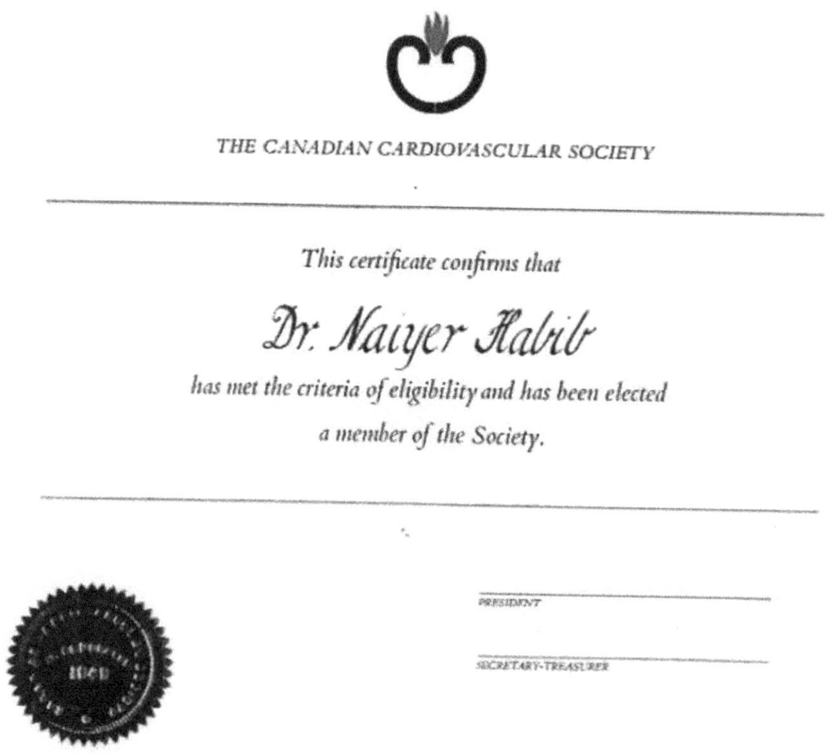

THE CANADIAN CARDIOVASCULAR SOCIETY

_____

This certificate confirms that

Dr. Naiyer Habib

has met the criteria of eligibility and has been elected
a member of the Society.

_____

PRESIDENT

SECRETARY-TREASURER

American College of Physicians

Be it known to all to whom these letters may come that

Naiyer Habib

has been elected a

Fellow of the American College of Physicians

In witness whereof the Seal of the College and the signatures of the proper officers are affixed

Given in the City of Philadelphia this   sixteenth   day of   April   in the year 1982.

Thomas F. Frawley
President

George T. Lukemeyer
Secretary General

American College of Chest Physicians

This is to certify that

Naiyer Habib, M.D.

has been elected a

Fellow

of the

American College of Chest Physicians
by the Board of Regents

the fourth day of October, nineteen hundred and eighty-eight.
In Witness Whereof, we have affixed our signatures.

A. Jay Block MD
President

Edward A. Rosberg
Treasurer

Academic Recognition

Pasque Hospital — Plains Health Centre — Wascana Hospital

INFO — MEDICA

The Medical Staff News Letter of the South Saskatchewan Hospital Centre

Spring, 1980, Vol. 1, No. 2

THE PLAINS HEALTH CENTRE

CARDIOVASCULAR INVESTIGATION LABORATORIES

The Cardiovascular Investigation Laboratories are located on Level 3, adjacent to Ambulatory Care and Nuclear Medicine. The Unit opened in April, 1979 under the direction of Dr. N. Habib.

It offers the services of Cardiac Angiography and Cardiovascular Exercise Tolerance Testing.

Cardiac Angiography is done using a Phillips Polydiagnost C. This equipment is capable of simultaneous multiple projections using A-P and lateral cameras. The A-P camera and tube are mounted on a motorized, push button controlled C-arm. This allows the patient to remain stationary on the table and the various views and projections are accomplished by manipulating the C-arm from the control panel on the table. In case of an emergency, the entire arm can be swung clear of the patient. The generator is capable of producing high quality film and automatically adjusts the exposure according to the girth of the patient. Computer technology forewarns the Technologist if incorrect technique is used. The equipment's bi-plane capabilities allow for two simultaneous views of the left ventriculogram with a single injection. This is particularly advantageous in patients with poor left ventricular function and those who are at high risk.

An analysis of one hundred cases studied highlighted the magnitude of the problem in showing that an improved diagnosis was obtained in 54% of studies with multiple projections for coronary angiography when compared with conventional views obtained with standard radiological equipment. In 33.5%, the lesions were upgrade and in 20.5%, lesions were unmasked (Aldridge).

The Laboratory is also equipped with a multi-channel physiological recorder for monitoring the patient's ECG and pressure wave forms. It is also capable of recording HIS Bundle Electrograms for the study of conduction defects.

From the information obtained from the physiological monitor and cine-film, calculations are done to determine valve areas, ejection fractions, intra cardiac and/or vascular shunts, valvular flow rates, cardiac outputs, L.V. myocardial contractility, O_2 saturations, etc.

The Cardiac Exercise testing equipment is a three channel ECG-automated treadmill. A 12 lead ECG is automatically recorded at three minute intervals during and after exercising on the treadmill. At the completion of the test, a histogram is produced showing speed and elevation or depression and the S-T integral. The equipment can be manually operated to suit the needs of the individual patient if so desired.

Besides routine Cardiac Exercise Testing, the facility is utilized in doing post exercise Thallium Cardiac Imaging.

DEPARTMENT OF MEDICINE

June 7, 1982

Dr. Naiyer Habib
Department of Medicine
Plains Health Centre
Regina, Sask.
S4S 5W9

Dear Naiyer:

I have received a copy of your May 25, 1982 letter to Dr. G.E. Sinclair in which you indicate your wish to resign your tenured academic full-time appointment as Associate Professor in the Department of Medicine, College of Medicine, University of Saskatchewan, effective September 1, 1982. The Department of Medicine regrets your decision in this regard but will assume you have arrived at this unequivocal decision for good reason after careful and considered deliberation. The Department of Medicine wishes to acknowledge and express its most sincere gratitude to you for your commitment and dedication to development of excellence within the Department of Medicine, particularly as related to teaching and patient care at the Plains Health Centre in Regina. The Department of Medicine recognizes your major accomplishments in establishing an excellent cardiology facility and service at the Plains Health Centre in Regina.

I would be most pleased, with recommendation from the Head, Department of Medicine, at the Plains Health Centre, to forward a recommendation that you be appointed as a Clinical Associate Professor in the Department of Medicine, College of Medicine, University of Saskatchewan, effective September 1, 1982.

I am aware that this has not been an easy decision for you to make throughout a period of most sincere deliberation. I wish to extend to you the most sincere thanks and best wishes, both personal and from the Department of Medicine, in your modified future career goals.

I would be most pleased to further discuss with you as related to any present or future details in your further planning.

Best regards.

Yours sincerely,

R. Marvin Bala, M.D., F.R.C.P.(C)
Professor and Head

RMB/mp

339

May 5, 2004

Dr. N. Habib,
Regina General Hospital,
1440 - 14th Avenue,
Regina, Saskatchewan.
S4P 0W5

Dear Naiyer:

Thanks very much for your letter. I wish you very well in your
retired and semi-retired life.

We will be pleased to have you maintain your hospital privileges
until the end of the year.

The Region and the Province owe you a tremendous debt of
gratitude for your service and your leadership. Your dedication
has been one of the single most important reasons for the quality
of the services that is being provided. I too am having
frustrations with the constraints imposed by the difficult
financial times.

May I also thank you for your friendship, your guidance and your
advice.

                        Best personal regards,

JDMcH/ep   James D. McHattie, M.D., FRCPC
                        Head, Department of Medicine
                        Regina Qu'Appelle Health Region

cc: Dr. O.P. Sood
     Dr. B. Laursen
     Mr. Dwight Nelson

Regina Qu'Appelle
HEALTH REGION

28 September 2004

Dr. N. Habib
3rd Floor Medical Office Wing
Regina General Hospital
REGINA, SK

Dear Dr. Habib:

I write on behalf of the Senior Management Team to express our best wishes on your retirement after 28 years of dedicated service to the patients of Regina and southern Saskatchewan.

Your retirement leaves a gap that will be hard to fill. Your expertise and leadership in the field of cardiology has been much appreciated by your colleagues in practice and also by those of us in administration. It is our sincere hope that you have a long and happy life following your retirement.

Yours truly,

Dr. B. Laursen
Senior Vice President Medical Services

BL/sl

c.c.   Senior Management Team
        Regina Qu'Appelle Health Authority
        Medical Department Heads

Recognition of my service of twenty-eight years at hospitals in Regina (1976-2004).
Dr. James McHattie, head of medicine; Dr. Naiyer Habib, administrator;
Dr. Chris Ekong, president, medical staff.

329

PATRICK PETTIT/The Leader-Post

Regina's Dr. Naiyer Habib was a clinical investigator in the HOPE study

Regina patients take part in international blood pressure study

By ANNE KYLE
of The Leader-Post

An international study which included 72 patients from Regina holds promise of lowering the death rate from cardiovascular disease for people with high blood pressure.

Patients with hypertension can reduce the risks of heart attacks, strokes and death by taking the blood pressure drug ramipril, according to the Canadian-led international study released this week.

"The study established that treatment with the anti-hypertensive ramipril (an antiotensin-converting enzyme (ACE) inhibitor) reduced the risk of heart attacks, strokes and mortality by 22 per cent in at-risk patients," said Regina cardiologist Dr. Naiyer Habib, a clinical investigator in the Heart Outcomes Prevention Evaluation (HOPE) Study.

"It's a unique study, the first of its kind directed towards the prevention of cardiovascular disease. We are pleased to be part of such a highly successful trial, in which 72 patients from the Regina area participated," Habib said.

Ramipril was shown to reduce the risk of cardiovascular death by 25 per cent, heart attacks by 20 per cent and stroke by 32 per cent, all of which are highly statistically significant, he said.

The rate of heart failure was reduced by 16 per cent and the rate of procedures including coronary angioplasty, coronary artery bypass graft and peripheral angioplasty dropped by 15 per cent amongst the ramipril users.

The study also showed a dramatic 39 per cent reduction in the risk of onset of type 2 diabetes, Habib said.

From a preventative point of view the role this drug plays goes far beyond just lowering blood pressure. It reduces the medical complications associated with hypertension thus reducing the number of cardiovascular procedures and hospitalization.

"The prevention and control of hypertension is important in reducing the burden of illness from heart disease and stroke, thereby improving the overall health of Canadians," Habib said.

The findings are significant and will have a major financial impact on our health care system and health systems around the world, he said, noting it is estimated this drug treatment will prevent one million deaths and cardiovascular events around the world.

Heart disease is still the leading cause of death in Canada, accounting for 37 per cent of all deaths in 1996.

About 4.1 million Canadian adults between the ages of 18 and 74 have high blood pressure, one of the primary risk factors in cardiovascular disease such as stroke, heart attack or atherosclerosis. In Saskatchewan, about 16 per cent of the population has high blood pressure.

Initiated in Canada, the HOPE study was conducted over a four-and-a-half year period, and involved more than 9,500 male and female patients in 267 centres from 19 countries across North and South America and Europe. In Canada, 129 clinical investigators and 5,721 patients (60 per cent of participants) took part in the study. Four clinical investigators and 144 patients were from Saskatchewan.

The HOPE study was halted in March 1999 by an independent data and safety monitoring board, consisting of international experts, because of the positive results.

The 55-year-old patients involved in the study had a history of coronary artery disease, peripheral vascular disease, stroke or had diabetes and were at high risk for heart attacks and strokes.

The study contained two treatment groups: one comparing ramipril to placebo in reducing cardiovascular events, and the other examining the effects of vitamin E compared to placebo in reducing the risk of heart disease and cancer. The vitamin E arm of the study is ongoing.

"The Regina Health District's Online Newsletter"

May 26, 2000

'The Ladies' Auxiliary, which will cease operations on May 31, 2000, after 70 years of caring for war veterans, recently presented a cheque for $44,000 to the Hospitals of Regina Foundation.'

What's Inside

Cardiologist Honoured
Accreditation Deferred
Playground Safety
Acting VP Appointed
Fitness Schedule
Teddy Bear Bash
Car Seat Safety Clinic

Regina Health District

Heart Outcomes Prevention Evaluation
Dr. Habib Honoured

Dr. Naiyer Habib has helped give some patients HOPE. The Regina cardiologist was one of four clinical investigators from Saskatchewan involved in the international Heart Outcomes Prevention Evaluation.

The HOPE study examined the potential benefits of the ACE inhibitor ramipril, a drug approved to treat high blood pressure, for patients at risk of cardiovascular problems. The Canadian-led study, which was terminated six months early due to the significance of the results, has been deemed landmark.

Aventis Pharma presented Dr. Habib with a plaque for his participation in the HOPE study.

The study showed that ramipril, which is sold as Altace, reduced the risk of cardiovascular death by 25 per cent, heart attacks by 20 per cent and strokes by 32 per cent. Ramipril also produced a 30 per cent drop in the number of expected new diabetes cases.

If ramipril is made available worldwide, it is estimated that one million fatal or non-fatal cardiovascular events could be prevented.

The HOPE study involved 9,500 patients at high risk for vascular disease and diabetes in 267 centres in 19 countries. Saskatchewan contributed 144 patients to the study, including 72 through Dr. Habib.

Withdrawal of Full Academic Support by the University of Saskatchewan from Regina

The university withdrew its full academic support of this institution. As a result, all the academic cardiologists and physicians who were appointed at the time of the initiation (1974) of the Plains Health Centre left, one by one. Eventually, very few of us were left at the Plains Health Centre.

This was a blow to me in my academic career. I stepped down from the tenured position but continued in a clinical position. Dr. Marvin Bala, then head of the University Department of Medicine, recognized my services in establishing the cardiac program, accepted my resignation, and understood why I had stepped down.

Closure of the Plains Health Centre and Now Repentance

This was another blow to me, as it was to many. Many raised their voices with petitions and rallies but to no avail. The Plains Health Centre was closed in 1998.

The Western Producer

Critics have become more vocal about Plains Hospital closure.

Posted Aug. 10, 1995, by Ed White

REGINA – The controversy surrounding the closure of the Plains Health Centre in Regina is beginning to heat up.

Health care across southern Saskatchewan will suffer if the Plains Hospital in Regina is closed, said a number of critics of the plan to close the hospital.

"If you allow the Plains Health Centre to close, you have just delivered a serious blow to health care in rural Saskatchewan," Brownlee farmer Ken Pottruff told a crowd of about 800 people at a rally in front of the legislature recently.

The Regina District Health Board denies health services. The board decided in 1993 to close the hospital and concentrate the city's health care in two other hospitals.

It said, "The cost of upgrading the Plains to meet safety standards is too high, and three hospitals in the city are too many. Instead, the two other hospitals will be expanded, and the Plains closed."

Board chair Dan de Vlieger said no health services will be lost in the consolidation. "The same services, the same programs will still be there," he said after the rally.

Many staff, former patients, and people in rural Saskatchewan have campaigned against the closure. Petitions have been circulated around Regina and through rural communities that use the Plains. They have so far collected about 26,000 names, and petition organizers hope to have 100,000 names by fall so the provincial government will call a plebiscite.

Rural hospital area people's concern

Hospital staff and patients addressed the rally. Robert Kosolofski spoke of his four-year-old daughter Karlee, who was revived after spending six hours outside her house in -22 C conditions. She was taken to the Plains, where her blood was warmed, and she was brought out of a near-freezing state.

Rally organizer and Plains nurse Darlene Sterling said about seventy percent of the patients in the hospital are from rural Saskatchewan.

"Why is the South Saskatchewan Plains Hospital even involved in the Regina Health District?" she asked rhetorically. "It's not a Regina hospital. They really don't have the right to shut it down."

But de Vlieger said all three Regina hospitals serve rural Saskatchewan, so characterizing the Plains as a rural hospital and the other two as city hospitals "is a complete misperception." If the board's plans are followed, the Plains will close by 1998. But the board, which was provincially appointed, faces an election before then. New Democratic Party MLA Andrew Thomson said, "Our chance to change the health board is coming this fall."

He said the government, which gave decision-making power to health boards as part of its "wellness" approach, thinks the board needs to answer many questions about hospital-closure plans.

The Progressive Conservative and Liberal health critics said the NDP's health-care policy is a shamble and the closure of the Plains is typical of government damage to rural health care.

Now, the inappropriate decision of the Romanow NDP government is being realized. The governing Saskatchewan party headed by Premier Brad Wall is planning to build out-patient services in the area where the Plains Health Centre was established.

The following poem, Ode to the Plains Health Centre, *expresses the feelings of those associated with this institution.*

Ode To The Plains Health Centre

There once was a place called the Plains Health Centre
It was a great place to work, if you went there.
All those colleagues you knew
Changed into friendships that grew
No matter the level or department you'd enter.

Remember that long walk from the parking lot?
Usually windy, ice cold or unbearably hot..
It was such a scenic location
To practice your vocation
And you could park there, more often than not.

The staff were friendly no matter where you went
There was cooperation wherever the patient was sent.
You knew people by name
All were treated the same
The sense of "family" was very much evident.

It seemed the Plains would always surpass an inspection
Amid the chaos in every direction.
We took pride in our site
Worked with all of our might
To make it a place thought of with affection.

It was a workplace that would always expect us
To diagnose and cure whatever was infectious.
The teamwork showed through
In all that we'd do
Quality care an ideal we thought precious.

Change to health care is a difficult decision
Every cut made with surgical precision.
The patients came every season
They asked us for the reason
Who expected all the support and opposition?

The Plains Health Centre shall forever be
Full of blood, sweat and tears, from you and from me.
So remember the great times we had
Both the good and the bad
And raise your glass to the old PHC.

Deb Lundy RTNM
PHC Homecoming 1998

334

My Outspokenness

I came from India as a foreign graduate, but I educated myself and received training such that I could establish myself in various countries. One should choose those options if fortunate enough to be given the choice to do so. Generally, it is seen that people coming from foreign lands and acquiring homes stay subdued. This was not me. I stood up for the right things all the time. My interviews in the media reflect that, be it in the medical profession or in community service. As head of cardiology, I had no hesitation in pointing out errors by anyone, but I never took any adverse action against such errors, even as head. It was mainly to point out so that the person involved may learn, rectify the wrong, and avoid repeating it.

My Resignation

Thus, facing the problems clashing with my life principles, giving up my section head position in 2001 because of various accumulating factors and being isolated from any participation in raising a voice for patient care and for physicians' needs, I decided to resign and retire and to move from my beloved city, where we had lived for thirty-one years, the greatest period of our life.

The healthcare system had changed. The doctor had become a smaller piece in the pie of planning and decision-making for patient care. Traditionally, doctors were the main decision-makers, and the role of the administration was to provide the facilities. This was my conclusion after serving as the builder of the cardiology part of cardiac science in various capacities -the vice president of the medical staff of the Southern Saskatchewan hospitals, chairing various committees, and sitting as a member on others. As time went by, I concluded, "Doctors were once the main decision-makers for patients, but now they are to walk on the path chosen by the bureaucrats running hospital affairs."

I felt that the medical association was too weak to provide strong leadership for the medical profession.

Health care was squeezed. Patient waiting periods started to climb, and the transfer of critically ill patients in a timely manner became too difficult. Over the course of time, I perceived that I could no longer provide my leadership according to the principles upon which I initiated, established, and maintained cardiology.

I really appreciated the sincere and untiring efforts of Dr. James D. McHattie, the then-head of medicine, and Mr. Jim L. Saunders, the then-acting CEO of the Regina Health District. Our correspondence and all facts noted are available in my file and will be over my lifetime as proof.

I highly appreciated the efforts and meetings in good faith by Dr. McHattie and Mr. Saunders to pursue me to continue as the head. Apologetically, I could not reverse my decision, although it was with a fatherly ache that I gave up the position through which I had established cardiology for Southern Saskatchewan and had continued to maintain it with up-to-date standards till the end.

Here is an email conversation between me and Mr. Jim Saunders, who was moving to a new position in Calgary; I wanted to say hello to him:

From: Habib, Dr. N., RHD

I submitted my final letter to Dr. James D. McHattie, head of the department of medicine, Regina Qu'Appelle Health Region, with copies to various authorities, including Mr. Jim L. Saunders. I had no intention of releasing the letter to the media. I refused an interview. I did send it to some of my very, very close staff, who, as I have said, were like my family. I did not expect its release to the media, but someone sent it to the Canadian Broadcasting Corporation. The news about my resignation, along with the comments from my letter and subsequent comments by Dr. James D. McHattie as head of medicine of the Regina Health District and Dr. Edward Busse, who was the newly elected chair of cardiac science on behalf of the Regina Qu'Appelle Health Region, is now accessible on the internet.

The following were, as it is said, the last straws that broke the camel's back. They were heart-breaking and insulting incidents to me as the head of cardiology. The administrative appointee was noted to use their authority indiscriminately. A nursing director moved my high-risk patient and ordered by me to be on a monitored bed to an unmonitored bed without contacting me. I took action without demanding penalization.

The other incident was that the director of nursing for the cardiac care unit withdrew the services of the nursing staff, who were to be available during off hours when the cardiac technological team was to arrive to perform emergency coronary angioplasty stenting in acute myocardial infarction according to the existing policy. There was no prior discussion about this—the requirement for any change. I took strong action as head, and it was pursued by other officials to its resolution.

I made various recommendations, but they did not bear any fruit. I note here one example of an important and very valid recommendation which could have been easily implemented but received no attention. Critically ill patients could not be brought from the outlying areas to receive timely cardiac care. The news media had covered these stories. I had recommended having a buffer bed activated in the cardiac-care unit to accommodate such situations and seeking approval of all authorities in the chain, i.e., the heads of nursing, cardiology, and administration. It was not approved, and my recommendation was not adopted.

My resignation letter and the responses from Dr. McHattie as head of medicine and of Dr. Busse as newly appointed head of cardiac science (a position offered to me that I had declined) are available through the media, but they do not include the responses to all my raised points.

The Media on My Resignation

RHD's head of cardiology will resign

Regina Leader Post

Last month Dr. Naiyer Habib reconfirmed his resignation as head of cardiology for the Regina Health District.

Habib, who had submitted his resignation some 10 months earlier, in a Sept. 13 letter to the district expressed his frustrations with the system and indicated that after more than 20 years as head of the section of cardiology he couldn't do the job any longer.

While attempts to contact Habib -- who is on holidays -- were unsuccessful, his letter advised the district that he felt the standard of care for cardiology patients was moving backwards.

In statements released Wednesday, Dr. James McHattie, head of the Department of Medicine, and Dr. Edward Busse, medical director of the district's new cardiosciences program, praised Habib for his contributions and expressed enthusiasm for new directions in cardiac care within the district.

"We are disappointed that Dr. Habib has resigned as the section head of cardiology but we are heartened by the fact that he will continue as a leader in clinical care and contribute to the advancement of cardiac care, although in a lesser role," said McHattie in a prepared statement.

"I think frustration over 'bumps in the road' in closing the Plains Health Centre and transferring and expanding cardiac care at the Regina General Hospital site has obscured Dr. Habib's appreciation of exactly how much progress has been achieved under his leadership in the section of cardiology," he said.

Integrating service delivery for cardiac patients. One of the goals of the new program is to co-ordinate and accelerate the pace of change in cardiac care, McHattie said.

The new program is under development now and will be launched in the first part of next year, according to Busse.

"While I respect Dr. Habib's skills as a cardiologist, I cannot agree with him that the standard of care has declined during the recent years of his leadership as head of the section of cardiology É," said Busse, expressing disappointment Habib resigned before seeing how the new program addressed his concerns.

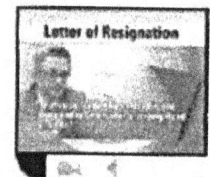

*Jennifer Quesnel reports for
CBC Television*

*Lorenda Reddekopp reports
for CBC Radio* [Download
Players]
Click on the Audio or Video
icon, right below the picture,
to view and listen.

Radio One Live

Latest Radio Newscast

Latest TV Newscast

CBC News Search

Saskatchewan ☑

CBC News ☐

All of cbc.ca ☐

search

Head of cardiology quits

REGINA - The Head of Cardiology for the Regina Health District has resigned. Dr. Naiyer Habib says he was frustrated with the system and couldn't do the job any longer.

"I personally felt... enough of this, I cannot progress cardiology and I'm just wasting my time," said Habib.

Dr Naiyer Habib is ending his term of more than 20 years, as head of the section of cardiology.

The CBC obtained a copy of a letter regarding his resignation. In the letter, he tells the Health District that the standard of care for cardiology patients is moving backwards.

Habib tells the health district there aren't enough beds for heart patients,meaning cardiac patients are sometimes put in other wards.

Habib says he's been raising these concerns for a long time, but that no changes are being made

Habib setting up practice in B.C.

By ANNE KYLE
Leader-Post

Leaving Saskatchewan was bittersweet for Regina cardiologist Dr. Naiyer Habib, who says he intends to continue his fight for improved health care for all Canadians in British Columbia.

"I'm just overwhelmed by the reception, the farewell and the good wishes from people in the community and the patients," said Habib, who left this week to set up a community practice in Abbotsford, B.C.

"Saskatchewan is a great province. It has been a great place to live and we love the people. We'll miss our many friends," he told the *Leader-Post* prior to his departure.

Born in India, Habib trained in the United States specializing in cardiology. He landed in Saskatchewan 31 years ago, working in ~~Prince Albert~~ before moving to Regina where he and his wife, Maushaba, raised their two sons — one of whom is pursuing a career in medicine as a kidney specialist and the other a B.C. lawyer.

Twenty-eight years ago, Habib was hired by the University of Saskatchewan's College of Medicine to establish a cardiology program at the Plains Health Centre for the people of southern Saskatchewan.

"When the Plains was established, the idea was to create a medical centre of excellence. I modernized the cardiac care unit and established the non-investigation and cardiac catheterization laboratory," said Habib, who was head of cardiology with the Regina Qu'Appelle Health Region until he resigned from that position in 2001.

An opponent of the closure of the Plains Health Centre, Habib said the cardiology department underwent enormous upheaval with the move to the Regina General Hospital, but things have started to turn around.

"The cardiology program in Regina Qu'Appelle Health Region is okay and progressing. In fact, our cardiac surgeons are second-to-none in the nation and are our cardiology program is of a very high standard and that will continue," he said.

Over the years Habib said he has seen a lot of changes in equipment and advances in the care of heart and stroke patients, which has improved their overall survival rate quite dramatically over the years. But, he said, there is still room for improvement.

Right now he shares a common concern with other doctors and health-care providers relating to providing patients with timely access to care.

"I think it is a struggle for physicians, nurses and those who manage the beds to accommodate these patients for whatever reason, whether it is economic or a shortage of beds, nurses or doctors. These things are being addressed slowly, but it takes time," he said.

The outspoken doctor said he is semi-retiring because the health-care system has changed significantly. Doctors, nurses and health providers, who are enthusiastic about working in the present health-care system, are either not able to or are not being accommodated by the system when it comes to their full participation in having a say on how to provide better patient care, he said.

Habib said he fully intends to make his views known in British Columbia. With B.C. Premier Gordon Campbell's Liberal government heading into a spring election next year, Habib said he'll have plenty of opportunity to lobby for improved health services in that province. *(& DID NOT PERSUE)*

QUOTABLE

66

It has been a great place (Sask.) to live and we love the people.

99

Dr. Naiyer Habib

[handwritten vertical text: SASKATCHEWAN]

I did not persue to let my views known in BC as stated in last paragraph of the media release

My resignation news

As word of my resignation got out, I received many, many telephone calls and some notes from well-wishers, staff, and patients. No doubt, I felt very bad regarding my patients. They were worried that I was leaving, and I had to reassure them that it was a resignation from mydepartment head post but not from my medical practice—yet. I would leave those responsibilities with my retirement, which came in October 2004.

So, we retired from Regina to do part-time office practice in Abbotsford, BC.

With sentiment on my resignation,I recalled the first visit of my family to my office on my appointment as Head and Assisstant Professor Of Carrdilogy: my wife with sons Arasalan on her right and Adnan on left

Dr. N. Habib's office closes permanently & Fax is disconnected as of 5 PM Thursday, September 30'04 after 31 years of service to Saskatchewan as he moves to semiretire in BC. Dr. Habib will continue hospital practice till further notice as per message on 766-6999 on which he could also be contacted till November 30'04.

He has seen all his patients with advice regarding follow up care. Information of chart on patients are available with the referring physicians. If chart copy is needed, it will be available at cost from 306-721-3779 (Vaughan's/Queen City Moving Systems). Dr. Aboguddah and Dr. Wojcik have agreed to accept his patients on referral.

He expresses his sincere thanks to all present and past administrators, hospital staff, administrative physicians, department of health in helping him establish cardiology program for people of southern Saskatchewan and for their support during his Headship of Cardiology from 1976-2001.

He, and his wife express their sincere thanks and appreciation to all Patients, their Families, Hospital staff, Physicians, News Media, Interfaith Community, Peace Coalition for their cooperation, respect, and devotion to them. They thank all people of Saskatchewan, a great people to be associated with and a great place to live where they lived the greatest part of their life.

OUR RETIREMENT

My life and its enthusiasm were not the same for me anymore!

One day in early or mid-2004, I told Naushaba, "I shall retire in October of this year." She was looking at my face. Generally, it is said that when the husband retires and starts staying at home, he becomes a problem for his wife. With that in mind, I asked her, "You do not seem to be happy?" She replied that she was shocked to hear of my abrupt decision. She further pointed out that we had not planned where we were going to go or what we were going to do and that we had so many things to close. I agreed but told her that once the decision had been made, we would do it. And we did.

So we both retired and went for dinner together at the superb Bedford House restaurant in Fort Langley, which closed its doors permanently in 2015. Our brains were storming with all the thoughts of our lives.

Us at the Bedford House restaurant (2011).

Me And Our Staff

I had a family relationship with our cardiac investigation staff at Cardiac Catheterization Laboratories. We started the tradition of an annual dinner party after our laboratory opened. The department of medicine would invite their staff to their party, but not our staff, so Dr. Hernandez and I decided to do it for them. When Dr. Hernandez left, I continued that tradition. Here are some pictures from our Cath lab's annual parties in the 1990s:

Patty, Wanda, Naiyer, Naushaba, and Froeda.

Clockwise: Cynthia, Patty, Wanda, Naiyer, Jacki.

343

Our Beloved Staff

Left 3: Jacki, Tom, and John.

Farewell By Staff and Colleagues

Finally, an elaborate and surprise farewell party was arranged by our family staff, to which many from the Regina Qu'Appelle Region hospitals, from the hospitals' various walks of life, were invited. Its memory will be everlasting.

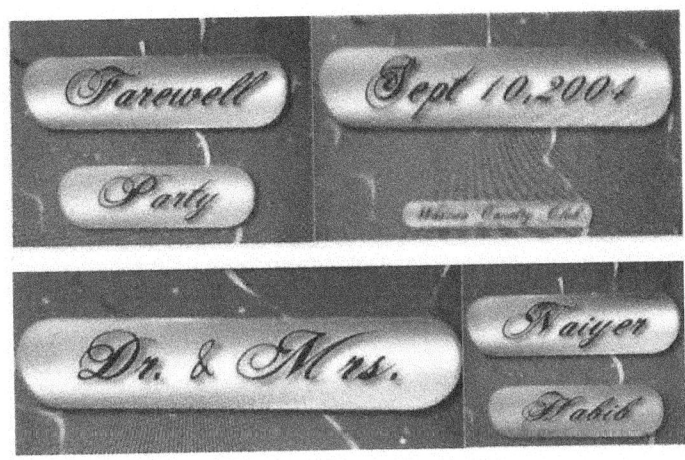

I was leaving the place I loved, had founded, and run, joining my staff as my family. They got together to give me a hearty and very emotional farewell. This is reflected in this "Farewell to us both." John Federiko led this, but the participation of all was obvious in their speeches, hugs, and gifts, especially in their memos to me and their presentation of an album with a caricature of me and pictures reflecting their attachment. Samples of these appear at the end of this chapter. I could not imagine the level of love and respect they had for us. I wish I had included all their mementoes here instead of just a few.

The Memos

I pursued any matter that I considered out of line by writing a memo to the individual concerned for rectification. That is what has been pleasantly talked about by my colleagues and staff. To celebrate this, they wrote memos for me and presented them to me in a folder. I included samples here, mine and theirs.

As John said, I was a serious guy, but not among them. Jokes, teasing, and laughter were a regular part of our existence, even during work. I undertook the annual cath lab party as a heartfelt tribute of my love and affection for the people with whom I worked. I was a man of my staff, much less than of my colleagues. But this chapter of my life had to end, as do all events in life.

John was the master of ceremonies at our farewell tribute. Here is an account of the event in their own words, with no editing, to maintain the originality as it happened:

John Federiko, master of ceremonies.

John's welcome

I'd like to welcome you all tonight. Thank you, everybody, for coming to recognize and pay respect to Dr. Habib. As you all know, Dr. Habib gave away, ending his career in cardiology in Regina. He is moving away to BC. We'd like to enjoy this evening, that will start with a meal, and we will have a few speeches afterward.

Speeches and Gifts

John: Dr. Habib, on a Wednesday morning, said to me, "I am going to retire. I am leaving. I got to go." I said, "You are not." It surprised me. It seemed strange. In a matter of weeks, he will not be around here anymore. Like bricks, he has been here since the beginning. He has been part of our everyday work and one of the pillars of the hospital. Dr. Habib has been in Regina working for cardiology for twenty-eight years and has been a pioneer in cardiology. He started cardiology in Regina; a memo master (he smiles). I have binders and binders of memos, just tons of them (he smiles). I was looking for them to throw in the garbage. I threw some of them away. But he will keep sending another memo, another memo. I did read them all. I responded to quite a few of them. Farieda will type them and discuss them with me. I will receive them. That is why (he points at me and says) I give *you* a memo today.

I'll try to remember a few stories about Dr. Habib. He has been a serious guy. Those of you who knew him twenty-some years ago almost like serious (John poses to be serious, then continues with his stories; one of which I will mention here). He was doing a stress test for a patient. This was the old machine. This could be shut at high speed. What happened that day when he finished his stress test on a patient? In the end, he started talking to the patient. While he was standing on the treadmill, the machine kicked in and shot him. That image is memorable. It is a great story (John smiles).

Dr. Habib not only did hard work in practicing medicine and cardiology in Southern Saskatchewan, but the part that's missed, thinking backward for years, is the huge burden of responsibility he accepted in the administrative

346

work—almost a thankless job at times, but he continued and carried out that responsibility with perseverance, along with that of patient care for Southern Saskatchewan. The most important work he did was establishing and maintaining a high level and standard of cardiology care for Southern Saskatchewan.

"We would be remiss not to say a few words about Mrs. Habib. Her quality of support with Dr. Habib has been for twenty-some years. For twenty-some years since I have known him. I have a gift for you, Mrs. Habib."

John gave us gifts: a binder with memos, a scrapbook, and a frame of the Victoria Bridge in Regina on behalf of the staff. These are memorable gifts that hold so many sentiments for us.

Looking through the scrapbook with Jeanne Falman.

Jeanne Falman.

Jeanne Falman

Dr. and Mrs. Habib, it is nice to see so many familiar faces to wish you farewell. I thank John for all the effort that he put into making this a very special evening for Dr. and Mrs. Habib. Dr. Habib, you did many things that nurses will remember you for. I am not going to talk about all of them. You have been so passionate about the cardiac care unit and how it is run. We know you are never wishy-washy about anything; you will grumble and do something. You may write a memo and grumble. I think most of us have seen more memos from you than anyone else. At one time, we had a wall in CCU plastered with Dr. Habib's memos. I was told I must mention this. I do not know who said that. . . .

I think most doctors love their toys, whether stethoscope, pager, phone, or car. You would have to agree that you enjoyed some of these, too. Just like a little boy showing us your new gadgets and what they can do. How many of you remember Dr. Habib's broken hand? Who would have thought he would print better with his left hand? Dr. Habib, do you remember printing orders with your left hand? I am not sure whose orders were harder to decipher: Dr. Habib's, Dr. Garbe's, or Dr. Wojcik's. I think it depended on the day.

When CCU moved from the Plains to the General, we really appreciated your attitude; you made a great effort to treat everybody the same. You also have an incredible memory of patients you looked after years and years ago. I think, after a while, some patients were more like family to you.

Dr. Habib, I never thought I would end up babysitting for you—not grandkids, but pond fish. I was pretty worried about one dying and hoped you wouldn't be able to identify yours. I just made sure I gave you back as many as I took home. Thankfully, it was never a problem, and I took them home for more than one year.

We tried to respect your Friday prayer time. Many nurses forgot this, but we always lived through it, and I have no memories of you getting terribly upset. You told me once that in your thinking, there is only one God, and we all just see him differently. I respected your openness of thought.

Dr. Habib, what tickled us most was when you became a grandpa. You said your first grandson was your boy. You were so very proud. I imagine Mrs. Habib was equally excited to be a grandma. You carried his picture next to your heart. You came into the unit one day and told us you had taken him for a ride in your sports car, and there was a special glint in your eyes.

We talked about what you would do when you actually retire. I think you should take up the sport of fly-fishing. There are wonderful fishing places in BC. You can trade MD for CA, or you could try being a lawyer or politician, but I think you had enough politics in Regina. You are happiest as a cardiac specialist. On behalf of your nurses, I wish you the best. Enjoy your new life in BC. I am sure Mrs. Habib will take care of you, and you have grandchildren there. Please keep in touch, and send us a memo sometime.

John asked Dr. Garbe to contribute: Dr. Garbe, please say a few words about Dr. Habib.

Dr. George Garbe

<u>Dr. George Garbe</u>

Thank you, John and others, for arranging this fabulous meeting. We are here to say farewell to Dr. Habib. I did not know much about him. He sent me a quick note and instructed me on which parts I was supposed to detail about him. I am just looking for it in my notes. Dr. Habib is from India. He did his MB, BS—equivalent to our MD—in 1963. An MD is something like a PhD, which he did in India in 1966. He was a resident at the hospital with Duke University, then Orange Memorial Hospital, and, finally, in a hospital affiliated with the Ohio State University. In 1973, he was in Saskatoon for a year in cardiology. He did his Royal College examination in 1972 for a fellowship. He joined the Plains Health Centre in 1976. Subsequently, he started the cardiology program in Regina.

In 1976, I was in Estevan as a general practitioner. Dr. Habib came out and gave us a talk; I remember that quite well. It was surprising to know about cardiology.

He changed the level of cardiology (read the content from Mr. Chinn's letter). He started the coronary intervention program, which was two weeks before I came. That was a lot of work. He built all the work. He established a high standard of cardiology from that time, and he maintained it.

Dr. Habib and Dr. Burgess established the Regina Cardiac Society together. This was an organization for Regina specialists of cardiology, vascular surgeons, and radiologists. We have speakers on various aspects of cardiology. Some speakers are internists, surgeons, and cardiologists, and some world-class speakers attend the Regina Cardiac Society educational meetings.

Since the time I worked with him, I had memos from him. I have one memo that I would like to mention. I could not find it. I did not have time to find it. I can remember some. My favourite memo he sent me said something like, "Dr. Garbe, I'd like to remind you that I sent you several memos, but you did not respond." (Big laughter.)

Nurses were talking. They said, "Do you remember when Dr. Habib came? We thought he was a resident. Then we realized that he was the director. He was a very serious character."

He used to give lectures to the nurses in the Cardiac Care Unit. I got one lecture from him when I ordered booze on the flight to Boston for the valvuloplasty demonstration course. We both were going.

One personal note. I will be serious. When I came here, when you look at us both, everything is very different about us. We have different backgrounds and different values. But somehow, despite those differences, we managed to find some common ground. I have a few strengths and many weaknesses, and Dr. Habib has many strengths and few weaknesses. The two of us worked together to achieve goals we felt we should be achieving. We could learn from the two of us about tolerance and about being different but finding common ground and values to work together. We worked together for twenty years. I appreciate having had the chance to work with him. (Dr. Garbe pauses and controls his tears.)

On behalf of the cardiologists of Regina, I would like to thank you for your leadership. People look at me as a tall guy who's somewhat serious, but inside, I am a little boy. My mother was sick. I was disturbed. I was told she would be OK. So, for all the sick people around our province, we need to worry about them as our family and continue to care for them.

Thank you for the opportunity. I wish Dr. Habib and Mrs. Habib well for their retirement.

Dr. George Garbe and his wife, Mrs. Lina Garbe.

Dear Nozomi + Naoshi

Best wishes for your future life in Nasushiobara. Thank you
for your support and cooperation in our work together over the last 20 years.

George + Lisa

Dr. John Tsang

Unfortunately, the transcript of his speech is not available. He represented the cardiac surgeons. He praised and thanked me on behalf of all the cardiac surgeons and remarked with a smile, "Dr. Habib had specific ideas about which patient to refer to which surgeon." This being a known fact, it was received with big laughter. It was a good team, and I enjoyed working with them. They were second to none. I had stopped sending patients out of the province.

Dr. Ayman Aboguddah

John introduces Dr. Ayman Aboguddah

John says I will ask Dr. Aboguddah to say a few words about Dr. Habib's role—not in our circle, but in this community.

Dr. Aboguddah

Dr. and Brother Habib and Mrs. and Sister Naushaba Habib, I would like to address you in an Islamic way: Assalam-o-Alaikum, peace be upon you all. We were in Regina. We clicked together sometimes. It was then that I knew Dr. Habib. I am very fond of a man of principle. Dr. Habib is a senior colleague. I especially consider him a mentor. I am proud to be given this opportunity to say a few words about him outside the hospital.

People talked about his memos. In the daytime, inside the hospital, he would write memos to hospital staff, and after hours, he would write memos to the board members. It was happy and nice. Dr. Habib served the medical community.

Dr. Habib welcomed the newcomers and helped quietly with dignity. He helped them by showing them the right direction. He looked after the members of the faith community and to see that they had Canadian values. He worked on this and chose the right channel to walk along. He established an Islamic school in his basement until it was moved to the Islamic Centre. Dr. and Mrs. Habib became examples for all in raising children with faith and Canadian values.

Dr. Habib maintained Canadian values. Nobody forced him to abandon his Islamic values.

Dr. Habib was the founder of the Islamic Association and was the president a few times. He also served as a member of the board. I was a member with him when he was the president. I took orders from him. Sometimes, I felt that he might not be right, but I would later conclude that he was and say as much. My impression of him was that he was an honest man. I never detected that he lied, nor heard of anyone proving that he lied. I am proud of his friendship. I think he is an honest man. Sometimes, he was too tough.

What was the interest? It was for everybody's interest, organized, no doubt about it, whether in office or in community service.

He is an active man. If he does not like anything, he will sit down and talk about it and take steps. You will often see his name in the media. He will write to the *Leader-Post*, the *Globe and Mail*, and *Time* magazine. They will publish his words. It was always about his ethics. You might have seen many groups and political activities in the community, but not Dr. Habib. All matters were the matters of principle with Dr.Habib.

For matters outside of the community regarding the rights of others, he will always favour telling people to get out and get involved. You are Canadian. You have Canadian rights. He practiced this himself.

He was involved in interfaith and never imposed his religion on others.

He was involved in mosaic and peace and justice. During the Iraq war, he had a poster against war. He was involved in the Canadian Islamic Congress and the National Advocacy Group in Canada for Muslims. After 9/11, he, along with other members, established an advocacy group, Muslims for Peace and Justice, to deal with any misunderstandings against Muslims. He dealt with these problems in the Canadian way.

Dr. Habib was never alone. Mrs. Habib was always with him. They formed a team. Mrs. Habib founded the women's group CCMW and asked women to come out in a Canadian way. They did a great job.

We need to maintain what was provided to us. God bless him and his family.

John calls Dr. Habib

Dr. and Mrs. Habib

Dr. Habib: I begin in the name of God, most kind, most merciful. I am surprised and very much overwhelmed to see so many well-wishers. I and Naushaba would like to thank you all for opening your hearts—not surgically, but literally (laughter). I would like to thank John and his team for arranging this occasion.

John asked me to confirm a date for this function. I discouraged him, but, as usual, like a spoiled child or a little brother, he said, "Do not let me down." This silenced me, and he got the result he wanted.

I am a bit of a shy guy. I did not have the courage to come here, but it was quite enjoyable. The happiness that Naushaba and I feel is difficult to express. There are so many people here and so many people who have come from out of town. I have met many of you. Susan has come from Moose Jaw, and she is the director of the operating theatre in Moose Jaw. There are other people here from Moose Jaw whom I haven't seen in many years. Shirley Carter, who worked in our cath lab in the beginning, is here, as are many others. The ups and downs we rode in Regina are memorable moments for me. Please keep up your tireless efforts. We will get there. We have excellent; knowledgeable staff and cardiac surgeons. As John said, all of you have lightened my burden. My stress is gone. We have a cardiac surgical team here that is second to none. We depend on that. I am relieved. In the past, it was stressful. I had to send some patients out of the country and province only to keep the care of them in my mind.

I would have thought to stay on, and I could change my mind, but I make a decision once and stay at that. Sometimes, I repent for them. We have an excellent team. As for myself, I have accepted that my loss of vigour means I can no longer walk on this changing path of health care. I have always chosen a path leading to where I felt we ought to go. Some friends call me a perfectionist. I reply that if demanding a standard of care is perfection, then so be it. I also tell them that I was born before my time. Things that I wanted to be done yesterday or even today are still undone and will be done in some distant tomorrow.

With the very different course our healthcare system is on, along with the affectionate pressure of my family, I have decided to walk away from this path.

A new page of life is to begin now. I am retired completely. I also want George Garbe to retire because he told me after a cardiac conference in the cath lab that he would do it before me. I asked if he would bet me, and he said he would (big laughter). John is a witness to that. So if I retire, George must retire, too. So, I will not retire. This will be my semi-retirement. It will allow me more time for the family, but I do not want to walk away if my health permits. I would like to have accountability, particularly from the politicians.

Now, a few comments about our family background, and the things that explain our relationships with our staff.

My and Naushaba's families are close relatives. Our mothers are sisters. Her family moved to Pakistan after the partition of India in 1947.

I was influenced by my maternal grandfather to be a doctor. He was a World War I veteran physician and served in China. He used to make calls to patients at their houses. I would go with him. At that time, patients used to pay a fee to doctors. Some would give him whatever money, eggs, vegetables, or pigeons they had. He would give away most of this to poor patients. I used to watch that. Then, I started playing doctor as a child. I used to inject ink mixed with water into my sister's dolls. In return, I would get a scratch on my face. Then we would be disciplined by Mom, who passed away here at the Plains Health Centre, in room 834. Thanks to all the staff for looking after her as well as the physicians.

I finally became a physician.

To many of you, I have been a man with a masked face and a cruel look, with no smile. To others, yes, I have been different. I overwhelmingly enjoyed teasing John. On some weekends, we used to be on call. I would call him and say that there was a patient in shock. He would say, "We will be there." Then we would expose the truth, and both laughed. He would express his madness with a smile on it—I mean that jokingly.

But he did get me one time. We had moved our office to the medical wing in Plains Health Centre to the General. He came to me very quietly and said, "Dr. Habib, I have something to tell you! But do not tell anyone that I told you." "What is it, John?" I asked. He told me: "The administration is in trouble. The city is not approving the medical office wing." So, I stood there for a moment. I said, "All right. I will get Tony Merchant." Then the staff started laughing.

I'd like to say a few things about my staff that demonstrate our relationship. I named my cordial staff Slim Red Head, Tweety Bird, and Wiring Lady (who helped me pass a wire in an artery during angioplasty). One staff member was short, and I always said I liked shorter people because I felt tall in front of them!

Here is also a joke about one of my cordial staff—the tallest one, whom I used to tease. "I don't like tall people. I feel small in front of them. One day, he came to me and said, "Dr. Habib, will you write a letter of reference for me because I am moving to Calgary?" I was very happy that he was leaving. Whether he deserved it or not, I wrote a very excellent letter to get rid of him. Months and months went by, and he was still around. One day, while he was helping me during a procedure, I asked him, "What happened? You have not gone yet?" He said, "I will stay."

I said, "My goodness. I tried writing an excellent reference to get rid of you, and you are still here. I want that reference letter back." He still has it. He is a nice young man with superb technical skills!

Then there was the person who, when I was limping for four or five weeks, asked me, "What happened to your foot?" Sometime later, I was dictating a summary in the health record, and I got called on the pager. It was her. She told me: "come over here." I asked why, but she just repeated: "You come over here." She was calling from the podiatry unit. The nurse looked at my foot, and then I got an appointment to see the podiatrist. Ultimately, I got a shoe. I used the shoe but did not like it. She would watch me to see whether I wore the shoe. If I wasn't wearing it, she would walk me around and tell me to go get it. I asked her to give me permission for Wednesday not to wear shoes because I do cath and on Friday because I go for prayer. She did.

I personally respect such individuals very much. Naushaba says you need a person like that. I love them as our own, and I never joked with anyone in my life as I did with them—so close. In an email, John Federiko wrote: PS. I miss our talk!

These are examples of the relationships I enjoyed with these people over the years. I can keep on telling you more. I respect them all. We have spent thirty-one years of our lives here—more than we've spent anywhere else. This has been a great, touching, everlasting memory! You have all treated my family so cordially!

Someone said Mrs. Habib is a very nice lady. You see her as quiet, but she is very firm with me and keeps me on a straight path. I must admit that I am immature. I follow her advice as a kid would. Once, I wanted to buy a new cell phone. It was available, and I started trying to convince her to let me get it. She is very conservative. I kept on talking for two or three days until, finally, she told me to go and get it. The next moment—not the next day—I called her with that phone, and she said, so you got it, did you not!? These are things that went on in my life and will stay in my memories for as long as I live. You all were with me for a long time—being with me, working with me, and joking with me.

We will begin leaving here in a few days. I shall be doing two or three days of office practice in Abbotsford. You may see us in the Yellow Pages. Please come and visit us and stay with us. You could e-mail me. We would appreciate that very much.

Thank you everyone for coming. God bless you all.

Dolores Fitzgerald, my secretary at PHC and Regina General Hospital, with Mrs. Habib, office manager.

Dolores, Frieda, and Debbie (nuclear medicine staff manager)

Susan Barber   Barb, former secretary   Fay Lazar, RN to ADCN

Dr. Wlad Wojcik, with his wife.

Dr. Ayman Aboguddah, with his wife, Mona.

Dr. Leith Dewer

Dr. Steve Korkola

Dr. Ahmad Mustapha

Some of our beloved nurses.

Naushaba Habib, Naiyer Habib, Lori Federiko, John Federiko, George Garbe.

Our Cordial Staff and Us

The caricatures—only a couple of many (from our staff).

I never did fish, remarking that it was "too boring for me" in our conversation;
hence their comments above.

Memos

March 28, 2001

> **TO:**   Dr....
> Medical director
> Cardiac Catheterization Laboratory

FROM: Naiyer Habib, MD

RE: **YOUR MEMO DATED MARCH 6, 2001, RE: TIMELY GENERATION OF REPORTS**

> I acknowledge your response.

One of the responsibilities as the director of the area is to ensure that reports are generated in a timely fashion in their departments and that they reach the physicians who need the service in a timely fashion.

In order to do that, the director is to see his own areas and follow up on where the problem is to rectify. If the problem is recognized in another area that's linked in some way or other and in your situation, health records of the Regina Health District,

I consider it your responsibility to communicate this concern to the director of health records. If the matter is not dealt with by simple communication and pointing out the problems, it could be forwarded to the section head—me, in this situation.

This remains your responsibility unless you communicate otherwise to me.

Naiyer Habib, MD, FRCPC,
Head, section of cardiology
NH/jp

Memo of Memories to Dr. Habib

From Frieda Koenig

This memo is to inform you that Regina is losing another great physician – a valued invasive cardiac specialist. It is known that Dr. Habib is the "father" of the Cardiology Program in Regina. It was under his direction, foresight and persistence that the Cardiac Catheterization Laboratory and associated departments such as the Stress Lab, Holter monitoring, Echo, etc. as well as other departments in conjunction with the Cardiac Cath Lab were established in 1979 at the Plains Health Centre in Regina.

I want to thank you for bringing this much-needed department to Regina. My years in the cath lab, 1983 to 2002, were filled with great memories, wonderful friendships, lots of hard work and a degree of stress especially during the closing of the Plains Health Centre. As much as you sometimes irritated us, we did respect you for your determination for the good of the patients and staff alike. Administration was not always kind to you, but respected you for the wealth of knowledge and organization that you brought to our city. You were stubborn and this paved the way for the great Cardiology program that we are now enjoying. A publicised honour was never bestowed on you, but your peers involved in the process do know and honour you for your dedicated work.

I want to thank you for the many social events that you sponsored – the Christmas parties, the summer barbeques, as well you would always attend functions which the staff organized – always being one of the guys. One Christmas party in particular that stands out in my mind is the one at the Parisian in Wolsely. You chartered a 48-passenger bus and everyone went out, we were treated to a wonderful meal and all of us had a most memorable time. Some of the other Christmas dinners were at the Applause theatre, the Hollywood dinner theatre - just to mention a few. Thanks for those wonderful times and memories.

I want to thank you for allowing me to be part of the start-up of the Regina Cardiac Society. Again, you had the foresight that an organization of specialists should be formed for dissemination of academic knowledge and teaching. I thoroughly enjoyed arranging the monthly meetings. This gave me an opportunity to work with the different pharmaceutical, equipment and appliance company reps to arrange the academic sessions utilizing the different venues here in Regina. It truly was a real pleasurable learning experience.

I want to thank you for including my husband and me in some of your family functions. I enjoyed learning of your faith, your customs and your gracious hospitality.

Since I have been retired for almost three years and have not been totally up to par with what has been going on in the cath lab, speaking to some of the "old" staff members they indicate that it will never be quite the same without you. Your presence in the lab seemed like the "rock pillar" and when in trouble or doubt, somehow - you were the one to turn to for advice and guidance. You will be missed more than you know.

As the years go by we all come to crossroads which take us in different directions. This is one of your crossroads. I wish you and Nashi much joy in your "golden years." You are blessed with two wonderful sons, daughter-in-laws and four grandchildren. That is a true treasure. Enjoy your family; take time to just relax and play with your grandchildren; tell them of your life experiences, your many travels, your upbringing in a different world and culture and teach them to pray, to respect and be honest to themselves and others. May God bless you and keep you and be gracious onto you as you proceed on your new journey of life.

Thank you for all your teaching, your patience and the wonderful memories and experiences.

Frieda

September 10, 2004

TomVanZyderveld
Cardiac Cath Lab/Pacemaker Clinic
Regina Qu'Appelle Health Region

RE: Dr. N. Habib

To Whom It May Concern:

I have known and worked with Dr. Habib since 1999. During this time I have come to know him as a man of precise judgement, compassionate views, and enviable skill as an Interventional Cardiologist. He has also demonstrated exceptional administrative ability during his tenure as Section Head of Cardiology for the Health Region.

To elaborate on his many achievements would be rather time consuming, so I will therefore just say this:

There was no Dept. of Cardiology until Dr. Habib arrived in Regina and started one nearly 30 years ago. He leaves us today with a Department that boasts one of the best patient outcome rates in the Country.

His patients, this city, the Health Region, as well as his many friends, colleagues and co-workers are better for having him here.

Sincerely yours,

Tom VanZyderveld, RRT/CVT

Memorandum

To: Dr. N. Habib

From: Val Roy

Date: 09/07/04

Re: A Final Memo

As you are well aware Dr. Habib , you and I have exchanged many memos over the years. Probably 99% of those were initiated by YOU, and required a response from ME. (eg: outpatient cardioversions, patient transfers , physician home care orders, addressograph issues....)

This being the case , I couldn't pass up the opportunity to send the FINAL MEMO.

I want to bring to your attention that it has been a privilege and an honor to work with you. I learned a lot from you clinically when I was a Cardioscience nurse. You taught me about problem solving and public relations when I became a Manager. The lessons in accountability , best practices and role responsibilities continued when I became a Director.

Our Cardioscience Program has retained many philosophies from the time when you were Head of the Department – to provide the best cardiac care to the people of Saskatchewan. I know you devoted decades of your life to that goal.

Thank you for being a wonderful teacher, role model and for remaining true to your principles and ideals. I will miss your subtle sense of humor and the impromptu conversations regarding the topic of the day in the corridors of the hospital .

Wishing you and Mrs. Habib all the best in beautiful British Columbia.

Val Roy

1

US IN REGINA: THE MUSLIM COMMUNITY

Regina was our home. We had never lived anywhere longer than there. We lived in Regina for thirty-one years and in Saskatchewan for thirty-four.

We were involved with many historical events related to this city. We both were heavily involved in community leadership and uplifting the community status there while integrating with mainstream society.

My cardiology career started, flourished, and ended there. Our life began there when I received my appointment at the Plains Health Centre. We moved to Regina in 1976. We purchased a house at 308 Habkirk Drive at a cost of $69,000. We had to get a loan from the bank. We had $35,000 from the sale of our house in Saskatoon. Diane Moore was the real estate agent in Regina. It was a three-split-level house and was reasonable for all of our needs. It needed some work. Its basement was not finished. Kiswhar, Naushaba's friend from university in Karachi, visited us with her husband and family. Her husband was a very nice person and was handy. He saw our unfinished basement and insisted on framing it while they were visiting. I helped him. I was not accustomed to such work.

The house needed electricity in the basement, so I took a course on electricity in the evenings and wired the basement. Then, Naushaba and I together purchased gyproc boards and carried them on our heads down into the basement. We both worked together to finish the entire basement. The ceiling was done beforehand. We also carpeted the basement. It became livable. Our children could play around in the basement and enjoy it. It was in this house that we started an Islamic school for the children. When the winter was over, we both painted the exterior of the house. It became windy, but we carried on and completed the work. The backyard was not finished. We needed to level the ground in the backyard, so I bought a roller. It was heavy stuff. When I picked up the roller from the dicky of our car, I injured my back. I was limited for a few weeks. Ultimately, the backyard was finished. It was seeded, and we planted some trees in the front and back of the house.

One could not imagine that we could do all this work, but we did. There was a need. There was also economic strain. We were young. There was space for a garage, and we hired people to build us one. My mother and sister then arrived.

Our needs were growing, and so we looked for another house. Our financial condition had also improved. We found a suitable house at 440 Habkirk Drive, just a few houses away from our previous home. We upgraded the house to suit us. Naushaba took training on drapery, and she prepared very good drapes for all the windows in the house.

My mother and my sister accompanied us to this house. My sister was married at this house. This was my mother's last residence before she passed away.

The next house we built of our own desire and wish was at 9227 Wascana Mews. It was a beautiful, double-story house with a basement and a large triple garage. We put a pond with fish in it in the backyard. We enjoyed that house. When we moved from Regina to Abbotsford, we sold it. The time passed.

9227 Wascana Mews (our third house in Regina).

Regina is a very cold city in the winter, but it is very good in the summer. Piles of snow used to collect all over in the winter. Saskatchewan is the province with the highest duration of sunshine in the whole country. Its temperature used to drop to -40. The snow would pile up, even to a height of five or six feet, in the median of the road. The city had a good arrangement for cleaning the snow. But they would not clean the outlying streets. Naushaba cleaned the snow when we lived in Regina. I tried to help her, but I was not the type. I was also very busy. Ultimately, when we moved to 9227 Wascana Mews, we had help cleaning the snow because the area was large.

When we arrived in Regina, we attended a community picnic. We met a few people there, including Dr. Haque and Akram Din. Dr. Haque did not pay attention to us. Akram Din looked like a philosopher wearing a worn-out, black, all-weather coat. I found out that he was alone. I tried to avoid him. After a short while, we were driving through Wascana Park, and I saw him walking with his wife and daughters. He had appeared interesting on our initial contact. We became very good family friends. I did not expect that he would drag me into community leadership, but he did.

We were heavily involved in the community. This is well illustrated in this book and the other book we wrote about the history of the Muslims of Regina and their organizations. Socially, we were limited to a few families. We got together every week for a potluck. It was a good life.

The Muslim community started to increase in number. I got involved in community leadership, as did Naushaba.

I ultimately retired from community leadership in 1998. Our community had changed, as had the policies and management of the hospital administration. The time came when I resigned from my position as department head and ultimately retired from the practice. We moved to Abbotsford, BC, where we are still living.

ABBOTSFORD

We moved to Abbotsford on October 28, 2004. It would be the site of my semi-retired life until 2011 when I retired completely. It was a strange experience. The plane was to land in Abbotsford directly from Regina. There was stormy weather, and we were diverted to the Vancouver Airport and transferred to Abbotsford by taxi.

I wished to be involved in a teaching program and to provide consultation services to the hospital in Abbotsford. I was surprised that they were not able to accommodate me and wanted me to take calls and do internal medicine with others. I declined and started my own office practice. It was first at Gladwin Road. It was a large area and the only one suitable and available when we moved.

Subsequently, it was moved to George Ferguson Way. Then, at the request of Dr. West, I moved to his office on Marshall Road and practiced there. From there, I moved to West Oaks Medical Centre on South Fraser Way under Denning Management, the same as my practice in Surrey. They established their branch there. I used to go to Surrey one day a week and to Hope one day a month. I enjoyed these days. Eventually, the time came when I decided to close my practice. I had equipped my office with an ECG, treadmill machine, ambulatory rhythm monitoring system, and 24-hour ambulatory blood pressure monitoring. All of this was sold.

Authorship

We took to writing during our retirement. It was in the form of an article publication. We wrote a well-known book, *History of the Muslims of Regina, Saskatchewan, and their Organizations... A Cultural Integration*. We completed this while in Abbotsford. The first book took approximately eighteen months, as did this book. Our book and other write-ups were published and well received. I have written other articles, too, which are posted on my website, and some are included here in this book.

Canadian Islamic Congress

I established the chapter of this organization in British Columbia from 2005 to 2011, when I stepped down.

Muslim Business Council

I served as a director on its board from 2010 to 2016 and on its advisory council from 2016-2017.

Islamic School At Abbotsford

We volunteered to teach children at our home from 2004 to this day. There are fourteen students at different levels, and two students are taught on Skype. The curriculum is the complete teaching of Islam. Naushaba and I run it every Sunday for three hours. We teach the following courses, which are mentioned in the certificates the students receive upon completion of their studies. We hold an Islamic School function at the end of every school year.

Our house in Abbotsford, BC.

COURSES TAUGHT AND TO BE COMPLETED BY THE STUDENTS FINALIZING THE SCHOOL:

1. Completion of the Quran in Arabic and English.

2. Hadith 500 and 40 Hadith by Imam Nawawi.

3. Islamiat: All Aspects of Practicing Islam.

4. Course on Marriage.

5. Etiquettes of Life in Islam.

6. Islamic History from IslamiCity.

7. Muslims in the Muslim and Western World (Geopolitical).

8. Many selected lectures and audio-video subjects from various sites.

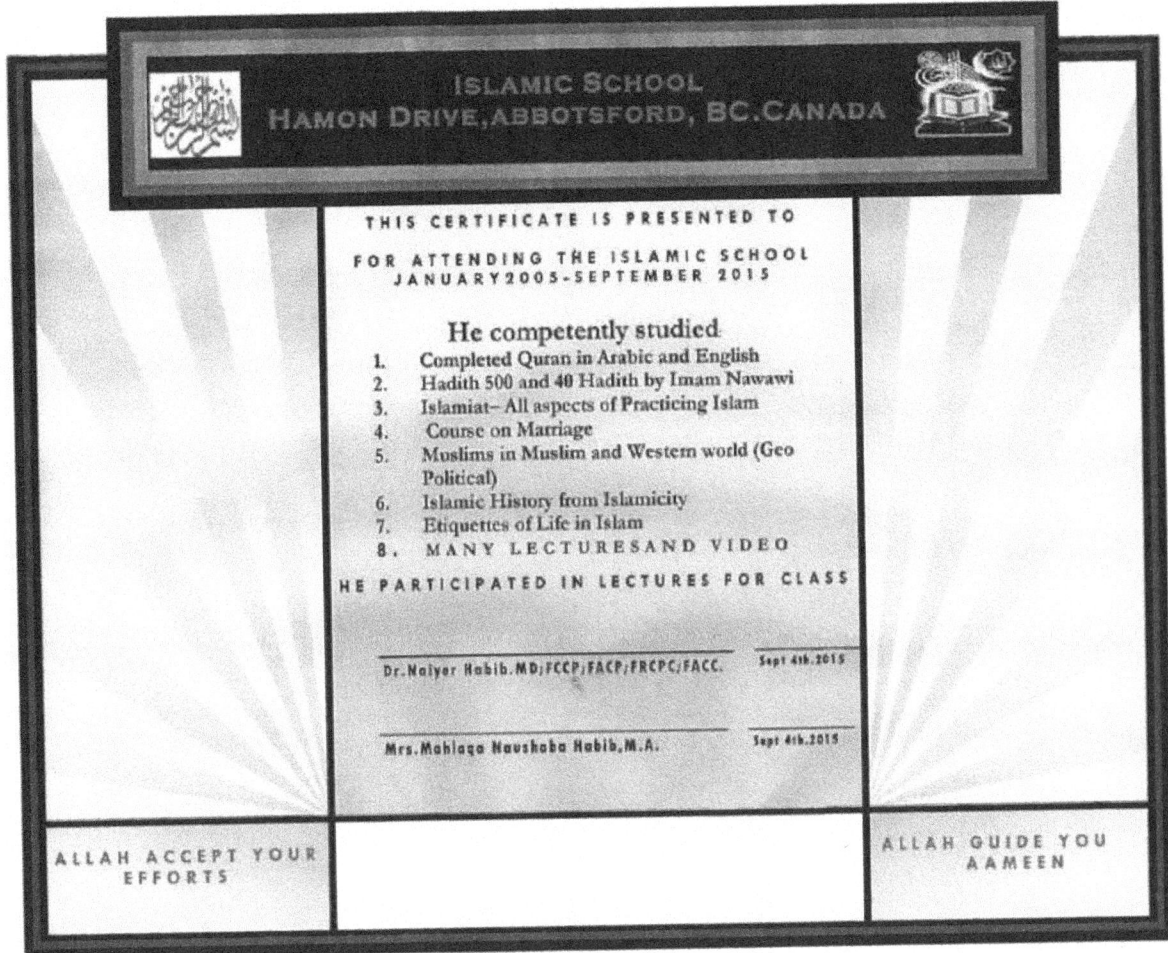

ISLAMIC SCHOOL
HAMON DRIVE, ABBOTSFORD, BC. CANADA

THIS CERTIFICATE IS PRESENTED TO

FOR ATTENDING THE ISLAMIC SCHOOL
JANUARY 2005 - SEPTEMBER 2015

He competently studied:

1. Completed Quran in Arabic and English
2. Hadith 500 and 40 Hadith by Imam Nawawi
3. Islamiat – All aspects of Practicing Islam
4. Course on Marriage
5. Muslims in Muslim and Western world (Geo Political)
6. Islamic History from Islamicity
7. Etiquettes of Life in Islam
8. MANY LECTURES AND VIDEO

HE PARTICIPATED IN LECTURES FOR CLASS

Dr. Nayer Habib. MD; FCCP; FACP; FRCPC; FACC. Sept 4th, 2015

Mrs. Mahlaqa Naushaba Habib, M.A. Sept 4th, 2015

ALLAH ACCEPT YOUR EFFORTS

ALLAH GUIDE YOU AAMEEN

Certificate presented to students.

COMMUNITY LEADERSHIP

by

Naiyer Habib

A detailed story of our community leadership is available in our book, *History of the Muslims of Regina, Saskatchewan, and their Organizations (HMRSO)*. It includes references to the Islamic Association, the Canadian Council of Muslim Women, and Muslims for Peace and Justice, "A Cultural Integration" (*HMRSO*), by Naiyer Habib and Mahlaqa Naushaba Habib[70]. Here, we provide some of the points that relate to us as persons who were involved in the leadership of the Muslim community in Saskatchewan.

We claim to have provided leadership with no preferential treatment to any one, irrespective of race, religion, family, or foe. We extended our hands to the community at large with open minds and no bias, offering our respect and friendship. Our other objective has always been to integrate with the community at large while maintaining our culture and religion. We never actively sought leadership, but when persuaded to assume a role, we would accept and do what we could do the best.

We had completed our education. We could not settle in either India or Pakistan and ultimately chose to settle in Canada. The culture and the religion of Islam were almost nonexistent in our Saskatchewan community. Dr. M. Anwar Haque and others had formed an association. We were few families—maybe six or seven, and that was it. We observed limited activities, such as Ramadan and Eid. There was not even any Juma (Friday) Prayer and no Islamic education for children. An attempt by Dr. Haque to initiate the teaching of the children in the Muslim community had failed. According to him, the community members, who were limited in number, did not show much interest. Dr. Haque had also attempted to initiate a Muslim organization in our neighbouring city of Swift Current, Saskatchewan, where there were a fair number of second and third-generation Lebanese families. Dr. Haque taught his children at home. Seeing the situation, Naushaba and I decided to have active involvement in the Muslim community.

---

[70] Available at www.amazon.com.

First Islamic School

We formed the first school in 1976 at our home in Regina, 308 Habkirk Drive, with Naushaba as the principal of the school.

Principal Mahlaqa Naushaba Habib.

The theme of education was based on the students knowing and practicing Islam without any bias against any religion or culture. We tried to emulate the standard of education suitable for our living in the West.

While Naushaba was the chair and principal, the school held an annual function with certificates and awards for the students. They were presented with a Quran and a Certificate of Completion of Islamic School. Their graduation from high school was also recognized as an achievement. A farewell function was held for them. The students also participated in the Islamic Association's functions. We had an established process to evaluate teaching in the school and get feedback from students. Students would be assessed and would receive a progress report.

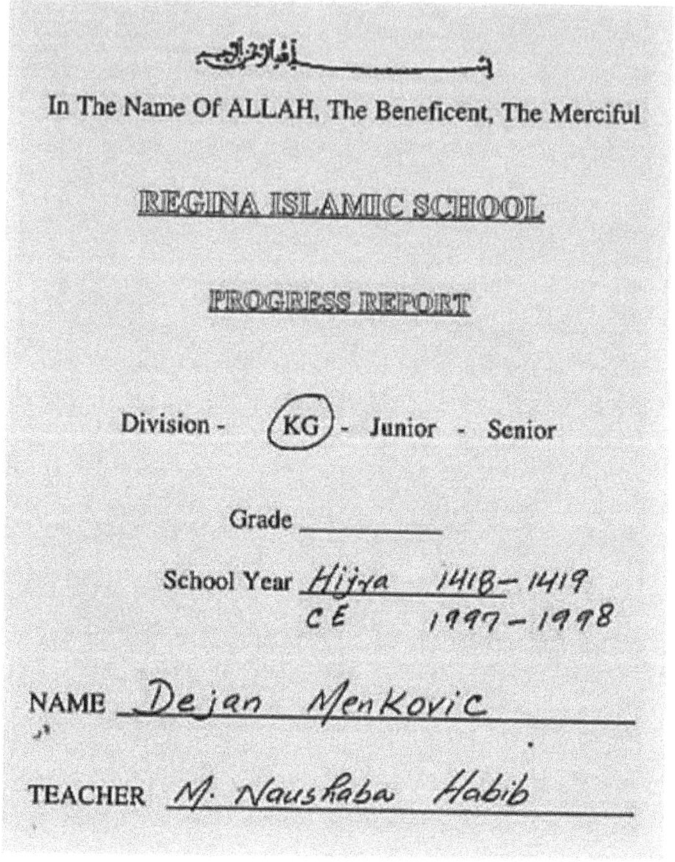

بسم الله الرحمن الرحيم

In The Name Of ALLAH, The Beneficent, The Merciful

REGINA ISLAMIC SCHOOL

PROGRESS REPORT

Division - (KG) - Junior - Senior

Grade _____

School Year _Hijra 1418 – 1419_
_CE 1997 – 1998_

NAME _Dejan Menkovic_

TEACHER _M. Naushaba Habib_

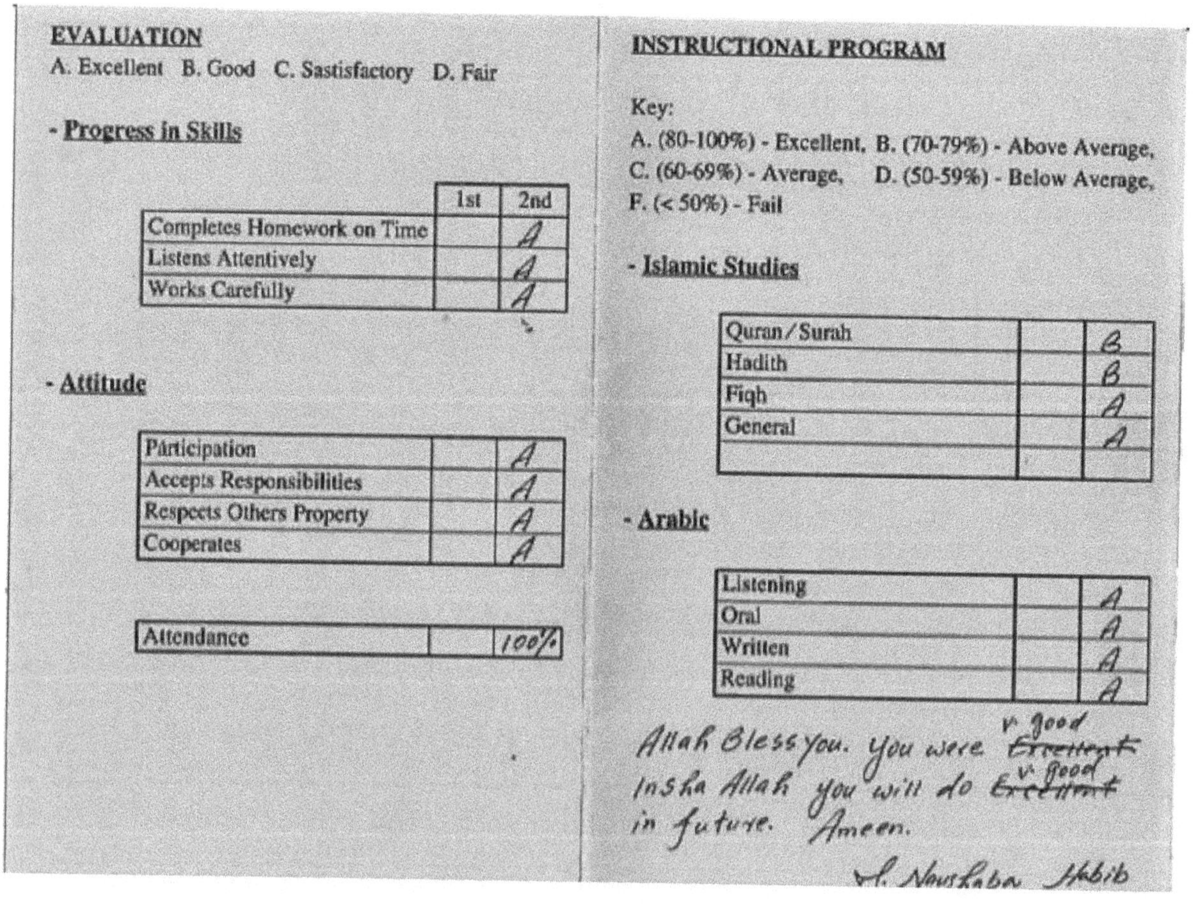

EVALUATION
A. Excellent   B. Good   C. Sastisfactory   D. Fair

- Progress in Skills

	1st	2nd
Completes Homework on Time		A
Listens Attentively		A
Works Carefully		A

- Attitude

Participation		A
Accepts Responsibilities		A
Respects Others Property		A
Cooperates		A

Attendance		100%

INSTRUCTIONAL PROGRAM

Key:
A. (80-100%) - Excellent,   B. (70-79%) - Above Average,
C. (60-69%) - Average,   D. (50-59%) - Below Average,
F. (< 50%) - Fail

- Islamic Studies

Quran / Surah		B
Hadith		B
Fiqh		A
General		A

- Arabic

Listening		A
Oral		A
Written		A
Reading		A

Allah Bless you. You were Excellent v. good
Insha Allah you will do Excellent v. good
in future. Ameen.

M. Naushaba Habib

An example of a 1997 progress report, found in our piles of papers.

308 Habkirk Drive (our first residence in Regina).

The school moved to the Islamic Centre at 240 College Avenue in June 1984. Naushaba stepped down as the principal when the school moved out of our home, after eight years of service. We volunteered for the school when Abdul Jalil was the principal as follows:

Abdul Jalil, principal, 1996-1998.
Naiyer Habib, president, 1996-1998.
Mahlaqa Naushaba Habib, voluntary teacher, 1996-1998.

Abdul Jalil, principal, welcoming.

Naiyer Habib, president; Abdul Jalil, principal.

Naushaba Habib (founder of Islamic School, 1976) distributing certificates.

ISLAMIC ASSOCIATION OF SASKATCHEWAN, REGINA INC.

I was informed by a member of the Muslim community that the community, including the then-president, Dr. M. Anwar Haque, wanted me to be the president of the Islamic Association of Regina (IAOS). I never wanted to compete with Dr. Haque, and I never wanted to be president. The community had faced some problems, and I had been involved as a negotiator. I had taken on this responsibility on the condition that I would not serve in any capacity on the board of the Islamic Association. It was at the last moment on the day of the election that I was given this message of election and me to be the choice for the presidency. There was no time for me to consult or confirm with Dr. Haque. The time for the annual general meeting was approaching. I was also told that I should just let my name stand for the presidency for a minute and that Dr. Haque would withdraw, and that would prove the point. I agreed, and that is what happened. In the later phase, I could not confirm, but I was suspicious that Dr. Haque had probably not said that he wanted me to be president. This suspicion occurred to me after a few years of serving the Muslim community.

Subsequent to that, I was re-elected as president. When I had served three years continuously, I asked someone else to be elected. It so happened that the community was getting split up on the candidacy of the individual and did not agree to that. I continued in this role for a fourth year.

During my fourth year as president, I decided that we should change the constitution to limit the term of serving on the board so that no board member would serve indefinitely. The constitution was changed.

No doubt, sometimes I made firm decisions in implementing certain policies, but I worked hard to ensure that the members of the community accepted my decisions with understanding.

One time, a member of the community pointed out to me regarding a certain matter that "it was a dictatorship." I humbly answered, "If a dictator is sincere and looking after the affairs selflessly for the benefit of the people, it is far better than a democratic leader who works to please people to stay on as their leader!"

Naushaba was part and parcel of my life in all my initiatives, helping and advising me. We embarked on our tasks and completed as many as we could. The community members were with us in helping us achieve what was needed.

We served the association in the following capacities and during the following periods:

I served as president of the association from 1977-1981, 1984-1986, 1989-1992, and 1996-1998. I served as a director on the board in 1981-1982 and 1982-1984. Naushaba served as a director from 1986-1988.

OUR ROLE IN THE MUSLIM COMMUNITY

It is of historic importance to cite the presidential report of my first term in office because it demonstrates our initiation of work and our vision for the future. These were achieved, as reflected in these pages, by the grace of God.

Juma (Friday) Prayer

This is a mandatory prayer in Islam. The prayer is offered weekly on Fridays in the city or village where the amenities of life are available. It has a social purpose so that people can meet and know about one another socially. At least three people are required to offer this prayer. There was no Friday Prayer in Regina when we moved there. Friday Prayer was started a little later, in 1978, on the initiation of Dr. Masood-Ul-Alam, who was the first imam for Friday Prayers.

Hadith, Quran, and views of other scholars were collected, and it was determined to fix the time of Friday Prayer, keeping in mind the necessity to avoid the period of Zawal (midday). This continued until 1998. With the change of the board, it was adjusted to 1:30 p.m. The youth disappeared from the Friday Prayer and attended only when school was closed.

Ayman Aboguddah, Naiyer Habib, Anwar Haque, Sajjad Malik, Hazam Raffat, and a member of the youth group participated by leading the prayer and khutbah[71] by rotation, a practice that continued until 1998. We did not want to have an imam funded by a foreign country, as we had seen situations where the imam would have his say and not listen to his community, and that led to considerable problems. We managed it fairly well.

I arranged a room at the University of Regina because I was also a professor of medicine there. But, we faced considerable difficulties in performing the Friday Prayer there. The room would sometimes be locked. Undaunted, we proceeded to buy a business building. We took a loan from the bank, rented the downstairs to a business to generate income for its support, and used the upstairs space for our purposes. It was located at 240 College Avenue.

Muslim Association of Swift Current

A large number of Muslims, particularly of Lebanese origin, had settled in Swift Current. They were now in their third generation. I, while the president of the IAOS, Regina Inc., accompanied by Abdul Qayyum, Mohammad Sadeque, and Zubair Akhtar, travelled to Swift Current. We wanted to drum up ideas and suggestions for initiating an organization of Muslims in that community. They were assured that they would be helped by the Regina and Saskatoon Muslim communities.

---

[71] Khutbah is an address (sermon) before Friday Prayer and after Eid Prayer.

I invited Salim Ganem and David Russell of the then-national organization, Council of Muslim Communities of Canada (CMCC), to a meeting with the residents of Swift Current.

Meanwhile, Mohammed Afsar moved from Hamilton, Ontario, to Swift Current, as an engineer for the city. He assumed the charge of forming the Muslim Association of Swift Current.

The Islamic Centre in Regina

First Islamic Centre, at 240 College Avenue, Regina.

The IAOS Regina purchased a business building in January 1982. The plan for this purchase was initiated in 1979 when I was the president. We were few in number. There was a financial constraint. We did not want to get money from foreign sources to avoid any influence from foreign countries on our affairs. Hisham Badran, an Islamic scholar and frequent visitor to Regina for our children, arranged a donation from the Rabita organization. The cost was still high. I spoke to the board members and the community. I told them, asking forgiveness from Allah, to get the building by taking a mortgage from the bank on a temporary basis. I emphasized that we were in dire need of a building of our own. There was a greater benefit for the Muslim community in this, to observe our Islamic duty—Friday Prayers, and to have a school for children and youth. I asked to ask Allah to forgive us if there was any sin in this reason. I also emphasized that banks never run losses and that interest is not a hardship, as other money lenders charge heavy interest and usurp property. After a heated discussion, the idea of applying for a loan was approved. The purchase was completed during the time that Dr. Haque was president. He registered the building with the corporation branch in January 1982.

Members of our community at 240 College Ave 1st Islamic Centre.

The opening was celebrated in 1984, when Abdul Qayyum was president, with Hisham Badran as the chief guest. He was told about the mortgage and the reason for it. He criticized the idea but was not harsh. He participated in the opening ceremony. A year later, we had paid the loan down. An Islamic knowledgeable person told me recently that this was an acceptable act under the circumstances (source not available). Recently, I saw commentary number 324 on Surah Baqra Ayah 275 by Abdullah Yusuf Ali in the 1938 edition, which was changed after his death by a group of Muslim scholars in the new and revised edition of 1989. I wonder how someone can modify the writing of the writer. One can write comments or criticism. However, a publisher, Tahrike Tarsile Quran, Inc., published it with no alterations of translation or commentary in 2012 and little grammar modification. I do not approve of any modification, including grammar, but it is a good step otherwise.

The Second at 3273 Montague Street

Our next move was to acquire a larger centre. Nasir Butt, then a member of the board, was instrumental in raising funds and acquiring a previous church to serve as our new home. The board also approached the Canadian Islamic Trust (CIT) for funding and received it.

The finalization of the agreement was completed and signed by Mohammad Ashraf, representing the Canadian Islamic Trust; Naiyer Habib, the president; and Nasir Butt, the secretary, on behalf of the Islamic Association of Saskatchewan, Regina Inc. This was notarized.

IN WITNESS WHEREOF, Trustee and Beneficiary have executed this Trust on this 1st day of November, 1989, and if this Trust is executed in counterparts, each shall be deemed an original.

THE CANADIAN ISLAMIC TRUST FOUNDATION

Per: _____

Per: _____

THE ISLAMIC ASSOCIATION OF SASKATCHEWAN, REGINA, INC.

Per: _____

Per: _____

PROVINCE OF:

COUNTY OF:

Before me a Notary Public in and for said County and Province, personally appeared ___

_____

_____

who acknowledged the execution of the foregoing TRUST.

Witness my hand and Notarial Seal this 1st day of November, 1989.

My commission expires: Signature: _Roberta M. Robertson_

Oct. 31/92   Printed: ROBERTA M. ROBERTSON

383

Islamic Centre & Mosque, 3273 Montague Street, Regina, purchased November 1989.

Nilofer Haque and Naushaba Habib, cleaning.

Nasir Butt and Sajjad Malik, renovating.

On November 10, 1989, Rabiussani 11. 1410 first Friday Prayer was held in this centre.

بسم الله الرحمن الرحيم

الله أكبر

ISLAMIC ASSOCIATION OF SASKATCHEWAN
REGINA INC.

ISLAMIC CENTRE AND MOSQUE
3273 MONTAGUE ST.
REGINA, SK. S4S 1Z8
RABI-2ND 11, 1410
NOVEMBER 10, 1989

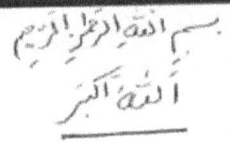

12:20   ADAAN: BR. MUSTAFA BARRE
12:30   KHUTBA: BR. SAJJAD MALIK
12:45   PRAYER: IMAM: BR. SAJJAD MALIK

NOTICE

THERE WILL BE ISLAMIC BOOKS ON SALE ON:
RABI-2ND 13, 1410
NOVEMBER 12, 1989

Mustafa Elbare calling Adhan. Sajjad Malik to lead the prayer.

<u>Opening Ceremony of the Islamic Centre and Mosque at Montague Street</u>

We held a very elaborate opening ceremony for this newly established centre on November 12, 1989, as detailed in *HMRSO*.

In the name of Allah, Most Gracious, Most Merciful

ISLAMIC ASSOCIATION OF SASKATCHEWAN, REGINA, INC.

OPENING CEREMONY OF THE NEW ISLAMIC CENTRE/MOSQUE
3273 Montague St., Regina, Sk.

Rabie the Second 13, 1410 A.H.   November 12, 1989 A.D.

PROGRAM

12:00 Noon	**Arrival**	
12:45 P.M.	**Zuhr** - Adaan: Br. Wa-el Sawan	
1:00	- Iqama: Br. Wa-el Sawan	
	- Imam : Br. Hazem Raafat	

1:15   **Pot-Luck Dinner** - Community Hall

2:15   **Function (Part I)** - Community Hall
Chairperson: Br. Naiyer Habib
- Recitation of Qur'an : Brs. Khalid Tuwaty & Munir-Ul-Haque
- Announcement of Program: Secretary (Br. Nasir Butt)
- President's Welcome Address: Br. Naiyer Habib
- Short Address: Representatives of Visiting Communities and National Organizations
- Recognition of Founding Members of The Islamic Association of Saskatchewan, Regina Inc.
- Recognition of Past Presidents
- Recognition of Founding Members of Islamic School
- Recognition of Past Principals of Islamic school
- Recognition of Founding Members of Muslim Youth Group
- Address by Guest Speakers:
    - Role of Islamic National Organizations in North America: Br. S. Imtiaz Ahmed
    - Role of the Mosque in the Community: Br. Mostafa Abd-El-Barr

3:30 P.M.   **Asr** - Adaan: Br. Mohammad El-Zawie
3:40   - Iqama: Br. Mohammad El-Zawie
           - Imam :   Br. Rasheek Rifaat

3:50   **Function (Part II)** - Community Hall
Presentation of Muslim Youth
Chairperson: Br. Ziad Malik
- Announcement of Program: Secretary (Br. Faisal Sethi)
- President's Address: Br. Ziad Malik
- Role of Muslim Youth: Br. Arsalan Habib

4:05   Presentation of Islamic School
Chairperson: Sr. Nasim Ahmed

4:50   Word of Thanks: Secretary (Br. Nasir Butt)
Dua'a and Official Ending of the Program
Snack - Community Hall

5:25   **Maghrib** - Adaan: Br. Jihad Rashid
               - Iqama : Br. Jihad Rashid
               - Imam   : Br. Mostafa Abd-El-Barr

Program for the opening ceremony of the Montague Street Islamic Centre/Mosque.

Presidential Address

Presidential Address on the occasion of the opening ceremony of the new Islamic Centre/ Mosque at 3273 Montague Street, Regina, Saskatchewan, Rabi 2nd, 13, 1410 AH, November 12, 1989 AD:

Dr. Naiyer Habib, president, past and present (1977-81, '84-'86, '89-'92).

In the name of Allah, most kind, most merciful.

My dear brothers and sisters in Islam and our guests. Assalam-o-Alaikum (peace be upon you). It is my pleasure to welcome you on behalf of the Islamic Association of Saskatchewan, Regina, Incorporated, as a third-time (not continuously) president of the Islamic Association on this historic moment for which we are grateful to Allah (SW).

We pray for all who put their efforts into establishing Islam in this part of the province, going back to the first Muslim who came to this part of the world, whoever he or she may have been, to those who are present today, that Allah accept their efforts and reward them for their deeds.

The various organizations and individuals who were supportive in one way or another for our community may be named. They are Rabita-Al-Alam, CMCC, Saudi Arabia via Rabita al Islamia (NY); and brothers Hisham Badran, David Russell (Hisham Ahmed), Asad Dawud, The Canada Islamic Trust, with the help Ashraf of the Canadian Islamic Trust associated with ISNA. I offer thanks to all our past presidents and their boards, and all members of the community of the past and present, for their help, and pray for them that Allah accept their effort and reward them for their good deeds.

I'd like to bring up the following facts that I feel are important to express on this occasion.

Our leadership is important, and it has to evolve continuously to lead us in this part of the world. Old or ex-leaders who served us are very valuable. It is important that we utilize their experience—and not put the old ones away as newcomers come.

Newer and younger generations must be incorporated into leadership under the guidance of the most experienced ones.

Remember "the present generation" who came from old countries and who have strived to maintain and flourish Islamic values with their families. They are our treasures, having the Islamic values of the old country and an understanding of how to follow Deen (the Islamic Way of Life) in this Western world. Please associate with them, with your family.

And we have another treasure: new Muslims. They know the negativity of the society they left because of what they experienced. They came to Islam because they were convinced of its values. Please love, respect, and adore them more than our own blood relatives. They have sacrificed a lot. To the new Muslims, I have to say that your belief in Islam and your achievement of Taqwa (God, conscience, and cognizance) are enough for you to be helped by Allah (SW).

It is our responsibility to demonstrate Islam to our neighbours, contacts, and non-Muslim wives through our practice—not our theory—and to invite them to Islam with wisdom.

Our actions and deeds (and failures) must be in accordance with our words (Qaul), which must be a representation of our Deen—Islam.

Remember two things:

1. Allah watches all the time and everywhere—with helping hands extended to us.

2. Our children, no matter how small they are, watch us—don't they?

A parent who is casual in the practice of Islam is a dual harmer. They cause:

1. Harm to their own family.

2. Harm to society by adding children whose Islamic values will dilute to degeneration, leading to the extinction of Islam to them and the society they will form (I hope and pray to Allah that this does not happen). Do we not see this happening?

By giving Islamic values to our children—from infanthood, when they are like green sticks for moulding, not when they have matured and become hard sticks that will break if you bend them—there will be a society for all; enriched with Islamic values.

It is hard or easy to practice Islam, depending on how we want to look at it. If it is hard, one can begin now with the least he or she can do—saying "Allah, La Ilaha Illallah"[72] at bedtime with all sincerity. Ask Allah (SW) for forgiveness. Ask Him to make it easier. He will help to achieve Taqwa in due course.

---

[72] There is no deity but God.

Why is it not possible to offer Fajr Prayer[73] and start our daily activity from then on? How can we get up at 4 a.m. to catch a plane at 6:00 a.m. and not manage Fajr Prayer? Why not get up to offer prayer and go back to sleep? Question yourself—as parents—about the bellyache in your children at midnight and whether to rush to the hospital or call a doctor? Or about the problem with your plumbing and the question of getting help from a plumber at an odd hour of night. Once a routine for prayer is adopted, all becomes easier while asking Allah SW to make it easier for us!

Let us change our lifestyle without interfering with the working needs of Western society.

Inhibition is a dangerous ailment in our society. By inhibition, I mean that some of us are too shy even to say we are Muslims, not to speak of offering prayers in public. The answer to inhibition is communication with people and society about our values and their significance.

Laziness—be it in ablution, offering prayers, or recitation of the Quran—is another ailment. Let there be copies of the Quran in your home wherever you sit. The investment you make in acquiring the invaluable Qurans is very little. It will not be a costly deed.

My dear brothers, sisters, and children, we live in the Western world. Let us make our presence known as individuals by becoming politicians, lawyers, journalists, doctors, farmers, labourers, and volunteers. Let us make our presence known as an Islamic society.

It is also important to make your voice known on day-to-day issues—be they abortion, alcoholism, or child abuse. We have answers. Discharge your duty to the country, province, city, and society in which you live. After you have established that, ask your right, as a Muslim society, without jeopardizing others. Following Islam is so flexible that it will not jeopardize individuals, neighbours, or others. Do not demand or impose things that will disturb or annoy people around us, especially when we have alternatives available.

I put forward an example of a demand to call for prayer on a loudspeaker that disturbs the neighbourhood when you could use many other modern ways to alert people to come to the masjid without disturbing others.

We as individuals make contributions to the development of this society as a whole, but little is known to this society. Our contribution as an Islamic society via news media is not known. No news media have come to publicize our opening ceremony despite my contacting them well in advance.

An immigration officer has been heard to say: "They are leaches to this country." Is that true? There are biases and they are because of misunderstandings and otherwise. *Satanic Verses* and the problems that arose out of it are as alive to me today as they were on the day this issue surfaced.

There are many lessons to learn and many steps to build from these lessons. Many things have been done and are being done. They must be done with wisdom. Can you imagine a writers' association reading *Satanic Verses* in public?! Ask if such an association has been able to prevent the agony that the author of this blasphemy is going

---

[73] Morning Prayer.

through because of the sin he has committed. Remember the words of our own prime minister, Mr. Mulroney, in March in London—which I have recorded—saying when the border authorities did not allow the book to enter Canada: "Who are they to decide what we can read and what we cannot read?" Remember, our foreign minister, with swift action, called the ambassadors of Muslim countries to condemn Iran (Fatwa of Ayatollah on Rushdie), but there was not a word—not a word—for Muslims to console them or any word against the author.

These things will change and are changing as we make our presence known with wisdom. Our population must increase by birth and sponsorship. And the issue of the economy will be solved by mutual effort. Migrating individuals should have quality and not quantity.

It is not practical to have a single Muslim organization. This would have been ideal, but as long as the goal is to act in accordance with the Quran-e-Karim and Sunnah of our prophet Muhammad (SAW), there is no problem. These organizations may complement and supplement one another but not compete for power or politics or ridicule one another. Therefore, my brothers and sisters and children, come together, come to the masjid, and resolve each and every day's issues, be they religious, social, familial, or political, as good citizens of the West as dictated by the Quran and Sunnah.

Hold the rope of Allah (SW), which he has extended to us, together. Help yourself and help one another, whoever you are, to whichever sect you belong, and whatever views you hold.

The carriage of Islam goes on—and will go on. That is the promise of Allah (SW). Please join it.

And those of you who are not of Islamic faith, you are our brothers and sisters in the human race, and we extend our values to you. Please use them and be benefited by them, whether you accept Islam. The choice is yours. Islam does not impose a conversion on you, but it does invite you. Jazakallah Khair (may God reward you with goodness). Allah bless you all!

Thank you.

Dr. Naiyer Habib, FACP, FRCPC, FACC. The President

Other Speakers

Their Speeches with their Photographs are published in our Book- History of Muslims of Regina and their Organizations "A CULTURAL INTEGRATION" amazon.com:

Anwar Haque, founding president;

Abdul Qayyum, past president;

Sajjad Malik, past president,

Dr. F. M. Alkatib, a founding member; Imtiaz Ahmed, ISNA Canada;

Mostafa Abd El Barr, U of Saskatchewan.

Mohammad Ejaz, president, IAOS, Saskatoon;

Mohammad Afsar, president, Muslim Association of Swift Current;

Ziad Malik, president, youth;

Arsalan Naiyer Habib, youth representative, Regina. Nasir Butt, Vote of Thanks

Muslims In Focus

We established the Muslims in Focus program on Cable Regina. Norul Ain Jaffery was the introducer, and Riazuddin Ahmed was the anchorman. The objective was to introduce the Muslim community of Regina to the population at large. There were interviews with invited members of the community to speak on various subjects of community interest.

Subsequently, Islam in Focus—a series by Dr. Jamal Badawi of Halifax—replaced Muslims in Focus. It was broadcast for a period. Cable Regina then did not want to continue the program, as it was not prepared locally. Available pictures[74] representing the program are shown here.

---

[74] Pictures as a courtesy of the Access Communications Co-Operative of Regina.

Riaz Ahmed interviewing Dr. M. A. Haque (centre) and N. Habib.

Sunday Monthly Islamic Symposium

A monthly Islamic symposium was arranged at the old university campus on College Avenue. Various subjects were chosen for the presentation. They were delivered and discussed in this symposium on a monthly basis. The participation of the speakers was from the Muslim community, on rotation. It included adult and youth members, and it was well received. However, over the course of time, this was discontinued because of the low number of participants. We also offered Friday Prayer in this building before acquiring our Islamic Centre at 240 College Avenue.

Old University of Regina campus on College Avenue, Regina.

Monthly Family Islamic Discussion

For the ongoing learning of Islam and for their participation in the community and national affairs, particularly focussing on the children, a few families joined together at our homes in the evening once a month. Children, youth, men, and women presented with various topics. A discussion followed under a co-ordinator elected for each session, irrespective of age and gender. Socialization followed.

Participant families included: Asif and Najma Mann, Dr. Abdul and Nusrat Jalil, Dr. Abdur and Rizwana Rahman, Dr. Naiyer and Naushaba Habib, Riazuddin and Samina Ahmed.

Muslim Youth of Regina

One of our objectives was to encourage our children to fully participate in the affairs of the community. Muslim Youth was their own initiative, and we supported it.

Muslim Youth Activities Muslim Youth Conference

Two youths from Regina attended the first conference for youth at the Council of Muslim Communities of Canada in Toronto in the early 1980s.

Monthly Potluck

Get-together at parents' houses, on rotation.

Voluntary Participation

Voluntary Participation in the functions and programs of the Islamic Association, as well as the Islamic School.

Educational Opportunities

Boys visited the masjid at 240 College Avenue after its establishment. They would recite the Quran and its translation. They would listen to Islamic tapes and have discussions. Subsequently, they went to restaurants such as McDonald's, Dairy Queen, etc., to have coffee and fun. Girls participated at their homes.

Al-Adhan Magazine

Al-Adhan Magazine was published by the youth.

Youth Camp

The youth arranged a camping trip to Camp Monahan in August 1985. This was the most important historic event arranged by the Muslim Youth of Regina. They made preparations by arranging the camp. Camp Monahan was a Christian camp, and they were happy to allow the facility to be used by our youth for a small donation. It is worth noting that the boys prepared a fence to put between them and the girls for swimming. The girls were primarily involved in making food, which they took to the camp.

At the camp, they held prayers, skits, swimming (partition for girls), games, campfires, and a Parents' Day.

Enjoying lunch, boys and girls.

Allah bless our youth. All of them achieved high status as Muslims in Western society, integrating with no bias or discrimination.

Subsequently, with changes to the Muslim Association board, the name was changed to Kids Camp, but this was the first and last event.

STAND TAKEN

Condoms In School

It had been recommended to the Regina School Board to equip public schools with condoms in an attempt to prevent teen pregnancy. This was a step in the right direction, given the prevailing problem of teen pregnancy.

However, from the Islamic point of view, it is the basic preaching of Islam that such practice should not come into play in society. The lack of this aspect of education and its practice was the root cause of teen and unwanted pregnancies. The placement of condoms in schools was perceived as an encouragement and acceptance of the acts leading to it by an institution responsible for teaching children.

In view of this, I took the initiative on behalf of the association, on the board's approval, to express our concerns to the Board of Education. The outcome of this is not available to me and is not recalled.

The correspondence between me and others is cited in *HMRSO*, but I note here what I wrote to start the discussion.

ISLAMIC ASSOCIATION OF SASKATCHEWAN
Regina Inc.

March 10, 1992

Mrs. Margaret Fern
Chairperson
Public School Board
1600 4th Avenue
Regina, Sask.
S4R 8C8

Dear Mrs. Fern:

I am writing to you on behalf of the Muslim Community regarding the issue of placement of condoms in the school. Public school system represents a broader public interest in the matters of education and is not to follow the morees of a particular group.

It is realized that teenagers are sexually active. Some parents want the school to take their responsibility to dispense condoms in schools or even teach sexuality in school from kindergarten. These are the parents who spend time in acquiring material success and have no time to spend with the family to raise the children with high moral and character. The family value is lost. It should be the responsibility of these parents to provide condom to their children themselves by organizing a volunteer place or home or as they consider fit outside the premises of the public school.

The public school funded by tax payers belonging to various cultures and religions must take into consideration views of all and must not act to support the views of a segment of the society only. If it has to involve itself it must give due consideration to the views of broader groups of the society based on culture, religion and morality respecting the principle of virginity.

We Muslims are a segment of the society. Our children attend the public school. I enclose here the following brief information which are self explanatory:
1. A brochure on moral system of Islam.
2. An editorial from Muslim Parent Magazine.
3. A recent statement of 'Magic' on virginity.

The subject in itself is vast. If the Department of Education wishes to have input of Islamic expert in developing any guideline we will be more than happy to provide you with list of resource personnel and will be happy to participate in any discussion that you may have.

3273 Montague St., Regina, Sk., CANADA, S4S 128   Tel:(306)585 0090

/2

President
(306) 584-6707 NH: bm

Encl,
Copies to: Trustees, Public School Board
His Worship Mayor Doug Archer
Hon. Mr. Roy Romanow
Hon. Mr. Grant Devine
Hon. Mrs. Linda Haverstock

Lord's Prayer in Public Schools

The Regina Board of Education proposed having the Lord's Prayer as a mandatory opening exercise in public schools. Since the schools had students of multi-religious beliefs, this raised concerns. The majority of the news released in the *Leader-Post* provided alternate suggestions.

I, as the president of the Islamic Association of Saskatchewan, suggested alternatives in a letter to the Board of Education. The letter was acknowledged by the board, and our concerns on behalf of Muslims were published in the *Leader-Post* on January 31, 1981. This appeared in an interview with *Maclean's* on February 23, 1981, on page 31. Other communities also spoke out.

The outcome was that the prayer would be optional and not mandatory—a decision that didn't consider the psychological impact on the students left out of such gatherings. These are the costs of living in a majority society. I believe that a democracy by a majority that neglects minorities is akin to a dictatorship.

Correspondence with the board of education and publication in the *Leader-Post*, courtesy of Marion Marshall, are included here. My opinion expressed in the *Maclean's* interview is also included, but not the pages of the magazine.

THE ISLAMIC ASSOCIATION OF SASKATCHEWAN
REGINA

PHONE

P O B 3572
Regina, Saskatchewan
Canada

بسم الله الرحمن الرحيم

وَاعْتَصِمُوا بِحَبْلِ اللهِ جَمِيعًا وَلَا تَفَرَّقُوا

"And hold together firmly to God's rope and do not separate."   The Quran 3:103

February 2, 1981

Chairman
Board of Education
Public Schools
1870 Lorne Avenue
REGINA, Saskatchewan.

Dear Sir:

I, on behalf of the Islamic Association of Saskatchewan (Regina), have been asked to express our concerns regarding the recent approval by the Board of Education of Public Schools, allowing the singing of Oh Canada, The Lord's Prayer and recitation of the bible as officially accepted practice in public schools from now on, as it appeared in the recent issue of The Leader Post. It is apparent that the Board did not consult any religious minority group while making this decision. It is also noted that this proposal was passed by the Trustees by a marginal vote of one only.

Approval of such practice is quite appropriate for any organization if all people come from the same background. However, Canada is enriched with people of various cultures and religions. All people, in whatever number they may be, are entitled to flourish equally and are not to be differentiated from one another on the basis of race, religion, culture, etc., Although the majority may not like to be dictated to by one or two (students/parents) people, majority also should not take steps to create circumstance to set aside the one or two persons from the mainstream of life. Those few persons could be of vital importance to the Nation.

Provision by the Board for the minority to be excused, yet asking the majority to proceed with its present recommendation as officially approved, creates considerable problem for the children of minority groups, particularly of a psychological nature. These children will be differentiated by other children in the schools. They may be suspected to be "unbelievers" when they may come from very religious communities. A vicious circle will be created. These schools which expected to bring up our children as good citizens, will become a source of differentiating one group of children from another and will become a centre of conflict for them. Children of minority groups thus singled out now and kept away from the main group of students with whom they have been united in performance of all activities, will be psychologically affected and tortured on a day to day basis if this proposal, which has been approved, is brought into practice.

I note the comments that many teachers conducted such exercises before and it is apparent that it was without approval of the Board. If it is so, the Principals of these schools, and the Board, should have tried to know the feelings of the minority groups in this context. If the Education Act allows the School Board to introduce both the Lord's Prayer and bible readings

399

in the schools as part of the opening exercises, we should look at this Act in the light of the views of the minority groups now.

After presentation of the above facts and comments, I put forward the suggestion of our organization to the Board for kind consideration and action for the public schools.

1. Singing of "Oh Canada" should be the opening exercise in all schools to stress Canadian nationalism, which we lack.

2. Although we realize that the Board is sincere to bring students to religion to make them better individuals, we feel that this approach should be left to individual families and religious communities, who should play active roles in our present Canadian set-up.

3. There should not be any recitation from any religious book, from any religion, either in the form of prayer or opening exercise.

4. The Lord's Prayer should not be included in the opening exercise. A prayer may be included on which all present or future minority group will agree. We would like to see the content of the Lord's Prayer for specific comment.

5. In view of the above discussion, all schools who are conducting religious exercises should be asked to discontinue such exercises.

6. The School Board should consult all religious groups whenever it considers any matter in relation to religion.

7. It is noted that Separate schools exist to bring up children of majority faith, whereas the minority lacks this facility and has to face much more hardship in teaching their children their religion and culture.

8. Our organization is apprehensive that if the Board does not take these points into consideration, and particularly if the Board continues to make decisions without consulting the minority religious groups, probably other religious difficulties may be encountered by the minority religious groups.

Having brought these points to your attention, some of which were amply focussed on by some members of the Board as well as some members of minority groups as it has appeared in the recent newspapers, it is our hope that the Board will withdraw its recommendation and will advise the various public schools accordingly.

We shall be waiting to hear regarding your action.

With sincere regards,

Yours truly,

Dr. Naiyer Habib
President.
4500 Wascana Parkway

The Leader-Post   Regina, Saskatchewan   Saturday, January 31, 1981

Moslems join protest against Lord's Prayer, Bible reading

By Matt Bellan
of The Leader-Post

Regina Moslems have joined the protest against guidelines allowing the Lord's Prayer and Bible reading in public school classrooms.

Dr. Naiyer Habib, president of the Regina chapter of the Islamic Association of Saskatchewan, called The Leader-Post Friday, saying his organization is upset about the guidelines, part of a package of procedures for opening exercises the board of education approved Monday.

"We favor the national anthem but do not favor any religious observance," Habib said. "Although we are Moslems and believe in God, we believe it should be kept separate."

Among other things, the guidelines give teachers the option of reciting the Lord's Prayer and reading passages from the Bible approved by the department of education.

Some trustees said many teachers already conduct opening exercises and board guidelines will standardize the practice.

The Education Act allows school boards to introduce both the Lord's Prayer and Bible reading in schools as part of opening exercises, they added.

Habib said although the guidelines allow teachers to excuse students from minority religious groups from participating, "I see a sort of pscyhological torture for those young children to be away from the majority."

He agreed with statements by Rabbi Sheldon Korn about the guidelines, he added. Korn, rabbi at Regina's Beth Jacob Synagogue, said in a Leader-Post interview this week that he objects to them partly because the Lord's Prayer is a Christian prayer.

"I suggest that the board of education, when it makes this kind of decision, should consult religious minorities." Habib said, adding that there are at least 100 students of Islamic faith in the city's public schools.

According to school board officials, total enrolment in the public school system is about 23,500.

Habib said his organization plans to write a letter to the board protesting the guidelines.

In a Leader-Post survey Friday of other religous minorities. Jack Hui, secretary of the city's Chinese Cultural Society, said he was also against allowing the Lord's Prayer and Bible reading in public schools.

"Even with excusing students I still say, in your heart you're isolated by the other people," said Hui, adding that he spoke for himself, not for the local Chinese community.

There are about 500 Chinese children in the city's public schools, he said. Some of their parents are Christian; the majority, including him, are of Buddhist background but not necessarily observant Buddhists.

His organization hasn't discussed the issue yet but may do so at a coming meeting, Hui added.

Dr. H. N. Gupta, a University of Regina professor and a Hindu, said parents should look at the Lord's Prayer before condemning its use in classrooms.

"Some prayers can be perfectly universal," he said, adding that he was speaking for himself, not for the local Hindu community. "One should not simply react angrily."

There are between 120 and 150 Hindu students in Regina public schools, Gupta said.

He said it's not just religious minorities who may object to religious practices in the classroom. Some parents of Christian background may also object.

"If anyone does not want to join in prayer, they should have a written request from parents," Gupta said. Teachers and principals should freely grant such students permission to be excused.

The following is my comment published in *Maclean's* under the heading "To Pray or Not to Pray" on February 23, 1981, page 31:

"It could actually amount to a form of psychological torture," warns Naiyer Habib, president of the Regina Chapter of the Islamic Association of Saskatchewan, after officially complaining in a letter to the school board. He further remarks, "There are mixed religions now in public school, and if some children do not join in or walk out, they will feel they are not a part of the group. Other students will see this and a feeling against the minority student might start seeding."

It was further remarked by the interviewer that, like other minority spokesmen, Habib complained that a committee established by the board to study the introduction of religious guidelines did not confer with parents or religious groups before reporting to the board.

Satanic Verses

Salman Rushdie, of Indian origin and living in the UK, was a writer. He wrote a book, *Satanic Verses,* which falsely accused the marriage of the Prophet (his wives) and Islam in dramatic language. This led to protests by Muslims internationally. Some Western countries had some humble comments against the book but were not opposed to its publication, claiming the right of the individual to self-expression in a democratic country. It is noted that many books were banned, as noted below in our announcement in the *Leader-Post.*

The former board of the Islamic Association in 1989 did not take any initiative. I assumed presidency again in September of 1989, but not during this crisis, which occurred in May-June of 1989. Having seen no action by the Islamic Association Board, I, being the chair of the Islamic Circle of North America, involved myself and was joined by a few members of the community to raise the issue. A large announcement was published in the *Leader-Post* on June 24, 1989. There were some media interviews, but that information is not available to be reproduced in this book. The Islamic Circle of North America published flyers and brochures and distributed them to the public across the nation.

Islamophobic Anti-Islam Conference

This conference was held by the Counter Terror Study Centre. Activities against Islam and Muslims were on the rise. Dr. Sadiq, the president of the Islamic Circle of North America in Edmonton, raised concerns with the group, and informed us so that we might do our part. Dr. Sadiq corresponded with various authorities. The outcome of his efforts was nil, but I am not aware of the responses to his letters.

Agenda

MAR 28 '90 12:54   FROM YYC 422-2811   PAGE.002

[ORGANISED BY " COUNTER TERROR STUDY CENTRE "
  200 DROMORE AVE
  WINNIPEG MANNITOBA R3M-0J3]

ISLAMIC TERRORISM IN THE 1990S AND THE THREAT TO NORTH AMERICA

April 20-22, 1990

* * * * * * *

Friday April 20 -	7:30	Registration and Reception at St John's College (Coffee and Desert)
Saturday April 21 -	9:00 - 10:30	"Islamic Fundamentalism and Hezbollah." Professor Ron Miller
	11:00 - 12:30	"The Relation between Internal Iranian Politics and External Revolution." Sean Andy Anderson.
	LUNCH	
	1:30 - 3:00	"Islamic Terrorism: the Threat in the 1990s." Professor Jerrold Green
	3:15 - 4:30	"Panel Discussion on Islamic Terrorism" Chairman - Professor Jim Ferguson
	7:00 - 10:00	Dinner at Holiday Inn South. Keynote address: Professor Jerrold Green
Sunday April 22 -	9:00 - 10:30	"The Threat to Canada." Federal, Academic and Specialist speakers
	11:00 - 12:30	"The Threat to the USA." Federal, Academic and Specialist speakers
	LUNCH	
	1:30 - 3:15	Panel discussion: "Islamic Terrorism and the Threat to North America." Chairman - Professor Peter St John

CONFERENCE ENDS

My Correspondence Regarding Islamic Terrorism

In the name of God, Most Gracious, Most Merciful.
ISLAMIC ASSOCIATION OF SASKATCHEWAN, Regina Inc.
3273 Montague Street, Regina, Sk. S4S 1Z8
CANADA
Tele: (306) 585-0090

April 12, 1990

Counter Terror Study Centre
200 Dromore Avenue
Winnipeg, Manitoba
R3M OJ3

Dear Sirs/Madams:

Re: Islamic Terrorism in the 1990's and
    Threat to North America

We came to know about the above conference lately. Although it is late for me to write to you about it because the conference is already scheduled to be held from April 20th to 22nd 1990. However, I could not shun this away and it is my responsibility to pass my comment to you on behalf of the Muslims of Saskatchewan. I am sure each and every Muslim of North America has the same feeling.

The theme of the conference is directed against Islam and Malign the Muslims in North America. We, those North Americans, loyal citizens of this part of the world have duty, to find such organization and group and do needful to save our countries from their evil plans not only against the Muslims but directed against anyone in this part of the world.

There is no terrorism in Islam. Islam teaches to live in peaceful co-existance according to the law of God and the guidance of the prophet, Muhammed (Peace be upon him). Islam protects the right of minority. We have materials and scholars in Islam. If you need to educate anyone or group about Islam we will be more than happy to assist you. This will remove various misunderstandings that exist in the western world because of the media and because of the west relying on information obtained from western non-Muslim sources. One must judge a Muslim on the criteria of Islam and one must not form opinion about Islam by looking at a Muslim who is Muslim by name and not in virtues. This also holds true for followers of other religions.

The definition of terrorism depends on which side of the fence one stands. Is Israeli terrorist for Palestinian making them homeless or are Palestinian terrorists against Israel to liberate their own land or even to find a home for themselves? There is no threat to North America from Islam (or Muslims). Islam is a society of people free from gayism, lesbianism, abortion, alcoholism, child abuse, drug addiction or trade. We Muslims are maintaining this kind of society in our homes and in our communities.

We wondered how educated people like the speakers and those who are taking part in panel discussions could take part in such a conference with such a theme to represent a unilateral biased opinion without inviting a single Muslim scholar from North America. This reflects a bias and giving one sided view of a group.

At this time if it is not possible for you to cancel this conference as it is too late, which is my demand you should kindly consider changing the name of the conference and its theme and invite a Muslim scholar from Muslim organization such as Islamic Society of North America or Islamic Circle of North America or Muslim Association of Manitoba who could analyze the discussion and will be able to give the views of the North American Muslims the way they will look at the content of the Conference.

The other alternative will be to arrange a conference in consultation with Muslim organizations under the heading of "Islamic Terrorism in the 1990's and the threat to North America - Counterview of North American Muslims, sponsored by Counter Terrorist Study Centre and Muslim Organizations of North America".

Please come together as human race and make the world a better place to live for all but not only for a group of people at the expense of another group of people.

I will hope we can count on your work towards just cause and with broad mindedness in future.

Yours truly,

Dr. Naiyer Habib
MBBS,MD,FRCP(C),FACP,FCCP,FACC
President
Islamic Circle of North America, Regina Unit

(306) 584-6707
NH:bm

ADDENDUM: I enclose a glimpse of the views of two non-Muslims of the West: H.G. Wells and George Bernard Shaw.

cc: Hon. Prime Minister Bryan Mulroney
    Hon. Marcel Mass, Minister of Culture, Federal Government
    Hon. G. Filmon, Premier of Manitoba
    Minister of Culture, Government of Manitoba
    President, Islamic Society of North America
    President, Islamic Circle of North America
    President. Muslim Associationof Manitoba

Dr. Naiyer Habib
MBBS, MD, FRCP(C), FCCP, FACP, FACC

CARDIOLOGY

PLAINS HEALTH CENTRE
4500 WASCANA PARKWAY
REGINA, SASK, CANADA
S4S 5W9
TEL: (306) 584-8707

September 30, 1990

Honorable Premier Mr. Gary Filmon
204 Legislative Building
Winnipeg, Manitoba
R3C OV8

Dear Mr. Filmon:

Re: Islamic Terrorism in 1990's and the Threat to North America

I congratulate you on being re-elected as Premier of Manitoba and I am sure you will be an asset to your province and to Canada as a whole.

I highly appreciated your response to my letter regarding the issue. Meanwhile, we had taken necessary step to change the situation and that the topic was changed to Terrorism in the Middle East. This is a very unfortunate happening and we expect that these things may prop up from time to time.

Although I agree with you and accept your regret that because of the arrival of my correspondence too late to persue this matter from your side.

However, it would have been nice if a letter should have gone to the Group from your side with appropriate comment expressing your views on the issue.

I personally feel that we Canadians respect one another as individuals whether they are black or white, Muslims or non-Muslims, Indians or non-Indians for their values and share common good ground to develop our society.

From our side we are getting increasingly watchful for such incidences and will take necessary step as time will go by. Certainly support of the politicians will be needed.

With kind regards.

Yours truly,

Dr. Naiyer Habib
FACP, FRCP(C), FACC
President
Islamic Association of Sask., Regina Inc.
Islamic Circle of North America, Regina Unit

NH:bm

THE PREMIER OF MANITOBA

Legislative Building
Winnipeg, Manitoba, CANADA
R3C 0V8

May 14, 1990

Naiyer Habib
MBBS, MD, FRCP(C), FACP, FCCP, FACC
President
Islamic Association of Saskatchewan, Regina Inc.
3273 Montague Street
Regina, Saskatchewan
S4S 1Z8

Dear Dr. Habib:

Thank you for your letter which arrived in my office on April 23, 1990 regarding the recent conference held at the University of Manitoba, titled "Islamic Terrorism in the 1990s and the Threat to North America"

I appreciate knowing your concerns about this conference and regret that the correspondence on this topic came too late for me to pursue this matter.

Please be assured that I share your desire to promote greater understanding between people of different races and religions and that I hold the highest regard for the members of the Islamic community who have contributed so much to our society.

Again, thank you for taking the time to write.

Yours sincerely,

Gary Filmon

NOTE: I received no response from anyone except from the premier, Honourable Gary Filmon.

Bosnian Crisis

The Bosnian crisis was an ethnic conflict that took place after the collapse of Yugoslavia. Slobodan Milosevic in Serbia and Franjo Tudjman in Croatia planned the creation of Serbia and Croatia as their own states with their ethnicity. Milosevic put all his resources together. He intended to include Bosnia-Herzegovina and Croatia.

The war began on April 6, 1992. Serbian forces killed men and boys and eliminated their intellectuals. They raped Muslim women and deported women and elderly people with children to neighbouring countries.

This crisis was dealt with very effectively by the Canadian Council of Muslim Women, Regina. We in the Islamic Association supported the group.

First Gulf War

The First Gulf War, under American President George Bush Sr., came into being after Iraqi President Saddam Hussein invaded Kuwait on August 2, 1990. Saddam Hussein proclaimed Kuwait a province of Iraq. This raised international issues. Iraq declared this step as a signal to the US to meet with an American official prior to the invasion. The US denied this. Operation Desert Shield began, led by the US, on August 7, 1990. The UN authorized deploying whatever force necessary to remove Iraqi forces from Kuwait. Hussein stated that an attack on Iraq would be a Holy War. This had an adverse effect on Muslims in the West. The Islamic Association of Saskatchewan, under my presidency, felt it was its duty to raise a voice against the war as a Canadian and Muslim organization representing Muslims. Prayers for peace were held regularly in the masjid.

A peace coalition of an interfaith group was formed. There were media interviews and a petition to the government against the war for a negotiated settlement of the problem. A large peace rally against this war was held at city hall on January 12, 1991. Naushaba, as well as others, addressed the rally as speakers.

Seeing what went on and what may happen to Muslims, I felt it mandatory to have a North American organization, including the USA, to form a confederation of Muslims. I wrote letters to all the organizations, including the Islamic societies of North America, the US, and Canada; the Islamic Circle of North America; the Council of Muslim Communities of Canada; and others, but received no response, let alone an acknowledgment. I also addressed the Muslim communities of British Columbia in the Richmond Masjid.

North American Muslim Confederation—A Proposal, 1992

A call for this much-needed organization received no response from any organization, but there was the formation of the American Muslims. Their role remained unknown as to such activities.

A copy of the circulated letter appears below. A second letter is missing, but its salient, handwritten content has been added.

In the name of ALLAH, Most Gracious, Most Merciful

ISLAMIC ASSOCIATION OF SASKATCHEWAN
Regina Inc.

February 24, 1992

Dear Brother in Islam:

Assalamo Alaikum!

You may recall my communication at the time of Gulf War in which I had expressed
my disappointments in our national organizations especially their inability to join
hands together to provide national leadership of Muslims at a time like Gulf War.
I had also spoken to some of you regarding the need and perhaps initiation to form
Muslim Federation. I had also communicated to you what we did at the time of War
with our small resources as to manpower and finance. We were pleased with the
outcome.

Now it is noted that American Muslim Council has been formed. It is expected that
this will be activated in Canada. Bearing this in mind I do not wish to pursue the
idea of Muslim Federation separately. The aim and objective of American Muslim
Council appears to be reasonable and good. It will be worthwhile that all Muslims
should join hands to see its success and see that it functions with input from all
according to Islamic democracy
From our local point of view we have continued to have our activity that we started
at the time of War and we appear to have established yourself fairly well. Certainly
I shall urge you that you must form your own local organization to deal with local
matters and to cooperate and assist the American Muslim Council when that comes
to being and extends hand to your area. *Local politically active group and national
politically active groups are requirement of today for all of us.

Wishing you the best in your Islamic work.

wassalam!

Yours truly,

Dr. Naiyer Habib
FACP, FRCP(C), FACC
President

NH:bm

*Meanwhile we must not
Wait for it. I urge you to start linking yourself
active & national watch prepare for political a with your adjoining aids & provinces.
Tato reflect you to see
These could then become national
organisation in one name or two.
He will be glad to join hands with
you at any time. Still I see
apathy hounds us.

3273 Montague St., Regina, Sk., CANADA, S4S 1Z8   Tel:(306)585 0090

410

Media Interviews And Broadcasts Related To Gulf War
INTERVIEW WITH HOLLY PRESTON, CBC
REGINA, JANUARY 9, 1991[75]:

HOLLY PRESTON: Later in the program, I will talk to a Regina Muslim leader and get his thoughts on the Gulf crisis. Joining me now is Naiyer Habib, the president of the Islamic Association of Saskatchewan, Regina Chapter. Good evening, Dr. Habib. What is your reaction to the failure of these talks in Geneva today?

DR. HABIB: I hope that we should not say failure. I hope they go back to the table again, and there should be some kind of negotiated settlement coming up. But if they do not, then we are heading for problems, as it appears from the news that we just heard, and I hope that people do become wise. The Iraqi, US, and Western allies as well as our own government, should get involved for a peaceful settlement.

HOLLY PRESTON: Do you support Saddam Hussein or the United Nations?

DR. HABIB: I think that is a good question. All along, all the Muslims, as with all the peace-loving people in the whole world, have been against the invasion of Kuwait by Iraq—there is no doubt about that. But the problem

---

75 Courtesy of CBC.

we perceive is with the United States. We expect the United States to act as a big, honest, just brother. We have not seen that perception.

HOLLY PRESTON: What do you expect the US and the UN to do?

DR. HABIB: Well, I think, first, I have to say that we perceive the United States to show a double standard. Let's go to China. When Tibet was attacked by China and taken over, what was done? It was the same situation with the Palestinian issue and the Israeli conflict. And now we have this problem.

HOLLY PRESTON: But the US is not acting alone. It is acting with the sanctions of a lot of other countries in the world.

DR. HABIB: Yes, I think the people are supporting—all countries are supporting—going after Saddam Hussein to get him out of Kuwait. But the way things are being done is not right. Things are being done quite hurriedly. The sanction has not been allowed to work. We have to allow the sanction to work, excluding the food and medications. We have heard from the United States analyst that Saddam Hussein's army is not going to last too long—maybe six or seven months—and is going to go, so I think the United States is hurrying the world to go for a quick settlement. They did not do that for sanctioning the African problem in South Africa. Our government should get into it and show good leadership for a negotiated settlement. I think it can still be done.

HOLLY PRESTON: We have heard tonight about Joe Clark's effort to do that. . . . What more can Canada do, then? Will you support the action the government has taken in this part? DR. HABIB: I think our government is now listening to us because we are forcing them to hear that we do not want war and that the majority of Canadians do not want war. We have formed a group, and you will be hearing about that tomorrow when there are ads in the news about the Interfaith-Intergroup. So I think the attitude of our government is changing, but we would have expected this attitude to start with for the Canadian government to follow its own agenda right from the beginning. The perception we have is that it went along with the United States.

HOLLY PRESTON: Thank you very much for coming in.

DR. HABIB: You are most welcome.

Interview with Steve Krueger, STV[76]

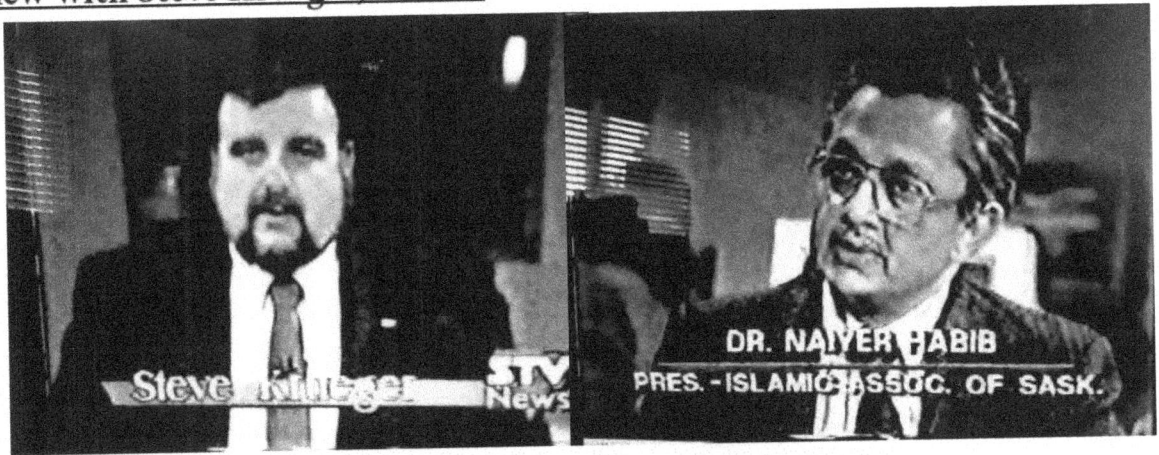

STEVE KRUEGER: Joining us now is Dr. Naiyer Habib. He is the president of the Islamic Association of Saskatchewan's Regina Chapter. Dr. Habib, thank you for joining us today. What is the feeling right now in the Islamic community in Regina about the events that are happening in the Persian Gulf?

DR. HABIB: Well, as any Canadian who loves peace, we are really shocked. We are shocked, and we are disappointed that all our efforts to resolve this issue peacefully have failed. We feel very sorry for all our young people who are fighting there in the armed forces, what is happening to them, and the onslaught or the result of what will happen to the families. They need a lot of support. We are quite concerned for people who are from the Middle East who have relatives there. They are much more shocked, so we are going into a phase of shock as any Canadian peace-loving people. As you know, with Islam being a worldwide religion, we have people from various parts of the world, so that is the feeling we have. This war could have been avoided. Economic sanctions were going to work in maybe months, as this war is out of our culture. But things were hurried, and we have run into such an escalation. I do not know the end to that.

---

[76] Courtesy of Global TV [formerly STV].

413

STEVE KRUEGER: Saddam Hussein has called for a holy war involving the Muslims of the world and the people of the Islamic faith. How are your people responding to that?

DR. HABIB: We do not consider this to be a holy war. There is no term like "holy war" in Islam. It is a misinterpretation of the word "Jihad," which is an Arabic word that merely means "struggle." Struggle for the right cause; struggle for even within yourself if you have any ill feelings; struggle if a Muslim is prevented from performing his religious duty; struggle against that will be Jihad.

STEVE KRUEGER: So, Jihad is not a holy war.

DR. HABIB: It is not. I think I have made a comment before that various leaders, whether of a Christian or Islamic sect, used religion to draw the attention of the people. So, this is not a holy war, but there is so much great sentiment for the shrines in Baghdad, and we are concerned. What is happening to those? Has the United States spared those areas? We have a lot of concern about that, and similarly, we have shrines in Saudi Arabia, so as world Muslims, we are quite concerned, and as Canadian Muslims, we are quite concerned about that part. STEVE KRUEGER: Is there anything that your community can do here in Saskatchewan to, in any way, express your concern or assist in what is happening here? I know that Iran this morning was saying that they are preparing to provide humanitarian assistance for the victims. They have opened their borders with Iraq and are allowing refugees to come in. Being this far away, is there anything that your community can do to help or is planning to do right now?

DR. HABIB: We have formed an interfaith group and are working through that. Presently, we are providing moral support to families who are from the Middle East and whose relatives are there. We are trying our best to negotiate a settlement by communicating with our government. And if we can offer economic help, we are looking at that and will try our best. We hope that there is a ceasefire and that a renegotiation will occur, and I hope that our government will take the initiative as a peacemaker rather than take a part in escalating the war. STEVE KRUEGER: How difficult is it right now for the Islamic community? Do they sense that there is any resentment directly toward your people because Canadian forces are in combat in this part of the world?

DR. HABIB: No, I have not perceived that in Regina or in Saskatoon, but I have heard some rumours that somebody by the name of Hussein in Edmonton is receiving phone calls, etc. My message to all Canadians, whether Muslim or Christian or Jew or Iraqi or Arab, is that we are all Canadians at this time and so should look at that. But if there is any person or group that is suspicious, we should go after them, and we should be looking into that.

STEVE KRUEGER: I would imagine it is the same case as we have with people who come here from every country of the world, hopefully, if problems at home are left at home.

DR. HABIB: We have to work as Canadians for the peaceful thing that is happening there.

We should not be singling out any individual or group for any matter.

STEVE KRUEGER: Any immediate plans right now in the Regina area?

DR. HABIB: We do not have any plans, no. As I said, we are shocked. We are as confused as any peace-loving people. We have joined the interfaith group, and we are working through them. STEVE KRUEGER: Thank you very much for joining us, and good luck. Hopefully, the tolerance that you are finding while staying in place here in Regina will pay off.

Media Representation

We attempted to respond to media publications related to Islam and Muslims. I monitored the media and acted accordingly. Other members of the Islamic Association took part. These are noted in our book, *HMRSO*. Here, we cite only matters related to us personally in view of the objective of this book.

The Leader-Post   Regina   Sat., Oct. 6, 1990

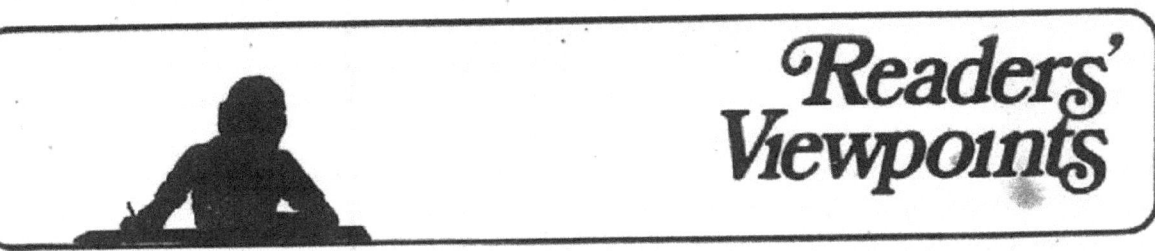

Solutions must address Palestinian problem

Some facts were left out by the reporter on my comments under the headline "Dartboard draws critics" (Leader-Post, Sept. 29, Page A17).

I had added, "However, I wonder why Hussein and Khomeini were selected for dartboards and not the Zionists who are responsible for killing Palestinians on an ongoing basis and making them homeless. From the Canadian point of view, they stand on the same level."

The situation in the Middle East is a complex one. Because of the complexity of the problem, I add the following comments.

Many leaders do not represent the masses. The West, which also includes a large, ever-growing Muslim population, must realize this fact. There should not be double-standards by people who claim to be of high morals and character.

Canadians used to be respected in the world, and that respect is dwindling. There is no doubt

that the aggression on Kuwait and its occupation are illegal. According to our present standard, so is the occupation of Palestine.

If Kuwait did belong to Iraq, Iraq had the option to solve the issue diplomatically through the United Nations. If the U.S. was inspired by the plea to protect Saudi Arabia and to liberate Kuwait, it should have shown its character by seeking a peaceful, honorable solution for the Palestinian people, rather than supporting wholeheartedly the state of Israel.

This comment is also for those western nations joining the United States in this endeavor. The solution must aim for a lasting peace with preservation of the home for Israel and creation of a homeland for the Palestinians.

It should be noted that the Muslim mass across the world is against the deployment of forces other than Arab ones in the Muslim holy land of Saudi Arabia. It is a serious matter.

We should all join together to seek a peaceful solution with honesty, justice and sincerity, so that we can all have a better world in which to live.

Let us not run in the race of competition of black or white, Muslim or non-Muslim, Indian or non-Indian. There is no end to that.

History shows us that the biggest powers do fall and the smallest rise. This rise and fall continues.

Dr. NAIYER HABIB
Habib is president of the Islamic Association of Saskatchewan, Regina Inc.

Wise, brave

The PLO leader, Yasser Arafat, and Israeli Prime Minister Yitzhak Rabin reached agreement. It is an unexpected, historic event.

They are wise and brave. They have come to the realization of the facts of history. History never stops; the cycle keeps going.

It is now the responsibility of the pro-Israeli and pro-Palestinian allies, friends or foes, to lend them helping hands to walk ahead on a very critical and difficult path for a permanent settlement.

The principles of tolerance, reconciliation, and give and take are the essence of coexistence.

I know Jerusalem may become a critical point. I do not think it should be. If wisdom prevails, it can be solved.

I have proposed (as an individual) that Jerusalem, with all its sacred places for Jews, Christians and the Muslims — "the children of Abraham" — be declared as a neutral zone for all three religions.

This neutral zone should be administered by representatives of these religions. Its chairmen could be elected from the Jews, Christians and Muslims in rotation.

This area could be a model, like the United Nations Organization.

Let us hope and work for everlasting peace for the Middle East and elsewhere.

NAIYER HABIB

Regina

416

'A new life'

The headline news on the front page of The Leader-Post, May 13, "Serbian refugee attacked", is inflammatory and is not in keeping with Canadian spirit. It is most important that when such a situation arises, we help people to reconcile their differences. They deserve our sympathy, from whatever background they come.

It is our responsibility to educate the people who come facing such circumstances in their old countries. The Canadian spirit, the spirit of beginning a new life in Canada, of respecting and tolerating one another for a new beginning, for the goodness of Canada and thereby for the goodness of the world as a whole.

People closely involved with such groups should sense the problems beforehand and take preventive measures. The media have a greater responsibility of what to publish and in what manner.

Dr. NAIYER HABIB

Habib is past president, Islamic Association of Saskatchewan, Regina. Inc.

417

Response to Time Magazine

Time magazine, June 15, 1992, had this cover line on its front cover: "Islam: Should the World Be Afraid?"

It had a picture of the top half of a mosque and that of a person apparently representing a Muslim from the Afghan area. My response, as president of the Islamic Association of Saskatchewan, Regina, was published by *Time* magazine in its issue on July 6, 1992, as follows:

ISLAM NEW MARCH

"By accepting an Islamic model, the world can be
a better place to live.
Naiyer Habib Regina.
Saskatchewan.

"ISLAM IS NOT A RELIGION OF RITUAL BUT a way of life. State and religion are not separate. Islam protects the rights of minorities and those who are oppressed, as well. By accepting the Islamic model, the world can be a better place to live."

Naiyer Habib, president, Islamic Association of Saskatchewan, Regina, Saskatchewan.

Community Events

We celebrated events and invited others as a gesture of outreach to society at large. Our men and women jointly participated in all the affairs of our organization. During our leadership, our objective was to maintain a high standard of society and to integrate into the society at large with no discrimination and not be ghetto dwellers. We maintained our culture and religion. We introduced them to the mainstream of society. With this intent, we proceeded with community events, such as Ramadan, Eid-ul-Fitr, Eid Milad-un-Nabi (observing the birth of the Prophet), Eid-al-Adha (feast of sacrifice), a family workshop, MOSAIC Festival (1977-78), Tri-Community get-together (Regina, Saskatoon, Swift Current), and the 125*th* birthday of Canada (1992). Details are in the book *HMRSO*, but some important highlights are noted here as well because of our active and leading role.

Ramadan

We held potluck Iftars[77] at our houses on rotation. We also did surah Taraweeh[78] by rotation at our houses before we had an official building.

---

[77] The evening meal when Muslims end their daily Ramadan fast at sunset.

[78] Taraweeh: This is an optional prayer offered every night during the month of Ramadan, reciting a part of the memorized Quran each night to its completion in the month. Some may use only a small part of it, as Sura.

Eid Prayers and Functions

We held Eid prayers, or Eid get-togethers, in the basement of the Red Cross building at the corner of College Avenue and Broad Street. Before we had our own building, we also performed Eid prayers in private houses. Eid Prayer was also held in the Arts Department Hall at the old campus of the University of Regina.

First Eid Function During My Presidency

We held an Eid function in the Landmark Inn at 4150 Albert Street in Regina in 1978, financed by family contributions. Eid gifts were presented to all children. It was very elegant. However, community attendance was small. We returned to a potluck format and held it at various places.

Dr. and Mrs. Anwar Haque's family and Riazuddin, facing back.

L-R: Wife of M. Hussain Khatri, Naushaba Habib, M. Hussain Khatri.

Akram Din family, Samiul Haque, looking at us.

Majid Khatri family.

Abdul Qayyum family.

First Eid Milad-un-Nabi Function

The observation of the birth of the Prophet (Peace be upon Him) was held at the Four Seasons Palace Banquet Hall in Regina on February 26, 1978. The chief guest speaker was Hisham Badran. The mayor of the city, Mr. Henry Baker, was invited as chief guest. Dr. David Russell, vice president of the Council of the Muslim Communities of Canada, and his wife were also invited.

420

THE ISLAMIC ASSOCIATION OF SASKATCHEWAN
REGINA

PHONE

بسم الله الرحمن الرحيم

P O B 3572
Regina, Saskatchewan
Canada

وَاعْتَصِمُوْا بِحَبْلِ اللّٰهِ جَمِيْعًا وَّلَا تَفَرَّقُوْا

'And hold together firmly to God's rope and do not
separate.'
The Quran 3:103

February 6, 1978

Dear Members,

Aslamaulakam :

It is with great sorrow that I have to mention the passing away of a
prominent member of our Community, Dr. Ishrat Hussain on January 22, 1978.
The burial took place at the Regina Memorial Gardens on Wednesday January 25,
1978 at 11.30 a.m. preceded by the Salat-Djinaza led by Dr. Habib. Quran
recital and prayers were held at Riffat Hussain's residence on Sunday January
29, 1978.

We all offer our deepest sympathies and condolence to his wife and
three children and to his brother Riffat Hussain.

Riffat Hussain wishes to convey through this news letter his appreciation
and gratitude to all friends for their sympathy and comfort at that time of great
sorrow.

Mawlid-An-Nabi

The Executive Committee is pleased to inform you that the Department of
Culture and Youth has co-sponsored the celebrations for Idd-Milad-un-Nabi this
year by approving a grant towards the expenses. The celebrations this year are
planned to be held on February 26, 1978 at the Four Seasons Palace Banquet Hall,
2401 Rothwell Street, Regina, between 11.00 a.m. to 4.00 p.m. with Luncheon
served at 1.00 p.m. Arrangements are being made for prominent speakers on
Islamic topics, invitations to guests and dignitaries from all walk of life.
Participation by all members of the Muslim Community is very vital and very warm
and sincere invitation is hereby extended to you and your friends, both Muslims
and non-Muslims. To facilitate and finalise the seating and catering arrangements in particular, it is very important the precise number of guests attending,
with a breakdown of adults and children, be obtained well in advance. You are
requested to complete and return the attached form so as to reach us by February
15, 1978. Alternately please phone 545-7430 and leave the relevant information
by February 16, 1978.

Please note this is NOT A POTLUCK PARTY. Lunch, refreshments and
Idd gifts to children will be served with compliments of the Islamic Association
and courtesy and co-operation of Department of Culture and Youth.

/2....

Head table, L to R: David Russell, Mrs. Russell, Anwar Qureshi (vice president), Naiyer Habib (president),
Akram Din (secretary), Zubair Akhtar, Aftab Ghani, Dr. Anwar Haque (founding president).

421

Welcome address by the President

My first address after assuming the presidency of the association on the first such elaborate function of this organization expressed the inclusiveness of the community at large with the Muslim community in 1978, the theme of which was put into practice.

Ladies, gentlemen, and my dear children: Assalam-o-Alaikum. I have the great honour of welcoming you to celebrate the birthday of our Prophet Muhammad (PBUH) today. I am thankful to his worship the mayor, Mr. Henry Baker, for accepting our invitation to be the chief guest, despite his busy schedule, even on the weekend. He is presently chairing the winter festival in Wascana Park and will be joining us at approximately 1:30 p.m. We greatly welcome the substantial grant by the department of culture and youth, thanks to the efforts of our secretary, Akram Din, without which a function of this scale would not have been possible.

On behalf of the Islamic Association, I welcome our chief guest speaker, Brother Hisham Badran, from Toronto.

We extend our welcome to the president, Dr. David Russell, the ex-president, Dr. Zahir Alvi, and other members of the Islamic Association of Saskatoon, who are with us today. We extend our warmest welcome to the guests and friends who have joined us, although many of them are of a different faith. This is a very good step in understanding one another, particularly in our Canadian society of multicultural origin. By mutual understanding, we can come very close to one another on many common grounds to improve society.

A religious community is a society of good human beings—a requirement of the world today. We hope we will have more and more opportunities to get together. Now, I shall comment on the importance of the day.

It is a day of great importance. According to the Islamic faith, it is the day when God sent his last chosen messenger, Prophet Muhammad (PBUH), to give a complete code of life in the form of Islam to all of mankind with a promise that it will remain applicable for all time to come.

Prophet Muhammad's life is a practical demonstration of Islam—a true and perfect human being. Time will not permit us to go into detail, but we will have an opportunity to get a glimpse at some aspects of the Prophet's life in the speeches of our speakers.

The message that came to Prophet Muhammad (PBUH) was of the same faith that came to previous Prophets. I quote the Quran, the holy book that came to Prophet Muhammad (PBUH), which says, "Say, We[79] believe in God and that which is revealed unto us and that which was revealed unto Abraham, and Ishmael, and Isaac, and Jacob, and the tribes, and that which was given to Moses and Jesus, and that which was given to all prophets from their Lord, we do not make any distinction between any of them and to Him do we submit" Quran 2:136.

---

[79] "We" does not mean multiple gods, but one and only one, with collective powers.

L-R: Mrs. David Russell, Anwar Qureshi (vice president),
Hisham Badran, Mayor Henry Baker, Naiyer Habib (president).

Second Eid Milad-un-Nabi Function

This was held at Empringham Hall on Pasqua Street on Sunday, February 11, 1979. The main presenters here were children, and Hisham Badran was again the chief guest. He spent a few days in Regina with the children.

Welcome by Naiyer Habib, president.

Hisham Badran, guest speaker.

Islamic School children participants.

L-R: Anwar Haque, Hisham Badran, Abdul Qayyum, Majid Khatri, Arif Sethi, Aftab Ghani.

Subsequently, the Eid Milad-un-Nabi and other functions continued in the Regina Community Hall as potlucks. A guest speaker would be invited, or a local speaker would be arranged. The ladies prepared the lunch/snacks.

I made sure that the children attended the functions, especially to hear the speaker and participate. If they were found to be playing in the playground and the speaker was about to begin the speech, they would all be called in. This is noted to emphasize the importance of children's participation in this society, where the Muslims were in the minority and facing the very different culture and religion of the majority, with the intent of integration while maintaining their culture and religion.

Eid al-Adha

Eid al-Adha Prayers were offered at Eid. Some of us—namely, Drs. Haque and Habib—went to a farm with our children for sacrifcing cow or goat. Brother Mohammad Sadeque used to accompany us. As our children grew up, we quit going to the farm while a few others continued.

Family Workshop

With my intent, along with the enthusiasm of having acquired our new centre, we wanted to expand our horizon of learning and practice what we wanted to learn, so we arranged a two-day workshop. We invited Dr. M. Sadiq from Edmonton, an internationally renowned clinical psychologist with a special interest in family, for the session. He was equally involved in serving the Muslim community and Islam.

426

There was active and good participation by our community, including men, women, and youth. Groups were arranged to follow on this so that the learning would be utilized by the entire community.

This was the only such workshop during our leadership, but we invited speakers from time to time on different occasions.

MOSAIC Festival

This is a multicultural exhibit and socialization event that started in 1977 in the city of Regina. Various members of the community at large from various countries and of various nationalities put their stalls in various buildings across the city. They have cultural shows, exhibits, and food. The Islamic Association participated in 1977. Unfortunately, there is no picture available of that MOSAIC. The next MOSAIC was held in conjunction with the 75th anniversary of the city of Regina. The Islamic Association participated in this with enthusiasm and presented a very successful program on May 25-27, 1978. Unfortunately, the association could only participate in the first two MOSAIC festivals. Our stall was called the Islamic World Pavilion.

Naiyer Habib in Islamic stall.

Naushaba Habib, cooking.

Fareda Sethi, leading the chorus with the children (Islamic School).

A cultural bridal preparation.

Cultural fashion show.

Tri-Community Get-Together

Abdul Qayyum initiated this in 1983. The objective was for the three Muslim communities (Regina, Saskatoon, and Swift Current) to get together once a year on rotation at the three community centres to socialize and have discussions of mutual interest, with an emphasis on youth and children involvement. It continued successfully for a few years but died down in 2001 or 2002. We were participants in it. Details can be found in our book[80].

Participation In The 125th Birthday Of Canada

This was celebrated at the Islamic Centre and Mosque at Montague Street. The Canadian flag was hoisted, and a sign was posted for the celebration. There was a community get-together. I, as president, along with past president Abdul Qayyum and Riazuddin Ahmed, an active member of the Muslim community, addressed the audience.

---

[80] History of the Muslims of Regina, Saskatchewan and their Organizations . . . "A Cultural Integration."

The children led the national anthem. The Quran was recited. Natasha Malik addressed the audience on behalf of the youth. A prayer was said for solidarity in Canada, and a promise was made to make our country an example of peace and justice for all.

Other Organizations

We stayed alert as we led our professional and family lives. Our family life included our community. We believe that community living with morality and character is the best way to maintain morality and character in the individual family, not to live in isolation.

The following two organizations were our realization for us and for our community. We have always consulted each other as life partners and then brought our thinking and plans to the open.

MUSLIMS FOR PEACE AND JUSTICE

by

Naiyer Habib

In the Name of God, Most Kind, Most Merciful

2001-2005

Local Muslims condemn violence

By PAMELA COWAN
and JANEL WHITE
of The Leader-Post

The sleep of a University of Regina professor was tormented Tuesday night as live TV images of the deadly terrorist attacks on New York and Washington continued to rerun in his mind.

"I still can't believe this has happened," said Dr. Ejaz Ahmed. "When I saw it on TV, it seemed like a movie, but this is reality.

"I think this is the most terrible event of the century. I had lots of difficulty sleeping."

Those responsible for the carnage should be punished, Ahmed said, but he hopes the U.S. waits until they have conclusive evidence before responding.

"If innocent people get killed it won't serve the purpose and the retaliation will be a disaster," Ahmed said.

TV coverage of Muslim leaders expressing fear on Tuesday night temporarily panicked Ahmed.

"I feel pretty secure in Canada as compared to the U.S. because the U.S. is a superpower and you can make lots of enemies, no matter if you do the right or the wrong thing," he said.

In 1995 and 1996, Ahmed served as president of the Regina branch of the Islamic Association of Saskatchewan. He estimates there are between 300 and 400 Muslim families in Regina.

Regina cardiologist Dr. Naiyer Habib called Tuesday "the saddest day of my life."

"To see this barbaric act on innocent people was most unexpected — I just couldn't watch the news last night," he said.

"We are quite concerned that these kinds of things are spreading instead of stopping ... whoever has done it has done it out of frustration because their goal or ideology could not be achieved. Not everybody can be ideal, but if people are fair and honest in dealing with things, it creates friendship and avoids these kinds of problems."

No matter who is responsible for the barbaric acts, Habib hopes an entire community does not pay the price for the actions of a smaller group.

This is a time of prayer and consolation, he said.

Priest Hafeez Ilyas of Regina's Islamic Association was busy answering calls and scheduling prayers dedicated to the tragedy.

Special prayers were held at the Islamic mosque Tuesday evening and more are planned for Friday.

Ilyas has received over 20 calls from Regina residents. But most of the calls he's answering aren't about prayer services.

"People keep calling here — just calling to make sure we are safe and the prayer place is safe," he said.

Ilyas said there is a concern that his ethnic group will be targeted.

But Regina residents have been showing their concern for his well-being.

"Some of the people come in and ask if we are getting a hard time," said Ilyas.

Three of Ilyas' neighbours, that have seen him and his family in traditional dress, have already told him to be careful because "they're worried we might be harmed."

Ilyas is grateful for the concern, but said there is nothing he can do.

"We are all human beings and are related to each other, but we are not part of it (the terrorism). But we are feeling bad," Ilyas said.

"All we can do is pray and we've done that."

INTRODUCTION

History Of Muslims For Peace And Justice Formation Timeline

The formation of Muslims for Peace and Justice (MPJ) was my brainchild and a reality to be established.

Crisis of 9/11

On September 11, 2001, a disaster occurred in the form of a terrorist attack on American soil, as discussed in my interview with the *Leader-Post*, noted below. Muslims became targeted across the world, and victimization started immediately. Muslim leaders received the jolt and had to stand up for the defence of all Muslims.

Tuesday, September 11, 2001

I heard this news when I was parking my car in the lot of my medical office at the Regina General Hospital. It shattered me. I called Naushaba immediately. At that time, I had stepped down from the leadership of the Islamic Association of Saskatchewan Inc., having been involved from 1977 to 1998. Naushaba had also served on its board. I perceived that the Islamic Association of Saskatchewan was not taking any active part. I felt that this was going to have a serious impact on the Muslims in the West. Not being involved in the leadership of the Islamic Association, I was at a loss as to what to do.

Thursday, September 13, 2001

The *Regina Leader-Post* published an interview with Professor Dr. Ejaz Ahmed and myself, both of us former presidents of the Islamic Association of Saskatchewan, Regina Inc., and our imam, Hafiz Ilyas.

Friday, September 14, 2001

I was in the masjid offering Friday Prayer. I saw Ejaz Ahmed (the past president) coming out from the masjid after me. Meanwhile, Abdul Jalil, the former secretary of the Islamic Association, also came out. The three of us looked at the issue and felt that something needed to be done. The *Leader-Post* interview had been published. We met at the residence of Ejaz Ahmed—11358 Wascana Meadows—that evening. We decided to invite a few people from our community who had worked with us and were also old-timers in Regina, members involved with the association in the past. So, it was finalized that we would form the organization of Muslims for Peace and Justice.

Sunday, November 4, 2001

A meeting was held in the University of Regina Union Centre. Ejaz Ahmed chaired it. There was also a press conference. STV and the *Leader-Post* provided coverage of the meeting. Here, the objectives of MPJ were finalized, and members were registered.

MPJ Meeting: June 2, 2002

This meeting was held at my residence, at 9227 Wascana Mews. On the basis of a motion, the following MPJ board of directors were elected, unopposed: Chair: Dr. Naiyer Habib.

Vice Chair: Dr. Mansoor Haque.

Secretary: Mrs. Zeba Hashmi.

Treasurer: Mr. Arif Sethi.

Community Liaison: Mr. Riazuddin Ahmed.

Subsequently, Kashif Ahmed was included as a communication director.

Sr. Tracy (Abdou) Shier was elected vice president in the general body meeting of MPJ, held on March 23, 2003. Dr. Mansoor Haque withdrew.

The board was authorized to appoint working committees from among MPJ members. The meeting closed after the elections.

MPJ Meeting: February 12, 2004

Founding members and trustees were finalized, and the constitution was approved by the trustee members. A new election was held, and the following directors were elected: President: Dr. Naiyer Habib.

Vice President: Sr. Tracy (Abdou) Shier.

General Secretary: Sr. Zeba Hashmi.

Treasurer: Sr. Qudsia Qayyum.

Board Members: Kashif Ahmed, Dr. Samiul Haque, Dr. Amr Henni.

The following general announcement was circulated to our community to engage them actively:

In the name of Allah, most kind, most merciful.

From: Muslims for Peace and Justice

To: The Muslim community of Regina,

Salaam (Peace be upon you)

You are aware that the "War on Terrorism" progresses onward and that Muslims residing in Canada have to deal with allegations and half-truths against Islam and Muslims in newspapers, magazines, TV, and radio. These media biases impugn Islam and Muslims. Whether they are done ignorantly or on purpose, we Muslims are obliged to defend our faith. We must defend our faith in this world and hereafter so that we can live a secure and peaceful life with our fellow Canadians without being harassed in Canada.

FOLLOWING September 11th, many establishments have yearned to learn more about Islam and Muslims in order to have a better understanding. MPJ directors and members have lectured at many sessions. MPJ is also involved in the Multi-Faith Forum, which is also essential for us in order to have a dialogue of understanding with other faiths. Imagine if we did not represent ourselves at inter-faith events or failed to fulfill a request to explain Islam; a void for the representation of Islam would be left, and all those allegations perpetuated against our faith would be deemed true.

Muslims need to be more informed concerning their rights. To address that, MPJ organized an information session on the "anti-terror bill."

Muslims for Peace & Justice has embarked on a sustained campaign of media relations, public/government relations, and anti-discrimination work. We have sent many press releases pertaining to major Islamic events and issues concerning Canadian Muslims. If you have been reading the *Leader-Post* for the last year, you will have noticed that many articles and letters on Ramadan and Eid have been published as a result of MPJ's continuous relations with Saskatchewan media. Inshallah, you will see more of our work in the media.

MPJ has also been supporting peace demonstrations, which have been organized by the Regina Peace Council. MPJ has demonstrated against the war in Afghanistan and has been demonstrating against the impending war in Iraq. MPJ continues to be active in making the governments of Saskatchewan and Canada aware of our just stance concerning political situations ranging from unnecessary deportations to unjustified wars.

MPJ has organized Eid events and an annual conference attended by important government officials and key community leaders. We were also extremely pleased by the attendance of many from the Muslim community. Global TV, CTV News, the *Regina Leader-Post*, and CBC News have covered these events. MPJ continues to communicate with the media and public officials for the purpose of advocating for Saskatchewan Muslims.

MPJ has devoted much time, effort, and money to improve our relations with the general public, media, and government in Saskatchewan and in Canada, but now **we need your help**. If you wish for us to continue with our advocacy work to defend the Muslim community in Saskatchewan and to promote the true image of Islam, please support us. Please donate whatever amount you can. Cheques can be made to "Muslims for Peace and Justice" and given to any of the following MPJ board of directors:

President: Dr. Naiyer Habib.

Secretary: Sr. Zeba Hashmi.

Acting treasurer: Br. Kashif Ahmed.

Community relations: Br. Riazuddin Ahmed.

Activities And Actions By MPJ

MPJ played an active and more elaborative role on an ongoing basis. We present here such activities of the year 2001-2002 to exemplify the role played by this organization.

1. Initial formative meeting organized and chaired by Professor Ejaz Ahmed, October 2001, following a preliminary meeting among Dr. Ejaz Ahmed, Dr. Naiyer Habib, and Dr. Abdul Jalil after the *Leader-Post* interview with Dr. Ejaz Ahmed and Dr. Naiyer Habib.

2. Press conference at the University of Regina to explain the purpose of this committee's formation from matters arising out of the impact of September 11 (a recorded tape version is available with me during my lifetime).

3. Informal group meetings held monthly to develop the objectives of the MPJ.

4. MPJ organized a multi-faith, multicultural reception to inform non-Muslims about Eid al-Adha, March 10, 2002. About ten faith and cultural organization representatives, two local MLAs, and six main media representatives (CBC, Global and CTV television, CBC and CKRM radio) attended the reception.

5. On June 2, 2002, twenty-four (24) members of the MPJ met under the chairmanship of Professor Ejaz Ahmed to elect a board of directors: Dr. Habib (chair), Dr. Mansoor Haque (vice chair), Mrs. Zeba Hashmi (secretary), Mr. Arif Sethi (treasurer), and Mr. Riazuddin Ahmed (community liaison).

6. The new board has now requested that Dr. Anwar Haque and Mr. Abdul Qayyum draft a constitution for the MPJ for presentation to and adoption by the general members. These members have accepted this responsibility.

7. MPJ supported and participated with the Regina Peace Council and the Regina Council for Peace in Palestine in a Peace Rally held in Regina on April 20, 2002. Dr. Habib spoke on behalf of the MPJ to support the Peace in Palestinian demands and the ending of Israeli occupation of Palestinian lands since 1967.

8. The University of Regina organized the annual meeting of the Peace and Education Association of Canada on June 6-9, 2002. Riazuddin Ahmed spoke on the Palestinian-Israeli conflict as a source of instability in the world.

9. Bill C 36:

a . A general information session was held for information to the community by hiring a lawyer by MPJ

b . A letter to the chair against the bill was sent to the chair of the senate committee with copies to ministers.

Letter to Honourable Mr. Graham re: Israel's aggression on Gaza, dated July 26, 2002.

To achieve the MPJ objective, to cultivate friendly relations between Muslims and the larger Regina community, and to enhance the understanding of the main teachings of Islam among non-Muslims, the MPJ members undertook the task of visiting various organizations, schools, and sites to introduce Islam/Muslim, and particularly to remove any misunderstandings about them.

Between 2001-2003, MPJ delivered more than forty presentations on Islam to a variety of institutions, including churches, government offices, schools, universities, and nonprofit organizations.

Finalization of Constitution

A meeting was held on February 15, 2004, at Regina Huda School at 40 Sheppard Street. The following trustees were present: Ayman Aboguddah, Kashif Ahmed, Riazuddin Ahmed, Samina Ahmed, Sheila Ahmed, Raza Bhimji, Kheliefa Daud, Naiyer Iabib, Naushaba Iabib, Abbas Iussainie, Zeba Iashmi, Anwar Iaque, Samiul Haque, Raabia Hatcher, Amr Henni, Abdul Jalil, Nusrat Jalil, Zarqa Nawaz, Abdul Qayyum, Qudsia Qayyum, Shahedur Rahman, and Tracy Shier.

Chairman: Naiyer Habib.

The meeting was opened with Surah(Chapter) Fatiha from Qur'an recited by Kashif Ahmed according to Islamic Tradition for opening a meeting or function.

L-R: Zeba Hashmi, Tracy Shier, Naiyer Habib, Riazuddin Ahmed, Kashif Ahmed.

This meeting was called to finalize the constitution. It was discussed in detail, and the constitution was finalized.

Election for the term, February 2004

Anwar Haque and Abdul Qayyum volunteered to be election officers. Abdul Qayyum explained the seven positions that were available: president, vice president, secretary, treasurer, and three directors. The following were elected:

President: Naiyer Habib   Director 1: Amr Henni

Vice president: Tracy Shier   Director 2: Samiul Haque

Secretary: Zeba Hashmi   Director 3: Kashif Ahmed

Treasurer: Qudsia Qayyum

The meeting was adjourned with supplication.

CONFERENCES—Annual Muslim For Peace and Justice

Annual Conferences were arranged on important topics relevant to the MPJ's objectives. Speakers of high calibre were chosen for lectures and discussions. Conferences were held for a duration of two days each year: 2002, 2003, 2004, and 2005.

The conferences were open to the public, with special invitations sent to dignitaries and politicians. Media were invited. Cable Regina recorded all the proceedings. Highlights of the program and its speakers are presented here. The recorded program on DVD is available through me.

Only the pertinent facts of each year of the conference are posted here. Refer to HMRSO for details.

2002 Program: Islam and Muslim Life in Canada Post 9/11

In the name of Allah, most Gracious, most Merciful
Muslims for Peace and Justice presents
a 2002 conference on

Islam and Muslim Life in Canada Post 9/11- Challenges and Opportunities

Saturday, October 12, 2002

Education Building, Main Auditorium,
University Drive South
University of Regina
Free Admission

Key Note Speaker:
ImamShabir Ally

For more information, please contact:
N. Habib 766-6999; M. Haq 949-7165;
Z. Hashmi 790-9789; A. Sethi 586-9049;
R. Ahmed 789-0416

Free Parking
East of Education Building. Lot 3 Middle
Section University Drive East, Lot 14,
University Drive South. With sign
"Authorized M permit holder area and
Lot 17 University Drive East.
Metered Parking is free on the weekend.

Morning Session

Session A: Moderator - Br. Omar Farooq

9:15 - 9:45 am — Opening Qur'an recitation - Br. Daoud Khalifa; Translation: Br. Kashif Ahmed
Observe one minute of silence for victims of violence and war in the world.
Welcome Address by MPJ President: Dr. N. Habib
Islam and Muslim Life in Canada Post 9/11- Opportunities and Challenges:
Sr. Zarqa Nawaz

Session B: Moderator - Dr. N. Habib

9:45 - 10:30 am — Islam - the Misunderstood Religion. Key Note Address by Imam Shabir Ally (Toronto)

10:30 - 10:45 am — Questions & Answers

10:45 - 11:00 am — Break

Session C: Moderator - Br. R. Ahmed

11:00 - 11:45 am — Canadian Political Perspectives on Waging War to Change Regimes in the Muslim World - Who is Next After Iraq?
Liberal
Mr. Roy Bailey (CA)
Honourable Lorne Nystrom (NDP)
Prof. S. Juyal (U of R)

11:45 - 12:00 am — Questions & Answers

12:00 - 1:30 pm — Lunch break - on your own (Zuhr Prayer - 1:15pm Stage of Auditorium)

Afternoon Session

Session D: Moderator - Dr. A. Aboguddah

1:30 - 2:15 pm — Peaceful Muslim Co-existence with Others: Let the Qur'an Speak by Imam Shabir Ally

2:15 - 2:30 pm — Questions & Answers

Session E: Moderator - Br. R. Ahmed

2:30 - 3:15 pm — Canadian Perceptions/Expectations of the Muslim Community Post 9/11
Presentation & Panel Discussion
Prof. F. V. Greifenhagen, Religious Studies, Luther College
Prof. Terry Marner, Chair, Regina Multi-faith Forum
Mr. Gerry Klein, University Editor, Saskatoon Star Phoenix

3:15 - 3:30 pm — Questions & Answers

Session F: Moderator: Dr. A. Aboguddah

3:30 - 4:00 pm — Place of Muslim Women in the Society - Home, Work, and the Mosque by Imam Shabir Ally

4:00 - 4:15 pm — Questions & Answers

4:15 - 4:30 pm — Closing remarks by Dr. N. Habib, supplication by Dr. M. Haq

Presidential address: Dr. Naiyer Habib.

Presidential Address at MPJ Conference 2002

Peace and blessings of Allah be on all of us.

I would like to welcome you all on behalf of the Muslims for Peace and Justice organization. This organization was formed soon after the incident of 9/11 to deal with this impact and to foster a mutual relationship and understanding between Muslims and others. We have chosen some of the topics that will reflect the matters that we are going to discuss.

I would like to add a few comments. There is a great deal of growing apprehension in the Muslim population in the West and suffering in the United States in the government's hands. The case of Mr. Baloch is well known. Mr. Baloch was a Pakistani Canadian waiting for an extension of his visa in the US, who was put in confinement in a five-by-seven-foot cell with no windows and a flashing light on the door for six months. He was later released with no fault found, and there are many who are suffering right now. The Canadian government did object, but it was not listened to. He was released only when the US wanted to release him.

Muslims left their home with the determination of no return. They live peacefully and are contributing to the nation as anybody else. With the time change, it was never expected of the treatment of Muslims after 9/11 similar to the treatment of loyal Japanese citizens at the time of the Pearl Harbor attack by the Japanese (December 1941). So far, Canada has not followed, and we hope it does not. We have to stand for Canada and its protection. Things are likely to worsen as the situation in the Middle East escalates. There is light in the tunnel, however, because the majority of Westerners—and especially Canadians—are standing by the side of the Muslims. It will be up to the Muslims to explore it, cooperate, and coordinate with them.

As to Islam, it has been misrepresented and misunderstood in the West. Many non-Muslim and Muslim authors admirably and truthfully have authored Islam, which nullifies these misrepresentations. There will always be Franklin Graham describing Islam as an evil religion, as well as Pat Robertson and, lately, Falwell calling Prophet Muhammad (PBUH) a terrorist.

On another topic, the topic of Muslim women in Islam seems to always attract the most attention of all. On the one side, women are to be covered from head to toe, confined in their homes, and even eliminated from some mosques. On the other side, women scholars are emerging. They indicate that Islam has been interpreted by men, who have interpreted it to suit themselves. These require our attention. They are embarking on having a Mosque for Women.

We see the existing and neglected Palestinian issues, False pleas to go to War in Iraq, and bias of the media on a day-to-day basis. These reflect the morality—or immorality—of nations, be it west or middle east. They are joining one by one and siding with one another. I hope Canada, as we understand it, or as we understood it when we decided to make it our home, will stand on justice and morality. As I said in the peace rally, when nations derail from the path of humanity and honesty, it ignites hatred and the flame of hatred which engulf nations to burn. There has never been a superpower everlasting, but the power of God, and when things have gone extreme, God has replaced them. I quote you from surah 6, Ayah 6 of the Quran, *"See they not how many of those before them We did destroy? —Generations We had established on the earth, in strength such as We have not given to you—for whom We poured out rain from the skies in abundance, and gave (fertile) streams flowing beneath their (feet): yet for their sins We destroyed them, and raised in their wake fresh generations (to succeed them).* God bless us all.

Thank you.

Dr. Naiyer Habib, FACP, FRCPC, FACC, president.

Imam Shabir Ally, keynote speaker.

Mr. Roy Bailey.

Honourable Lorne Nystrom, MP.

Professor S. Juyal.

441

Professor F. V. Greifenhagen.

Professor Terry Marner

Mr. Gerry Klein, editor, *Saskatoon Star Phoenix.*

2003 Program: Breaking Barriers & Building Bridges

In the name of Allah, Most Gracious, Most Merciful

**Muslims for Peace & Justice
2003 CONVENTION**

Co-sponsors:
**Canadian Islamic Congress (CIC)
Muslim Students' Association (MSA)**

"Breaking Barriers & Building
Bridges"
Saturday, October 4, 2003

University of Regina & Delta Hotel
10:00 AM – 3:30 PM & 5:30 PM – 8:30 PM

Admission
Day Program: $5.00 / person
(may be paid at the Convention entrance)

Evening Banquet Fees: $25.00 / person
(Register in Advance by September 20, 2003)

Full Convention Discount : $25.00 / person

**Under age of 12 & Students with proper ID
are FREE for the Day Program Only**

KEY NOTE SPEAKER
DR. MOHAMED ELMASRY
National President of
Canadian Islamic Congress

FREE PARKING
East of Education Building, Lot 3 Middle
Section University Drive East, Lot 14,
University Drive South, With sign
*Authorized M permit holder area and Lot 17
University Drive East Metered Parking is free
on the weekend.
Free Parking at the Regina Delta Hotel

Morning Session	Main Auditorium, Education Building, University of Regina Master of Ceremony Dr. Samiul Haque
10:00	Registration
10:30 – 10:45	Opening & Prayer – Fatih Hamad Welcome: Dr. Naiyer Habib – MPJ President & CIC Regional Director
10:45 – 11:15	Session A: Moderator - Riazuddin Ahmed - MPJ Community Relations Director Canadian Muslims & the Media – Award Winning CIC Research Dr. Mohamed Elmasry
11:15 – 11:30	Question & Answer
11:30 – 12:00	Session B: Moderator – Hamid Javed – Muslim Civil Rights Activist Panel Session – Anti-Terror Law & Canadian Civil Liberties Speakers: Prof. Allan Blakeney, Canadian Civil Liberties Association Representative from Justice Canada
12:00 – 12:15	Question & Answer
12:15 PM	Lunch – Provided by MPJ at a cost to Convention participants
Afternoon Session	Master of Ceremony Zeba Hashmi – MPJ Secretary
1:30 – 2:15	Session C: - Moderator – Tracy Abdou – MPJ Vice President Keynote Address: Dr. Mohamed Elmasry Spiritual Fitness for Life
2:15 – 2:30	Question & Answer
2:30 – 3:15	Session D – Moderator Dr. Ayman Aboguddah – President, Regina Huda School Panel Session - Canada's Relationship with the Muslim World Speakers: Lorne Nystrom, Member of Parliament, NDP Larry Spencer, Member of Parliament, CA Foreign Policy & International Trade - David Orchard, Former PC Party Leadership Candidate
3:15 – 3:30	Question & Answer
3:30	Closing Remarks: Dr. Naiyer Habib
	MPJ Evening Banquet – Regina Delta Hotel Master of Ceremony – Zarqa Nawaz
5:30	Reception
6:00	Welcome: Dr. Naiyer Habib – MPJ President & CIC Regional Director
6:10	Greetings from the Government of Canada
6:15	Greetings from the Government of Saskatchewan
6:20	Greetings from the City of Regina
6:30 – 7:30	Banquet Dinner (7:15 Maghrib Prayer – Led by Dr. Mohamed Elmasry)
7:40	Keynote Address: Dr. Mohamed Elmasry Breaking Barriers, Building Bridges Moderator: Kashif Ahmed – MPJ Communications Director
8:15	Closing Remarks: Dr. Naiyer Habib - MPJ President & CIC Regional Director

If you have any questions or concerns, please contact MPJ at 1-866-284-5910

Presidential address, Dr. Naiyer Habib, October 4, 2003.

Presidential Address at MPJ Conference 2003

In the name of God, most kind, most merciful. I greet you with the Islamic greetings of Assalam-o-Alaikum.WRB—i.e., peace be upon you and the mercy of God be on you.

I would like to extend our welcome to all of our audience: the general public, speakers, political leaders, and members of churches, synagogues, and Hindu temples, to all of whom we have extended our invitation.

We welcome the representatives of the press, police force, and intelligence services.

We thank all our speakers, the majority of whom have travelled from far away; their moderators will introduce them in detail in their sessions.

I am very much disappointed with our governing party, who, despite advanced notice and requests to send even an alternative, sent a simple regret by phone from the office, not even a letter to be read here. They did the same last year. The minister of justice's office was also unable to send a speaker on anti-terror law.

This tells the Muslims to get involved in politics vigorously. However, you all are here. It is encouraging and a great pleasure and honour to have you with us. Our mutual understanding of the Canadian mosaic will help us to co-exist peacefully with prosperity. It will make our new home, Canada, which we all cherish, a more unique country, from economy to morality.

I will give you a brief background on Muslims for Peace and Justice. This organization was formed after the incident of 9/11 to remove the misunderstanding about Islam and Muslims and to deal with any injustice. Nine-Eleven was one of the most recent acts of horror but not the only one in human history. This one occurred next door. This reminds us of other horrors of the past. There were approximately 1,500 Muslims killed in this horror, but we did not hear this in the media. This act of terror was launched by a group of Muslims misquoting the Quran out of context to justify terror. Similarly, other religious books can be misquoted out of context. Nine-eleven brought terror to Muslims and Arabs and to the people who resembled them—namely, Sikhs and Hindus in the US as well as in Canada—by the government and the people.

Many Muslim organizations stood up to the challenge, including the Canadian Islamic Congress, the Council of American-Islamic Relations, and Muslims for Peace and Justice. We limited our activity to Saskatchewan, but there are many other organizations in the US and some in Canada.

The public has started to understand. We do not see much positive response from the government, but they have started to realize our presence. Muslims are primarily professionals and workers. They are working, minding their business, and serving the country and society.

They are not much of a people of media know-how. The media also ignored their contribution to the country and society. You will hear more of this from Dr. Elmasry. Things have started to improve. The Saskatchewan media have been cooperative with us all along.

Muslims are here to stay. The majority of them came here to enjoy democracy. Democracy has received a dent for them because of recent incidents and their treatment by the government and the public—to some extent in Canada but much more so in the United States of America.

We need the support of the public and justice from the government. We all should remember that it was the Japanese and Italians then, and now the Muslims. Who's next?

We must build a society and elect a government that must stand above all of what we see happening today.

Dialogue by all and with all, especially with Muslims now, will create a healthy and just society and establish an appropriate government.

Now, regarding the conference last year, we had topics on important aspects of Islam. These have been shown by Cable Regina throughout the year. Thanks to Cable Regina for this community service.

This year, we have parted from it. Next year, we will bring a mixture of topics, God willing! This year, we are focusing on important topics related to the program.

Muslims in Canada and the media will reflect who and what the world knows about Muslims and Islam. This is improving. The Saskatchewan media have been fair to us.

We must know the anti-terror laws and how they affect civil liberties. We need protection, but is this the way to get it?

The Patriot Act of the US and the anti-terror law in Canada have terrorized Muslims and Arabs. These have turned the US and Canada into almost police states. According to recent articles in *The New York Times*, the Patriot Act is being used for many other crimes.

It seems the anti-terror law and Patriot Act were made by a majority group of people whose populations would not be affected by them. It is the minority—Muslims and Arabs—who are the subjects of these acts of legislation. Their representation was heard but not taken into account.

The topic of Spiritual Fitness for Life will be self-explanatory in the words of our renowned speaker and national Muslim leader, Dr. Elmasry.

As to Canada's relations with the Muslim world, I will leave this question to the speakers. Is it the Muslim world of Muslim mass or the world of Muslim mass ruled by kings and dictators appointed or supported by the West, out of which some are turning terrorists? Should we attempt to bring democracy to these countries?

Our foreign policy must be Canadian, based on justice, honesty, a caring attitude, and dignity. I think our Iraq experience seems to point in the right direction for our government.

However, we have to do more. The world is a global village. Justice, honesty, a caring attitude, and dignity are respected. They last forever. Thank you, and God bless us all,

Dr. Naiyer Habib, President.

Dr. Mohamed Elmasry.

Honourable Allan Blakeney, former premier, Saskatchewan

Mr. Mervin Phillips, lawyer.

Larry Spencer, MP.

Honourable Lorne Nystrom.

Mr. David Orchard, farmer, author.

Evening Banquet at Regina Delta Hotel

Chief guest Dr. M. Elmasry. Dr. Elmasry was recognized for lifelong service to the Muslims and other Canadians as the founding president of the Canadian Islamic Congress.

OTHER MPJ Awards of Excellence to:

Tracy Abdou, vice president MPJ.

Kashif Ahmed, public relations, MPJ.

Members and guests.

Left to right: Farzana Mohsin, Samina Ahmed,

Ruksana Nadeem (in the back), M. Naushaba Habib.

446

MUSLIMS FOR PEACE & JUSTICE

In the Name of Allah, Most Gracious, Most Merciful

3rd Annual MPJ Conference

Islam in the 21st Century: Discovering Contemporary Muslim Religious Thought

Speakers

Prof. Jamal Badawi

Prof Jamal Badawi, PhD is the Director of the Islamic Information Foundation and is a professor of Management at Saint Mary University, Halifax. He has authored many books and articles on Islam and produced 350 half hour segments TV shows on Islam. He lectures extensively on Islam in North America and abroad

Shaikh Ahmad Kutty

Doctorate degree from McGill University, He is specializing in Shariah. Imam and lecturer at the Islamic Institute of Toronto and non-Resident Imam of various Islamic Centers

Prof. Amir Hussain

Is a member of the Department of Religious Studies at the California State University. He is an Islamic Scholar, Author, Researcher and Award winner.

Registration

Conference: $10/person or $15 Per family
(may be paid at the Conference entrance)
Students with ID—Free for Conference
Discount : Conference & Banquet: $35/person
Evening Banquet Fees: $35/person
(Register in Advance by September 5, 2004)

University of Regina & Hotel Saskatchewan
September 18th, 2004
9:00 AM – 5:00 PM & 6:30 PM – 9:00 PM

MUSLIMS FOR PEACE & JUSTICE

P.O. Box 28044
Regina, SK S4N 7L1
Tel: 306.538.0188
E-mail: info@mpjsask.org
Website: www.mpjsask.org

Please contact us for more information.

447

In the Name of Allah, Most Gracious, Most Merciful

Muslims for Peace & Justice 2004 CONFERENCE

ISLAM IN THE 21ST CENTURY: DISCOVERING CONTEMPORARY MUSLIM RELIGIOUS THOUGHT

Friday,
September 17, 2004

Regina Huda School
40 Sheppard Street
Regina, Saskatchewan

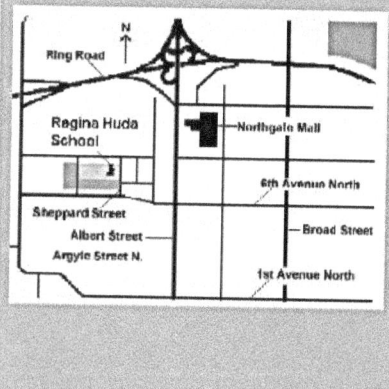

Meet the Speakers Reception – Regina Huda School

7:00 PM	Opening – Recitation of Quran
7:05 PM	Welcome: Tracy Shier, MPJ Vice President
7:05 – 7:30 PM	Meet the Speakers Reception
7:30 – 7:45 PM	Isha Prayers
7:45 – 9:00 PM	**Moderator: Riazuddin Ahmed, MPJ Member**
	The Currents in the Contemporary Muslim Religious Thought In the West and East
	Panel Discussion by all invited guest speakers
	Closing Dua

Speakers

Prof. Jamal Badawi
Prof. Jamal Badawi is the director of the Islamic Information Foundation, Halifax, Canada. Prof. Badawi is a professor of Management at Saint Mary University in Halifax.
He has authored several books and articles on Islam and designed and participated in the production of nearly 350 half-hour segments of a TV series on Islam.
He has lectured extensively in North America and abroad, and is an excellent speaker on a variety of topics including Islam & Christianity. He is expert in Christian-Muslim Dialogues.
Prof. Badawi is also a member of the Islamic Society of North America (ISNA) Fiqh Council. An Egyptian by birth, he obtained his Ph.D. in Business Administration.
Active in journalism and broadcasting he has had a series of programs concerning Islamic belief and practices shown on Canadian television throughout the world.
In Canada, he is the author of a number of books and articles on Islam.

Shaikh Ahmad Kutty
Educational background
- 1975-1980: McGill University, Montreal: Doctoral Studies; Specialized in Shari'ah Thought.
- 1972-1973: University of Toronto: Masters in Islamic Studies.
- 1968-1972: Islamic University of Madinah, Saudi Arabia: Licentiate in Usul al-Ddeen (first rank).
- 1957-1967: Islamiyya College: Graduated in the Traditional Islamic Sciences and received the 'Ijazah (title) of al-Faqih fi al-ddeen (first rank).
Career/experience
1. Presently: Senior Lecturer/Imam at the Islamic Institute of Toronto & and a non-resident Imam/Khatib (orator) at the following centers/mosques in Toronto: Islamic Center of Canada, Islamic Center of Canada, Bosnian Islamic Center, and Ansar Mosque
2. 1984-1994: Director/Imam Islamic Foundation of Toronto
3. 1979-1982: Director/Imam: Islamic Center of Toronto
4. 1973-1975: Assistant Director: Islamic Center of Toronto

Prof. Amir Hussain
Prof. Amir Hussain is a member of the Department of Religious Studies at California State University, Northridge, where he teaches courses in world religions. His own particular specialty is the study of Islam, focusing on contemporary Muslim societies, specifically those in North America. His academic degrees (BSc, MA, PhD) are all from the University of Toronto where he received a number of awards, including the university's highest award for alumni service. Amir's PhD dissertation was on Muslim communities in Toronto. Amir taught courses in religious studies at several universities in Canada. He is active in academic groups such as the American Academy of Religion (where he is co-chair of the Religion, Film and Visual Culture group, and serves on the steering committees of the Study of Islam section) and the Canadian Society for the Study of Religion, publishing and presenting his work at conferences. Amir is also interested in areas such as religion and music, religion and literature, religion and film and religion and popular culture. Amir has won a number of awards at CSUN, both for his teaching and research. In 2001 he was selected for the outstanding faculty award by the National Center on Deafness. For the academic year 2003-04, he was selected as the Jerome Richfield Memorial Scholar. Amir will be on sabbatical in the Fall semester of 2004, working on a textbook entitled Muslims: Islam in the 21st Century.

In the Name of Allah, Most Gracious, Most Merciful

Muslims for Peace & Justice 2004 CONFERENCE

ISLAM IN THE 21ST CENTURY: DISCOVERING CONTEMPORARY MUSLIM RELIGIOUS THOUGHT

University of Regina & Hotel Sask
Saturday, September 18, 2004
9:00 AM – 5:00 PM & 6:30 PM – 9:00 PM

Admission
Conference: $10/person or $15/family
(may be paid at the Conference entrance)

Banquet Fee: $35/person
(Register in Advance by September 5, 2004)

Under age of 12 & Students with proper ID are FREE for Conference only

A BLOCK OF SEATS ARE AVAILABLE FOR LADIES WISHING TO SIT SEPARATELY

FREE PARKING

East of Education Building, Lot 3 Middle Section University Drive East, Lot 14, University Drive South, With sign *Authorized M permit holder area and Lot 17 University Drive East Metered Parking is free on the weekend.

Main Auditorium, Education Building, University of Regina
Master of Ceremony: Tracy Shier – MPJ Vice President

9:00 – 9:05 AM	Opening Prayers
9:05-9:15 AM	Welcome Address by Dr. Naiyer Habib, MPJ President
9:15 – 10:00 AM	**Session A - Moderator: Dr. Naiyer Habib, MPJ President** *Normative Muslim Beliefs and Practices in the Interfaith Context (Areas of Commonality and Particularity)* **Speaker: Prof. Jamal Badawi**
10:00 – 10:15 AM	Question & Answer
10:15 – 11:00 AM	**Session B - Moderator: Kashif Ahmed, MPJ Communications Director** *Concept of Jihad and Traditional Practices– Do Ends Justify Means in Islam?* **Speaker: Shaikh Ahmad Kutty**
11:00-11:15 PM	Question & Answer
11:15-12:00 PM	**Session C - Moderator: Prof. F. Greifenhagen, Religious Studies, U of R** *Human Rights and Responsibilities in Islam – Current Practices and Challenges for the 21st Century* **Speaker: Prof. Amir Hussain**
12:00-12:15 PM	Question & Answer
12:15 - 1:25 PM	Lunch on your own (available for advanced requester $7.50/person) Zuhr Prayer

Master of Ceremony
Dr. Samiul Haque, MPJ Community Relations Director

1:30-2:15 PM	**Session D – Moderator: Zeba Hashmi, MPJ General Secretary** *Gender Equity in Islam – Scripture VS Culture* **Speaker: Prof. Jamal Badawi**
2:15-2:30 PM	Question & Answer
2:30-3:15 PM	**Session E – Moderator: Dr. Ayman Aboguddah, President, Huda School** *Traditional Islamic Fiqh (Laws) –Its Development and Implementation* **Speaker: Shaikh Ahmad Kutty**
3:15-3:30 PM	Question & Answer
3:30-3:45 PM	**Coffee break**
3:45-4:30 PM	**Session F – Moderator: Riazuddin Ahmed, MPJ Member** *The Impacts of Contemporary Muslim Religious Thought* **Panel Discussions by All Guest Speakers**
4:30-4:50 PM	Question & Answer
4:50-5:00 PM	Closing Remarks: Riazuddin Ahmed, Vote of Thanks: Dr. N Habib Closing Dua: Dr. Samiul Haque, MPJ Community Relations Director

MPJ Evening Banquet – Hotel Saskatchewan

6:30-7:00 PM	Reception Quranic Recitation – Prof Amr Henni & Welcome by Tracy Shier
7:00-8:00 PM	Banquet Dinner
8:00-9:00 PM	**Moderator: Riazuddin Ahmed, MPJ Member** *A Clash or Dialogue of Civilizations?* **Prof. Amir Hussain**
9:00 PM	Closing Remarks: Riazuddin Ahmed, MPJ Member Closing Dua: Prof. Amr Henni, MPJ Director

Presidential address, Dr. Naiyer Habib, September 18, 2004.

Presidential Address at MPJ Conference 2004

In the name of God, the compassionate, the merciful. Praise is to God the Lord of the universe, and peace and prayers are upon all of the prophets and His final prophet and messenger, Ahmed Mujtaba Mohammed Mustafa (SAWS). The peace and blessings of God be with you all. I welcome you all to our third annual conference.

A special welcome to our guest speakers alphabetically: Dr. Gamal Badawi of St. Mary's University, Halifax; Professor Amir Hussain, California State University; and Sheikh Ahmed Kutty, Islamic Institute of Toronto. They will be introduced in detail in their sessions. Our sincere thanks to them for sparing the time for us from their ever-busy schedules. God bless them.

This conference would not have been successful without your participation and financial support. We thank you for that. We hold such conferences to highlight some aspects of Islam that are relevant to the time. We formed Muslims for Peace and Justice immediately after 9/11 to remove misunderstandings about Islam and Muslims and to defend Muslims who were maligned or victimized. They are still facing problems today on an ongoing basis—not as much in Canada, but certainly in Canada and almost regularly in the US.

Some of the remarks that follow are in no way for our audience or the majority of the citizens of the world but for an aggressive minority who are able to drive their agenda very dominantly against us. These are the feelings that some or many of us have. I remain apprehensive that some Muslim enemies, be it a nation, a group or an individual, may create terrorism in Canada to malign Muslims to say: "Look what is happening," and to compel them to act against us. Canada has remained peaceful. It has not participated in mistreating Muslims and Arabs as fully as expected by the neoconservatives. I was not expecting that Muslims would be victimized in the West— the modern and civilized world of today. A friend of mine, who is present in the audience, remarked with a grim face during the ethnic cleansing that was occurring in Bosnia, "I hope this does not happen to us here." I told him with a smile, "No!! It will not happen here in the West. They are civilized people. There is repentance for what happened with the Japanese." But, lo and behold, what is happening in the civilized society of the West? Who is the worst violator of human rights? Please note this statement: "To Arab Americans, they are fortunate not to be treated the way Japanese Americans during World War II were - that is, fortunate not to be thrown into concentration camps and have most of their property seized, never to be returned." **John Ashcroft, 79th Attorney General**. Do you know whose words these are? These are the words of Ashcroft, one of the very few high-ranking and very close members of the Bush administration who are driving the agenda of our friend country and the world. We are here to stay. We have burned our boat. We are loyal to our new land as second to none, yet doubts are perceived about our loyalty. There are demands for condemnation of events occurring elsewhere. There is criticism of the degree of condemnation done by us to do more. Some of the talk show audiences reflect poisonous views about Muslims. Some talk show moderators and some news media choose topics that target Muslims. No doubt, it is not the majority but the minority. The biased minority has an aggressive personality that dominates their thoughts and acts.

I am apprehensive. The worst is still to come. The second win of Bush will have a mandate to go further unless it learns from its mistake and rolls back. Of course, that will only happen if it considers its policy to be a mistaken policy.

Problems occur elsewhere. The impact is here. People in Chechnya, Palestine, Kashmir, and elsewhere are fighting their battles for their causes in the manner they can and by the means that they have. It so happens that they are Muslims—downtrodden by the British Empire and ruled by kings and dictators appointed or supported by the West.

What do we have to do with them in this regard?

Islam is a religion of peace, but war is permissible to maintain peace if required. It is permissible in Islam to fight the aggressor who drives people from their homes or confiscates their property. Such permission is reasonable and practical. Different groups may interpret this differently. This is like using pretexts in some circumstances. Pretext has been used and is being used by nations to wage war against innocent nations for self-gain. History tells us that. The use of pretext must be condemned.

The Oklahoma bombers and fighters in Ireland are not different from these people who happen to be Muslims.

Let us understand one another, be just, and not lose civility or practice double standards. These are important for everlasting peace.

It will not be out of place for me to pass some comments on the situation of women and Muslim leadership.

As Muslims are targets of various elements, Muslim women are targets of Muslims and non-Muslims. Their status in society is yet to be defined. They are being banned or put behind curtains or placed in the most rejected room of the mosque. Their children are abandoning the mosque. Their men—fathers, brothers, and husbands—have taken back seats as obedient disciples of some imams from the pulpit. This was not the case at the time of the prophets or in the early '60s or '70s when we came here. A change is to be brought, and it will be, God willing. The majority of Muslim women in the West feel threatened by Islamic law, not the Quran. Over the course of centuries, the Quran and prophetic traditions have been interpreted—and I say interpreted—differently by scholars, sub-scholars, or non-scholars. By non-scholars, I mean people with the least knowledge but claiming the most. This has created confusion and controversies all over. This needs to be looked at.

The women scholars of Islam, although few, based on their research, claim that Islamic law, not the Quran, has biases and prejudices against women as they were made or interpreted by men. This needs our attention jointly, with the open and cool minds of both men and women.

The hijab or headscarf is one of the greatest targets. Muslim women with hijab are discriminated against. Yes, many non-Muslims do respect them. It is considered to be a sign of oppression as well as a sign of a terrorism breeder. France banned it. Others are looking at it. The majority of Canadians did not approve of the ban, but a fair number were in favour of it. Thanks to our prime minister for reassuring Muslims. I wonder whether such comments and steps might have been made if our respectable nuns had continued to wear their respectable attire. The majority of Muslim women do not wear hijab for these reasons, although some have reacted against mullahs. I like to see the Muslim women wearing hijab and sitting in the parliament. This was the case at the time of the prophet when women used to interact. I would like them to get back into hijab to support those who are battling to keep hijab, including the non-Muslim girls who supported their Muslim girlfriends by wearing hijab at the time of 9/11.

Lastly, it is my appeal to Muslim leaders and to you to ask your Muslim leaders to join hands to sit together to deal with problems jointly in a concentrated effort to have credibility for the governments, the media, and the public. No doubt, each leader in his or her organization is doing a marvellous job, but it is like blowing their own trumpets in different directions.

With these words, I urge the Muslims and other citizens to be just and sincere, to not follow a double standard, and to make efforts to co-exist with respect, justice, and honesty, and to help others to do the same. Let us make our land and the world a better place for all to live.

My friends, this is my last address to you all as the president of the Muslims for Peace and Justice, as I leave Saskatchewan after thirty-one years to begin a new chapter of our life in the next few weeks. God bless you. God bless Saskatchewan and Canada. Ameen

Speakers Of International Repute

Evening Banquet at Hotel Saskatchewan

Welcome by the president, Naiyer Habib.

Riazuddin Ahmed, moderator.

Award and recognition of Dr. Anwar Haque, founding president of the
Islamic Association of Saskatchewan (1971), serving in the position from 1971-'77,
presented by Dr. Naiyer Habib, founding president of MPJ, on behalf of MPJ.

Award of Excellence to Zeba Hashmi from MPJ.

Riazuddin Ahmed, receiving an Award of
Excellence from MPJ for his long-time service to
the community in MPJ and the Islamic
Association of Saskatchewan.

Recognition of Dr. Naiyer Habib, founding and outgoing president of MPJ, presented by vice president Tracy Shier and director Riazuddin Ahmed.

In the Name of God, Most Compassionate, Most Merciful

Muslims for Peace & Justice (MPJ)

Appreciation Award

Presented to

Dr. Naiyer Habib

In recognition of your many years of service, leadership, and dedication to the Muslim community of Regina

2004

Tracy Shier
Vice-President

Zeba Hashmi
Secretary

L-R: Naiyer Habib, Kashif Ahmed, Ahmed Kutty, Samiul Haque, Jamal Badawi,

Amir Hussain, Amr Henni Qudsia Qayyum, Tracy Shier, and Zeba Hashmi.

Events- Participation
Honouring Ramadan by Ikea, Bay, Home Hardware, and Zellers

Welcoming Ramadan sign at the door of the Bay.

Naiyer Habib, presenting a certificate of appreciation to the Bay representative.

Muslims for Peace & Justice (MPJ) recognized the Hudson Bay Company at the Cornwall Centre for its outstanding commitment to religious diversity through its Ramadan advertisements that were featured in flyers and posters across Canada.

Ramadan Recognition by Ikea in The Toronto Star and Habib's interview:

(Courtesy of the *Star* is greatly appreciated.)

November 17, 2003. 12:14 p.m.

Nod to Ramadan, a trend in retailing: IKEA launches a low-key campaign that puts Muslims in the mainstream.

LESLIE SCRIVENER

FAITH AND ETHICS REPORTER

When does a minority know it's become part of mainstream culture? When are temples and mosques as much a part of the cityscape as churches? When Muslim women wear head coverings without attracting stares? When a home furnishings company recognizes that shoppers spend not only at Christmas but also at Diwali, Ramadan, and Hanukkah.

In a new public relations campaign, IKEA has highlighted Ramadan, the month-long Muslim fast that began October 27. The campaign shows women wearing hijab and South Asian dress, photos of Mecca, sweet trays used for end-of-fast celebrations, and a text explaining the religious meaning of the holiday.

The series of photographs showing IKEA carpets, candles, table settings, and gifts for children—ways of decorating the home for the holiday—is not a nationwide mail-out campaign but will be on the IKEA Canada website today.

It's the first for IKEA and part of a trend for retailers to acknowledge minority celebrations.

Hudson's Bay Company, for the first time this fall, included Ramadan greetings in flyers for The Bay, Zellers, and Home Outfitters, plus posters and door signs. It will do the same for Hanukkah and other holidays.

"We realize that millions of Canadians are shopping in our stores, and we should be celebrating the cultures and diversity of all our customers," said spokesperson Hillary Stauth. The company's efforts have already been recognized. The Multicultural Council of Regina and Muslims for Peace and Justice Saskatchewan sent the company a citation of thanks.

"We are a minority, and these are especially bad times for us.

"We appreciate this first initiative to recognize Muslims as part of mainstream Canadian society," said Dr. Naiyer Habib, president of Muslims for Peace.

Keka Das Gupta, whose first project was home decorating for Diwali, created the IKEA campaign in the store's public relations department for the Hindu festival of lights last month.

She drew from her Bengali background to show how the festival is celebrated at home. For Ramadan, she interviewed Muslim staff and was advised by Aneesa Razakazi, a design consultant at the North York store.

"It's important to look at how people of all backgrounds live," Das Gupta said. "It's not just about the products; it's about sharing what we've learned."

Muslims were generally appreciative, though wary that they would become another demographic group targeted by retailers. They don't want to see their holy month commercialized.

Ramadan ends November 24, depending on the moon sighting, with Eid celebrations. With it comes cleaning and updating the home and buying new clothes or furnishings. ("Eid is a time for cleansing both the heart and the home," the IKEA copy reads.)

Showing ways to beautify the home and make it welcoming in a culturally sensitive way is valued, Muslims say.

"My first reaction was that this is good, that we're part of the mainstream, we have a voice, we are in large enough numbers to be recognized, but there's definitely a flip side," said Farheen Hussain, program manager for a Mississauga non-profit group.

"Islam isn't about consumerism. We don't come from a commercial, disposable culture. If Eid sales become part of a company's bottom line, I really don't like it. Eid is about spending time with family; it is a religious time, remembering people less fortunate, and comes at the end of the month of self-denial and prayer."

(IKEA's campaign includes charity references: ". . . one way to teach children these values: ask them to pick one gift they received for Eid and have them donate it to a family in need.") While it's clear retailers are looking at Muslims as consumers, the overall message is welcome, said Riad Saloojee, executive director of the Council on American-Islamic Relations Canada. "What I like is that Muslims are humanized, as are our cultures and traditions, and we are portrayed strictly as part of Canadian culture," he said. "It's not a foreign celebration." IKEA is doing just what Muslim stores do, though on a bigger scale, said Imam Abdul Hai Patel, coordinator of the Islamic Council of Imams Canada.

"There is always a commercial side to every festival. At Eid, we traditionally get something new."

CBC Learn at Lunch, March 11, 2003:

What's it like being Muslim in Canada today? A Regina summits.

About 100 people brought their lunch to the Regina Public Library to hear from three prominent Saskatchewan Muslims. The discussion opened with Dr. Naiyer Habib, president of Muslims for Peace and Justice. He described his perceptions about portrayals of Muslims and misinformation about what Islamic believers feel.

459

Second to speak was Kashif Ahmed, a University of Regina student whose comments exposed the biases that exist in the media and how they serve to perpetuate stereotypes about Islamic people.

Finally, filmmaker Zarqa Nawaz presented her light-hearted approach to the painful and often absurd experiences of being a devout Muslim in a Judeo-Christian world.

The public discussion exposed a great desire for understanding between cultures.

L-R: Zarqa Nawaz, Dr. Habib, Costa Maragos.

Media Invitation: the Meeting with CTV

In the name of Allah, most gracious, most merciful

Mpj Officials Meet With Ctv News Group

(December 17, 2003) Representatives from Muslims for Peace & Justice

(MPJ), a Saskatchewan-based Muslim outreach and advocacy organization, met with the directors of the local CTV news station at a Monday luncheon meeting to discuss CTV's coverage of issues pertaining to Islam and Canadian Muslims.

Representatives from the Regina Huda School and the Canadian Council of Muslim Women (CCMW) joined MPJ at the meeting. The meeting was aimed at opening up communication between the Saskatchewan Muslim community and CTV and for Muslims to provide feedback on CTV news coverage.

MPJ officials expressed appreciation for the positive coverage of Muslim and Islamic events yet raised concerns regarding misinformation and stereotypes that are still present in the mass media about Islam and Muslims. Aspects concerning how the coverage could be improved were also discussed. The CTV news officials were very receptive to the feedback and encouraged Saskatchewan Muslims to keep them informed.

The meeting was a very fruitful and positive session, and MPJ looks forward to working with the Saskatchewan media to improve the image and coverage of Islam and Muslims in the public sphere.

—END—

CTV Television Inc.

216 - 1st Ave. N.
Saskatoon, Saskatchewan
Canada S7K 3W3

Tel 306.665.8600
Fax 306.665.0450

Thank you for attending our third Editorial Board Luncheon Meeting!

The meeting will focus on news issues affecting the Muslim community, and how these issues are covered by the Regina CTV news cast. The following individuals have planned to attend:

Dr. Ayman Aboguddah – Cardiologist ; President of Huda School (Public and Islamic education)

Mr. Kashif Ahmed – University Student and Communication Director of Muslims for Peace and Justice (MPJ)

Mr. Riaz Ahmed – City Planner / Director or Public Relations for MPJ

Dr. Naiyer Habib – Cardiologist; Former Head of Cardiology for Regina Health District; Former President of the Islamic Association of Saskatchewan (Regina); President of MPJ

Mrs. M. Naushaba Habib – MA (Political Science); President of Canadian Council of Muslim Women (Regina Chapter)

Dr. Samiul Haque – Child Psychiatrist

Zeba Hashmi – Homemaker and Secretary of MPJ; Bilingual Medical Office Administration Certification

Zarqa Nawaz – Journalist and Film Maker

Carl Worth - News Director - CTV Regina

Dale Neufeld - News Director - CTV Saskatoon / Prince Albert

Brian Zawacki - Director of Community Relations

Angela Loewen - Human Resources Specialist (Saskatchewan)

Geoff Bradley - Creative / Promotions Manager (Saskatchewan)

Wade Moffatt - Sales Manager - CTV Regina / Yorkton

Tara Robinson - News Anchor - CTV Regina

Manfred Joehnck - News Anchor - CTV Regina

Nelson Bird – Video Journalist; Host of Indigenous Circle

We want critical feedback on CTV Regina's news stories and interviews. We would like you to consider the following discussion questions:

1. How do our news stories cover issues affecting the Muslim community? Give specific examples.

2. Comment on how Muslim people are presented in the news.

3. What issues are being ignored? Give specific examples.

4. What news program do you watch all the time? If it's not CTV, explain why you prefer it.

5. Describe what you like about our station's approach.

6. What suggestions do you have about how we could improve our ability to serve your community?

a division of
Bell Globemedia

Muslims reach out to larger community

By Frank Flegel

REGINA — The Sept. 11, 2001, events in New York, Washington and Pennsylvania focused attention on the Muslim faith, but a Saskatchewan group is using that interest in a positive manner. Muslims for Peace and Justice (MPJ) in Saskatchewan began shortly after 9/11 to reach out to the general community and at the same time face internal changes. Its third annual conference, held Sept. 17 - 18 at the University of Regina, attracted some 200 people to hear Muslim speakers discuss their faith.

MPJ President Dr. Naiyer Habib said in an interview that some people blamed Islam because some Muslims took the name of Islam in the events of 9/11. That has led to new challenges for Muslims, he said, but the old challenges remain.

"There is a perception that Islam is a religion of war, particularly a war against non-believers, and that Islam considers everyone non-believers. That is not the case." The word jihad is often misinterpreted, Habib said. It allows Muslims to engage in war for liberation and if being oppressed, but not otherwise. Christians, Jews and Muslims all come from one Abrahamic faith, he said, and Muslims respect the other faiths.

The old challenges are that different scholars have different views of what the Quran says, and their interpretations and comments have led to controversy. The same thing, he said, is happening to the tradition of the Prophet Mohammed and what he said and did.

The status of women within Islam has divided Muslims into two categories, according to Habib: conservatives who wish to exclude women from the mosque and active participation in virtually all areas of society outside the home (as the Taliban did in Afghanistan), and those who support women. Habib said excluding women is totally wrong: "That is not what it was like at the time of the Prophet."

Habib said there is a group of people who look at Islam in a different way. "They are saying that the presence of women creates evil desires. It is stupidity to make this kind of statement." Many Muslims are concerned that excluding women from the mosque has also kept children away, and there is a fear that the younger generation will leave the faith.

Habib came to Canada from India more than 30 years ago. An American-trained heart specialist, he worked in Saskatoon for several years and then headed the cardiac unit at the old Plains Hospital until his retirement. He said that when he came to Saskatchewan, women and men interacted according to the tradi-

— MPJ, page 9

Flegel

Dr. Naiyer Habib

MPJ looking to Prophet

Continued from page 3

tions of the Prophet and the Quran, but that has since changed to the more conservative view. Habib said MPJ is trying to "rechange it to the time of the Prophet."

Riazuddin Ahmed, one of the founders of MPJ, said the organization has had success in Saskatchewan changing some attitudes about Islam, but less success in the rest of Canada and the United States. "But the kind of speakers we have here are going to make a difference and are going to have an impact, and that's the purpose: to create better understanding between communities."

Acknowledgement: As a courtesy of *The Prairie Messenger*, Regina.

MPJ Participates in the City of Regina Centennial Celebration

We celebrated the seventy-fifth anniversary (mosaic of the city) and were around to celebrate its 100 years. Our community members joined us. Details are in our first book (*HMRO*)[81].

Our Stall

---

[81] *History of the Muslims of Regina, Saskatchewan... "A Cultural Integration,"* available from Amazon.

1st Row, L-R: Zeba Hashmi, Zeba's daughter, Nargis Bhimji, and Tracy Abdou Shier.
2nd Row, L-R: Sana Ahmed, Naushaba Habib, Samina Ahmed, and Qudsia Qayyum.
They were joined by others who cooked traditional multicultural food and offered it
to visiting guests.

L-R: Naiyer Habib, Abdul Qayyum, Arif Sethi, and Mansoor Haque.

END OF HABIB ERA 2001-2005, MPJ

I initiated and joined MPJ as one of three. I was elected founding president.

I decided to wind up and move from Regina with my family to Abbotsford, British Columbia. In preparation for this, I wanted to finalize the constitution and wind up various matters related to Muslims for Peace and Justice. These were done.

Final Meetings

A meeting was held at the residence of Amr Henni at 4243 Wascana Ridge on Saturday, February 26, 2005. The following points were discussed and were to be dealt with in the meeting of the MPJ on February 27, 2005.

1 . Opening with Quran recitation.

2 . Review of the minutes of the general body of February 15, 2004.

3 . Matters arising out of that meeting.

4 . Review of the minutes of the previous board meeting, time permitting.

5 . Matters arising out of the minutes of the board meeting, time permitting.

6 . Conduction of election for all positions.

7 . Review of the nomination papers and ballot papers.

8 . Membership fee collection and ID card distribution.

9 . Safe-keeping of the constitution.

10. Various items belonging to MPJ. Others, time permitting, as advised by the board members.

11. Invitation to Brother Ahmed Abodheir.

AGM Sunday, February 27, 2005, at Regina Huda School, 40 Sheppard Street:

Ahmed Abodheir and Naiyer Habib.

L to R, back row: Aijaz Hussai, Khalid Barzouti, Ayman Aboguddah,
Fateh Hamad, Abdul Jalil, Arif Sethi, Abbas Hussaini.
Front: Nargis Bhimji, Samina Ahmed, Riazuddin Ahmed, Raza Bhimji,
Fatah Wasty, Samiul Haque, Sheila Ahmed, Amr Henni.

The following trustees were present; Samina Ahmed, Riazuddin Ahmed, Amr Henni, Khalid Berzoutit, Ayman Aboguddah, Fasahat Wasty, Samiul Haq, Fateh Hammad, Sheila Ahmed, Shahid Rehman, Abdul Jalil, Khalifa Daudi, Raabia Lacher, Tracy Shier, Naiyer Habib, Kashif Ahmed, Ejaz Hussain, Abbas Hussainie, Arif Sethi, Raza Bhimji, Nargis Bhimji, Zarka Nawaz, Zeba Hashmi.

Ahmed Aboudheir (guest), president, Islamic Association of Saskatchewan, Regina. Inc.

Chairman: Naiyer Habib.

Opening recitation of Surah-Fateha by Amr Henni.

Welcome address: Tracy Shier (Abdou).

The agenda was adapted, moved by Ayman Abguddah, seconded by Fateh Hammad, and carried unanimously.

The minutes of the meeting of February 15, 2004, were reviewed and re-circulated. All accepted this.

As chair, I indicated that the constitution would be submitted to the corporation branch for incorporating the MPJ in the province, and, subsequently, MPJ would apply to Revenue Canada for tax-exemption status for donors. If the corporation branch recommended any modification in the constitution, it would require the approval of the trustees. All accepted, and it was the responsibility of the elected board to carry this out.

I also spoke about the importance of retaining an original copy of the constitution, stating that two original copies, signed and initialled on every page by the president and secretary, would remain with the president and secretary, and any new amendment was to be signed and initialled on the pages of the amendment by the current secretary and the president on an ongoing basis. I called Riazuddin Ahmed in the year he was elected to find out if the constitution was incorporated by the elected board as assigned in the general meeting held on February 26, 2005. I contacted some others as named by him. Ultimately, I concluded that no one pursued this.

A membership card was issued, and it was pointed out that future renewal may require placement of the year of renewal for the membership, that is, the trustee.

Invited Guest

Ahmed Abodhier, president of the Islamic Association of Saskatchewan, was invited by the MPJ. He showed appreciation to the founders, members, and volunteers whose cumulative work went into forming the Islamic Association. He further stated that the Islamic Association of Saskatchewan constitution was a great achievement and that he would work toward maintaining it. He expressed his vision to activate every article and protect the rights of every community member. He further mentioned that different committees had been formed. He wanted to see people become members of good standing of the Islamic Association of Saskatchewan.

An election was held, and the following candidates were elected:

Riazuddin Ahmed: president, two years.

Tracy Shier: vice president, one year.

Zeba Hashmi: general secretary, two years.

Sheila Ahmed: treasurer, one year.

Kashif Ahmed: director, one year.

Samiul Haque: director, two years.

Amr Henni: director, two years.

Note: This election was undertaken according to the newly finalized constitution.

Before adjournment, Riazuddin Ahmed thanked everyone for their confidence in him and stated that he would try to build on the success of Naiyer Habib's achievements. The chair acknowledged Riazuddin Ahmed's contributions.

Riazuddin Ahmed spoke about the Security Roundtable objectives and mandate. He spoke of other Muslims on the roundtable. He emphasized that it was important for the Muslim community to involve itself in national-level discussions and make them aware of the concerns of Muslims.

Note: For details about the Security Roundtable, you can go to the Government of Canada website or the internet. I had recommended Riazuddin Ahmed to be on the roundtable. He was successfully placed on the roundtable board.

Finally, I thanked all board members for their extraordinary and sincere help with the work of MPJ over the years and wished them well.

The meeting was adjourned with a recitation of the Quran by Amr Henni.

Trustees No More

It was time for us to step down as trustees. There was a provision for us to continue as trustees, but we decided not to, as we would not be able to contribute anything to it, living so far away.

On Friday, June 25, 2005, we wrote an email to the board from our home in British Columbia:

Assalam-o-Alaikum WRB.

We pray to find you all in good health and happiness.

After considerable deliberation, we have decided not to continue as trustees of MPJ.

We are living here. We will not be active participants to contribute anything to MPJ. It is best that the seats are vacated to bring in new trustees. The participation of new members will further the progress of MPJ. We highly appreciate your cooperation with the work of MPJ. We appreciate much more the love and affection of our community in Regina over the years and, in particular, for giving us such a fond farewell. We will always remember everyone.

Your brother and sister in Islam,

CANADIAN COUNCIL OF MUSLIM WOMEN

Saskatchewan, Regina Chapter, 1981

By

Mahlaqa Naushaba Habib

INTRODUCTION

The Canadian Council of Muslim Women (CCMW) is a national non-profit organization with chapters across the nation, established to assist Muslim women in participating effectively in Canadian society, and to promote mutual understanding between Canadian Muslim women and women of other faiths. It is an example of realization by Muslim women to establish an organization to focus on the recognition of their talent and social, cultural, religious, and political status in society at large. The Canadian Council of Muslim Women was established by the Edmonton educator, Sister Dr. Lila Fahlman.

The first national meeting was held in the Manitoba Islamic Centre on April 24-25, 1982. Representatives from across Canada attended the meeting.

I attended this meeting. I was the founding president of the Regina chapter, which was formed even before the national organization when Sister Lila Fahlman visited Regina.

History Of The Canadian Council Of Muslim Women (CCMW), Regina

Dr. Lila Fahlman visited Regina, her province of birth, at our residence, 308 Habkirk Drive, while touring the nation, where a meeting of a few women was held. This led to the establishment of the Canadian Council of Muslim Women, Regina, as a chapter of the national organization in the fall of 1981. An election was held, and the following women were elected to the board of this newly formed Canadian Council of Muslim Women. I was the founding president.

Mahlaqa Naushaba Habib, founding president.

Fareda Sethi, vice president.

Rashida Nawaz, secretary.

Qudsia Qayyum, treasurer.

The women who were actively involved in running the organization from the beginning and later joining actively included: Mahlaqa Naushaba Habib, Samina Ahmed, Rashida Nawaz, Nilofer Haque, Zia Afsar, Nusrat Jalil, and Qudsia Qayyum.

After being established in the fall of 1981, the CCMW Regina chapter played a major role for Muslim women in Regina. We interacted with other women's groups in the province and participated in many activities. CCMW Regina was recognized and respected by various organizations and received their praise.

Besides various other important roles, CCMW Regina played a vital and exemplary role during the Bosnia crisis, especially paying attention to the treatment of women in Bosnia. There was a demonstration, a rally, and media interviews. Zia Afsar of CCMW Regina, and Kathleen Thompson of United Women, along with others, played leading roles in rallies. We embarked on various fundraising projects.

By the time I left Regina in 2004, the Canadian Council of Muslim Women had achieved a very high profile during my presidency, along with other presidents, and supported by all members of this organization. I moved with my husband to British Columbia.

Activities

The activities of CCMW Regina are detailed in *HMRSO*. Here, only a glance is represented.

- Hijra Bazaar.

- Holiday International Market.

- Monthly meetings.

- Launched baby-sitting scheme for better parent relationships.

- Visiting the sick in hospital, with cards and flowers.

- Involved with youth program.

- Supporting mosque with fundraising as women's contribution.

- Donation to Human Concern International.

- Self-Education—religious education.

- Other community contact.

- CCMW National Conference.

- Workshops.

- Financial management and building workshop, November 1994.

- Mother/Daughter Tea, January 1999.

Programs

- Display booth at the University of Regina's International Women's Day celebrations. This allowed for the opportunity to network with other women's organizations, publicize the functions and contributions of the Regina chapter, and promote a positive image of Muslim women.

- Interfaith Council—Zia Afsar (president) attended an interfaith workshop in Davidson, and spoke on women's rights in Islam. The workshop presenters were members of Jewish, First Nation, and Muslim groups. The audience was the local Interfaith Council in Davidson and other interested individuals.

- Seniors Class.

- Regina Council of Women.

- Community for Children Project: the United Way funded this project.

- Sister Nargis Bhimji represented the CCMW in many volunteer organizations.

Media

- Press conference, March 1995.

- Insights: Zia Afsar (president) was interviewed by a local cable TV show. She was invited to speak on Islam. The show received positive feedback from both Muslims and non-Muslims.

Affiliations, Memberships, And Participation

- Amnesty International annual general meeting.

- Breakthrough Fear of "The Other," hosted by CCMW with panelist Zeba Hashmi.

- Participation in World Religion Day.

- Canadian Cancer Society: Door-to-door fundraising campaign, Naushaba and Nargis.

- Canadian Institute for the Advancement of Women and National Organization of Immigrant and Visible Minority Women of Canada.

- Immigrant Women of Saskatchewan.

- Lions Club.

- Member of Regina Council of Women.

- Multicultural Council of Saskatchewan.

- Immigrant Women of Saskatchewan, Regina Chapter.

- Shared Values Forum, J. A. Burnett Education Centre.

- Muslim for Peace and Justice.

- Packing of Eyeglasses by Lions Club: Sister Nargis.

- Participated in workshop and recommendation on access to legal services for women, conducted by SCAR; attended by Naushaba.

- Peace Council.

- Public Health Nursing: an informative meeting with the following subjects discussed: lecture on Islam by Nargis; Muslim patients and their circumstances in hospital, Naris; pamphlets on abortion, the Muslim diet, and Ramadan, distributed; celebrated International Women's Day, hosted by immigrant women and the CCMW; lecture on "Value of Women in Islam," by Mrs. M. Naushaba Habib.

These activities helped to develop networks with other women's groups and to publicize the existence of the Regina chapter. Through these networks, the Regina chapter was invited to participate in other important councils and activities. It was suggested that we make ourselves aware of local activities; the display booth at the

International Women's Day celebration was organized by reading the paper, attending the celebrations, and asking the organizers on the spot if the Regina chapter could have a booth. This brought about positive feedback and results.

THE BOARD OF EDUCATION OF THE
REGINA SCHOOL DIVISION
NO. 4 OF SASKATCHEWAN

J.A. Burnett Education Centre   Ph: (306) 791-8200
1600 4th Ave., Regina, Sask., S4R 8C8   Fax: (306) 352-2898

December 1, 1997

Mrs. Naushaba Habib
9227 Wascana Mews
Regina, SK
S4V 2W3

Dear Mrs. Habib:

Re: __Shared Values Forum - September 24, 1997__

Enclosed please find a copy of the Shared Values Forum Report, as well as the summary of small group discussions that took place that evening. The summary contains detailed notes from each small group discussion, and were used to compile the condensed Report of the Forum.

Thank you for taking time out of your busy schedule to attend this most important event. Your contribution to the data gathered will go a long way towards creating an awareness and strengthening shared values, not only in Regina Public Schools, but in the wider community as well.

The information that was received from the participants at the Forum will be used by the Advisory Committee to make recommendations for future initiatives in the area of shared values.

Please feel free to call me at 791-8212, if you have any questions, or require further information.

Sincerely

Barbara Young, D.Ed
Superintendent
Curriculum and Support Services

BY/ms

Canadian
Cancer
Society

Société
canadienne
du cancer

Dear Naushaba:

I'd like to take this opportunity to thank you for the donations you have collected for the Canadian Cancer Society over the years and taken the time to support us once again this year.

Your dedication very clearly demonstrates your enthusiasm and commitment to our vision. You are a partner in the important work being done by the CCS.

This year you have helped raise :
$199.00
and we thank you for it.

The Canadian Cancer Society is leading the way to a new and better world: a world in which no man, no woman, no child need live in fear of cancer. Our research programs and our direct-help services depend upon the support of people who share our vision and our commitment— People Like YOU

Sincerely,

Saweena Seth
Special Events Coordinator
Canadian Cancer Society: 1910 McIntyre Street, Regina. Tel: 790-5818

Other Roles Of The Canadian Council Of Muslim Women

This organization played various important political roles on occasions that prompted its involvement—in particular, the Bosnia crisis, the Gulf War, and the University of Regina student scholarship program. Some brief reflections on these are cited below:

Bosnia Crisis

Women United And The Bosnia Crisis

We invited local women's organizations to join hands and raise a strong collective voice against the violence toward women in Bosnia-Herzegovina. Sixteen such organizations came together, and an ad-hoc group called Women United was formed. We developed an action plan to write letters to our respective sister organizations in other cities to raise their voices against the atrocities in Bosnia; also to write letters to the secretary general of the United Nations and other concerned heads of state to take immediate action and declare rape as a war crime, and to stop rape camps and ethnic cleansing. We gathered approximately 1,100 signatures, and petitions containing these signatures were forwarded to local MPs. We held a protest rally in Regina. We accomplished all we planned.

All media in Regina overwhelmingly and sincerely supported our cause. Media coverage was excellent, and representatives of the CCMW Regina chapter and others were interviewed for television (CBC Regina, STV, CKCK), the local newspaper (*Leader-Post*), and local radio stations, who also covered the protest march. Zia Afsar and Kathleen Thompson were up front, and Sabreena Haque, Samina Ahmed, Saleena, Lydia Fuller, Widy Davis, and I were active with them.

NEWS: Bosnia (courtesy of Global TV).

Naushaba Habib

82 Published as a courtesy of Global TV, CKCK, and CBC Regina.

Gulf War

CCMW was an active participant in the Iraq War Crisis II, along with the Islamic Association. We held a protest march and rally. As the president, I addressed the Regina City Hall rally.

Address On The Iraq War At Regina City Hall,
By Naushaba Habib, February 15, 2003

Assalam-o-Alaikum, peace be upon you all.

I represent the Canadian Council of Muslim Women. We stand with you against this war. I am going to summarize to you an article from Physicians for Global Survival (Canada) with my added comments. "This organization is concerned with human health, well-being, and security. We assert that the planned attack on Iraq is inconsistent with international law designed to protect vulnerable populations and that it is inhumane and unthinkable because there are alternative ways to achieve any legitimate goals in this conflict."

This is what the Physicians for Global Survival are saying. They go on to say, "We are opposed to this war and therefore call on the Canadian government not to provide military or moral support for it." We at the Canadian Council of Muslim Women fully agree with this.

"Contrary to international law, human life is not being respected, be it for children or otherwise.

"It is recognized that there is an increasing awareness of the rights of children, and particularly the plight and rights of children in armed conflicts. The 1989 Convention on the Rights of the Child applies under all circumstances—peace or war. The child has a right to live, to a family, to adequate nutrition, to education, to health care, and to play. Usually, non-governmental organizations are called into action after a war has been waged when the lives of thousands of children have been lost. In this case, we look ahead to try to prevent this deliberate act.

"This war will result in tens of hundreds of thousands of civilian causalities, including children. Civilians, likely half of them children, will be slaughtered in the internal conflict between Shia and Kurdish. We cannot accept this. The life of each child is precious. The lives of men and women in the armed forces matter, too, whether US, UK, or Iraqi.

"Recent Canadian experience tells us that many will be incapacitated by the psychological aftermath of the horrors of armed conflict. We do not accept this unnecessary suffering. We are concerned that the lives of ordinary Canadians will be placed at greater risk of terrorism if our government participates in this planned war. Far from seeing this as a war to counter-terrorism, we see it as a war to provoke terrorism.

"Violation of a country's sovereignty with pre-emptive war is, frankly, illegal under the UN charter. Furthermore, President George Bush, on December tenth, stated that the US would consider the use of nuclear weapons against Iraq if Iraq uses chemical or biological weapons.

"Canada must not even contemplate giving support to such an act.

"Additionally, the International Court of Justice advised in 1996 that the use and threat of nuclear weapons is generally illegal. The strictest interpretation of threat in the ICJ's advisory opinion included the threat to use nuclear weapons against a specific country under specific circumstances. In Afghanistan, US forces dropped thousands of cluster bombs, dispersing hundreds of thousands of cluster bombs left there.

"Cluster bombs have high failure rates and lay waiting for the touch of civilians, especially curious children, to trigger their explosion. It is highly probable that the US will use cluster bombs in Iraq.

"This has humanitarian consequences. The efforts to remove Saddam Hussein through sanctions and the last war have already cost the lives of well over a million Iraqis. These efforts have also caused the destruction of civilians and civilian infrastructures, including water purification, sewage treatment, and electrical and power generation.

"The impact of the sanction contributes to damage to the social fabric through an increase in crime and family disruption. Together with the direct effects on healthcare systems and the punitive blocking of medical supplies and information technology, there is a high toll on the physical and mental well-being of Iraqis.

"We cannot accept this and, as health professionals, we strongly resist Canada's involvement in this contemplated war as indicated by the Physicians for Global Survival."

They further stated that they strongly resisted Canada's involvement in this contemplated war. So do we.

There are various alternatives suggested by this organization to achieve the objective for which this war is being waged. We fully agree with the alternatives proposed by this organization.

- There is a UN inspection process, which should be supported, not undermined.

- The inspection process would also gain enormously in moral strength and form genuine moves on the part of the nuclear weapons states to follow through on their own promises to abolish nuclear weapons, get rid of biological and chemical weapons, and support inspection and verification regimens to monitor these processors. Similarly, if it is demanded by a previous UN resolution to achieve a Middle East region free of nuclear, biological, and chemical weapons, this should be supported.

- Sanctions affecting the basic needs of the Iraqi population and the economic development of Iraqi society should be discontinued.

- Convene a regional conference jointly by the UN and the organization of the Islamic Conference to examine security and cooperation in the Middle East. After two appalling wars in Europe, there has been a slow evolution of the European Union and the organization for security and cooperation in Europe. Peace in the Middle East would be no more miraculous than this.

- Nurture democratic movements within Iraq. Democratic development cannot be imposed by outsiders or conferred by war. Numerous examples of strenuous nonviolent movements exist in many countries, e.g., Marcos, Suharto, military regimes in Latin America, and communist governments in the Eastern Bloc were deposed without military intervention. Such non-violent movements can best be supported by both regional and international non-governmental organizations.

478

In the end, I would like to say that we must oppose this unwanted and unjustified war. We must not allow our government to participate. We pray for a peaceful result for all conflicts. Ameen.

M. Naushaba Habib

President, Canadian Council of Muslim Women.

CCMW Established Scholarship

CCMW established a milestone scholarship at the University of Regina in the name of the Canadian Council of Muslim Women, Regina chapter. I led the establishment of the scholarship, with the support of others, to be awarded to students, particularly Muslim girls, and if no Muslim girl was available, to any other as decided by the university. The university was very appreciative.

UNIVERSITY OF
REGINA

February 12, 2004

Mrs. Naushaba Habib, President
Canadian Council of Muslim Women-Regina Chapter
C/o Medical Office Wing
3rd Floor
1440 – 14th Avenue Regina, SK S4P 0W5

Dear Mrs. Habib:

Thank you to Samira Ahmad, Nusrat Jalil and you for meeting with me on Friday, January 23, 2004 to discuss the terms of reference criteria for a new scholarship funded by the Canadian Council of Muslim Women, Regina Chapter.

The Terms Of Reference have now been prepared and, hopefully, reflect the wishes of your organization. The Assistant Registrar, Student Awards and Financial Aid, has assisted in the preparation of the Terms Of Reference. Therefore, I would ask that you review the Terms Of Reference as attached and let me know if your concur with the criteria as prepared for the **Canadian Council of Muslim Women – Regina Entrance Scholarship**. Please telephone me once you have completed this task so that we may prepare formal copies for approval signature.

The scholarship will be presented for the first time in fall 2005 to a University of Regina student who has successfully met the admission requirements to enter the University of Regina as well as other criteria as cited under ELIGBILITY. As discussed, the donation amount of $5,000 will be held in an interest earning account for the time the scholarship is active.

The University of Regina recognizes our donors to scholarship initiatives and the recipients annually in the May and October Convocation Programs. As well, a complete listing of undergraduate awards can be viewed on the University of Regina home page, www.uregina.ca/awards and in our annual University of Regina Undergraduate Awards booklet.

A gift of scholarship enriches the lives of our entering students in so many ways. Once again, thank you for choosing to create this most precious gift of scholarship through your CCMW chapter.

I look forward to hearing from you should you have any questions, my direct telephone number is 585-4446 or by e-mail, darlene.freitag@uregina.ca.

Sincerely,

Darlene Freitag
Development Manager, University Relations

REGINA 2005
Jeux du
CANADA
Games

Enclosure   Terms Of Reference:
                 Canadian Council of Muslim Women-Regina Entrance Scholarship
                 Education

Cc: Betty St. Onge, Assistant Registrar, Student Awards and Financial Aid

University Relations Campaign Office · IIO - 2 Research Drive · Regina, Saskatchewan, Canada S4S OA2
Ph: 306.337.2446 Fax: 306.337.2447 · e-mail: urcampaign@uregina.ca · Toll-free: 1-866-667-7500

480

UNIVERSITY OF REGINA

Terms of Reference
CANADIAN COUNCIL OF MUSLIM WOMEN – REGINA ENTRANCE SCHOLARSHIP

The Canadian Council of Muslim Women Regina Chapter is an affiliate of the national CCMW non-profit voluntary organization started in 1982 to assist Muslim women participating effectively in Canadian society and to promote mutual understanding between Canadian Muslim women and women of other faiths. As an initiative to support and promote post-secondary education within the Regina Chapter community, an annually funded entrance scholarship has been established in 2004 to encourage students to begin their university studies at the University of Regina.

DONOR Canadian Council of Muslim Women – Regina.

FUNDING $5,000 to be received by the University Relations Office in May 2004.
- At the time of approval of the Terms of Reference, the donor wishes to establish an annual award of $800 for a six year period, years 2005, 2006, 2007, 2008, 2009 and 2010.
- In year 2010, the scholarship will be presented for a combined value of $800 plus any residual funds in the trust account.
- The award funding is open to receive additional donations from the Canadian Council of Muslim Women – Regina Chapter membership.

AWARD $800 in support of tuition, course and semester based fees.
- Annually. Fall semester. Commencing in Fall 2005.
- Student who has received other awards is eligible.

ELIGIBILITY The scholarship will be presented annually to a University of Regina entering student who meets the following criteria:
- University of Regina scholarship entrance average of 80%, based on early conditional average which consists of five courses from the approved subject areas common to all faculties for admission to the University of Regina;
- registered in 12 or more credit hours of study in the semester the scholarship is paid out;
- financial need will be considered;
- preference to an entering female Muslim student or male Muslim student, if no application is received from a Muslim student, the award is open to any student who has met the other eligibility criteria;
- demonstrate through application in writing, not to exceed 250 words, highlights of volunteerism within the Muslim community and their familiarity with the Muslim faith.

APPLICATION Must be submitted by April 30th.
- Applications are available from the:
  - Student Awards and Financial Aid Office, Riddell Centre, Room 229
  - or on the web, see www.uregina.ca/awards.
- Return completed application to:
  - Student Awards and Financial Aid Office.

SELECTION University of Regina Undergraduate Scholarship Committee.
- The University of Regina Student Awards and Financial Aid Office shall notify a representative of the Canadian Council Of Muslim Women Regina and the student recipient, in writing, each year the scholarship is presented.

NOTES (1) If, in the opinion of the University, it should become no longer practical or possible to use this funding for the specified purpose, (for example, if a program to which it relates is restructured or discontinued), the University will seek the written consent of the donor to redirect the gift to a new purpose. The support provided by the gift will continue to be clearly identified with the name of Canadian Council of Muslim Women-Regina Entrance Scholarship.
(2) Continued receipt of the award is conditional upon the student's compliance with all of the terms, conditions, guidelines and regulations as set out in the University Calendar from time to time. The University may suspend or cancel the award at any time if the recipient has committed any misconduct (academic or otherwise) as described in the University's Calendar.
(3) The Canadian Council of Muslim Women-Regina Entrance Scholarship amount will be presented in accordance with these Terms Of Reference or until such time the donor organization wishes to increase funding support.

Signature: Representative Canadian Council of Muslim Women-Regina

May 10/04
Date

Signature: Betty St. Onge, Assistant Registrar, Student Awards & Financial Aid

May 12/04
Date

Events

Eid Celebration at Islamic Centre (1996)

We invited people of other faiths, officials, and political and community leaders.

Naushaba Habib, with guests.

Guests and CCMW members

Eid at Huda School, CCMW 2003:

Welcome address by Mahlaqa Naushaba Habib, president of CCMW

This was an address of welcome and also an address as the outgoing president to the community at large.

Honourable Minister Doreen Hamilton, City Councillor Sharon Bryce, and distinguished guests and members of the Muslim community. Assalam-o-Alaikum (peace be upon you all).

Indeed, it is my honour and pleasure to welcome you here today. You have been invited to celebrate Eid-ul-Fitr (the festival of fast-breaking and thanksgiving) with us. This past week, Muslims all around the world celebrated the completion of Ramadan, a month of fasting adhering to the tenets of Islam. To celebrate this, Muslims meet each other, saying Eid Mubarak. I extend this Eid greeting to you and wish all of you an Eid Mubarak.

Your participation encourages us, and we hope to continue such interaction in the future.

Now, I will give you a brief introduction to the Canadian Council of Muslim Women. Sister Dr. Lila Fahlman was a woman representative on the board of the Council of Muslim Communities of Canada. She felt that she was not serving any useful purpose on the board for the women. She discussed this with the board and was given the responsibility to organize Muslim women in Canada. Twenty years ago, she travelled to each city across Canada, beginning in St. John's, Newfound Land, and Labrador, and ending in Vancouver. She visited and talked with Muslim women in each community. The goal was to bring these women together into a national body.

In April of 1982, Muslim women representatives from each city met in Winnipeg, where we founded the Canadian Council of Muslim Women. I represented Regina. Chapters were established in various cities. The Canadian Council of Muslim Women is a national non-profit organization established to assist Muslim women to participate effectively in Canadian society, and to promote a mutual understanding between Canadian Muslim women and women of other faiths.

The national organization is geared toward organizing and strengthening our bond as women in Islam at the community and national levels. Muslim women must strive to achieve a balance among divergent cultures, traditions, family values, and religious beliefs. As women, we experience many of the same difficulties as other Canadian women of different religious backgrounds. At the same time, pride in our own values should also be developed through a strong organization through which we can improve our lives as women and, more importantly, as Muslims. We are proud of the fact that the CCMW had its twentieth anniversary last year.

It is quite an achievement for a small volunteer organization to not only have survived but also to have lived up to the vision created twenty years ago. It has provided a voice for Muslim women and demonstrated that Islam is a women-positive faith. And it has brought Muslim women into the mainstream of society. It has done this through conferences, newsletters, networking, initiating projects, holding regional meetings, and publications.

We also have an active chapter in Regina. It was formed in 1981, even before the national organization. Our membership is small, but we are actively participating in various organizations and expanding. We have extended ourselves outside the Muslim community. We initiated the formation of Women United in Regina at the time of the Bosnia War, which was an exciting experience, getting to know one another and learning about our different cultural and religious backgrounds.

In the larger Regina community, we have contacts with the Regina Council of Women, Immigrant Women, Open Door Society, Amnesty International, Multicultural Society, Lions Club, SCAR, and SCR, among others.

We raised funds for the Canadian Cancer Society, Soul Harbour, a women's shelter, and a food bank. We hope we can continue to work together and develop a mutual understanding to enrich our Canadian society.

Eid Mubarak to you all; God bless us all. Amen. Thank you for your attention.

Mrs. Mahlaqa Naushaba Habib
President, CCMW, Regina

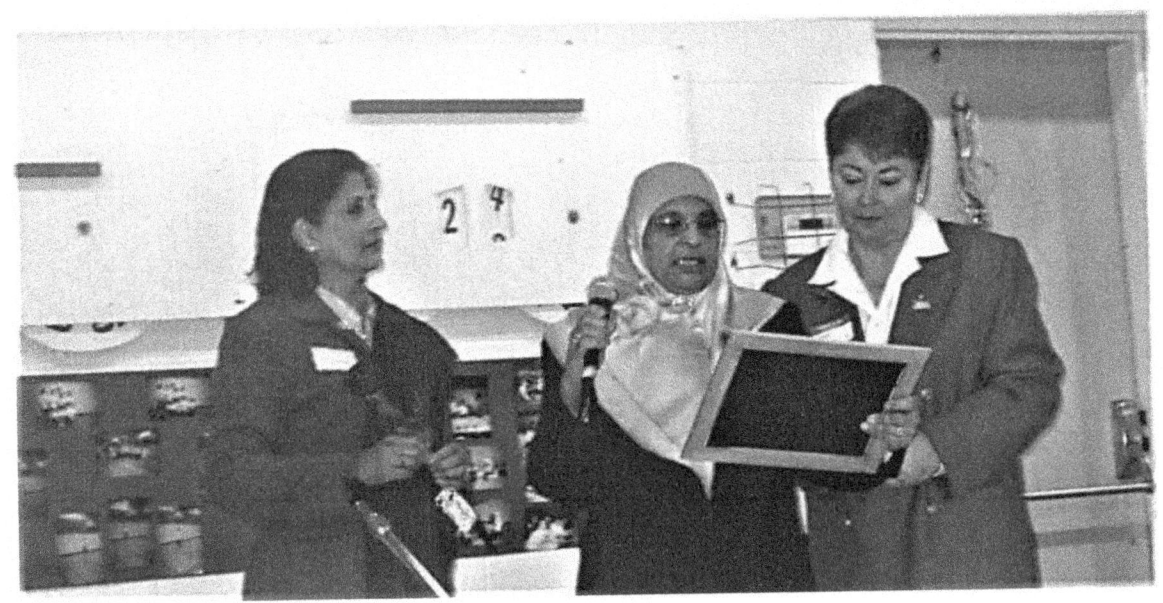

Presentation to Honourable Doreen Hamilton, by President Naushaba Habib, and Samina Ahmed.

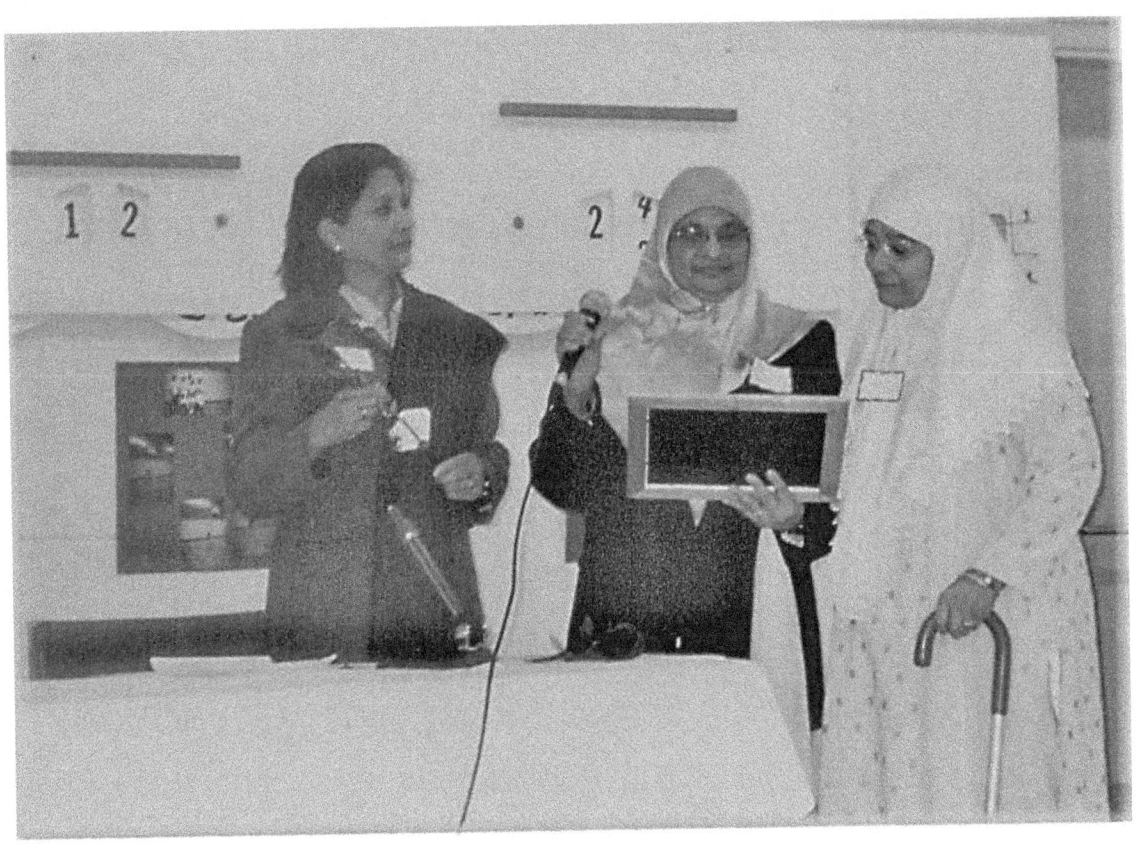

Presentation to Naris Bhimji for her contribution to CCMW and the community at large by President Naushaba Habib, and Samina Ahmed.

Participation in International Women's Day

Naushaba Habib, president of CCMW, addressing the participants on International Women's Day.

Participants in International Women's Day.

It gives me great pleasure to welcome you on behalf of the Canadian Council of Muslim Women on this International Day of Women. It is a great and important day for women who are mothers, sisters, and daughters in society.

Prophet Muhammad, Peace be Upon Him (PBUH), said, "Woman as a mother is the best school." The children form the society and nations are raised under the guidance of mothers. One can imagine what an important responsibility God has assigned to us. Prophet Muhammad PBUH also said heaven lies under the feet of mothers. This simply means that a mother carries the child in the womb and nurtures that child to adulthood. Therefore, God assigns this responsibility to the children to have very high regard for the mothers. Women have been mistreated in society. It is a credit to the women in society who provided leadership by forming various organizations to raise the status of women as they are today. We pay respect to them on this International Day of Women. We have to go further. We hope and pray that we continue to progress toward the achievement of our goal to have women recognized and to work cooperatively with men, and for women to achieve equal status and play a complementary role in society. God bless us all. Ameen.

Mahlaqa Naushaba Habib

Ctv Invites Ccmw And Others

Mahlaqa Naushaba Habib attends on behalf of CCMW

CTV Television Inc.

216 - 1ª Ave. N.
Saskatoon, Saskatchewan
Canada S7K 3W3

Tel 306.665.8600
Fax 306.665.0450

Thank you for attending our third Editorial Board Luncheon Meeting!

The meeting will focus on news issues affecting the Muslim community, and how these issues are covered by the Regina CTV news cast. The following individuals have planned to attend:

Dr. Ayman Aboguddah – Cardiologist ; President of Huda School (Public and Islamic education)

Mr. Kashif Ahmed – University Student and Communication Director of Muslims for Peace and Justice (MPJ)

Mr. Riaz Ahmed – City Planner / Director or Public Relations for MPJ

Dr. Naiyer Habib – Cardiologist; Former Head of Cardiology for Regina Health District; Former President of the Islamic Association of Saskatchewan (Regina); President of MPJ

Mrs. M. Naushaba Habib – MA (Political Science); President of Canadian Council of Muslim Women (Regina Chapter)

Dr. Samiul Haque – Child Psychiatrist

Zeba Hashmi – Homemaker and Secretary of MPJ; Bilingual Medical Office Administration Certification

Zarqa Nawaz – Journalist and Film Maker

Carl Worth - News Director - CTV Regina

Dale Neufeld - News Director - CTV Saskatoon / Prince Albert

Brian Zawacki - Director of Community Relations

Angela Loewen - Human Resources Specialist (Saskatchewan)

Geoff Bradley - Creative / Promotions Manager (Saskatchewan)

Wade Moffatt - Sales Manager - CTV Regina / Yorkton

Tara Robinson - News Anchor - CTV Regina

Manfred Joehnck - News Anchor - CTV Regina

Nelson Bird – Video Journalist; Host of Indigenous Circle

We want critical feedback on CTV Regina's news stories and interviews. We would like you to consider the following discussion questions:

1. How do our news stories cover issues affecting the Muslim community? Give specific examples.

2. Comment on how Muslim people are presented in the news.

3. What issues are being ignored? Give specific examples.

4. What news program do you watch all the time? If it's not CTV, explain why you prefer it.

5. Describe what you like about our station's approach.

6. What suggestions do you have about how we could improve our ability to serve your community?

A DIVISION OF
Bell Globemedia

Welcome To A Presentation
On

The Contribution of Women in the Development of Muslim Society During The Life of The Holy Prophet PBUH and The Rightly Guided Caliphs In' ISLAM

Dr. Riffat Hassan
Head Of Religious Studies
University of Louisville, Kentucky USA

Cathedral Neighbourhood Center
2900-13th Avenue
Regina
February 20th 1999
7:00pm Sharp

Sponsored By Muslim Women of Regina and Canadian Council of Muslim Women-Regina Chapter

Guest Speaker, Dr. Riffat Hassan

L to R: Erum Afsar, Samina Ahmed, Naushaba Habib.

COMMUNITY FAREWELL

by

Naiyer and Naushaba Habib

We were leaving the community that was an important component of our life. It was here where our permanent settlement started and was established with ongoing learning, facing circumstances, and dealing with them in the march of time. It was professional, political, and social. All of these have been put together in this book for those who care to read and be inspired.

The community arranged this farewell, led by Sr. Zeba Hashmi and Brs. Abdul Jalil and Ayman Aboguddah.

Master of Ceremonies, Dr. Abdul Jalil, welcoming.

Assalam-o-Alaikum

This evening, I want to say something that is difficult. It is a reality that Dr. Habib and his family decided to move from here, Saskatchewan, to British Columbia. Normally, people move to Alberta. There are very few who skip Alberta and move to British Columbia. So, he has taken the decision not to move to Alberta. We are certainly going to miss him. I am also hoping that he will consider Regina as his second home—not his first home—and that he will be visiting Regina more often than many others who left Regina. He will break that tradition. With that, I do not want to stay in between you and the other folks who want to say a few things, including some who have said that this may be their last chance to roast Dr. Habib. I am looking forward to that opportunity. I will ask Dr. Ayman Aboguddah to say a few words.

Dr. Ayman Aboguddah.

Who can roast the roaster? I was asked to say a few words, but to roast Dr. Habib, I will speak my mind. When I came to town, it was he who helped me and got me to Regina. Allah Subhanahu Wa Ta'ala set me to work with him.

When my father came to Regina, Dr. Habib was at the airport to receive him. Whenever I called my father, he would ask how our brothers in Regina and Dr. Habib were doing. He would tell me, "Call Dr. Habib your uncle, not a colleague."

I started working with him. My admiration for him was because I learned many things from him. I thought sometimes that he was wrong, but time would go by, and after a few months, I would conclude that he was wise and absolutely right. I will not go into details. It appeared to me that he was a good man. We worked, and everything he promised he did and more. He will say Assalam-o-Alaikum openly. He would like to see a Muslim saying Assalam-o-Alaikum to another Muslim. Many people will shy away from their religion, but not Dr. Habib. If it was not for him, there would not have been the small mosque or this mosque or Muslims for Peace and Justice.

The newcomers may not have had a chance to work with Dr. Habib and others who established this community; Allah knows the best. I will miss him. I cannot imagine that I worked with him and now will not see him. We will see you in Vancouver, Insha Allah. Assalam-o-Alaikum **Abdul Jalil:** Thank you, brother.

I knew even before I started that it was going to be an emotional and tough evening, not only for me but for everyone here. So that is why I was trying to set the stage that we are going to endure. The second in line is someone whom I am sure you know very well, Dr. Anwar Haque. He has been here for thirty-eight years and, as some of you know, is a founding president of the Islamic Association of Saskatchewan here in Regina. He is one of those pioneers who started here and worked very closely with Dr. Habib, not only in the medical profession but in establishing the foundation for the Islamic Association in Regina.

Dr. Anwar Haque, roasting Dr. Habib.

Thanks for allowing me to address this gathering of respected brothers, sisters, and respected elders. I do not see too many elders; they are mostly youngsters. That was done with respect. I mean that I do not have to respect them by saying respected brothers and sisters, but the old tradition of Assalam-o-Alaikum.

When I was asked to talk about respected Brother Dr. Naiyer Habib, I was not sure what to talk about. They are hosting. I thought they would say something. If I could not say something about the leader of the community, then I would be in trouble. I needed help. So, to be on the safe side, I decided to talk about the history of Muslims in Regina because Dr. Habib *is* the history of Regina.

Now as far as I know, the first Muslim came to Regina in 1903. When I met an aboriginal Muslim, he told me that the first Muslim to come to Regina was from Mongolia through Alaska. When I asked him to give me proof, he did not have any.

To my mind, the first Muslim was Muhammad Ali Ta Haynee. He came to Regina in 1903. He actually came from what is currently known as Lebanon. He was an army officer of the Ottoman Empire. He came to North Dakota in 1900 and, from there, moved to Regina in 1903. When he moved here, he was single. He started a business as a vendor, going door-to-door, selling items. Then he opened a store. The store was on the corner of 12th and 5th Avenues.

When I came, I saw the store. It had been preserved by the Heritage Foundation (which doesn't exist anymore). It was under the Heritage Buildings of Regina, Saskatchewan, because it was the first store. You could buy anything there but medicine.

In 1911, at the age of forty-eight, Muhammad Ali Ta Haynee went back to Lebanon to get married. Then he came back. He had seventeen children. Gradually, other people came, mostly from Lebanon at that time. Salim Ganem and his family came from Turkey. He was working in the CPR. A few families came and started businesses. One opened a general store in Craven. Then another man came with his family from Czechoslovakia. His name was Raymon (?Aymon), but I do not know his first name. He settled here and became a teacher. Then, a family from Damascus came.

When the Muslim community got bigger, they wanted to form an association. Haynee formed the association and became its imam, or probably its president. The secretary was Salim Ganem. Back then, his name was Muhammad Ali Ta Haynee, but people could not pronounce it. So he changed his name in 1905 to Haynee. When he died in 1972, he was the oldest person in Saskatchewan, 108 years old. The city honoured him by naming a street in Regina Haynee. When Haynee died, the association was dissolved.

When I came to Regina on January 4, 1969, there were four other Muslim families, and one of them was that of Arif Sethi. After a few months, we decided that we would form an association of some sort so that we could practice our religion. All the four families got together. Zack Haynee, the son of Haynee, was there. We five families decided to make a one-page constitution. It took us almost a year to finalize it. We formed the association in a meeting in the university cafeteria in Regina on November 7, after the Eid prayer. That was the second association in Regina. I became the president.

The purpose of the association was to organize religious activities, teach our children, and get to know the Muslim community of Regina through get-togethers. We had dinners, religious festivities, and prayer. We used to pray in someone's garage and in someone's basement, or wherever, because we did not have any money until we got the mosque.

We also got a school started, but we could not find a place to start it. We did not have many students to start a school. In 1977, a man came, Dr. Naiyer Habib. When he came, he wanted to start a school. That was very good. That is what he wanted. So, he started the school, but I did not know that he wanted his wife to be the principal. That was OK. So he started with a school with two teachers and gradually added more teachers and students. I could not figure out why Dr. Habib wanted his wife to be the principal and not himself. I found out later. He said, "I want to be president." I said, "No, you couldn't be the president." So we argued with each other and decided that we'd just share the responsibility. So he became the president, and he did very well.

Another person came in, too, and became president. His name is Abdul Qayyum. He is out of town. So we were doing very well here. I would like to tell you that, in those days, the three of us—you can call us the Three Musketeers or whatever—worked together well. We fought and argued, and we were friends.

We had Eid functions. We had potlucks every month and then every two months. We had children's festivals. This is the way we got to know the whole community. We knew almost everybody, and we had feelings for each other. If something good happened to someone, we would feel happy, and sad if it was something not good. This is the way you work. *(He starts roasting Dr. Habib now—a superb roast.)*

Then I thought, Dr. Habib is the president; that should be enough. But he had other angles in his mind. One day, he came out and said he wanted to form another association here, a women's association. I said it was a wonderful idea. I thought that it was a very good idea. But he made his wife the president. One day, he suggested having a youth camp, a summer camp, for all the youths. I said it was a good idea, but I found out that he had made his son president. Then I thought: I am left with nothing.

He had one more son, so I asked him, "What do you need to do because everything is taken away from me?" He said, "Do not worry. I am not going to stay here," and that was a relief to me. OK, I thought. I will be president again someday.

Still, Dr. Habib was not very happy. He had to do something else. He wanted to introduce a different type of Islam in the community. He did not tell me what he accomplished under the table. What is that called? He asked. He himself responded that it (under the table) was taking money to hide a deal. But he was not taking money (laughter). He was training his nephew to be the president. I questioned him. He said Islam would come to Regina so fast that you wouldn't be able to cope with it. I have never seen Islam come so fast as what he was doing before, then all became (fanatic) un-Islamic. Everything was cancelled and when Dr. Habib came to know that, he went to talk to him about the result. The nephew ignored him.

Then Dr. Habib came to me and asked, "Dr. Haque, what do I do?" I said, "There is only one thing you can do. You go into exile somewhere." He told me, "I cannot do that because I have a big house and a farm." I told him, "You are in trouble." So then he asked, "Where should I go?" I said, "There is a place in BC called Abbotsford Forest. You should go there." He agreed and said, "OK, I will go there." Then I told him, "When you are there, form an association and become president, and your wife can become president of a women's society. Make a youth committee and make your son the president. But never try to form a grandchildren's association." He asked, why not? And I told him: "You will lose. I have eleven of them."

This is serious and tough. I am sure that you will join me and Naushaba in wishing him good luck in whatever they are going to do there. They will be successful, and Allah will guide them. Dr. and Mrs. Habib, this is personal to you. If Nilo and I have hurt you in any way and at any time, knowingly or unknowingly, forgive us.

Recites Arabic farewell.

Abdul Jalil: Now I think we are moving to the ladies' part, where two sisters are going to say a few things about Sister Naushaba. The first one in line is Sister Nargis Bhimji.

Assalam-o-Alaikum

Dear brothers and sisters,

I must exclude my husband because he does not qualify as a brother. It gives me great pleasure to thank Dr. Habib and Sister Naushaba, who are really shortly leaving us with the goal of establishing themselves in British Columbia. It is a pleasure to say that they will be with their grandchildren, whom they both love very much. However, it is sad for us all in the sense that we will be deprived of their good company, guidance, and belonging. As far as I know, both Dr. Habib and Sister Naushaba contributed to our community and our province in several ways. You, in all modalities, know that Dr. Habib has given kindness and also some of his knowledge to the Islamic Association of Saskatchewan and to the cause of Muslims in this province. His contribution to the medical profession, and particularly to cardiology, has been immense. I have no doubt that his patients will miss him greatly. Sister Naushaba has not only been a driving source, inspiring Muslim women as an active participant and chairperson of the Canadian Council of Muslim Women, but she has also been instrumental in introducing the CCMW to the Regina Food Bank, the Canadian Council of Women, the Multicultural Council of Saskatchewan, and the Regina Open Door Society.

We live in Saskatchewan. If you break down this word, one can say Sas Katch One. What I am trying to say is that we were successfully catching one Dr. Habib, but he is very soon going away. However, we hope that here in Saskatchewan, he will keep coming back again and again with Sister Naushaba to inspire us and offer his wisdom and guidance. My husband has always insisted on delivering short speeches, and I should maintain his principle of keeping things short and simple.

Finally, I would like to end by saying that yesterday was history, which Dr. Habib and Sister Naushaba established in this province. Tomorrow is a mystery, and we do not know what the plans are going to be for BC. Today is present, which can be translated into a gift: the gift that both Dr. Habib and Sister Naushaba have given to us, our community, and our province. May Allah bless them both (Ameen).

Jalil: I would like to ask Sister Samina to come and say a few words about Sister Naushaba.

Bismillah ir-Rahmanir-Rahim, Assalam-o-Alaikum.

Brothers and sisters, everybody has spoken about Dr. Habib, so I am going to talk about Naushaba. I have known Naushaba and Dr. Habib for many years, more than twenty-eight. Fortunately, Naushaba has been a very close friend of mine. She has been there whenever I needed her.

She has charm and is always smiling. As far as our community in Regina is concerned, she has been a good community leader and spokesperson for the Muslim women of Regina. She has helped numerous newcomers in our community and has also helped some refugee families in the past of Bosnia and Iran.

Since 1982, she has been an active member of the Canadian Council of Muslim Women International. Here in Regina, she has served as the president many times and has been a member since 1982. At present, she is also the president of the CCMW of Regina. She has organized community events on various occasions, and I have had the pleasure and privilege of working with her side by side. When she organized community events in Regina, she was always very calm and confident about them.

The Canadian Council of Muslim Women of Regina organized a scholarship fund for the Muslim women in the University of Regina under her leadership. It will be given to Muslim girls for five years. I am wondering if there is anyone in the community who could not be touched by her kindness and friendship. Naushaba, I never thought that you would be leaving Regina so soon. I thought we would go together. I am going to miss you a lot. You and Dr. Habib have been great assets to our community. On behalf of all the Muslim women of Regina, and especially the Canadian Council of Muslim Women of Regina, I thank you for your leadership, great help, and support. Also, on behalf of our friends who are present here today, I wish you and Dr. Habib all the success in your future, and a healthy, happy, and prosperous life with your family in Abbotsford, British Columbia.

Jalil: Now, I just go to the floor to ask anyone who wants to say something to take the chance.

Dr. Raza Bhimji: Dr. Habib, dear brothers and sisters, including Naushaba. It gives me pleasure today to talk to you tonight. Dr. Habib is my cardiologist. I thank them because of so many things that you both have done for the Muslim community, particularly in Regina. We really wish you success wherever you go. In order to end my little talk, I would like to tell you that I have written this note, which has been modified to suit the occasion of Dr. Habib's and Sister Naushaba's departure. If you cannot stay back, then you are free to go. The only request we all have is to keep remembering us. We will never be able to forget you. So please do go if you must, but all of Regina will be sad with your departure; their hearts will be broken with your leaving. Your softness and kind-heartedness will be remembered. Please do go if you must. Thank you very much.

Riazuddin Ahmed

There is a small story. Behind every successful man is a woman. This is very true for Dr. Habib. When we came, myself and Samina, as a young couple twenty-five and twenty-seven years ago, I was still young. We both were still young. At that time, it was a custom in Regina, established by Drs. Haque and Habib, that whoever came was invited to their house for a sort of welcome and get-together. We had to come in Ramadan, then we had an Eid party where we met the families of Regina—about six or eight families—and then we had the pleasure of being invited to Dr. Habib's house. After my supper and conversation, tea time and dessert came. Now we know how Dr. Habib was a very busy man. He had established the cardiology department in areas of the Regina hospital, and he hardly had time to do many things. But we did not know the extent to which he was dependent on Naushaba.

When the tea came, I got up and said I would start making tea for people sitting around the room. I was passing the tea around, and asked Dr. Habib how much sugar he took. He called Naushaba, and she knew how much sugar he took. (laughter).

Jalil: I think—no, I am sure—there are many more stories like this one, which people are hesitant to share, but certainly, at any point you want to, you are welcome to do so. I think I just personally had the opportunity to work with Dr. Habib in various capacities, and when I say in various capacities, I don't mean in the medical profession but in the Islamic Association. When we moved to Regina, Dr. Habib was just one house down on the street, but I do not know whether it was me or something else, but as soon as we moved there, he decided to move. I have not asked him since that time whether it was me or something else, but maybe today, as he is moving away to BC, I will ask him why he moved. Was it me?

I think I can say one thing for sure. I have met many people around the world, and I have seen many men whom I considered men of principle who would not compromise their beliefs or their principles no matter what. And I can say with conviction, and I am proud of this, that I know one person who whom I genuinely consider a man of principle. He has not let his principles be compromised, no matter what, even when he's stood alone, so that is the quality of a leader. That is the quality of a good person, and I am proud that I know him.

With that, I think if there is no one else, there are a couple of formalities I would like to cover right now. One of them is Dr. Habib. On behalf of the Muslim community of Regina, there are a couple of tokens of appreciation and thanks for the service you have done for this community and Islam in this part of the world, and I would like to recognize those. First of all, I would like to present to you, on behalf of this Muslim community, this box.

In the Name of God, Most Kind, Most Merciful

Appreciation Award
presented to

Dr. Naiyer Habib
&
Mrs. Naushaba Habib

For your outstanding contributions
to the Muslim community
of Regina

Thank you
and may Allah (SWT) bless you both,
Muslim Community of Regina

2004

And there is one more present, Dr. Habib and Sister Naushaba, that the Islamic community of Regina will present to you. It will remind you that you had a good time here in Regina.

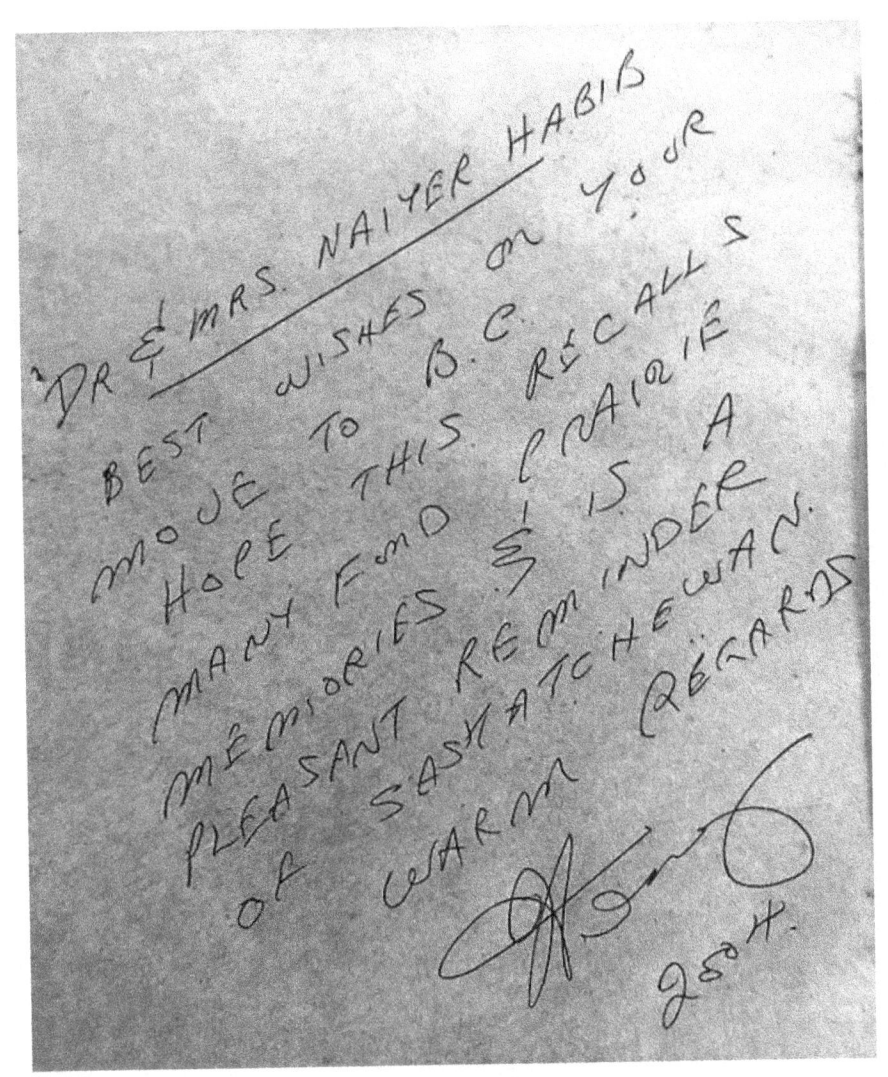

Note on the back of the painting.

Sister Zeba Hashmi has been working very hard behind the scenes for so many days, maybe more than a month, for this occasion. I would like everyone to thank her for the work. I would like Sister Naushaba to come and receive another gift of appreciation. Sister Zeba, please present the gift.

Sister Zeba Hashmi, presenting a bouquet to Naushaba.

Samiul Haque: I would like to thank Dr. Habib and Mrs. Habib for the time we spent at their school. I tell you, there were four of us of the same age. Dr. Habib bought a car for Adnan. We had fun. I would like to thank Dr. Habib for this.

Samiul Haque

Mustafa Elbare: I was single. We met in the mosque. We came to their house. I knew nobody. Dr. Habib is my older brother. He invited me to his house with food, and they helped me get married. He said you are my brother. He helped me with Sister Naushaba every time and for anything. He was there. When I was going home, they helped me. Dr. Habib and Sister Naushaba helped us. It is hard to describe. I'd like everybody to know this. From the bottom of my heart, I'd like to thank the family. Insha Allah, we wish you well.

502

Mustafa Elbare

Jalil: I wanted to give the Habib family the last word. Dr. Habib, kindly say a few words.

Naiyer Habib

Assalam-o-Alaikum

Peace and blessing of God be to our prophet and to you all.

We are quite overwhelmed by the feelings that you all expressed. I do feel sad to decide to move to BC. I do not want to hide my age. I have turned sixty-three now—too early to retire—but I did make a decision. When I told Naushaba, she kept looking at me and was dumbfounded. I took this as an expression of dismay or surprise. I am not the kind of husband who will when retired, bother Naushaba. She knows that. So it was a bit of a surprise to her. I expected that she would be very happy. I asked her, "Are you not happy?" She said, "I do not know. You have made the decision. What are you going to do, and how will you enjoy your retirement, being so busy!?" So, I said, "I am somewhat unpredictable. I decided. So that is what it is."

For that decision, there could be various reasons, but this is a move. Besides, both my children were insisting that I retire, and I thought I should do that. They were watching the deep involvement of my work with the community over the years. With that went some stress to achieve the goals that I did by the grace of God. This was

503

a move. So we are moving. Nobody knows me there as a physician. We already have a house. We already have an office. The phone and the fax are active. So, I will just land there. There is the MSA Hospital there, with my offer to them that if they want to arrange cardiology, I will be happy to do so. I will be happy to be involved in education, but I have no intention of doing hospital practice[83].

We are sad to leave Regina. I did not walk away from Brother Jalil pertaining to his remark to create some smiles on our faces, but I did build the house to stay in Regina. That was the intent. However, things change. I never knew that Dr. Anwar Haque, having done so many Hajj, lies (I know he did a superb job of roasting and here was my little response). LAUGHTER! I was approached by people to become the president. I told them I should never contest Dr. Haque. I did become one. I have always respected him as an elder brother, and I acted on his advice, so if anything good was done, it was by me, and if anything went wrong, it was his advice! This is my roasting of him. LAUGHTER. I have respected him all along, and I still respect him. As for the CCMW president, I had no say if Naushaba became president, or my son in youth. One of our friends did say the Habib dynasty in a Friday Khutba. (When I was away, Dr. Haque raised the issue with him.) But God knows I never was a part of it. We enjoyed my roasting, and it will be a treasure in my memory. So we did evolve here in Regina, as time went by, working shoulder to shoulder, inclusive of Brother Qayyum.

I have a presentation[84] showing some of the reflections of the past to remember the things that we tried to do.

It was a pleasure to achieve what we did by working together. I do not think I did anything alone. One thing I'd like to remind you is that we, as a family, gave priority to our community work, and our personal gain was kept behind that. Yes, I was sometimes called a dictator. I responded by saying that a strong leader taking a stand for the betterment of the community was better than a weak one with interests in continuing to get elected by keeping everyone pleased.

You all have shown so much love and affection. We might have made some mistakes. We would like you to forgive us. We will keep in touch as long as my mind works, and also my health. But, generally, doctors who retire die within a year from a heart attack or cancer. Big SIGHS!!! AND NO, NO!! Maybe I will survive longer.

Naushaba has been with me all along. She looks to be very simple, but she is very firm with me and keeps me on the right path.

Thank you all. We have come a long way. You must keep moving forward. We must put Islam to what it was at the time of our Prophet and according to the Quran. We tried, but perhaps we might not have done all that was required. There are still things to be done, which I leave in the capable hands of you people. I will try to come to some of the functions, such as Eid, to meet you all.

---

[83] This did not work out. I was asked if I would take calls and practice internal medicine with them. I laughed this off, telling them: "Why should I do this after retiring and leaving such a successful career?" I established and maintained a well-equipped office practice until I retired completely in 2011.

[84] A pictorial historical slide presentation on the community work since 1977 was shown. May read the book HMORS foot note[1].

Assalam-o-Alaikum

Jalil: Sister Naushaba, would you like to say anything?

Naushaba, overwhelmed by emotion, did not say anything. But her expression was there!

Jalil: Thank you, Brother Habib.

This concludes our program of formal farewell.

Certainly, Dr. Habib, I think if we look around, we will see that we have seventy or seventy-five people with family members. Be prepared; we will be visiting Abbotsford quite often. I hope you have bought a big house.

Some community members, attending the event.

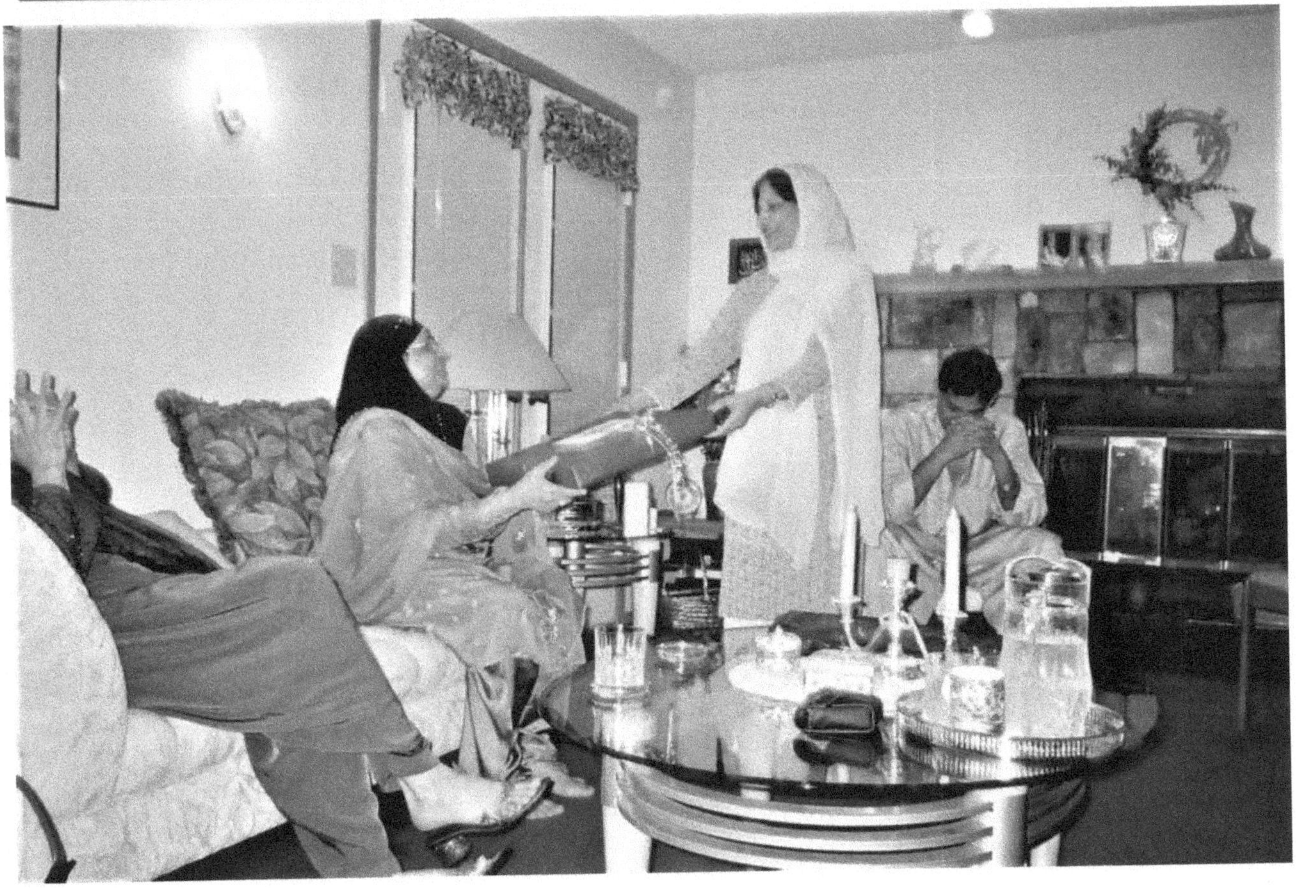

508

DEPARTURE to Abbotsford from Regina Airport

Few came to see us off at the Regina Airport, even on a weekday. All are not in the pictures.

L to R-Aijaz Ahmed & Nasreen Aijaz, Samina Ahmed, M. Naushaba &Naiyer Habib, Riaz Uddin Ahmed.

L to R: Zabiba, Naiyer Habib, Nasreen Aijaz, M. Naushaba Habib front, Samina Ahmed behind Naushaba

L to R: Standing: A Lady?, Shareef ,Idris.
Sitting :M. Naushaba & Naiyer Habib, Aijaz Ahmad @ Regina Airport

CANADIAN ISLAMIC CONGRESS NATIONAL AND BRITISH COLUMBIA CHAPTER

by

Naiyer Habib

From its origins with an idea developed by Dr. Mohamed Elmasry in 1970, the Canadian Islamic Congress (CIC) went through nearly three decades of groundwork and preparation until it was finally launched as a fully fledged national entity on April 5, 1997. Dr. Elmasry was the first national president and held that post from 1997 to 2009. It ceased to function two years after Dr. Elmasry stepped down.

Political Advocacy

The CIC's mission was to work as a proactive facilitator for political advocacy, enabling Muslim Canadians to contribute more fully to the well-being of their country, defend their Constitutional and Charter rights, and work supportively for Canada with other groups.

The CIC acted promptly and competently on matters affecting the status, rights, and welfare of both Muslim and non-Muslim Canadians. The CIC worked to assist with and improve the social, economic, educational, and spiritual condition of Muslim Canadians and Muslims throughout the world, with the overall goal of promoting universal peace with justice. The CIC's mandate was to be an autonomous, independent, and respected voice for all Muslims— Sunni and Shia, men and women, youth and seniors. It also stood for Canadian in general.

Activities

The Canadian Islamic Congress (CIC) chapter of BC was established in 2007 by Dr. Naiyer Habib. He served as a director, and Luay Kawasme as the regional director in BC. This chapter ceased to function when Dr. Habib stepped down in 2011.

Scholarship Program

It pioneered a scholarship program for Canadian Muslim university students entering the fields of journalism, law, social sciences, or political science.

Additionally, the CIC had established a peace studies scholarship in the name of Captain Nicola Goddard, the first Canadian female soldier killed while on duty in Afghanistan. It was in sympathy for the family, while the CIC opposed the war in Afghanistan. The CIC sent its representative to the Canadian foreign minister to register its opposition to the war and its plea to withdraw our soldiers from Afghanistan and to provide humanitarian aid to the country.

Media

The CIC stayed in close touch with the Canadian media and policymakers by issuing regular communiqués and opinion articles about issues affecting Muslims and Canadians at large. Many of these were reported on or published in mainstream Canadian daily newspapers, including *The Globe and Mail, The Toronto Star, The Ottawa Citizen, The Montreal Gazette, The National Post*, and others. They also appeared in the Muslim and multicultural media, such as *Al-Ahram, Arab News, Egyptian Gazette*, etc., and in various community journals.

It did comparative research on Canadian media about their biased and non-biased attitude to Islam-Muslims. This led to an improvement in media presentation. It also graded Members of Parliament for a period as to their favourable and unfavourable attitudes toward Islam-Muslims.

Expert Witness

The CIC maintained and increased its positive political profile by serving in expert witness capacity for the Maher Arar, Bill C-38, Bill C-36, and other items of proposed legislation affecting the rights and freedoms of Canadian Muslims and of Canadians in general.

Conferences And Community Functions

The CIC also hosted various conferences to increase the political awareness of Muslims and to dispel non-Muslims' fears and misunderstandings about Islam and Muslims.

Islamic History Month

The CIC initiated the Islamic History Month (IHM), energizing other Muslim organizations for an ongoing event annually. It is a Brain Child of Dr.Elmasry.October was declared IHM by the Canadian Parliament. Islamic History Month has become a permanent part of Canada's multicultural calendar, with events across the country... The main objective of IHM was to introduce the historical aspect of Islam and Muslims to the Western world, something that has remained hidden. The secondary objective was to inspire the younger generation about the past of Islam and Muslims.

First Canadian Islamic Congress Community Function 2006, in Surrey, BC:

Dr. Mohamed Elmasry, national president.

Dr. Naiyer Habib, a national director.

Naushaba Habib, in front, in black scarf hijab.

Annual Parliament Award Dinner

Canadians were recognized for their outstanding service with an award at an annually held dinner in the Parliamentary building in Ottawa. Dignitaries were invited. In one such function, we received an award from the CIC for lifelong service to the community.

Dr. Mohamed Elmasry, president of the CIC.

Honourable Minister Bill Graham.

A section of the invited guests, us, and Dr. Elmasry included.

Awards or recognition received during functions of various organizations are included in the functions of the respective organizations.

<u>Recognition of Mahlaqa Naushaba Habib and Naiyer Habib for COMMUNITY SERVICE:</u>

Canadian **I**slamic **C**ongress

675 Queen St. S., Suite 208, Kitchener ON
Canada N2M 1A1
Tel: (519) 746-1242
Fax: (519) 746-2929
email: np@canadianislamiccongress.com
http://www.canadianislamiccongress.com

October 5, 2005

Dr. Naiyer and Mrs. Mahlaqa Naushaba Habib
103-2975 Gladwin Rd.
Abbotsford BC V2T 5T4

Dear Dr. and Mrs. Habib:

It is my pleasure to confirm that the Canadian Islamic Congress has awarded you The Canadian Islamic Congress 2005 Community Service Award: To honour those with a lifelong record of serving the Canadian Muslim community. It is an honour to know that fellow Canadians can have you as a mentor for many future generations. The award will be presented to you during our CIC Ottawa dinner on Monday, November 14, 2005 at Parliament Building, West Block, Room 200 at 5:00 pm.

You and your spouse will be our guests at the dinner; please find two invitations. If you need extra tickets for the event, you may buy them online.

See http://www.canadianislamiccongress.com/dinner/ottawa.php

Sincerely,

Prof. Mohamed Elmasry,
Ph.D., P.Eng., FRSC, FCAE, FIEEE
National president,
Canadian Islamic Congress

515

Naushaba and Naiyer Habib receive the Community Service Award, 2005.

Abdul Jalil, a respectable, humble, very close community friend, joined our community award celebration in Ottawa. He was a most sincere and helpful friend in the affairs of the community

MUSLIM BUSINESS COUNCIL

by

Naiyer Habib

The Muslim Business Council (MBC) of British Columbia, established in 2008, is an organization representing a number of businesses, professionals, and students in British Columbia. The members are drawn from diverse sectors of the provincial economy. Through its collective talents and strengths, it has the capacity and ability to research, develop, and advocate credible policy positions on economic and related issues that influence the government, business community, and public of British Columbia.

The Muslim Business Council is rapidly evolving as the de-facto advocacy organization for business in the province of BC. Membership provides opportunities to participate in roundtable meetings, working committees, and conferences, which will allow them to stay informed about current developments and stay connected with other business leaders and the government.

Besides various educational activities, the council raised $55,000 in 2014 to furnish high-tech mattresses for palliative care at the Surrey Memorial Hospital, raised $30,000 for a transport monitor for Royal Columbia Hospital in 2015, and $27,000 in 2017 to buy a van for an organization supporting the family with a disabled child.

I have been a member and director from 2010 to 2015 and on the advisory council for one year, 2016-2017. I headed the first two fundraising events for hospitals along with other members of the board, and in particular, Mr. M. Yasin, a founding member and the then-chair of the council.

Naiyer Habib, addressing an MBC conference.   Recognition of Service Award by the MBC.

Front row, L-R: Naiyer Habib, M. Yasin, Feroze Deen.

Muslim Business Council helps hospice patients rest more comfortably

Thanks to the generosity of the Muslim Business Council of BC, patients at Laurel Place Hospice will soon be sleeping on high-tech mattresses. Naiyer Habib, a member of the council and a clinical professor of medicine at the University of Saskatchewan, headed the efforts to raise the funds, along with other key members of the council.

The group's generous $55,000 donation to Surrey Hospital & Outpatient Centre Foundation (formerly Surrey Memorial Hospital Foundation) will be used to purchase Isogel mattresses, specially designed to help protect the delicate skin of frail patients receiving palliative care.

Why palliative care? "We felt palliative care was an appropriate area to donate towards because it's a way to help seniors in their time of need," Dr. Habib says. "In our community we consider it our duty to help our elders and this was a great opportunity to do just that. If we can give some comfort to somebody nearing the end of their journey in life, then that's just great."

"One of our mandates is to contribute towards community service, making a difference in our local community whenever possible."

For the last few years, the council has been a major donor for hospitals in need throughout the Lower Mainland. "One of our mandates is to contribute towards community service, making a difference in our local community whenever possible. There was a need and we were happy to help address it," he notes.

Kathleen Johnston, patient care coordinator at Laurel Place Hospice, says that the mattresses will make her patients much more comfortable.

"Thanks to the donation by the Muslim Business Council of BC our patients can now have a good night's sleep without being in pain when they turn or move around. The mattresses help to alleviate that problem for them."

Mohammed Yasin, chairman of the council, had initially approached Dr. Habib to get involved in supporting Surrey Memorial Hospital as it continues to grow. Mr. Yasin helped to lead the fundraising activities, hosting a dinner earlier this year at a Coquitlam hotel to help raise the funds. Dr. Habib said that Mr. Yasin is a leader in the Muslim community and his involvement was much appreciated.

Established in 2008, the Muslim Business Council of BC includes approximately 100 businesses, professionals and students. Members are drawn from diverse sectors of the provincial economy,

Muslim Business Council of BC members try out the new mattresses on a recent visit to Laurel Place.

including real estate, financial services, law and health care. They believe strongly in the importance of giving back to local causes with a focus on hospitals throughout the Lower Mainland.

Laurel Place Hospice is located across 96th Avenue from Surrey Memorial Hospital and operated by Fraser Health. Families, or any member of the community interested in supporting the hospice can direct their donations to Surrey Hospital & Outpatient Centre Foundation.

RECOGNITION OF COMMUNITY SERVICE

Royal Columbian Hospital Foundation

WALL OF THANKS

We are honoured to acknowledge the individuals, businesses, and community organizations that have generously donated to support Royal Columbian Hospital, its health care providers and the patients who arrive from throughout the region and beyond.

Royal Columbian Hospital provides the highest level of care to some of the most critically ill and injured in the province.

With your help, Royal Columbian Hospital Foundation is working to help save lives, restore health and provide comfort by raising funds which directly benefit patients.

Catalysts
$5,000 – $9,999
[Individuals]

Arthur Diels	Dr. Robin & Barbara Kuri
Dr. Laura Duggan	Phyllis Kuzmicki
Mr. Dunsmore	Tony & Narinder Lal
Robert & Beryl Duxbury	Chuck & Stacey Lavis
Robert Evans	James F. Law
Michael & Melinda Fabbro	George & June Lawrie
Mr. & Mrs. William Fairburn	Chun-Nan & Ya-Ling Le
Robert & Jean Featherstone	Dr. Dick & Stella Lee
James & Ebba Fenkarek	Esther Leung
Dr. Norman Ferguson	Yuk Ying Lo
Leonard Fidgett	Lawrence Loong
Dr. Marcia Fleming	Spencer & Jessie MacCosha
Susan Fox	Angus & Grethe MacLeod
Dr. Gordon Fyffe	Morva Reid Maerki
Michael Grunewaldt & Dr. Carol Galley	Gary Mah
Dorothy Galer	Clinton & Lynne Mahiman
Colin & Marion Galinski	Tom & Claire Manion
Jim & Julie Szabo	Cyril & Frances Maplethorp
Martin & Judy Gifford	Ian & Debbie Matheson
Bill Gilson	Gladys Mathieson
Dr. Winston Gittens	Mammud & Salima Mawji & Fan
Della Grant	Owen & Marilyn McQuarrie
Kenneth Bradley Oliver	John Mendes
Dr. Naiyer & Mrs. M. Naushaba Habib	Robert Miller
Mansell P. Hambly	Millicent Milne
Edward & B. Gaile Hameluck	Warren & Diana Mitchell
Thomas & Barbara Hanna	Annelis Moesti

Premier of Saskatchewan
Legislative Building
Regina Canada S4S 0B3

September 17, 2015

Dr. Naiyer Habib and Mrs. Mahlaqa Naushaba Habib
34720 Hamon Drive
ABBOTSFORD BC V2S 1H5

Dear Dr. and Mrs. Habib:

Thank you for your letter of September 10, 2015, and copy of your book titled, *History of the Muslims of Regina and Their Organizations*.

Your thoughtfulness is appreciated. Saskatchewan's Muslim community represents a significant and growing segment of our province's diverse population. As active members of Saskatchewan's Muslim community for over three decades, you can take pride in your pioneering work in support of your community and for advancing cooperation with other cultural communities throughout our province.

Best wishes and thank you for your kind words.

Sincerely,

Brad Wall
Premier

peu-regina

523

July 15, 2016

Congratulations! I am pleased to announce that the name "Habib" has been added to the Master List for Street and Park Names.

The Civic Naming Committee approved "Habib" in honour of Naiyer and Mahlaqa Naushaba Habib at their October 28, 2015 meeting. The men and women on the list have all made significant contributions to our city, our province, country or the world. Naiyer Habib's work in establishing a cardiology program in Regina, his work in the founding of Regina and Saskatchewan's Islamic community, and his role as a spokesperson for peace and justice has made Regina a better place to live, work and raise a family.

As our community grows, names are chosen from the list by developers for streets in new areas. Park names are selected from the list by community groups and developers and are ultimately approved by City Council.

I am pleased that the City of Regina can celebrate Naiyer's achievements in this manner.

Sincerely,

Michael Fougere
Mayor

OFFICE OF THE MAYOR
Queen Elizabeth II Court•Box 1790•Regina, Saskatchewan S4P 3C8•Ph: (306) 777-7339•Fax: (306) 777-6824

524

THIS CERTIFICATE
OF APPRECIATION
IS PRESENTED TO

DR. NAIYER & NAUSHABA HABIB

IN RECOGNITION OF YOUR SUPPORT TO THE

HOST PROGRAM

A SINCERE "THANK YOU" IS EXTENDED FOR HELPING MAKE THE
PROGRAM A SUCCESS.

COORDINATOR: HOST PROGRAM   CHAIRPERSON: BOARD OF DIRECTORS

27 May 1993
DATE

IM-209/5/92

Host
Program, Open Door Society (Helping New Immigrants).

525

AUTHORSHIP: MAHLAQA NAUSHABA AND NAIYER HABIB

http://www.theusreview.com/reviews/History-Habib.html#.Vw6xtfkrJG8

History of the Muslims of Regina, Saskatchewan, and Their Organizations . . . "A Cultural Integration"

by Naiyer Habib and Mahlaqa Naushaba Habib (at Amazon.com)

Reviewed by Barbara Bamberger Scott.

"God bless us all in our new home and bless our new home, Canada."

This book represents the tireless efforts of a retired husband and wife team to document and preserve the history and culture of immigrant Muslims who have settled in Saskatchewan, Canada. Arriving in Canada in 1973, Naiyer Habib (a cardiologist and medical administrator) and his wife, Mahlaqa, who holds a master's degree in political science, began establishing numerous civic and cultural organizations based on their faith, such as the Islamic Association and the Canadian Council of Muslim Women. Their intention was to establish and strengthen connections with other Muslims scattered throughout the region. Now, both having retired, they have sought to document the presence of an established Muslim community in the region for themselves and future generations.

The book reads best as a reference volume, primarily consisting of photos and photocopied letters, newspaper articles and documents. There are, however, some important preambles before the presentation of certain documents expressing Islamic Association concerns over such public-policy issues as condoms in schools and the Gulf War. These preambles and the material collected indicate a clear and continuing concern for matters outside the local region. The book admirably highlights the intention of this immigrant group to integrate into local society while sustaining critical aspects of their own culture and religion. It is exhaustively researched, presenting extensive information about Muslim civic activities in the greater Saskatchewan area in an organized format.

History of the Muslims of Regina, Saskatchewan, and Their Organizations . . . "A Cultural Integration" can serve as an excellent reference for anyone needing to gather material about the history of Muslim expatriate communities in Canada, either for family or civic purposes.

RECOMMENDED by the US Review of Books. ©2015 All Rights Reserved•*The US Review of Books*

Book Review: History of Muslims of Regina and their Organizations, A Cultural Integration

By
Lisa Kenney, Eagle Eye Editing, Harrison Hot Springs, BC

Cultural Integration: What does cultural integration mean? I am a 4th generation descendent of

Irish/English immigrants to Canada. Ships crossing to North America were so crowded back then that very few actual belongings were allowed on board; all they could bring was their culture – language, music, food, social values, traditions...and religion. As Catholics/Presbyterians who spoke English, they didn't have to do much to "integrate".

Dr. Naiyer Habib is not only a medical pioneer in Canada, but he and his wife, Mahlaqa Naushaba, arrived in Saskatchewan at a time when there were only a handful of Muslims. As true pioneers do, they forged forth to establish a Muslim faith community, and together with that handful of men, women, and youth, they created places of Muslim worship and education. Mrs. Habib operated a fledgling Islamic School out of their home. A youth group was eventually organized by the youth, including a summer camp. Special celebrations were held and attended by the entire community in recognition of high school and Islamic School graduates. Notably, most of these mentored youths went on to become doctors, lawyers, accountants, and other professionals.

The Habibs were not only involved with their Muslim community but also encouraged, joined, and founded multifaith groups and events in order to provide interfaith support systems, fostering discussion and friendships instead of the fear that comes from a lack of knowledge and subsequent assumptions.

527

<u>History of the Muslims of Regina, Saskatchewan, and Their Organizations</u>: A lot of history can be made in three decades. Most major organizations keep an archive of their founding and subsequent activities. Dr. and Mrs. Habib moved to British Columbia after they retired, and with them came the paper records of the many associations that they had joined, founded, and guided. Once the idea of retirement actually set in, Dr. & Mrs. Habib set to work on meticulously sorting, organizing, and digitizing hundreds of papers, photos, videos, newspaper and magazine articles; an odyssey of documentation that became a book called Cultural Integration, which is not only an important historical account of Muslims in Saskatchewan but also an important part of the overall history of Saskatchewan and Canada.

This book was written as a chronological history of events that Dr. and Mrs. Habib were involved with during their time in Saskatchewan. The original intention was for it to be a permanent record of who, what, when, why, and where for the benefit of future generations, so it is packed with lists of board members, verbatim speeches, meeting minutes, and conference agendas. At the same time, it provides a basic overview of the Muslim faith.

I first "met" Dr. Habib back in March 2015 through an email urgently requesting my assistance with some glaring errors that became apparent during a read-through of the galleys. As the manuscript was already making its way to the printing press, I was given one week to review the 700-page tome. Due to the sheer volume and complexity of the work, we had to extend the deadline by many weeks in order to check and compare, check and research, compare and change.

a progressive Canadian newsmagazine

www.briarpatchmagazine.com

BRIARPATCH

Volume 33, Number 2

March 2004

$3.00

Voices of the Sisters

Protect ME with Justice not excuses

GENUINE CANADIAN MAGAZINE

A look at the special barriers that First Nations Women and Women of Colour face to full participation in our communities, workplaces and society in general.

WHEN CULTURES DIFFER

A glimpse into the experiences of an immigrant Canadian family.

by M. Naushaba Habib

photo: Debra Brin

My family immigrated to Canada in 1973 and our links are to India and Pakistan. We left both of these countries because of discrimination. In India, Muslims faced discrimination from a predominately Hindu population, and Indian Muslims who moved to Pakistan faced discrimination as immigrants.

Our first stop on the way to Canada was the United States. My husband had come for medical training and I was pregnant with my first child.

The primary barrier we faced was ignorance and continues to be ignorance. Most of the people around us did not know anything about our faith, or if they thought they did it was often a mistaken understanding. We avoided activities which were contrary to our cultural or religious upbringing.

Accommodation

When we first arrived, access to food was a problem. We eat *Halaal* food, animals slaughtered in a special religious way. Pork, pork products and alcohol are forbidden for Muslims. Because of the lack of food suitable for our eating, we remained vegetarian for a while. Subsequently, we arranged to slaughter cow, lamb and chicken on farms. Now *Halaal* food is available in many grocery stores. Hotels arrange for our kind of food when we invite people for marriages and other events.

When we started to receive invitation from our local friends and neighbours we did not know how to tell them about our food requirements. We thought we would be imposing on them. Therefore, we would go and eat whatever was suitable for us to eat. One day a family invited us for a meal and served only foods containing pork. Therefore, we could not eat. When the hosts found out, they were very embarrassed and we felt guilty for not telling them. Because of this experience we have decided to let our hosts know and we request that they not bother with any special preparation. In spite of this request, people go out of their way to make sure that there is some food for us. Thus, it was a process of learning to be frank and cordial.

When we arrived here we were welcomed by the larger society and participated in social and community gatherings, but we did not have a place to offer congregational worship. Churches were generous to offer their places without hesitation when approached. Now there are Mosques in every city, from small houses to palatial buildings.

When we first arrived here, and until lately, children were allowed to leave classes for our holidays but were marked absent. The children are no longer marked absent, and schools are even providing a place and allowing the children to pray at the required times. Employers now allow their Muslim employees to go to offer prayer; the Muslim employees compensate by working for the total hours they are expected to work. Workers generally have to use their annual holidays to celebrate our religious holidays, except in Ontario. We are appreciative of these accommodations.

Racism

My children faced racial discrimination in schools. Our home and car were vandalized and I faced taunts over my head scarf; I was walking one time in the downtown area and a youth poked my head from behind and ran away. Another time I was walking in the park in my neighborhood and a boy called me "Hebrew lady" and tried to hide. I went to him and told him, "I am a Muslim lady." It was gratifying that a white woman came to me and told me, looking at my traditional dress, "You look different and nice. Do not change yourself." It was encouraging for me to be reminded that there are kind people! I also have a fond memory of our first landlady when we lived in the USA. Jackie was a registered nurse and was like a mother to us. She even took time off work to attend to me during my pregnancy, and to my child when he became very sick.

Muslim Community

Over time my family became involved with the Muslim community. I was, and am, President of the Regina Chapter of the Canadian Council of Muslim Women and my husband was President of the Islamic Association for many years. We established Muslims for Peace and Justice after the 9/11 incident in order to address misunderstandings about Islam and Muslims, and to deal with the ensuing rise in discrimination. My children were active with the Muslim youth and were also involved in the society at large.

I started an Islamic school in my home to teach religion to the children and did so for a number of years. The school started with nine children of different age groups. By the time we acquired our own centre or Mosque, the number of children had grown to 30. The Mosque now provides religious study.

Some of the Muslim families felt the need for a full time Muslim school and Regina Huda School was started in 1999 with 20 students. Two years later it became an associate school with the Public School Board. Saskatchewan School Board curriculum is followed and taught by five certified non-Muslim teachers. Three Muslim teachers teach Islam and Arabic. The school has 85 children from pre-kindergarten to Grade 8. These families are originally from 15 different countries. The school maintains a very high standard and has excellent facilities. There is a plan to eventually include high school.

We are active in university programs for Islamic discussion, folk festivals, work related functions, and in interfaith and intercultural activities. My children, now grown up, were involved with us, and continue to be active in the Muslim community and in society at large.

Prior to 9-11, I believed that Muslims were gaining greater acceptance by the mainstream society. After 9-11, I became apprehensive for the future of my family and my country, Canada. While I see the rise of all kinds of bigotry, at the same time I am reassured to see many of my sister and brother Canadians outside my faith group standing up for us.

Ignorance is the biggest disease of the human being. I believe that the best way to overcome something is to face the problem head on and deal with it. We have to develop understanding and respect for one another to live and progress as individuals, as society and as a nation. We are created by God as one.

As God says in the Holy Quraa'n: "O mankind, We have created you from a single male and female and made you into nations and tribes so that you may know each other. The most honorable in the sight of God are surely the Righteous."

M. Naushaba Habib is an immigrant citizen of Canada with a Master's degree in Political Science. She is a homemaker, medical office manager, community volunteer worker and a founding member and the President of Canadian Council of Muslim Women, Regina Chapter.

Blaming Converts for Terrorism

By: *Naiyer Habib* Source: *IslamiCity*

Featured on: January 31, 2015

Category: *Articles, Faith, Featured, New Muslims, Society*|

Topic: *Converts*

Views: 1,892

Media, politicians, and Muslim scholars are pointing fingers at converts as being the source of terrorism in recent trends. Some Muslims pass such remarks at the coffee table. This is similar to the media, politicians, and other groups with anti-Islam and anti-Muslim biases that blame the Muslims after 9/11 for it. One could glance at the *Human Rights Watch report* to see what happened to the Muslims after 9/11. In the aftermath of the September 11, 2001, terrorist attacks, Arabs and Muslims in the United States and those perceived to be Arab or Muslim, such as Sikhs and South Asians, became victims of a severe wave of backlash violence. The hate crimes included murder, beatings, arson, attacks on mosques, shootings, vehicular assaults, and verbal threats. This violence was directed at people only because they shared or were perceived to share the national background or religion of the hijackers and al-Qaeda members, who were deemed responsible for attacking the World Trade Center and the Pentagon.

Islamophobia is still on *the rise*. Indeed, the tragic events of 9/11 not only caused a sharp rise in Islamophobic attitudes in the immediate aftermath thereof but continue to account for the violence and discrimination of Muslims and Islamic institutions still facing it *today*.

It has taken more than a decade for some sections of the population to start to differentiate between the minority group of Muslims who are responsible for terrorism and the Muslim masses and all who stood for their support (in *Canada, Germany*, and *Australia*).

One could also look at the targeting of the new Muslims or converts as terrorists. When statistics are reviewed, their number is not different from the terrorists', especially among young ones who come from being lifelong Muslims. It also calls the broad *branding* of Muslim converts as a terrorist threat inaccurate and misleading and points out that there are, of course, far more Muslim converts who do not become terrorists than those who do.

It remarks further that there are 100 media articles on "Muslim Convert Terrorism," the majority of which are inaccurate and speculative and only reinforce an inaccurate negative stereotype of converts (*CONVERSATION*).

The vast majority of Muslim converts are law-abiding, decent citizens. It is only a small minority of converts that find the extremist message attractive (*Moosavi*).

Many new converts flourish, and few become radicalized. Many people become inquisitive about Islam because of what it truly is or sometimes because of the public defamation against it. A majority of them, by their own initiative or with helping hands, test the waters of Islam for a long time before conversion. They flourish. They acquire their own status and their own prestige. The contributions made to Islam by converts are immense and exemplary.

"Converts in the West are bridge builders for the communication of Islam between non-Muslims and Muslims because of their language, colour, and culture (*Moosavi*). It will not be justified to name only a few, but examples are required for those who are not familiar with their ongoing contribution. This includes Ibrahim Hooper of CAIR, Yusuf Estes of Share Islam, Hamza Yusuf of Zaytuna College, Imam Suhaib Webb of Boston, Lauren Booth, a journalist and a human rights activist, Yvonne Ridley, a Taliban prisoner and a British journalist, and numerous others.

Some accept Islam through the bond of marriage, and some perceive what a Muslim practices and how it is different from their life. Thousands of people converted to Islam after 9/11 when they started to explore what kind of religion it is. The figure varies, including a quote of 25,000 in the US annually, "Prior to these attacks, there were an estimated 1.2 million Muslims in the United States, with a rate of about 25,000 conversions a year (*afterwards*).

The Charlie Hebdo cartoon affair will likely accelerate the conversion. Just four days after this incident, *Matic* accepted Islam in that very land, posting her remark about the Prophet (Peace Be upon Him).

Many converts fall victim to isolation and desperation. They face abandonment by Muslim hosts and non-Muslim friends and family.

When they convert to Islam, they are only received with enthusiasm by the Muslims in the beginning and then are left out in the wilderness, in the words of these *converts*. The converts find it hard to fit into Muslim *culture*.

Many converts expect Muslim communities will compensate by welcoming them and providing a new support network, as is encouraged by Islamic teachings. But in reality, this welcome is not always forthcoming. Rather, converts can be ostracized by lifelong Muslims because they are still perceived by some as outsiders (*Moosavi*).

Non-Muslims abandon them in view of the portrayal of Islam in general as a backward, violent, women-suppressing religion, which is far from fact. They are unwelcomed by Muslims and become misfits in society at large (*Booth, Allott*). Thus, they are faced with both isolation and desperation.

Many of these converts do not have the time, ability, means, or environment to learn Islam. They wander from one mosque to another and from one Islamic scholar to another and come across different versions of Islam. Even translations and interpretations of the Quran can be different. Some examples of misinterpretation could be about beating a wife or apostasy or Jihad, etc. Such examples and others create confusion in their minds. The outcome is to shun Islam or adopt the principle of following self-analysis and exploration until the right answer appears. This falls in line of the *conscience* given by God.

The vast majority of Muslim converts are law-abiding, decent citizens. However, there is a minority of converts whose previous lifestyle involved criminality, gang culture, and general hostility toward authority. These converts may seek redemption in Islam or a clean break from a troubled past. In some cases, though, the past remains within their psyche, and it is in extremism that they find a familiar framework. It is these innocents who may be indoctrinated by the extremist preachers (*Moosavi*) who are looking for them, as well.

One example of this took place when Al Qaeda leader *Ayman al-Zawahiri* suggested that Al Qaeda consider recruiting *converts* in Western countries on the basis that they could provide tactical and strategic advantages.

They were brainwashed by the so-called Jihadists, who have, as a common denominator with the Islamophobes, misunderstanding and misrepresenting Islam *(Mahdi Hasan)*.

Only a fraction of converts is similar to lifelong Muslims who fall prey to extremism.

It is very sad to see this blame coming from Muslims, including scholars of Islam, *warning* the converts point blank rather than to all the intenders of terror, in general. A checklist here on which imam to follow and the suggestion of what Islam to follow, offered under the prevailing circumstances may fall into controversy. These should be generalized for all Muslims and not limited to the converts. Which mosque to follow cannot be relied upon, as the case of Damian *Clairmont* demonstrates.

A publicly announced recommendation to screen new Muslims and potential new Muslims, whether they be *drug* addicts, alcoholics, or criminals, will drive them away from approaching an imam for fear of being contacted by law enforcement and facing an unexpected outcome. It is these individuals who hear or read some aspects of Islam and come to accept Islam to walk away from such a life. This fear is highlighted in the article by *Erren*.

It is not my intent to elaborate on terrorism and its causes or even go on to recommend how this can be dealt with. There is much written on this. However, I will suffice to leave some remarks here.

An individual, group, or nation that takes the recourse of terrorism by whatever means they can accumulate considers themselves to be subjected to unjustified acts by the powerful against them. This is their way of dealing with the injustice they perceive. Canada is not an exception. This existed for a long time, even in *Canada*.

This vicious cycle will continue under the shadow of ego, selfishness, and double standards. The birth or excuse of birth of Al-Qaeda, ISIS, Boko Haram, and others are being claimed to be for these reasons.

Neither the terrorists listed by the West nor the West itself will roll back. The Muslim world, as the *situation* exists, is not expected to play any role.

The Western Muslims, by their own efforts, victimized from all sides and kept isolated in a cage of suspicion, are very slowly being recognized in some corner for help, which may play a role.

They need dignified and honest approaches for such assistance, something that the West never thought of at the beginning.

Live and let live in peace!

http://www.islamicity.org/6458/blaming-converts-for-terrorism/

Angela Merkel—A Leader of Vision

By: Naiyer **Source:** Views

Featured on: Aug 21, 2015

Category: *Articles, Europe, Featured, Politics*

Topic: *Angela Merkel, Germany*

Views: 611

Violence and terrorism, in some form or another, have been part of the human condition from day one. History is full of wars and atrocities inflicted by people over other people that they saw as weak, and therefore to be exploited, or for various other real or fake reasons.

After the Second World War, the world had calmed down to a large extent, except for a few pockets of violence here and there. A few reasons for some of this violence centred in the Middle East and led to the infamous 9/11 incident. After that, all hell broke loose, and now, it seems, it is the "Age of Terrorism."

Followers of some self-appointed leaders who misrepresent Islam are resorting to acts of violence, not only in the Western countries but in their own.

Terrorism is not exclusive to the Muslim groups in the past or present. People resort to terrorism and violence when they perceive themselves to be weak or they perceive injustice at the hands of the more powerful, be that from within or without a foreign country or their own corrupt government. Unfortunately, innocents suffer directly or as collateral damage.

These terrorists feel that the West is doing an injustice to their Muslim-populated world. Western writers are themselves pointing at the power of the West as the cause for the upsurge of Muslim group terrorists such as ISIS, Al-Qaeda, and the like.

As it looks, the leaders of the Muslim-populated world are silent and non-participating, even though their countries claim to be harbouring terrorists or to be associated with terrorism.

In this chaos, one hears the human, justified, well-understood, and sincere voice of a Western leader—Angela Merkel, the chancellor—on different occasions making statements about various problems.

"Former president Wulff said Islam belongs to Germany. That is true. I also hold this *opinion*," Merkel said at a news conference, hours before marches by the movement of Patriotic Europeans against the Islamisation of the West were to begin in several German cities.

In another statement, the chancellor said, "Every exclusion of Muslims in Germany, every general suspicion, is forbidden," emphasizing that the free practice of religion, including Islam, was protected under the German constitution. She further added, "We will not let ourselves be *divided*."

Paul William quotes her: "Our country is going to carry on changing, and integration is also a task for the society taking up the task of dealing with immigrants," Ms. Merkel told the daily newspaper. "For years, we've been deceiving ourselves about this. Mosques, for example, are going to be a more prominent part of our cities than they were before." Williams also quotes the figures of the rising *Muslim population in Europe*. And Merkel has a very valid question directed at Muslim leaders: "They want to know why terrorists have so little regard for the value of human life and why they tie their crimes to their faith. They ask how they can trust the phrase that murderers who claim to act in the name of Islam have nothing to do with *Islam*.

"I want to emphasize that these are *valid questions*. I believe we urgently need a clarification of these questions by Islam's religious leaders. This issue can't be evaded any longer," she said. Terrorists may believe that they are "allowed to act, punish, kill on God's behalf," she said, "but for me, this is nothing but *blasphemy*."

No doubt, and rightly so, she is acting expeditiously to take all security measures for protection from terrorism. She favours freedom of speech, in my opinion, not speech that may cause hatred that leads to violence.

All of this suggests that she has a vision to rectify the existing situation related to terrorism. In my opinion, it is also an invitation to the world as a whole.

She is the only leader, along with her predecessor, who has made such bold statements amongst both supporting and opposing Germans at large. She made these statements in the German parliament and attended anti-Muslim and pro-Muslim rallies, the latter held not by Muslims but by the German population. Is there any leader in the West who is paying attention to stand up and support her, which I believe that she wishes as part of the plan? Thus, she has a vision for the future of Germany, which, if implemented, will serve as an example for others to follow.

Various Western leaders have lately made statements differentiating the general Muslim population from terrorists and putting the same challenge on the shoulders of Muslim leaders, asking them to take responsibility and point to terrorism in their countries.

She displays knowledge of controversies in Islam by various Islamic scholars and points to the acts of terrorists being perpetrated in the name of Islam as blasphemous. She wants answers from Muslim leaders. She wants to know what she should tell the people when they ask her what Islam she meant. They want to know why the terrorists have such little value for human life and why they always link their deeds to their faith.

The answer should come from the German Muslim community across the country in consensus. In my experience of three decades of service to the Muslim community with people of other faiths in various capacities and under various conditions, this expectation is unlikely to be met. The Muslim community has diverse origins. It is an established fact that various versions of Islam are preached by various Islamic scholars according to their backgrounds. There is a pope in Catholicism, but no such authority in Islam. The *grand imam* of al-Azhar, Sheikh

Ahmed el-Tayeb, has shown concerns regarding the misrepresented Islam in the West. He is an accepted and respected authority by the majority of Muslims.

For these valuable initiatives to succeed, steps ought to be taken by the chancellor. Otherwise, they will die on the vine. I put forward some suggestions here.

A council under the authority of the government and working with the government will be required. The council should consist of Muslim scholars born and raised in the West or who have lived the majority of their life in the West. Their credentials should show knowledge and non-biased opinions. Jamal *Badawi*, Tariq *Ramadan*, Hamza *Yusuf*, and non-Muslim Islamic scholars like John *Esposito* and Karen *Armstrong* are a few people who are suitable for the task of sitting on this council.

An Islamic scholar nominated by the German Muslims should also be included. The council should prepare an informative document that answers these raised questions and is presented to the chancellor. Any other new problem that might occur from time to time should be addressed by this council. The respected chancellor, Angela Merkel, ought to be the chair with a vice chair responsible for the day-to-day running of the council with a caveat that all decisions will require the final approval of the chair.

All decisions are to be according to the Quran and authentic Hadith (told and practiced by the Prophet). In rare circumstances, the council ought to use the God-given conscience as stated by the Quran, as well as the consultation, as per the Quran and Hadith. Islam is a very practical and accommodating religion. It also advises Muslims to obey the law of the country in which they live. And it, of course, asks them to raise a constructive voice with authorities against inappropriate matters.

If wisdom permits, public opinion may be sought on such documents in a democratic country, but not approval if it violates the Quran and cannot be accommodated by the authentic Hadith. The respected imam of Al Azhar may be an asset for consultation and a speaker on the subject of a misunderstood Islam.

What about the rising Muslim population in the West? This fact is confirmed by the chancellor in the article by Paul Williams. Some Western writers are alerting the West of this rising population (P. *Williams/Mark Steyn*). So, what is the solution? Genocide, mass deportation, or shutting down immigration? Are these possible solutions? The world has seen an attempt at genocide in Bosnia and the genocide of native Indians. No doubt, the West stood up to help in Bosnia, although it was too late. The world has also seen mass deportation by Idi Amin of Uganda, who ended up in exile. The West depends on immigrants, Muslims among them. Their contributions aid the West in sustaining itself and enjoying progress at no cost to the West. The Muslims are not part of the economic loss that occurs on a day-to-day basis in dealing with alcohol abuse, gambling, and other problems of Western countries. Many immigrants come for a better economic life; others come because of rampant corruption and undemocratic acts by the democratically elected leaders in their home countries. The administration of the government falls in the hands of these democratically elected leaders who rule over their populations. This may be limited to some families who have ruled the country for decades upon decades.

Live in peace and let live is the ideal goal for the world. But this goal is not achievable. There's nobody to reconcile or negotiate for justice to prevail. The UNO's efforts on this front are obviously powerless. Ego and greed for selfish objectives are forcing everyone against everyone else, and chaos prevails. This is very obvious across the world.

All Muslims across the board have been considered to be associated with terror. The situation that occurred with the Italians, Japanese, and others during the World Wars has been repeated. Some from among the Muslims became determined to act violently, considering the injustice done to them. This was a group feeling hurt that isolated itself and minded its own business, although living in fear. The chancellor has made a point of paying attention to these people, as noted in her statement above.

It would have been a wiser step to incorporate the Muslims as participants in solving this problem right from the beginning, a fact that's being pointed out now by Westerners (*Ian Buruma*). They would have felt dignified serving their country, as their religion dictates that they do. They would have worked shoulder to shoulder. Unfortunately, they were the target of mistrust and victimization. There has been a plot to lure Muslims into fake terror plots, and the Muslim community has reacted to that. Of course, it is necessary to be alert and vigilant to any whiff of terror, but not to create an atmosphere of suspicion and degradation for Muslims. They ought to be included as partners with dignity. Islam upholds dignity and respect. A shy attempt to initiate this has started to some extent.

Still, Islamophobia continues. Indeed, it is on the rise. The leaders of the Muslim-populated world have remained silent all along instead of trying to protect themselves in their positions. They could have played an important role right from the beginning. They could have contacted those parts of the West that were maligning and victimizing innocent Muslims. They should have entered into negotiations with terrorist groups and educated them, sought to learn their grievances, and worked toward a peaceful settlement. They could have asked the West to deal with terrorism jointly, even if the West didn't invite them to do so. They could stand up now to start such participation with still-rising Islamophobia. There are reasonable voices of support from some members of the public, the media, and churches.

While Islamophobia continues, there is sympathy and help forthcoming from some corners of the world as lessons to be learned by Islamophobes. Where there is an anti-Muslim rally, there is also a pro-Muslim rally by the general population in larger numbers in such places as *Germany, Australia*, the *UK*, and *Canada*. Muslims thanked non-Muslims who helped clean a vandalized mosque in Cold Lake, Alberta.

There is a lesson to be learned from the persons of *Rachael Jacobs* and *Stacey Eden* in their exemplary defence of victimized Muslims. These waves of understanding and support may be heartening.

There is an anti-christian drive in some Muslim- and Hindu-populated countries that requires attention. The chancellor is sincere in her statements in Germany and in her desire to put them into practice.

Doing so will require a reciprocal response from the German population at large and much more from the Muslims to stand and show the Germans who they are and what they can do to live in peace in accordance with their new home, even if they have to make sacrifices. They must not stand openly or secretly demand Germany be an Islamic. They must not demand anything that will offend the German population, and that is what Islam tells them to do.

It requires cultural integration while maintaining their own culture happily, as demonstrated in our book, *The History of Muslims of Regina, Saskatchewan, and their Organizations... "A Cultural Integration,"* whose background theme is the integration of *culture*. Making that work calls for a two-way lane of respect and accommodation.

As to Germany, under the leadership of the chancellor, it can stand alone with its large German population and new German Muslims who can teach the world that they can coexist in peace. The suggested council and others can serve as a resource in the UNO that might be followed by other countries.

http://www.islamicity.org/9240/angela-merkel-a-leader-of-vision/

Islamic Education At A Family Level

AUGUST 3, 2015 NAIYER HABIBEDIT

Dr. Naiyer Habib M.D; FACP; FCCP; FRCPC; FACC

Islamic Education at a Family Level

Dr. Naiyer Habib, MD; FACP; FCCP; FRCPC; FACC. Abbotsford. 3-27-2012.

There is a sincere desire and effort by families to provide Islamic education to their children. Parents face many hurdles in seeing this through. Some are fortunate to live near a full-fledged Islamic school or a weekend Islamic school. Some travel a long distance to acquire Islamic education for their children. Some are too busy to make ends meet economically. If parents wait too long for an Islamic education opportunity to be made available to them, it may be too late. Children may grow up in Western societies without Islamic education. And the longer they go on this road, the more difficult it is to attract them to the idea of an Islamic education. Islamic education should begin when the call to prayer is said upon the birth of the infant.

It is easier to bend a green stick to mould it than when it is mature. Forcing Islamic education at a mature age brings family violence to the extent of unwanted and un-Islamic honour killings because of the tussle that begins between the grown-up children and parents who woke up too late.

Islamic education at a family level and by the family is an asset whose value needs to be acknowledged by those who cannot avail themselves of the education opportunities for their children or who face hurdles in attempting to do so. It should be considered a source of lifelong learning for the family. If conducted sincerely and seriously, it could be superior to other schooling. This method of education has been proven to be a success in the majority of cases in which the family's senior members are in their sixties and seventies. It was a time when non-biased Islamic literature was almost nonexistent, a far cry from the availability of Islamic education material today. Those who paid attention to the family while meeting the community's needs of praying and gathering at home, in churches, or in community halls were able to raise their children with enriched Islamic knowledge and culture by the grace of Allah (SWT). These can be seen today in the form of the children's Islamic capacities. It is unfortunate that they have not been incorporated into the mainstream community to provide or participate in the leadership, though there seems to be some effort being undertaken in that regard.

Islamic family education must include the involvement of all members of the family in educating themselves about Islam and culture based on the Islamic way of life. Each member of the family, including children, no matter what age, must take an active part according to their age and ability.

The parent is to play the role of supervisor. Grown-up children who have participated in family education can take up that supervisory responsibility in due course. Let the education even be coordinated and chaired by the children. The distributed responsibilities may include scheduling, collecting or sorting out educational material, and collecting money for charity within the family, even if it is a meagre sum. This approach prepares them for community involvement and leadership.

The family needs to understand that all of this is mandatory for them to have Islamic education for their family. It needs to be scheduled at a time and day when it can be regularly performed. It must not be taken casually. Children must be convinced to pay as much attention to such education as they do to their regular school. In the case of a failure to attend a scheduled event due to unavoidable circumstances, that event ought to be rescheduled.

The educational material should be planned and collected for the next event ahead of the scheduled time by the person in charge of the education of the family. It ought to be an ongoing effort without fail. In order to emphasize, I will not avoid referencing a friend's family who used to turn everything off, including the phone, every Saturday morning while they had their session of Islamic education at home. This family may not be the exception. The ultimate outcome of this was that the son took up the presidency of the association according to the constitution and not by inheritance in the fourth decade. The daughter started to wear a hijab when she finished high school. I felt that, although they were very sincere with their family education, the parents did not force the daughter to put on hijab, believing she would with time. And she did.

In such education, some points have always to be kept in mind. Children are intelligent and close observers. They observe and learn what parents do. Parents have to be the models for them. If they cannot do what they are required to or what they should do for valid reasons, they ought to explain to the children why. If this is not done, they will look to be double-faced in the eyes of their children. The children will be resentful and confused.

The other point of importance is that Islamic education must be open. Children ought to be given the opportunity to ask questions about whatever comes into their minds, including about what they're facing outside of the home. A legitimate explanation should be provided, even if it means seeking input from outside sources. We all live in a Western society, so our children cannot be isolated. However, they need to be told about the good and bad of society without bias. When children happen to visit the old country, they see many contradictory things to what they learned Islamically. They need to be told about these and not to judge Muslims by Islam or Islam by the acts of Muslims.

The family is to decide and select material while keeping in mind the intellect and age of the children. Islamic education materials are available in abundance on websites and in printed forms. Islamic educators are also in abundance. For my part, I offer the following suggestions.

Our fundamental faith requires that we be convinced that there is only one god, that the Quran is from Him, and that Prophet Mohammed (PBUH) is the last prophet. Children need to be convinced and provided with proof to the extent that it is available so they might defend these facts if challenged by others. Knowledge of the Quran, Hadith, Shariah, and history is essential.

The mere reading of the Quran in Arabic is not enough. For non-Arabic-speaking students or for all, they should be taught an English translation in simple English such as "The Noble Quran—the Arabic text and English translation by Dr. Thomas B. Irving (Al-Hajj Talim Ali), or any other chosen by the parents. They should recite Arabic, followed by a translation as they start reading the Quranic. For advanced study or to seek explanations, one could refer to Tafseer by Ibn Kathir online (Tafseer **Ibn Kathir**: A compilation of the Abridged Tafseer **Ibn Kathir** Volumes 1-10 in the English language with Arabic verses. **ibnkathir**.atspace.com/**ibnkathir**) or Tafheemul Quran in print or on line (http://www.tafheem.net/main800.html).

I also suggest emphatically that children read the collection of Ayahs according to the subject matter in the Quran. They are: *Commandments by God in the Quran*, compiled by Nazar Mohammad, available from the ICNA book store, and another book with a similar theme, *Modern Day Qur'anic Guidance*, a collection by Ehsanul Karim. Another source of lessons and interesting stories is the two-volume *Stories From the Qur'an* by Maulana Hifz ur-Rehman Sevharvi. These are useful books to keep for reference.

I also suggest downloading 500 Hadith collections of MSA. These are simple but have some difficult English words that require translation by parents and the dictionary for the understanding of their small children. (*http://www.iium.edu.my/deed/hadith/other/hadith_500.html*).

Of course, for more elaborate study, Hadith such as Bukhari is online and in print. It is also searchable online. The authentic book on Shariah is *Fiqh-us-Sunnah*, by As-Sayyid Sabiq. It is available online (*www.muslimaccess.com/sunnah/fiqh/Default.htm*) and in print in five volumes. Parents looking at these books may conclude that they are voluminous. They are, however, very simple and have material from Purification to Umrah—critical knowledge for us.

Having offered some suggestions for seeing through the fundamental need of our faith to educate children, I shall take you to two websites: www.islamicity.com and www.shareislam. com. A review of them will show you the richness of materials therein. Parents could be selective in demonstrating them to children and using them to assign tasks. Islamicity has all the material that one could need, including history, translations, and audio memorization of the Quran. Share Islam is full of Islamic knowledge in the form of videos, including those for children, as well as lectures and articles. These resources should suffice, although websites are full of resources. Be careful to avoid misrepresented websites designed to mislead Muslims. I do not believe that there will be a need for more material to confuse the family.

A session of two hours a week should suffice for such studies. The subjects could be alternated week by week, with some subjects for one week and others for the next. I feel that just one family itself should hold these sessions. However, if it is desirable, two or three families in the neighbourhood may join the event. Multiple family sessions can become an imposition on families and may become cumbersome in due course as far as scheduling, rescheduling, and even getting together at one another's houses. Sometimes, these gatherings become more of a social than an educational event for children, and they may fail.

Such educational sessions have been, and are being, practiced with success. Even now, there is trend toward home schooling, particularly in the US. *Article Source*: ALAMEEN POST *http://alameenpost.com/articles.aspx?categoryname=faith&newsId=3666#sthash.LLYAdGPi.dpuf* (no more on its website).

SERVING THE MUSLIM COMMUNITY

Honour Killing

Dr. Naiyer Habib MD; FACP; FCCP; FRCPC; FACC. Abbotsford. 2-14-2012. http://alameenpost.com/articles.aspx?categoryname=viewpoint&newsId=3562 (copy and paste in URL).

Honour killing is the killing of a family member (or social group) by members who feel that the victim has dishonoured the family (or community).

According to the expert Dr. Shahrzad Mojab (on honour killing in Wikipedia), the followers of all major religions have used their religions as the rationale to commit honour killings. She maintains further that this does not have any definite connection with religion at all. She points out that honour killing has been practiced for a very long time, even before any major religion came into existence.

The question does arise: why are honour killings more common among followers of Islam, especially given that they are forbidden by their religion? Followers of other religions have adopted Western culture. The majority of Muslims have adhered to their religion. Contrary to Western views that women are oppressed or considered inferior in Islam, Islam has a very high regard for them.

The honour killers are cherishers of their honour, like anyone else, but they deviate from what Islam says about such killings and the guidance it provides around preventing such happenings, especially as they occur among families who migrated to Canada (West). They walk the path of honour killing and reach the extreme end. Domestic violence is not uncommon in such circumstances. They spend all their efforts on economic achievements. They, along with the entire family, engage in work to have houses, cars, and other material goods, as they see in their neighbourhoods and communities. They spend their time, day and night, working to achieve these goals.

They rarely spend time with their children. They are so involved in their economic goals that they are unable to watch where their young are heading and what to do for them. To the young, the Western lifestyle appears glamorous: wining, dining, dancing, and all that goes with these. This clashes with their Islamic values and culture, but parents generally realize this too late. The eyes of their own in their old countries stare at them. They retaliate. There is domestic violence. Some go to the extreme of honour killing, thus ignoring what Islam forbids.

Islam, which demands raising the children born of rape with honour and justice, makes the family and community accountable. If it didn't, how could it favour honour killing?

Children follow their parents. If the parents are not around, they follow their friends and what they see in society. Grandparents and other relatives are not around. A friend circle of the type they need is rare. Society is different.

Parents have to decide what their children should be like. Children need to be nurtured and moulded from infancy. They need not to be isolated from society. They should be told about the good and bad elements of

543

society according to their culture and religion without creating any bias about any religion or culture. If they do not follow these principles according to the guidelines of Islam, they are the wrong-doers, not their children.

The community and its leaders have an equal responsibility here. Everyone needs to pay attention to the community at large and keep their eyes and ears open to individual society members or individual families. The public glamour of leaders does not help the individual or the family. They need to bring the good and bad aspects of society to their attention with their solutions on an ongoing basis. We regularly see these domestic problems affecting the individual and the family, don't we?

Article Source: ALAMEEN POST

View Original Article (no more on its website)

Canadians Against Atrocity

Dr. Naiyer Habib, Abbotsford, BC

2-22-2017

Muslims live in guilt and fear. Guilt because of the atrocity by their fellow Muslims in various places when they themselves are not at fault. They fear and suffer because there are similarities in both. They look alike, they dress like each other, and they both pray. Sikhs have suffered this because of their Muslim look.

Anyone who takes arms or discriminates against other religions does not know his/her religion or that of any other. The Quran is misquoted and cut and pasted out of context to serve certain objectives. The Islamophobes are one example, and DASH/ISIS is another.

I recall a friend during the Bosnia conflict being sad and telling me he was apprehensive that the same thing might happen to us here. I laughed it off. I reassured him that it was West. People are educated and unbiased here. I further added that the government was apologizing to the Japanese for what had been done to them. Unfortunately, my friend's apprehension was correct. The world has plunged into chaos. We all are witness to this. This has been and is accelerated by some religious and political leaders for false gain at the cost of humanity.

Immigrants who ran away because of atrocities in their home countries and to have peaceful and better lives see the future as dark. All of us are immigrants here. I noted a satirical comment with the picture of our respected native Indian at the time of the Trump campaign: "I do not like immigrants."

The killing of six innocent people in a Quebec mosque has aroused our nation to rise against terrorism, whatever its source. It is unprecedented, heartening, and inspiring to see such overwhelming support for a community that has been seen with suspicion.

Politicians and the public across the nation and the world (and even Trump) have come out in support of and with sympathy for them.

Particularly remarkable was the invocation in parliament by MP Joel Lightbound for all to rise in the House of Commons Wednesday and vow "never again." He addressed his statement to Quebec's Muslim community with whom he grew up. "I also want to apologize to them. I apologize for having observed stigmatization and ostracization over the past few years, having seen the mistrust, the fear, and the hatred among my peers, and having tried to respond but not having done enough." Lightbound added a warning that "silence also has consequences. You are at home in Sainte-Foy. You always will be."

Our prime minister, Justin Trudeau, said, "We will defend you, love you, we will stand by for you." Rona Ambrose said, "An attack against the place of worship on people praying is the most heinous attack on freedom of us and on which Canada was founded." Tom Mulcair added, "We mourn with you, we pray with you. We promise to stand united and fight the forces of bigotry and Islamophobia.

The voices of Green leader Elizabeth May, Quebec premier Philippe Couillard, and the Quebec and Montreal mayors.

Members of the public, including Francois Legault and Kathleen Weil, gave similarly thoughtful messages of sympathy and support. They all reassured Muslims that their home is here. No doubt, the fire of hatred has not been extinguished. The night after the incident, another mosque was vandalized, and former Conservative leadership candidate Kellie Leitch, without any hesitation, repeated her stand on immigration.

Of course, we trust our leaders to have guidelines for immigration with the underlying principle of fulfilling the needs of our nation and not separating families. Those who stand against immigration should clarify, in civilized terms, what they mean, and who they mean. They ought to put forward their and their ancestors' contributions to Canada and have them compared with those of immigrants.

It is pathetic to see virulent comments and protests against Islam and Muslims following the proposed motion against Islamophobia by MP Iqra Khalid. Though it is, again, inspiring to see support and condemnation against such bigotry from the majority of Canadians. Thus, we need to march with the Canadian flag to eliminate bigotry and establish Canadian values.

We should maintain this tempo of support and stay alert to those spreading bigotry across our nation, be they political leaders, would-be political leaders, or any uninformed part of the public. Any bigotry should unite and energize us much more to act. We all are Canadians.

Long live Canada!

Article Source: ALAMEENPOST.COM

ALIGARH MUSLIM UNIVERSITY AND ITS FOUNDER

by

Naiyer Habib

Sir Syed Ahmad Khan was the founder of Aligarh Muslim University. He was an important personality on India's soil. Hence, a chapter with pertinent information on this man is appended to this write-up, along with an account of the renowned Aligarh Muslim University.

I felt it important to include the personality of the respected Sir Syed Ahmad Khan, a visionary and a social reformer despite many odds.

I have noted some details about him as follows. I edited and abbreviated the information from the reference: https://en.wikipedia.org/wiki/Syed_Ahmad_Khan.

His life and legacy may be explored in various resources by searching the internet, books, and their cross references.

Sir Syed Ahmad Khan

Syed Ahmad bin Muttaqi Khan CSI (October 17, 1817-March 27, 1898) was the founder of the Aligarh Muslim University. He was born to a noble Syed family in Delhi. His mother, Aziz-un-Nisa, played a formative role in Sir Syed's early life, raising him with rigid discipline with a strong emphasis on modern education. Sir Syed was taught to read and understand the Holy Quran by a female tutor, which was unusual at the time. He received an education that was traditional to the Muslim nobility in Delhi. He read the works of Muslim scholars and writers. Sir Syed assumed editorship of his brother's journal and rejected offers of employment from the Mughal court.

He took an active part in the Mughal court's cultural activities. He took part in sports, wrestling, and swimming. He was an Indian Muslim pragmatist, Islamic philosopher, and social activist of nineteenth-century India. He was a jurist for the British East India Company.

In1842, Mughal Emperor Bahadur Shah Zafar II conferred upon Sir Syed the title of *Javad-ud*

85*Daulah* Wikipedia (Edited), maintaining the title originally conferred upon Sir Syed's grandfather, Syed Hadi Jawwad bin Imaduddin Khan by Emperor Shah Alam II around the middle of the eighteenth century. In addition, the emperor added the title of *Arif Jang*. The conferment of these titles was symbolic of Sir Syed's incorporation into the nobility of Delhi.

Born into nobility, Sir Syed earned a reputation as a distinguished scholar while working as a jurist for the British East India Company's rule in India. During the Indian Rebellion of 1857, he remained loyal to the British Empire and was noted for his actions in saving European lives. After the rebellion, he penned a book, *The Causes of the Indian Mutiny*– a daring critique, at the time, of British policies that he blamed for causing the revolt. Believing that the future of Muslims was threatened by the rigidity of their orthodox outlook, Sir Syed began promoting Western-style scientific education by founding modern schools and journals and organizing Muslim entrepreneurs. Toward this goal, Sir Syed founded Muhammadan Anglo-Oriental College in 1875, the first residential college with the aim of promoting the social, scientific, and economic development of Indian Muslims, which later developed into the famous Aligarh Muslim University. The movement of Muslim awakening associated with Syed Ahmad Khan and MAO College came to be known as the Aligarh Movement.

Prior to the Hindi-Urdu controversy, Sir Syed was interested in the education of both Muslims and Hindus and visualized India as a "beautiful bride, whose one eye was Hindu and, the other, Muslim." As a result of this view, he was regarded as a reformer and nationalist leader. There was a sudden change in Sir Syed's views after the Hindi-Urdu controversy. Hali wrote, "One day, as Sir Syed was discussing educational affairs of Muslims with Mr. Shakespeare—the then-commissioner of Banaras—Mr. Shakespeare looked surprised and asked him, "This is the first time when I have heard you talking specifically about Muslims. Before this, you used to talk about the welfare of the common Indians. Sir Syed then told him, "Now I am convinced that the two communities, Muslims and Hindus, will not put their hearts in any venture together. This is nothing; it is just the beginning. In the coming times, ever-increasing hatred and animosity appear on the horizon simply because of those who are regarded as educated. Those who will be around will witness it (Hali, 1993).

At the outbreak of the Indian rebellion on May 10, 1857, the conflict had left large numbers of civilians dead. Muslim powers such as Delhi, Agra, Lucknow, and Kanpur were severely affected. Sir Syed was personally affected by the violence. He lost several close relatives who died in the violence. Although he succeeded in rescuing his *mother* from the turmoil, she died in Meerut, owing to the *privations* she had experienced.

Sir Syed and many other Muslims took this as a defeat of Muslim society. Sir Syed Ahmad Khan established the MAO College, which eventually became the university. He patterned MAO College after Oxford and Cambridge universities, which he saw on a trip to London. He wanted this college to act as a bridge between the old and the new, the East and the West. His objective was to build a college that was in line with the British education system but without compromising its Islamic values. He opposed ignorance, superstitions, and evil customs prevalent in Indian Muslim society. He firmly believed that Muslim society would not progress without the acquisition of Western education and science. As time passed, Sir Syed began stressing ideas of pragmatic modernism and started advocating for strong interfaith relations between Islam and Christianity.

Maulana Altaf Hussain Hali wrote in the biography of Sir Syed:

"As soon as Sir Syed reached Muradabad, he began to write the pamphlet entitled 'The Causes of the Indian Revolt (Asbab-e-Baghawat-e-Hind),' in which he did his best to clear the people of India, and especially the

Muslims, of the charge of mutiny. In spite of the obvious danger, he made a courageous and thorough report of the accusations people were making against the government and refused the theory which the British had invented to explain the causes of the mutiny."

Rae Shankar Das (a Hindu), a great friend of Sir Syed, begged him to burn the books rather than put his life in danger. Sir Syed replied that he was bringing these matters to the attention of the British for the good of his own people, of his country, and of the government itself. He said that if he came to any harm while doing something that would greatly benefit the rulers and the subjects of India alike, he would gladly suffer whatever befell him. When Rae Shankar Das saw that Sir Syed's mind was made up and nothing could be done to change it, he wept and remained silent. After performing a supplementary prayer and asking God's blessing, Sir Syed sent almost all the 500 copies of his pamphlet to England, one to the government, and kept the rest himself.

When the government of India had the book translated and presented before the council, Lord Canning, the governor-general, and Sir Bartle Frere accepted it as a sincere and friendly report. The foreign secretary Cecil Beadon, however, severely attacked it, calling it "an extremely seditious pamphlet." He wanted a proper inquiry into the matter and said that the author unless he could give a satisfactory explanation, should be harshly dealt with. Since no other member of the council agreed with his opinion, his attack did no harm.

Later, Sir Syed was invited to attend Lord Canning's durbar in Farrukhabad and happened to meet the foreign secretary there. He told Sir Syed that he was displeased with the pamphlet and added that if he had really had the government's interests at heart, he would not have made his opinion known in this way throughout the country; he would have communicated it directly to the government. Sir Syed replied that he had only had 500 copies printed, the majority of which he had sent to England, one of which had been given to the government of India, and the remaining copies of which were still in his possession. Furthermore, he had the receipt to prove it. He was aware, he added, that the view of the rulers had been distorted by the stress and anxieties of the times, which made it difficult to put even the most straightforward problem in its right perspective. It was for this reason that he had not communicated his thoughts publicly. He promised that, for every copy that could be found circulating in India, he would personally pay 1,000 rupees. At first, Beadon was not convinced and asked Sir Syed over and over again if he was sure that no other copy had been distributed in India. Sir Syed reassured him on this matter, and Beadon never mentioned it again. Later, he became one of Sir Syed's strongest supporters.

Many official translations were made of the Urdu text of *The Causes of the Indian Revolt*. The one undertaken by the India Office formed the subject of many discussions and debates. The government of India and several members of parliament also translated the pamphlet, but no version was offered to the public. A translation, which had been started by a government official, was finished by Sir Syed's great friend Colonel G. F. I. Graham, and finally published in 1873.

Sir Syed began to realize the advantages of Western-style education, which was being offered at newly established colleges across India. He began feeling increasingly concerned for the future of Muslim communities. The animosity between the British and Muslims before and after the rebellion (Independence War) of 1857 threatened to marginalize Muslim communities across India for many generations.

Sir Syed intensified his work to promote cooperation with British authorities, promoting loyalty to the Empire amongst Indian Muslims. He committed to working for the upliftment of Muslims. He established schools for scientific and other education. He also worked on social causes, helping to organize relief for the famine-struck people of North-West Province in 1860.

Despite being a devout Muslim, Sir Syed criticized the influence of traditional dogma and religious orthodoxy, which had made most Indian Muslims suspicious of British influences. Dr. Sir Mohammad Iqbal observed: "The real greatness of Sir Syed consisted in the fact that he was the first Indian Muslim who felt the need for a fresh orientation of Islam and worked for it—his sensitive nature was the first to react to the modern age."

His view of Islam was rejected by Muslim clergy as contrary to traditional views on issues like jihad, polygamy, and animal slaughtering. Clerics of the Deobandi and Wahhabi schools condemned him harshly as a Kafir(Unbeliever). In the face of pressure from religious Muslims, Sir Syed avoided discussing religious subjects in his writings, focusing instead on promoting education.

By 1873, the committee under Sir Syed issued proposals for the construction of a college in Aligarh. He began publishing the journal *Tahzib al-Akhlaq (Social Reformer)* to spread awareness and knowledge on modern subjects and promote reforms in Muslim society.

Sir Syed worked to promote reinterpretation of Muslim ideology in order to reconcile tradition with Western education. He argued in several books on Islam that the Quran rested on an appreciation of reason and natural law, making scientific inquiry important to be a good Muslim. Sir Syed established a modern school in Aligarh and, obtaining support from wealthy Muslims and the British, laid the foundation stone of the Muhammadan Anglo-Oriental College on May 24, 1875.

He retired from his career as a jurist the following year, concentrating entirely on developing the college and religious reform. Sir Syed's pioneering work received support from the British. Although intensely criticized by orthodox religious leaders and hostile to modern influences, Sir Syed's new institution attracted a large student body, mainly drawn from the Muslim gentry and middle classes. The curriculum at the college involved scientific and Western subjects, as well as Oriental subjects and religious education. The first chancellor was Sultan Shah Jahan Begum, a prominent Muslim noblewoman, and Sir Syed invited an Englishman, Theodore Beck, to serve as the first college principal. The college was originally affiliated with the Calcutta University. Near the turn of the twentieth century, it began publishing its own magazine and established a law school. *In 1920, the college was transformed into a university.*

Sir Syed Ahmad Khan lived the last two decades of his life in Aligarh. He was regarded widely as the mentor of nineteenth- and twentieth-century Muslim entrepreneurs and politicians. He remained the most influential Muslim politician in India, with his opinions guiding the convictions of a large majority of Muslims. The university he founded remains one of India's most prominent institutions. Prominent alumni of Aligarh include Muslim political leaders Maulana Mohammad Ali, Abdur Rab Nishtar, Maulana Shaukat Ali, and Maulvi Abdul Haq, who is hailed in Pakistan as *Baba-e-Urdu (Father of Urdu)*. The first two prime ministers of Pakistan, Liaquat Ali Khan and Khawaja Nazimuddin, as well as the late Indian president, Dr. Zakir Hussain, are among Aligarh's most famous graduates. In India, Sir Syed is commemorated as a pioneer who worked for the socio-political upliftment of Indian Muslims. Battling illnesses and old age, Sir Syed died on March 27, 1898. He was buried beside Sir Syed Masjid inside the campus of Aligarh University.

Aligarh Muslim University (AMU)

I, my father, and other relatives were educated at this institution. I studied here from 1956 to 1958. Sir Syed Ahmad Khan was geared for the uplift of Muslims as presented above. A brief summary is presented here about the university.

Aligarh Muslim University was established by Sir Syed Ahmad Khan as Mohammedan Anglo-Oriental College in 1875. The Mohammedan Anglo-Oriental College became Aligarh Muslim University in 1920.

Transformation into University: Around 1900, efforts began to make the college its own university. The Aligarh Muslim University Act of 1920 made it a central university.

H. H. Sir Mohammad Ali Mohammad Khan and the Aga Khan III also played a major role in realizing the vision of Syed Ahmad Khan by collecting funds to build the Aligarh Muslim University.

In 1927, a school for the blind was established, and the following year, a medical school was attached to the university. By the end of the 1930s, the university had developed an engineering faculty. Syed Zafarul Hussain joined the Aligarh Muslim University in the early 1900s as head of the philosophy department and dean of the faculty of arts. He was a pro-vice chancellor before his retirement.

Before 1939, faculty members and students supported an all-India nationalist movement. After 1939, political sentiment shifted toward support for a Muslim separatist movement. Students and faculty mobilized behind Muhammad Ali Jinnah, and the university became a centre of the Pakistan movement.

The AMU faced various challenges from the British period to the period of independence. The university was independent but came under government control in 1965. It held a minority status that has been challenged in the courts as recently as 2015. The court has agreed to withdraw this status. The AMU is to appeal. The minority status had allowed the university to reserve seats for the education of Muslims and other minority groups in India. It was a university built for the sole purpose of educating the Muslims who were falling behind in education in the British system because of Muslim religious leaders' resentment of it. (Wikipedia)

PARTITION OF INDIA

by

Naiyer Habib

The Indian independence movement that was aimed to end the East Indian Company rule of 1757 to 1858 and the British Indian Empire of 1858 to 1947 in the Indian Subcontinent was a stormy, bloody effort by the Indians (in the company of people of all races and religions). British control of India spanned a total of 190 years. It was the largest mass migration in human history, of some 10 million. As many as one million civilians died in the accompanying riots and local-level fighting.

The Indian Self-Rule Movement was a mass-based movement that comprised various sections of society. It also underwent a process of constant ideological evolution. These ideologies were: Congress, Muslim League, Khudai Khidmatgar(1919-24), Khaksar Tehreek, Hindu Mahasabha, JanSingh, and others.

Allama Mashriqi founded Khaksar Tehreek to direct particularly the Muslims towards self-rule.

The division of our country did not have the beneficial outcome for the population that we see today. It left two countries in a state of chaos from which they could not come out. Abul Kalam's prediction in his book *India Wins Freedom* is self-explanatory. The masses were not the participants in decision-making.

India, our motherland, never had its sons and daughters to keep her happy. This time, it received a non-healing injury from them.

Today, the families are divided, a reality that especially affects the Sikhs and the Muslims. For one reason or another, they cannot visit one another—or rarely do—because of the rejection of visas. I am originally from India. I lived and was educated there, and my wife from Pakistan (a refugee from India in 1947) could not settle in either country. So, we took settlement in Canada. In an attempt to settle in Pakistan after five years of stay in the US, I had to get Pakistani citizenship due to unavoidable circumstances. We came to Canada after less than a year of stay in Pakistan. It took us three years to get visas to visit India, my home. Of course, we were no longer Indian citizens, but we had dual citizenship with Canadian passports. I am focussing on the problem faced by us, and I am critical of the division of India.

Exploring the facts of the Partition of India, I came across various pieces of information online referred below. Interested individuals may explore the references.

References for Partition of India

1. https://en.wikipedia.org/wiki/Indian_independence_movement 2. https://en.wikipedia.org/wiki/1946_Cabinet_Mission_to_India
2. https://sites.google.com/site/cabinetmissionplan/nehrupressconference10july1946
3. http://www.bbc.co.uk/history/british/modern/partition1947_01.shtml
4. https://en.wikipedia.org/wiki/Radcliffe_ Line
5. https://en.wikipedia.org/wiki/Constituent_Assembly_of_India
6. https://www.telegraphindia.com/1050605/asp/nation/story_4828954.asp
7. Jinnah: India-Partition, Independence by Jaswant Singh
8. http://news.bbc.co.uk/2/hi/south_asia/6926464.stm
9. India Wins Freedom by Maulana Abul Kalam Azad, Orient Blackswan Private Limited
10. 1/24 Asaf Ali Road. New Delhi110 002. India

EPILOGUE

This ends the story of our journey on Parallel Roads.

See Ancestry Char No 11 Page 27 for Ancestry link& Chart No 11 B page 556 for Shasms Uz Zaman

Ancestry Chart 11 A

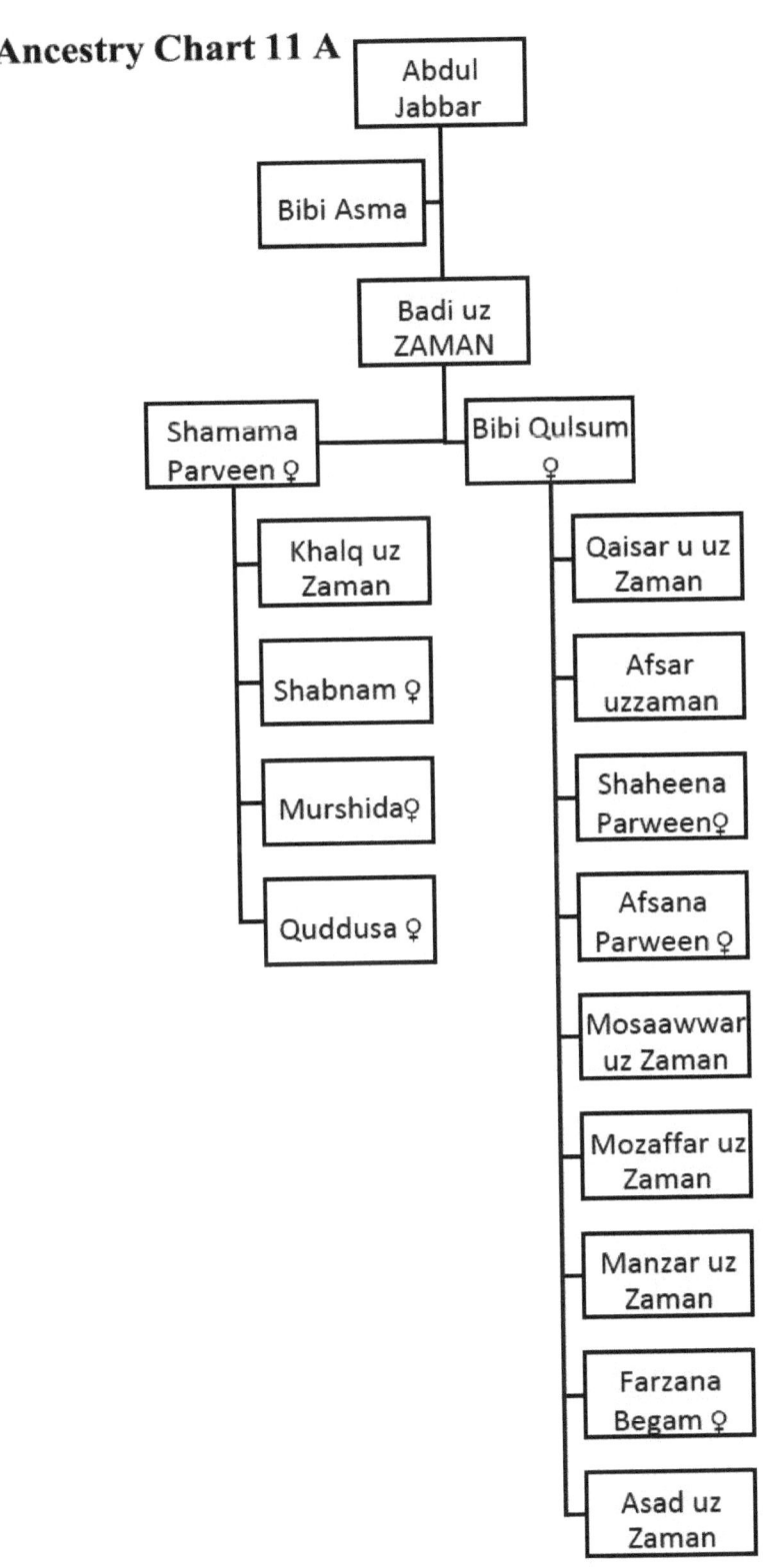

ANCESTRY CHART NO 11 B

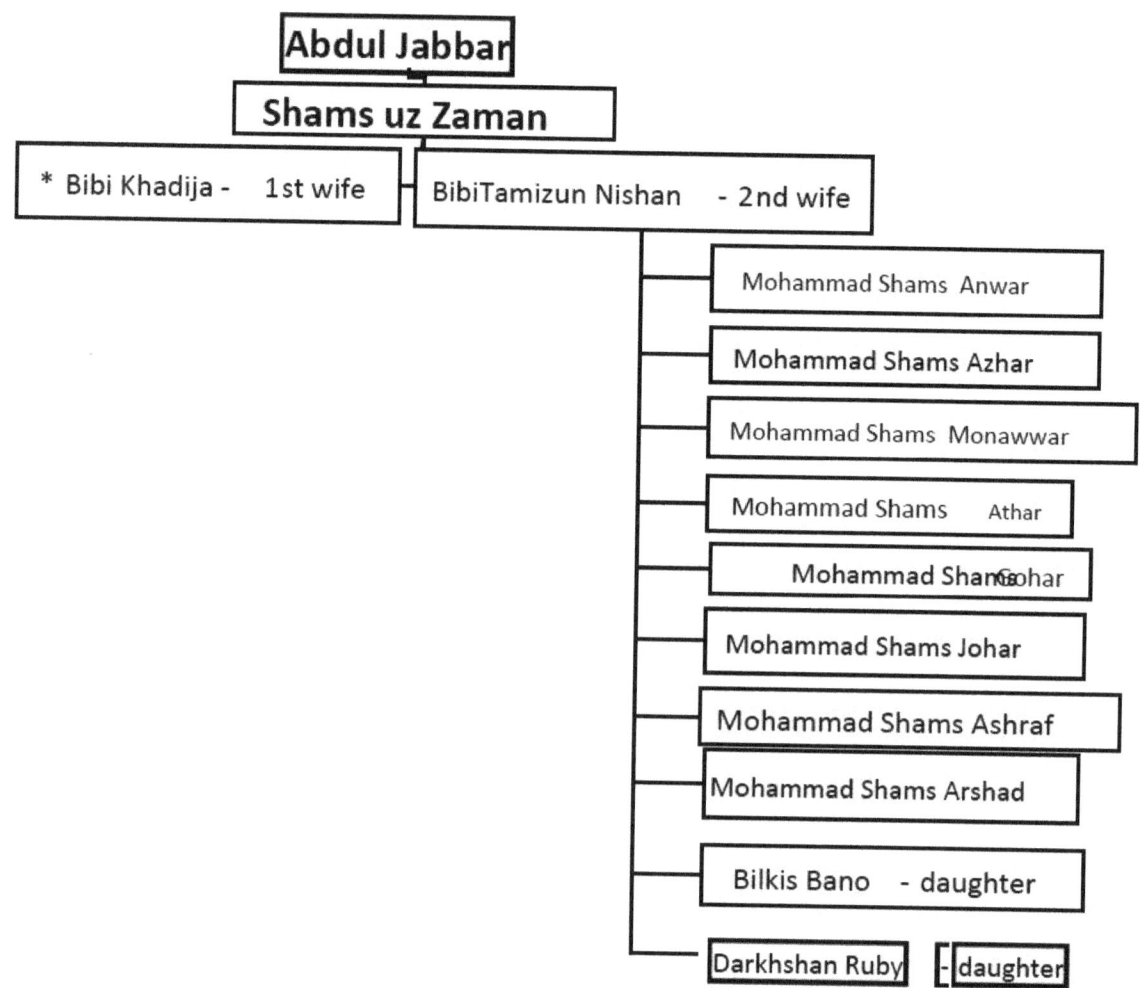

Abdul Jabbar

Shams uz Zaman

* Bibi Khadija -   1st wife

BibiTamizun Nishan   - 2nd wife

Mohammad Shams Anwar

Mohammad Shams Azhar

Mohammad Shams Monawwar

Mohammad Shams   Athar

Mohammad Shams Gohar

Mohammad Shams Johar

Mohammad Shams Ashraf

Mohammad Shams Arshad

Bilkis Bano   - daughter

Darkhshan Ruby   - daughter

See Chart No 11page 27 for Ancestor link and Chart No 11A page 555 for BadiUz zaman *
Bibi Khadija-See Ancestry Chart 16 Page 32 for her siblings etc.

US Book Review

THE US Review of Books

Journey on Parallel Roads: Autobiography and Memoir

by Naiyer Habib and Mahlaqa Naushaba Habib Friesen Press*

book review by Dylan Ward

" We dedicate this book to those who loved and respected us during our l ives."

In this touching autobiography, an immigrant couple recounts their rich and fulfilling lifelong journey of more than fifty years together. Immigrants (Canadian Citizens) from Ind ia and Pakistan, the Habibs have penned a memoir that is a labor of love. It is a testament to their lasting bond with each other, honoring their marriage, successes, and heritage. But it is also a dedication to the community at large

in which they serve and have come to know and affectionately consider as extended family. Additionally, they convey thanks to Canada for opening its arms to them following the partition of India, a complex social and political history that still affects them today. The book splits the focus between Naiyer and Mahlaqa, portraying their lives before and after India. The beginning pages ardently trace each ancestry with maps, pictorials, and detailed family trees. From there, they depict their upbringings, extensive educations and careers, and active retirement with civic roles devoted to the Saskatchewan Muslim community. Part of their efforts here is to shed a positive light upon the Muslim faith and traditions, endeavoring erase challenges, stigmas, and fears against their culture. Their prominent positions with organizations helping t o better the Muslim population are also admirable and vital to its prosperity.

Altogether, this is a comprehensively structured but elegantly assembled memoir. At first glance, their book appears to be a hefty read. However, in actuality, there is a considerable amount of photographs and other documents highlighting their lives along with regional histories, articles, and other materials. Yet nothing is wasted or superfluous here, and all of it is pieced jointly into one chronicle that beautifully illuminates this generous couple' s sacrifices and contributions. It is surely a lasting legacy worthy of being passed down to their descendants.

Return to USR Ho me

Journey on Parallel Roads is more than a memoir—it is a legacy etched in time. This heartfelt autobiography traces the intertwined lives of Dr. Naiyer Habib and Mahlaqa Naushaba Habib, two remarkable souls whose parallel journeys converged amid tides of history, migration, and purpose. From Partition-era India and Pakistan to the far reaches of North America, their story is one of love, resilience, sacrifice, and an unwavering dedication to family and community.

Shaped by displacement and a deep search for belonging, their early years were marked by upheaval and hope. As they crossed continents—from the vibrant streets of India and Pakistan to the United States, the United Kingdom, and finally the multicultural mosaic of Canada—their path became emblematic of quiet heroism.

In Regina, Saskatchewan, Dr. Habib was appointed by the University of Saskatchewan to establish the cardiology program for Southern Saskatchewan—a visionary endeavor he led with excellence, building a service second to none. He is widely recognized as the pioneer of cardiology in the region. Together, Dr. Habib and Mahlaqa Naushaba Habib became pillars of their community, offering leadership and unwavering service for over two decades. In recognition of their shared contributions, both were honored as pioneers by the Premier of Saskatchewan for their leadership and service. Dr. Habib is awardee of the Fellowship of the American College of Cardiology - FACC, American College of Physician - FACP, American College of Chest Physician - FCCP and is Fellow of the Royal College of Physician of Canada -FRCPC.

This narrative is more than a personal history—it is a tribute to generations past and a beacon for generations to come. It honors the inheritance of values, the pursuit of meaning, and the strength it takes to build anew while carrying a legacy. Poetic and profound, Journey on Parallel Roads flows like a river through time and memory—expansive in emotion, yet held within the intimate reflections of two lives lived with extraordinary grace and purpose.

www.ingramcontent.com/pod-product-compliance
Lightning Source LLC
Chambersburg PA
CBHW041109120626
46547CB00019B/2633